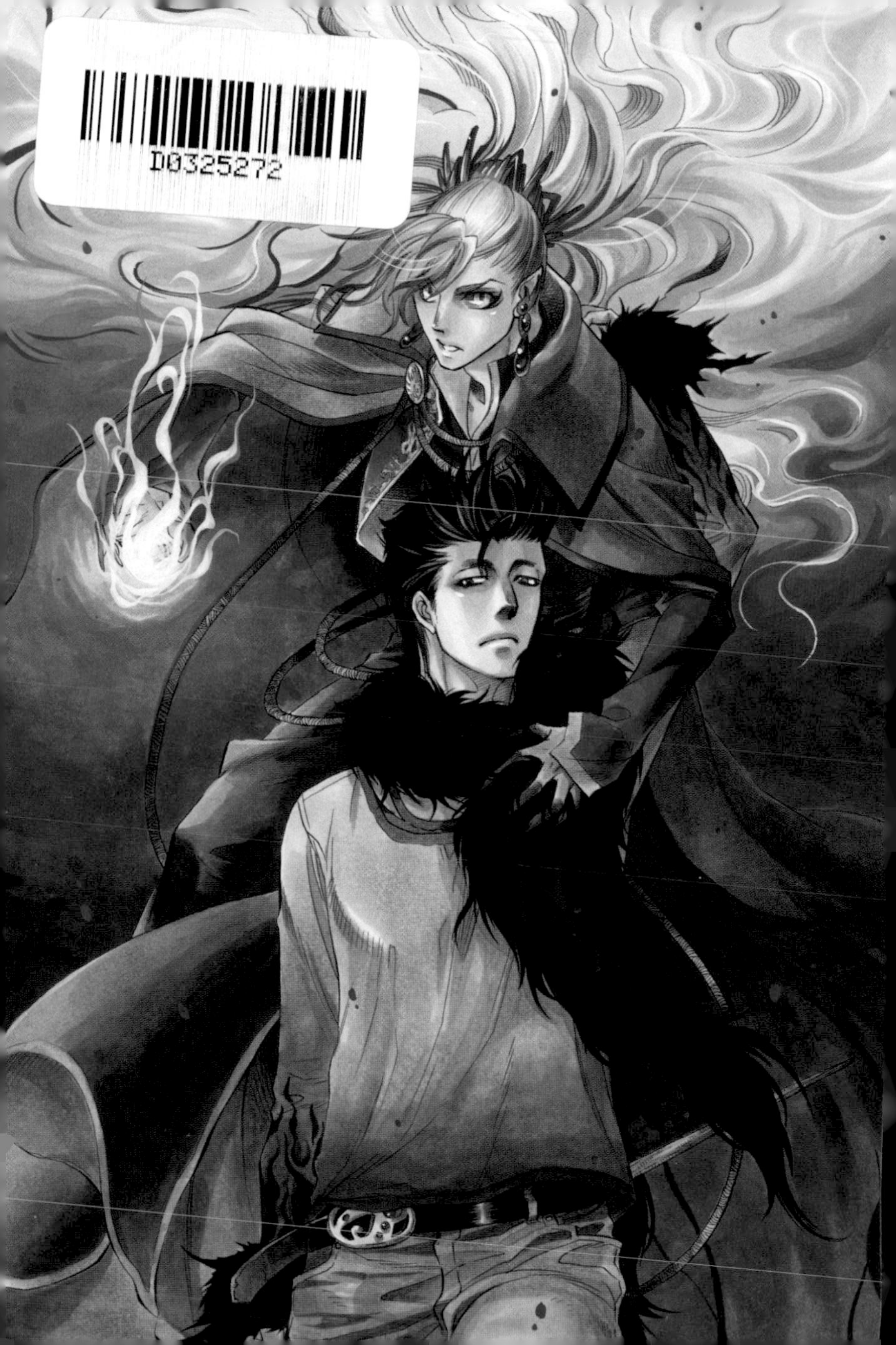

Midnight Stranger

Story and Art by **Bohra Naono**　　volume **2**

CONTENTS

SUBLIME

SuBLime Manga Edition

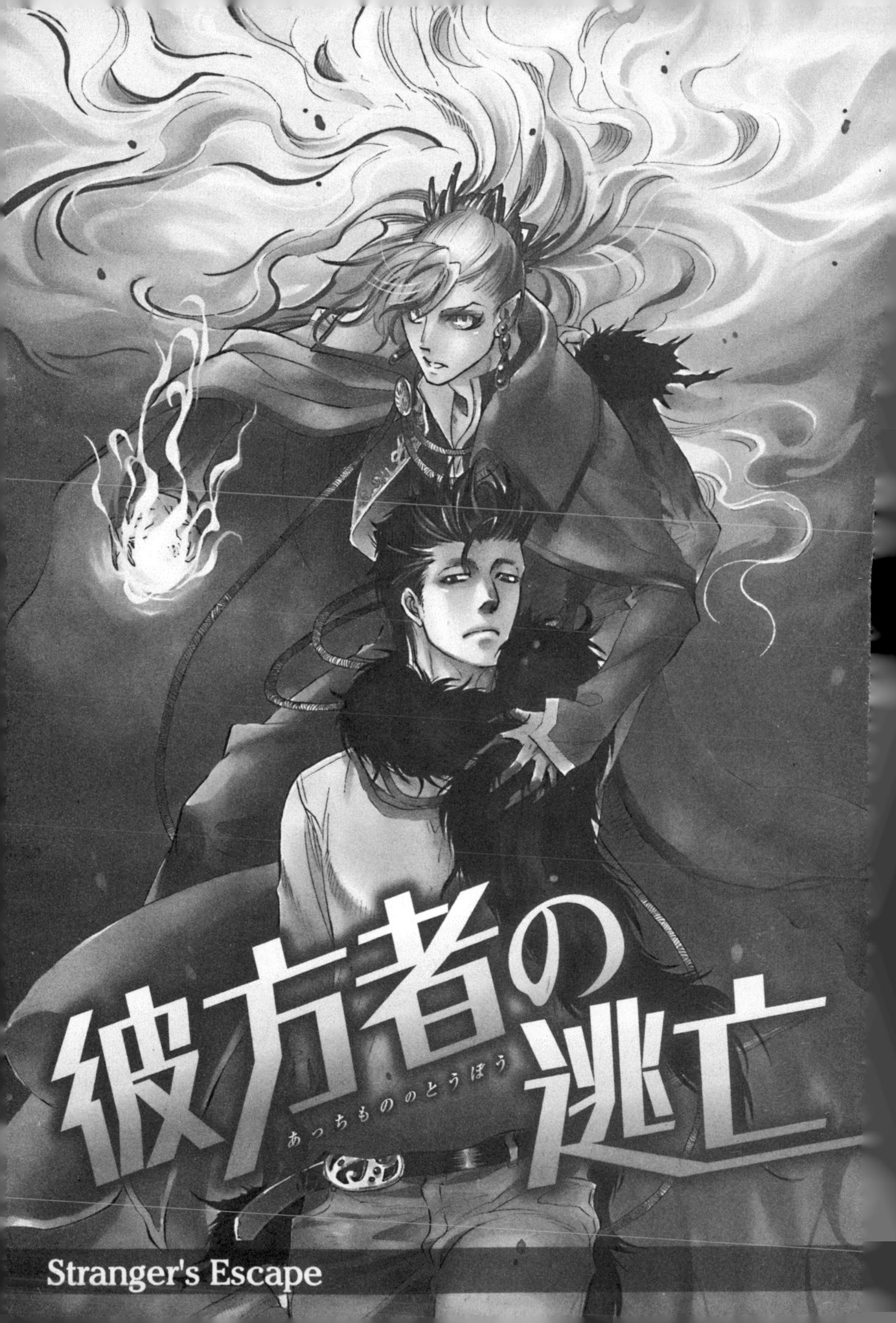
彼方者の逃亡
あっちもののとうぼう
Stranger's Escape

彼方者の
困惑
あっちものの こんわく

Midnight Stranger

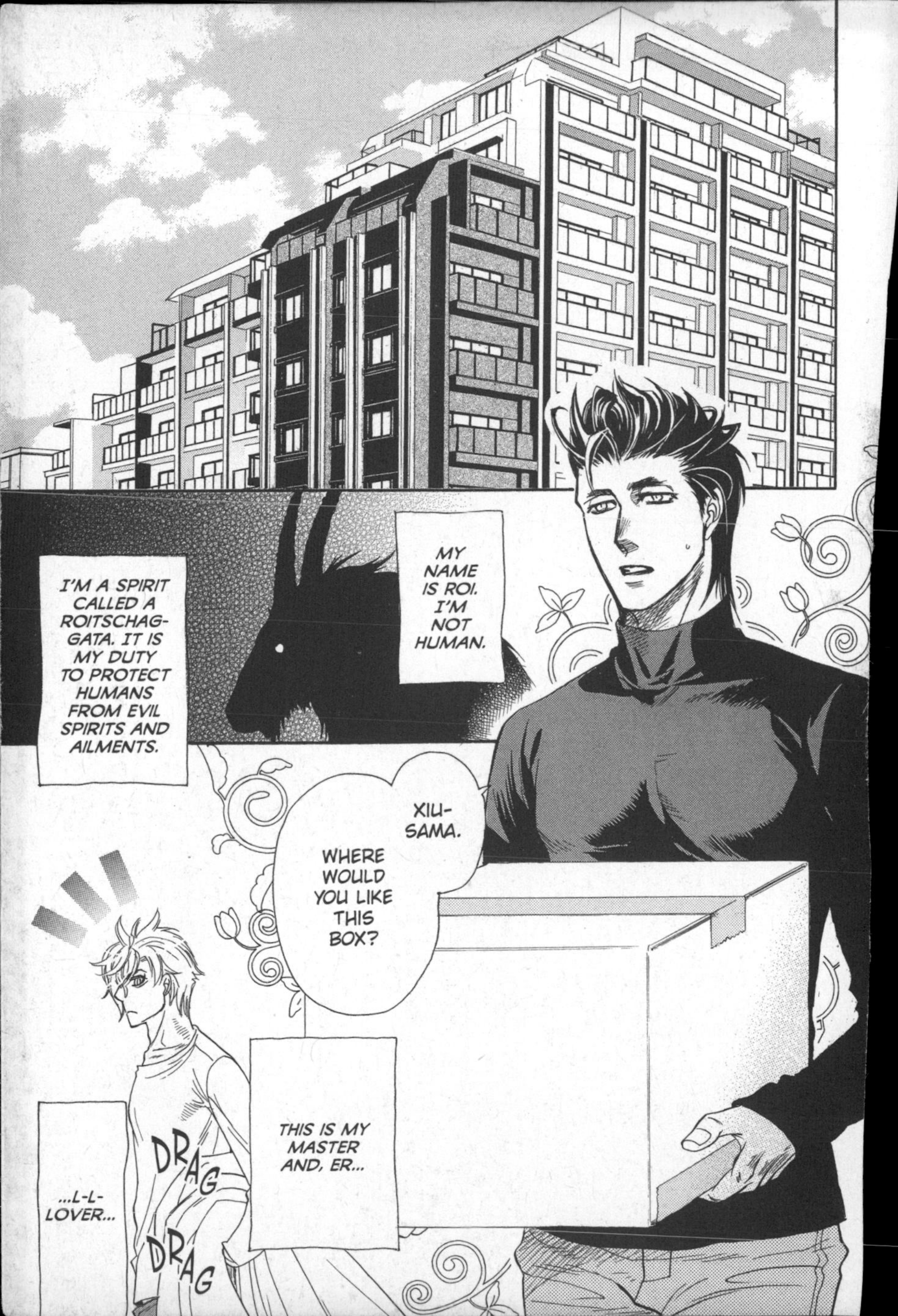
MY NAME IS ROI. I'M NOT HUMAN.
I'M A SPIRIT CALLED A ROITSCHAG-GATA. IT IS MY DUTY TO PROTECT HUMANS FROM EVIL SPIRITS AND AILMENTS.
XIU-SAMA.
WHERE WOULD YOU LIKE THIS BOX?
THIS IS MY MASTER AND, ER...
DRAG
DRAG
...L-L-LOVER...

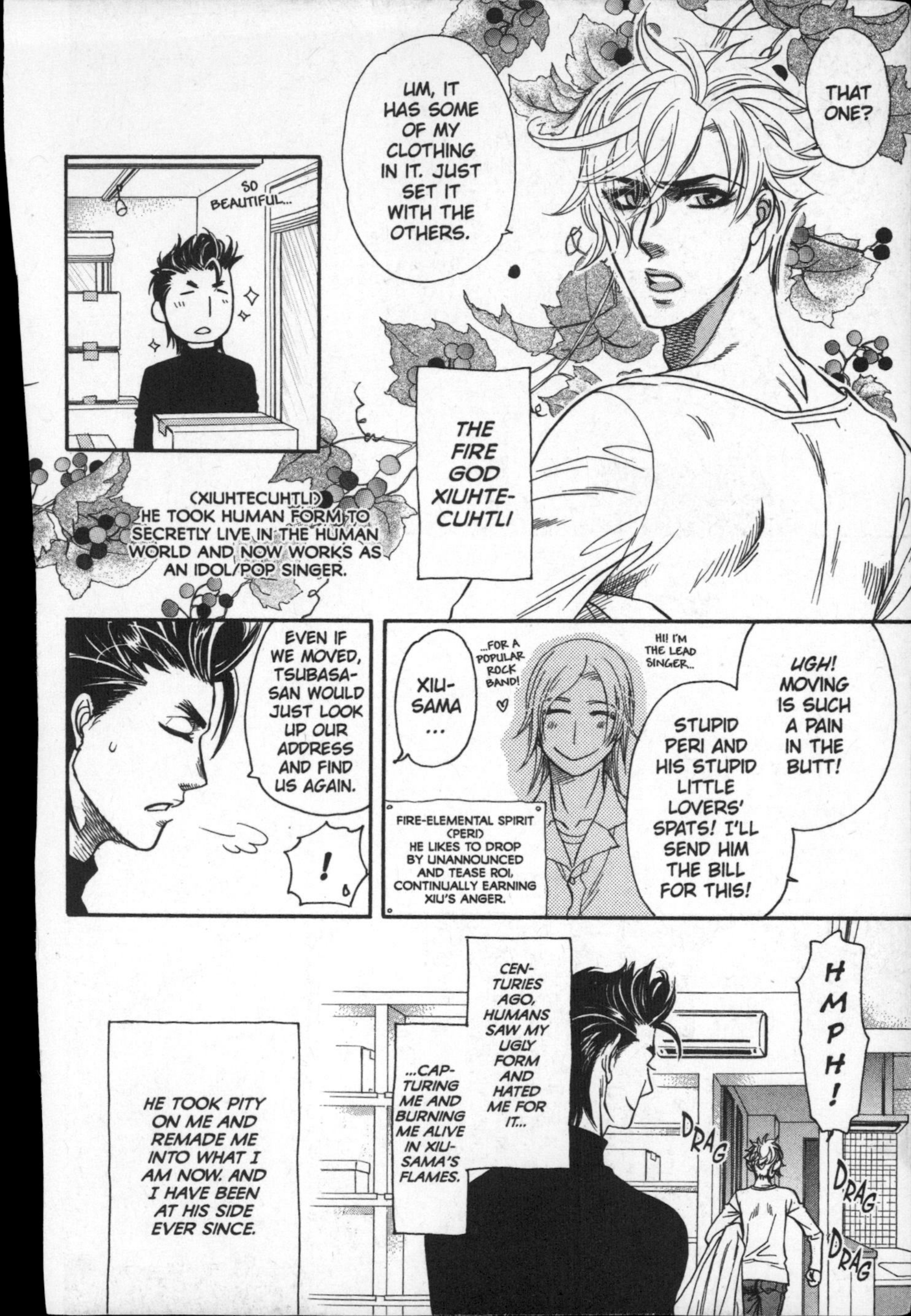

THAT ONE?
UM, IT HAS SOME OF MY CLOTHING IN IT. JUST SET IT WITH THE OTHERS.
SO BEAUTIFUL...
THE FIRE GOD XIUHTECUHTLI
(XIUHTECUHTLI) HE TOOK HUMAN FORM TO SECRETLY LIVE IN THE HUMAN WORLD AND NOW WORKS AS AN IDOL/POP SINGER.
UGH! MOVING IS SUCH A PAIN IN THE BUTT!
STUPID PERI AND HIS STUPID LITTLE LOVERS' SPATS! I'LL SEND HIM THE BILL FOR THIS!
HI! I'M THE LEAD SINGER...
...FOR A POPULAR ROCK BAND! ♡
XIU-SAMA ...
FIRE-ELEMENTAL SPIRIT (PERI) HE LIKES TO DROP BY UNANNOUNCED AND TEASE ROI, CONTINUALLY EARNING XIU'S ANGER.
EVEN IF WE MOVED, TSUBASA-SAN WOULD JUST LOOK UP OUR ADDRESS AND FIND US AGAIN.
!
HMPH!
DRAG
DRAG
DRAG
CENTURIES AGO, HUMANS SAW MY UGLY FORM AND HATED ME FOR IT...
...CAPTURING ME AND BURNING ME ALIVE IN XIU-SAMA'S FLAMES.
HE TOOK PITY ON ME AND REMADE ME INTO WHAT I AM NOW. AND I HAVE BEEN AT HIS SIDE EVER SINCE.

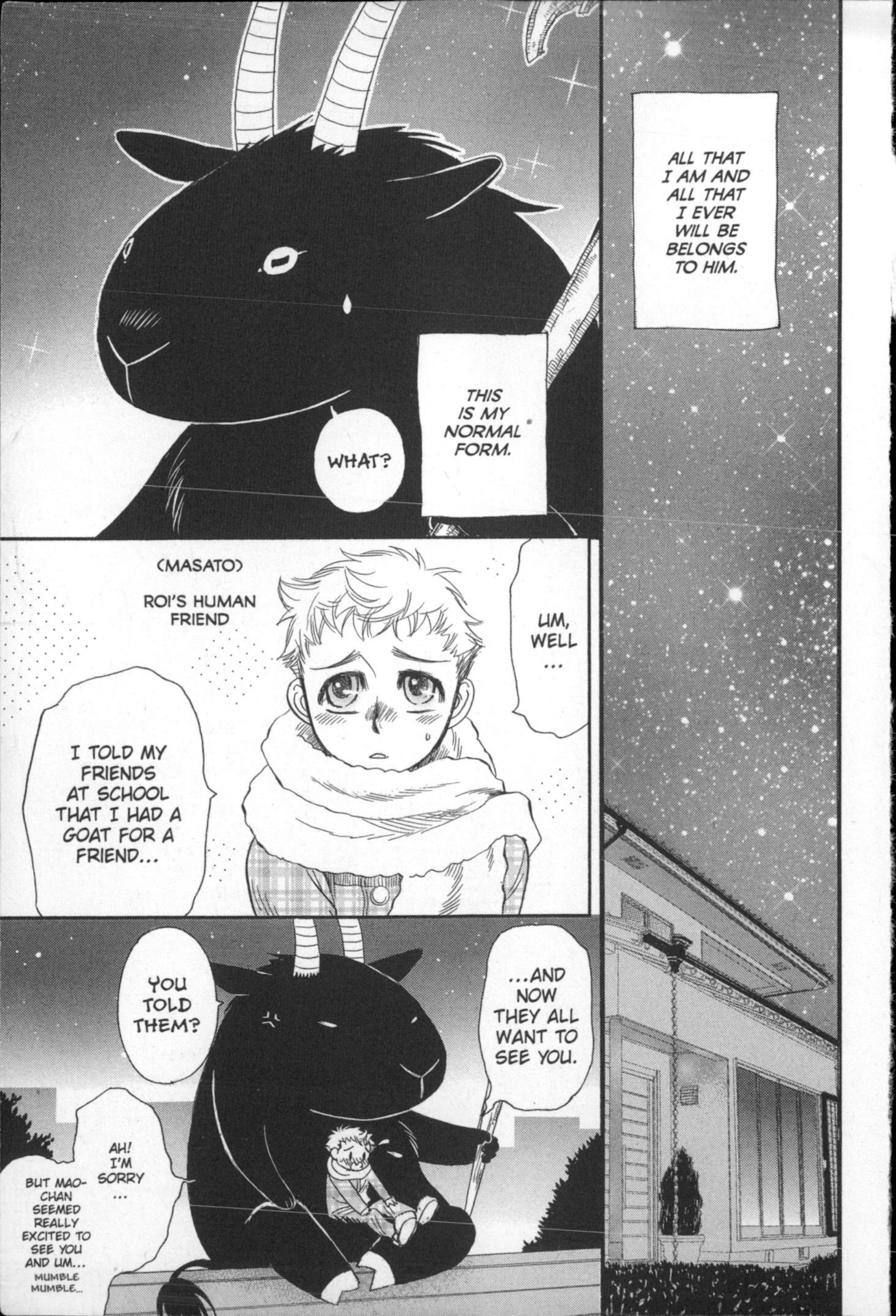
ALL THAT I AM AND ALL THAT I EVER WILL BE BELONGS TO HIM.
THIS IS MY NORMAL FORM.
WHAT?
UM, WELL ...
(MASATO)
ROI'S HUMAN FRIEND
I TOLD MY FRIENDS AT SCHOOL THAT I HAD A GOAT FOR A FRIEND...
...AND NOW THEY ALL WANT TO SEE YOU.
YOU TOLD THEM?
AH! I'M SORRY ...
BUT MAO-CHAN SEEMED REALLY EXCITED TO SEE YOU AND UM... MUMBLE MUMBLE...

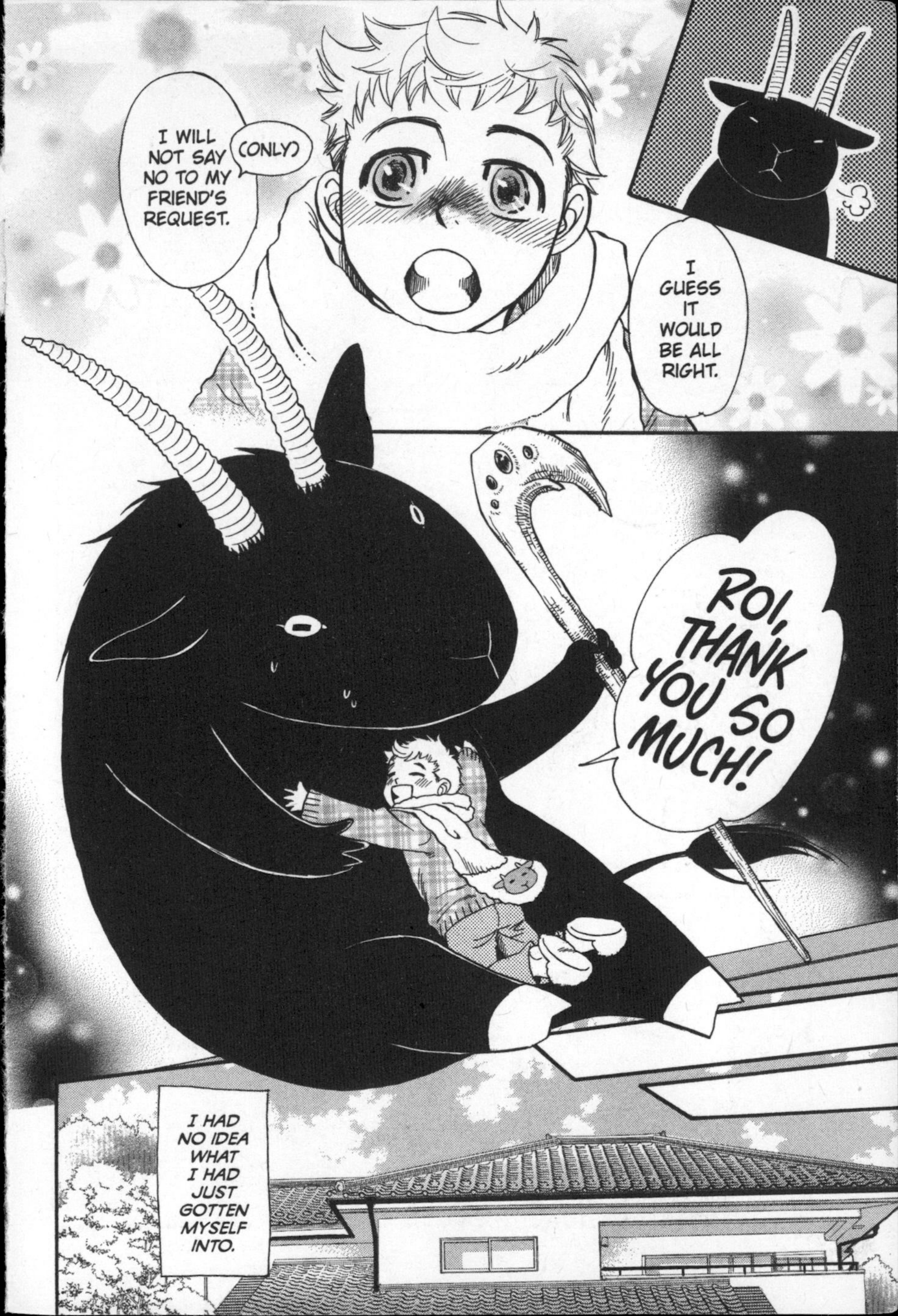
I WILL NOT SAY NO TO MY FRIEND'S REQUEST.
(ONLY)
I GUESS IT WOULD BE ALL RIGHT.
ROI, THANK YOU SO MUCH!
I HAD NO IDEA WHAT I HAD JUST GOTTEN MYSELF INTO.

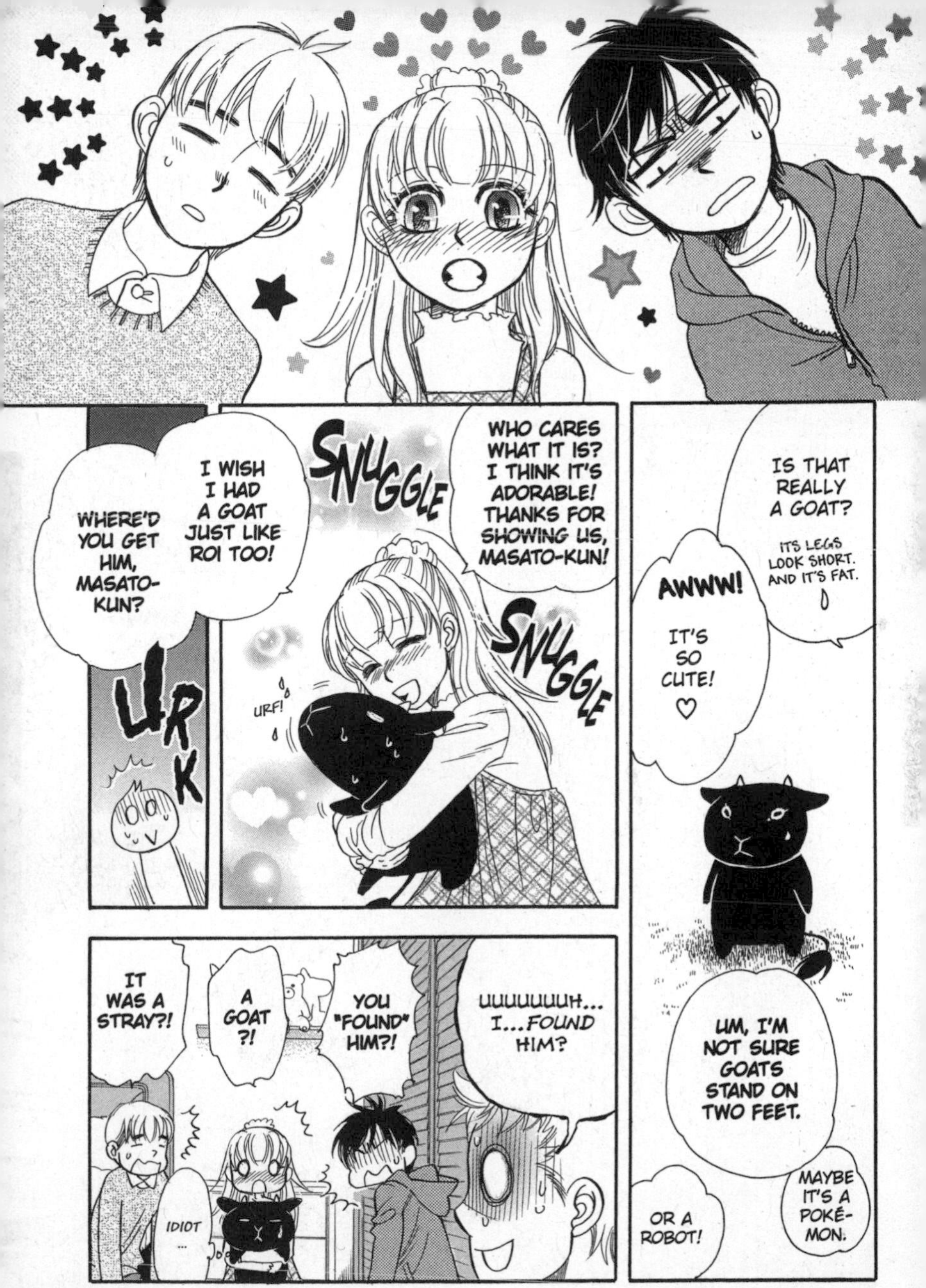
IS THAT REALLY A GOAT?
ITS LEGS LOOK SHORT. AND IT'S FAT.
AWWW! IT'S SO CUTE! ♡
UM, I'M NOT SURE GOATS STAND ON TWO FEET.
MAYBE IT'S A POKÉ-MON.
OR A ROBOT!
WHO CARES WHAT IT IS? I THINK IT'S ADORABLE! THANKS FOR SHOWING US, MASATO-KUN!
SNUGGLE
SNUGGLE
URF!
I WISH I HAD A GOAT JUST LIKE ROI TOO!
WHERE'D YOU GET HIM, MASATO-KUN?
URK
UUUUUUUH... I...*FOUND* HIM?
YOU "FOUND" HIM?!
A GOAT?!
IT WAS A STRAY?!
IDIOT...

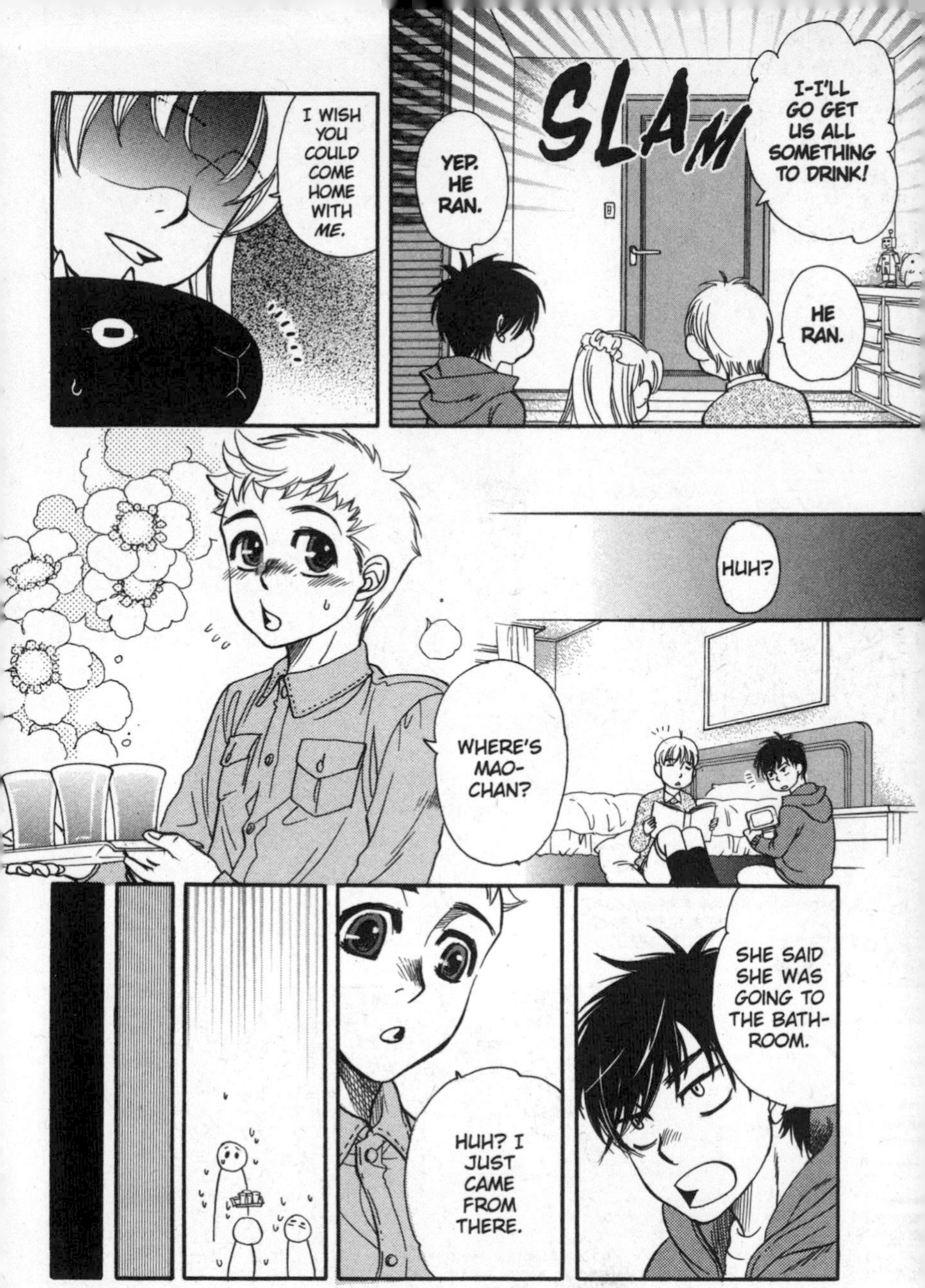
I-I'LL GO GET US ALL SOMETHING TO DRINK!
SLAM
HE RAN.
YEP. HE RAN.
I WISH YOU COULD COME HOME WITH ME.
HUH?
WHERE'S MAO-CHAN?
SHE SAID SHE WAS GOING TO THE BATH-ROOM.
HUH? I JUST CAME FROM THERE.

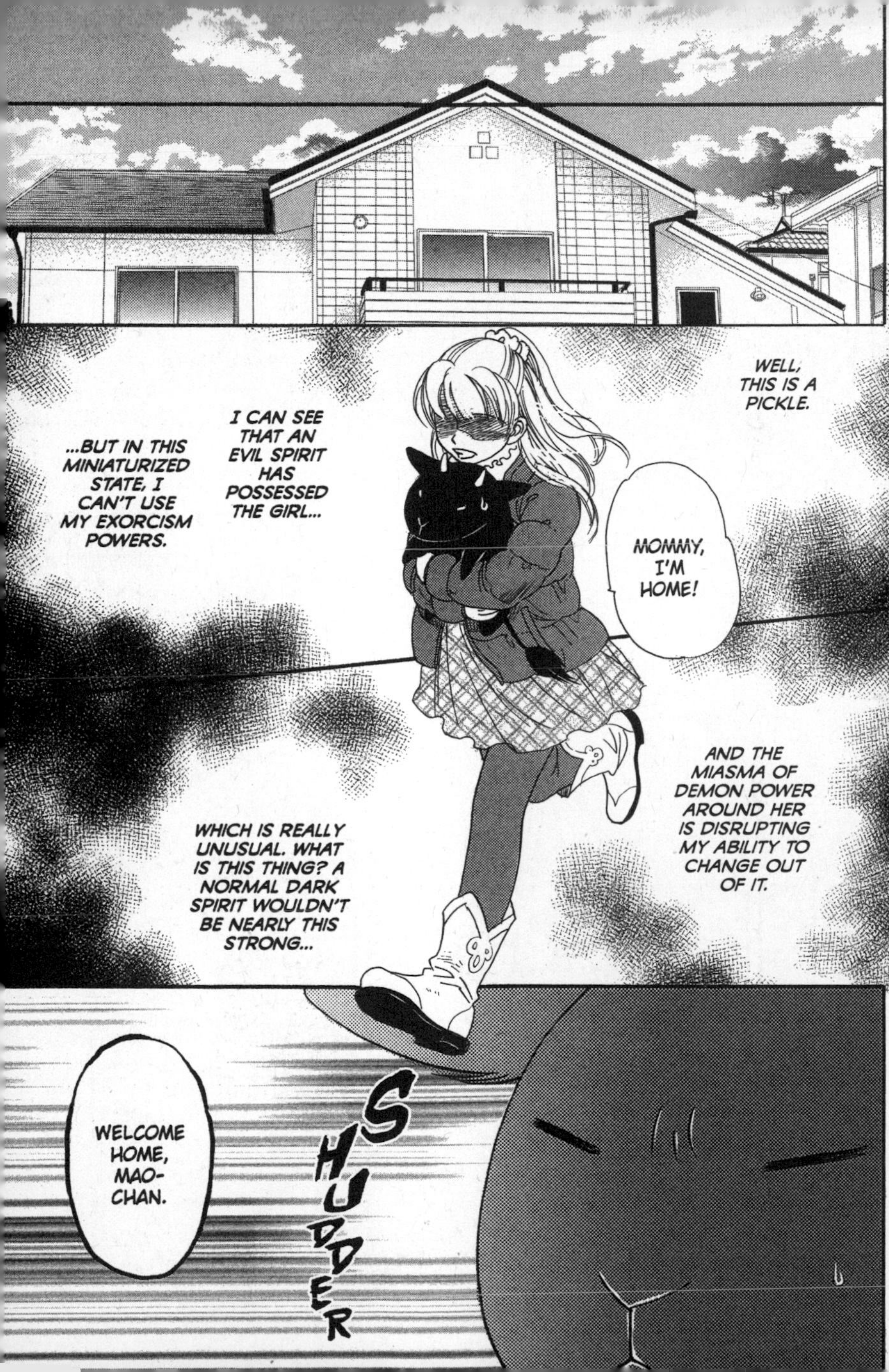
WELL, THIS IS A PICKLE.
MOMMY, I'M HOME!
I CAN SEE THAT AN EVIL SPIRIT HAS POSSESSED THE GIRL...
...BUT IN THIS MINIATURIZED STATE, I CAN'T USE MY EXORCISM POWERS.
AND THE MIASMA OF DEMON POWER AROUND HER IS DISRUPTING MY ABILITY TO CHANGE OUT OF IT.
WHICH IS REALLY UNUSUAL. WHAT IS THIS THING? A NORMAL DARK SPIRIT WOULDN'T BE NEARLY THIS STRONG...
SHUDDER
WELCOME HOME, MAO-CHAN.

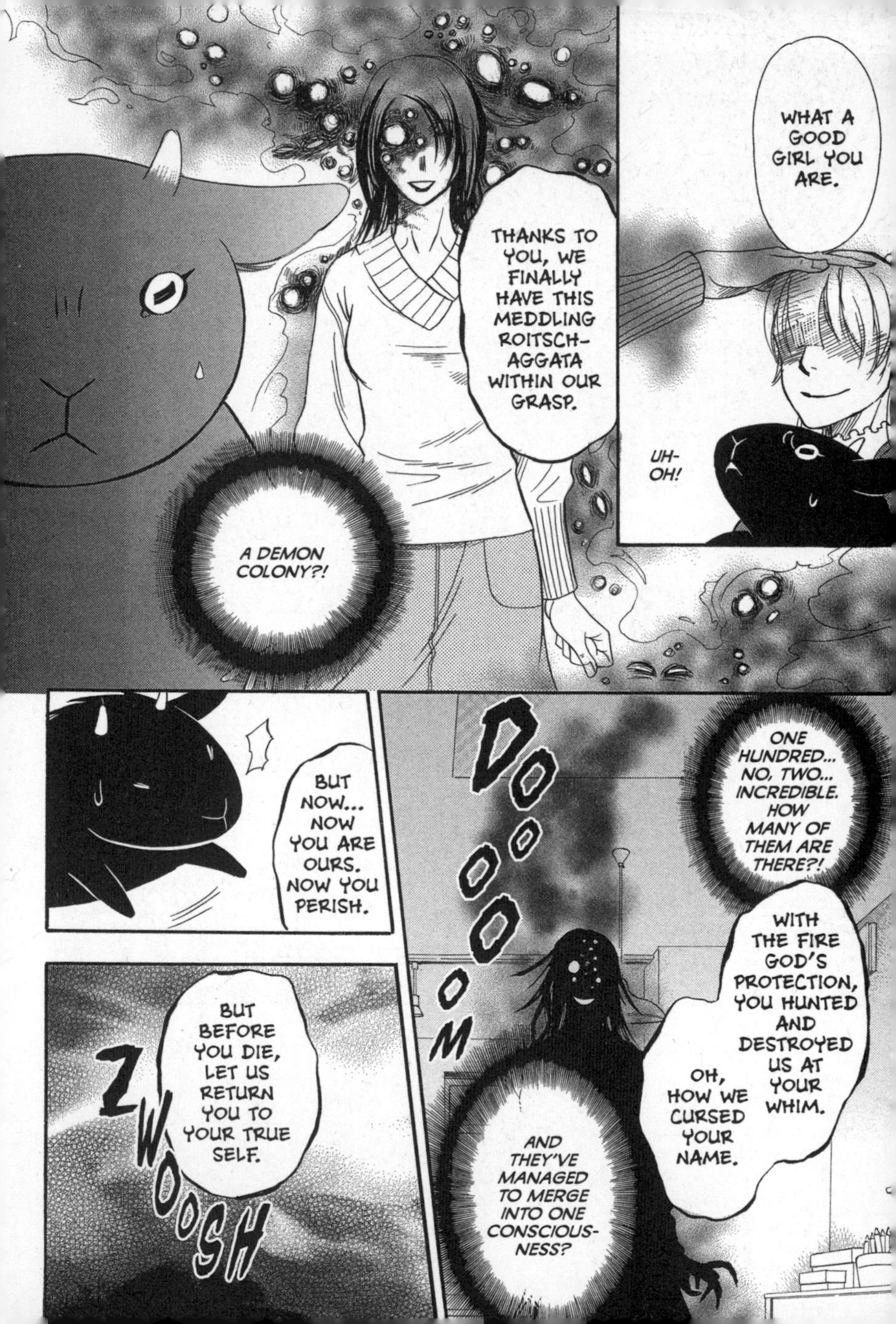
WHAT A GOOD GIRL YOU ARE.
UH-OH!
THANKS TO YOU, WE FINALLY HAVE THIS MEDDLING ROITSCH-AGGATA WITHIN OUR GRASP.
A DEMON COLONY?!
ONE HUNDRED... NO, TWO... INCREDIBLE. HOW MANY OF THEM ARE THERE?!
DOOOOOM
WITH THE FIRE GOD'S PROTECTION, YOU HUNTED AND DESTROYED US AT YOUR WHIM.
OH, HOW WE CURSED YOUR NAME.
AND THEY'VE MANAGED TO MERGE INTO ONE CONSCIOUS-NESS?
BUT NOW... NOW YOU ARE OURS. NOW YOU PERISH.
BUT BEFORE YOU DIE, LET US RETURN YOU TO YOUR TRUE SELF.
ZWOOSH

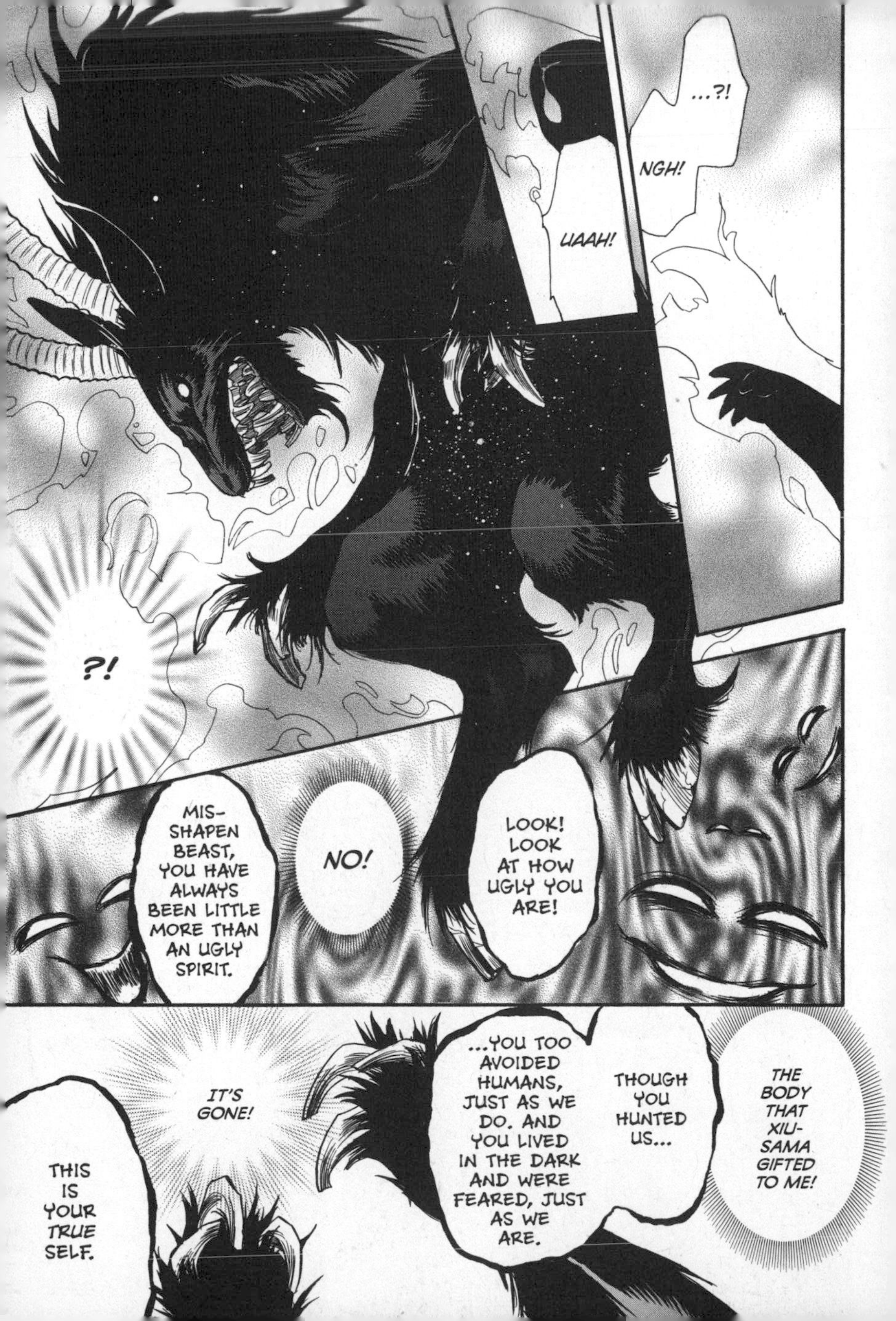
...?!
NGH!
UAAH!
?!
LOOK! LOOK AT HOW UGLY YOU ARE!
NO!
MIS-SHAPEN BEAST, YOU HAVE ALWAYS BEEN LITTLE MORE THAN AN UGLY SPIRIT.
THE BODY THAT XIU-SAMA GIFTED TO ME!
THOUGH YOU HUNTED US...
...YOU TOO AVOIDED HUMANS, JUST AS WE DO. AND YOU LIVED IN THE DARK AND WERE FEARED, JUST AS WE ARE.
IT'S GONE!
THIS IS YOUR TRUE SELF.

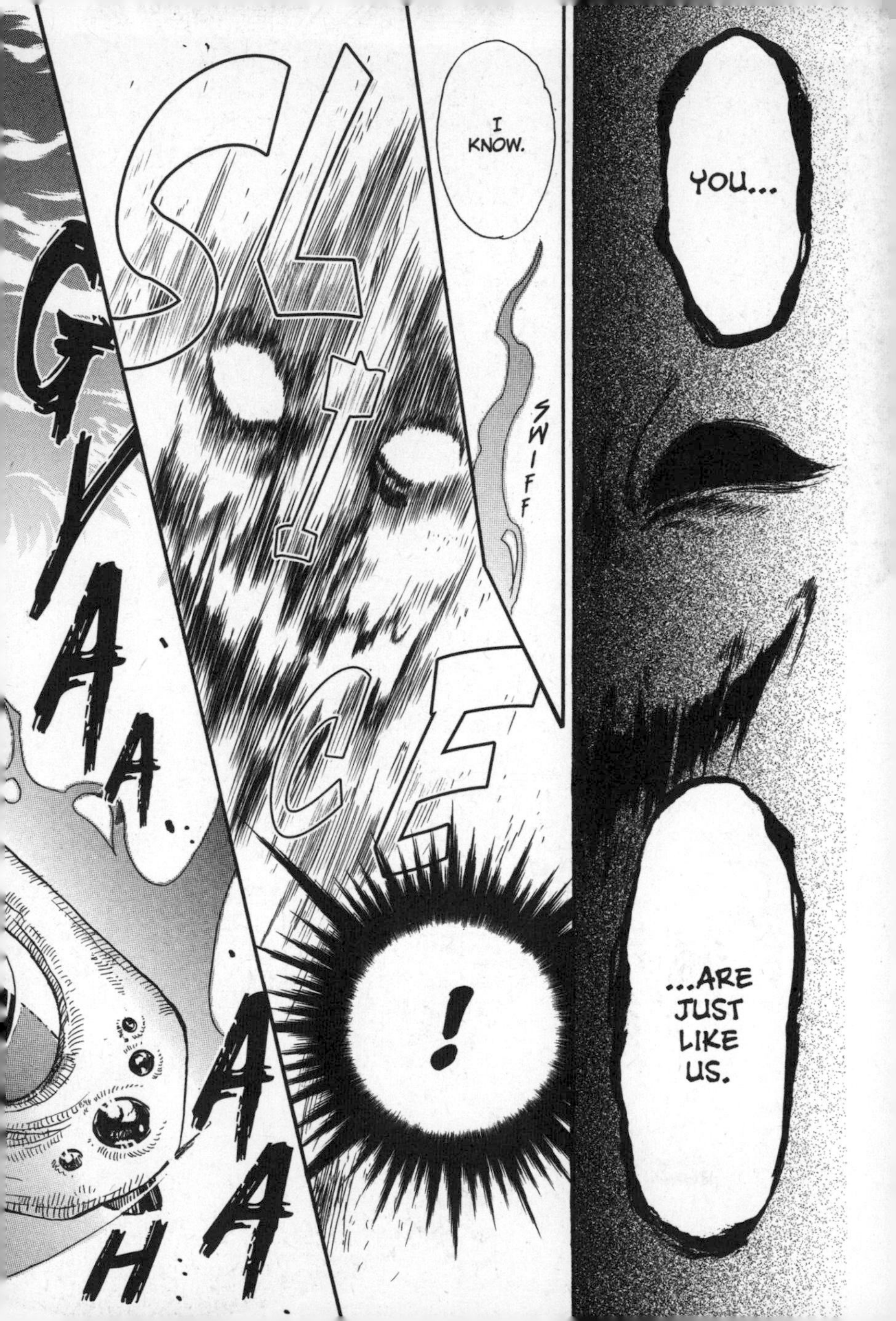
YOU...
...ARE JUST LIKE US.
I KNOW.
SWIFF
SLICE
!
GYAAAAH

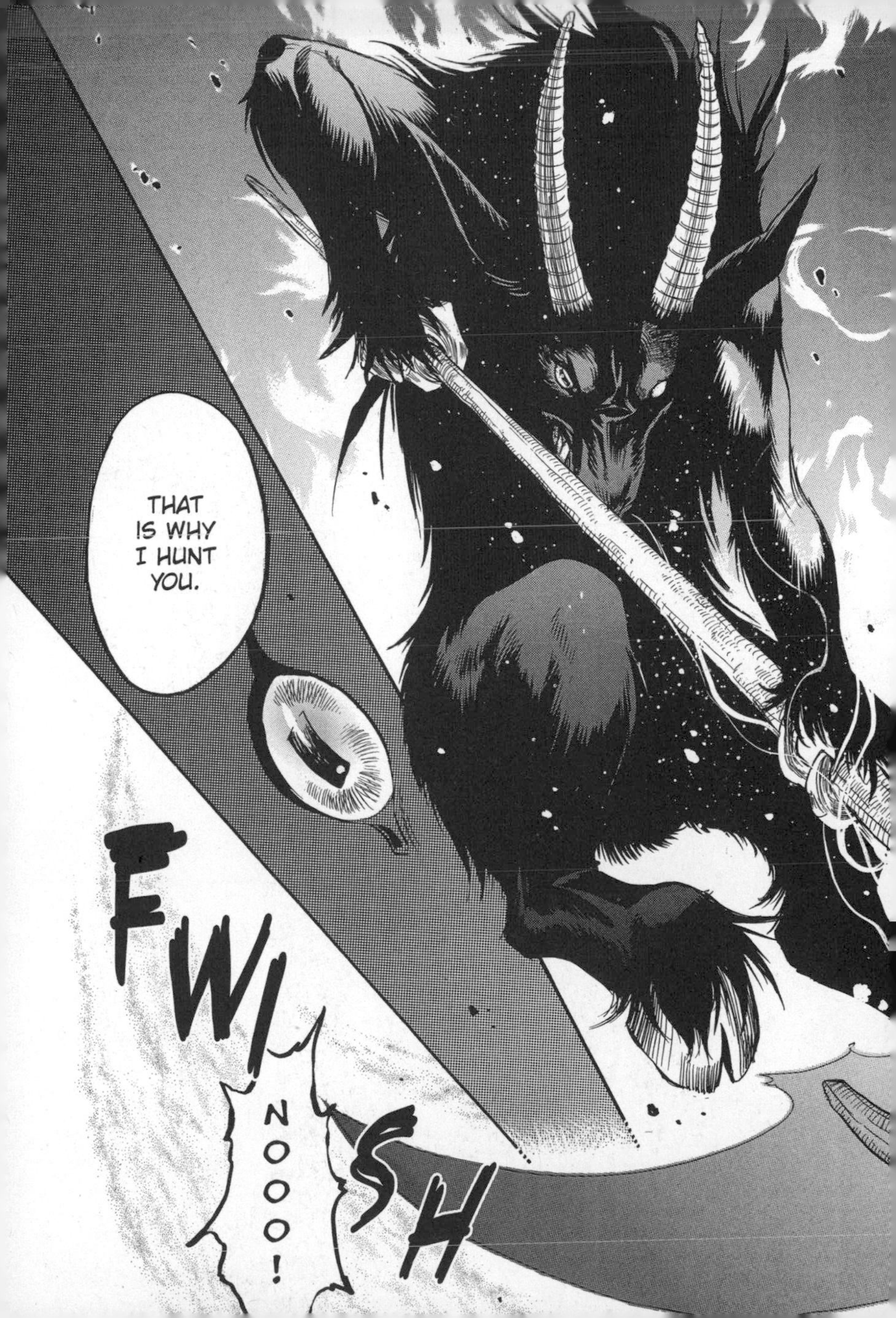
THAT IS WHY I HUNT YOU.
FWISH
NOOOO!

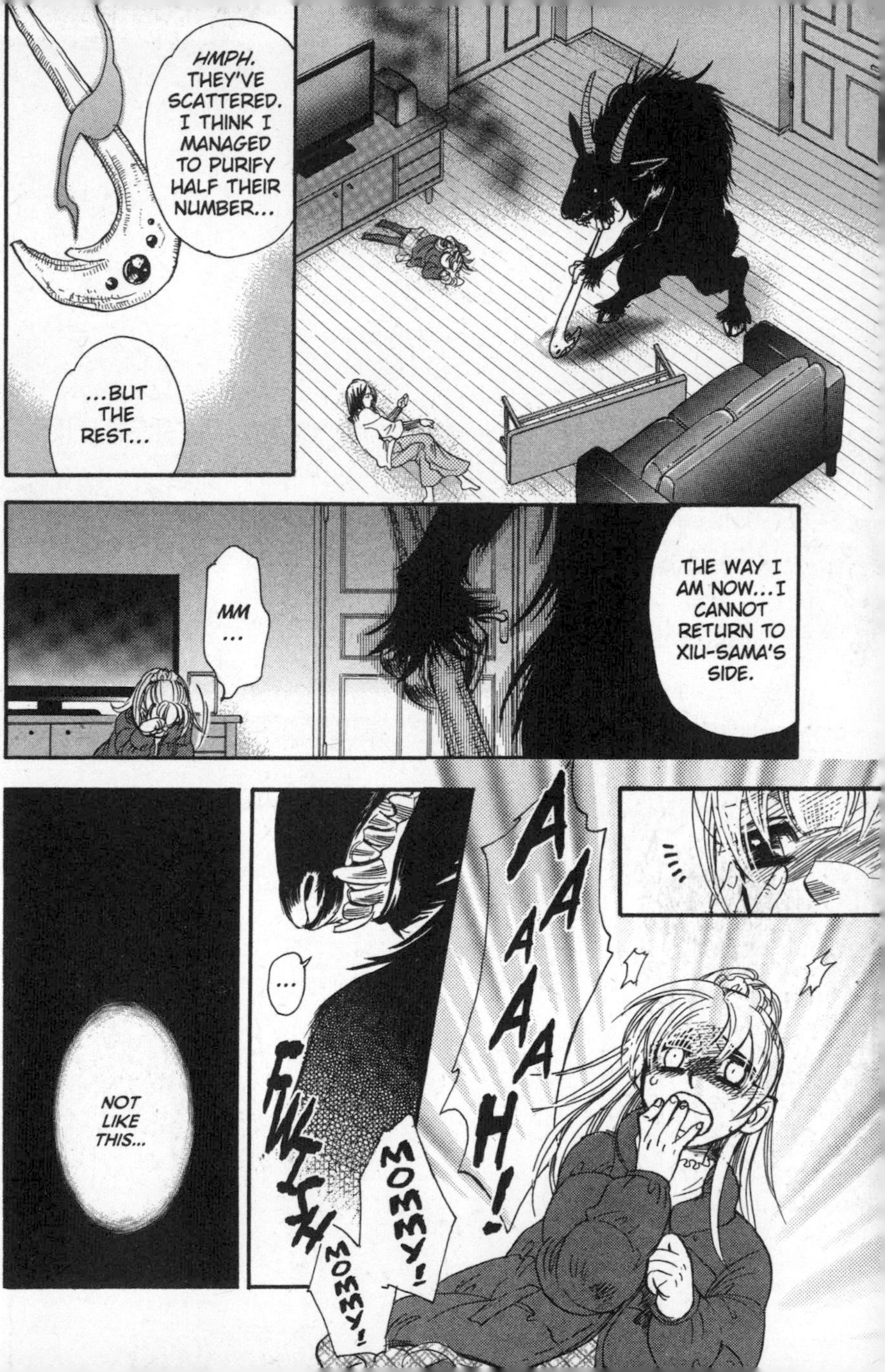
HMPH. THEY'VE SCATTERED. I THINK I MANAGED TO PURIFY HALF THEIR NUMBER...
...BUT THE REST...
THE WAY I AM NOW...I CANNOT RETURN TO XIU-SAMA'S SIDE.
MM ...
AAAAAAAH!!
...
FWISH
MOMMY! MOMMY!
NOT LIKE THIS...

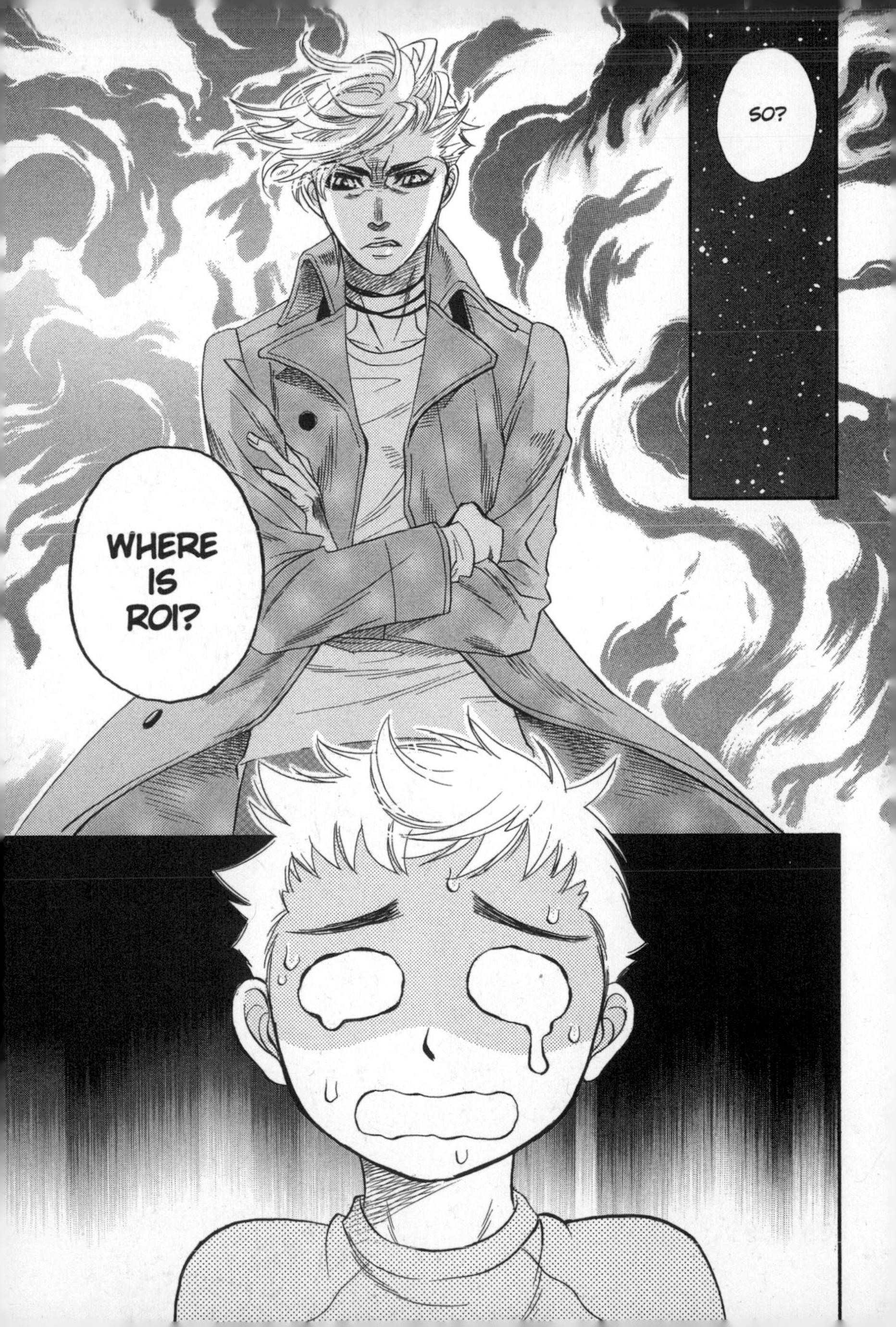
SO?
WHERE IS ROI?

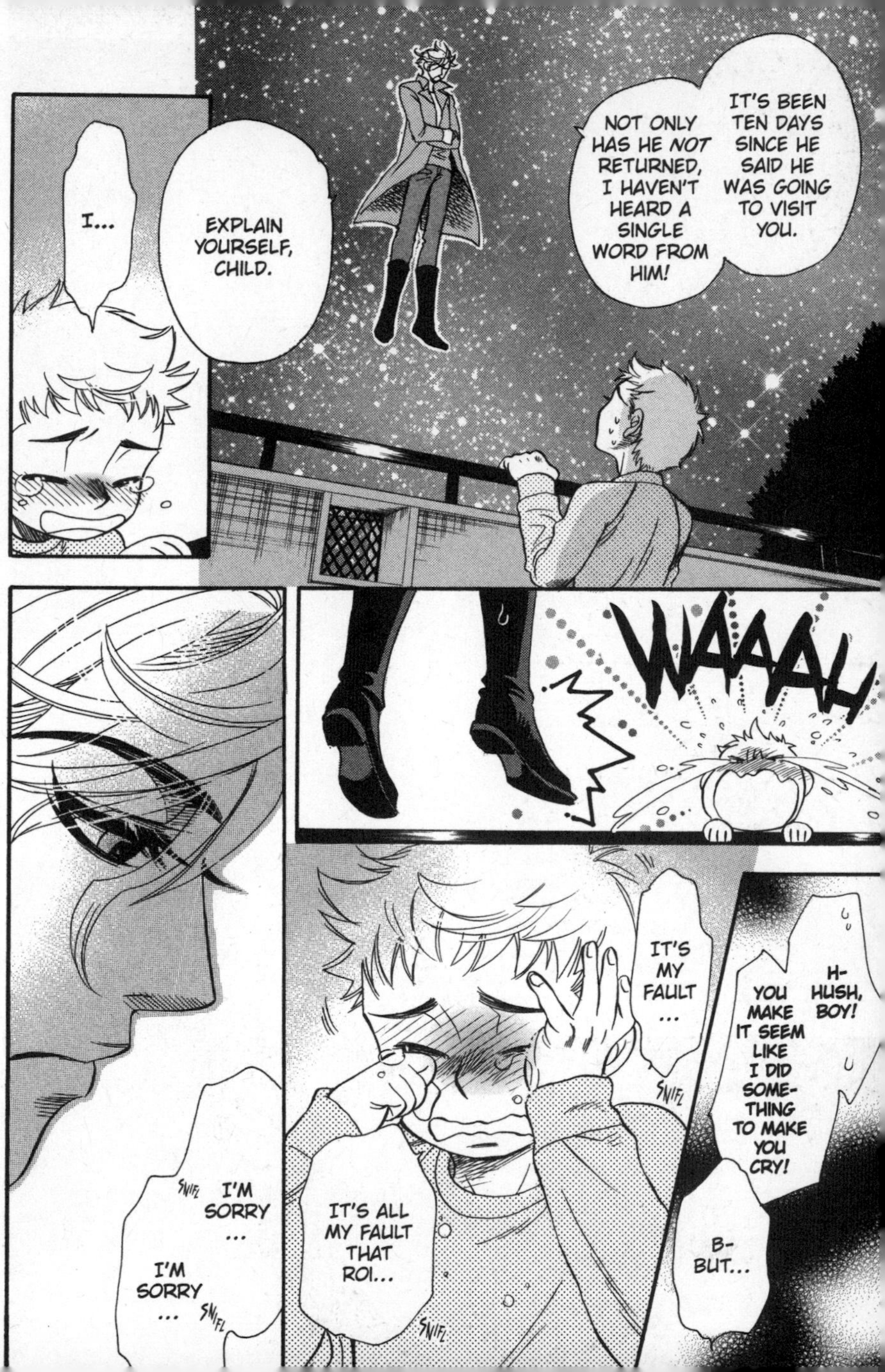
IT'S BEEN TEN DAYS SINCE HE SAID HE WAS GOING TO VISIT YOU.
NOT ONLY HAS HE *NOT* RETURNED, I HAVEN'T HEARD A SINGLE WORD FROM HIM!
EXPLAIN YOURSELF, CHILD.
I...
WAAAH
H-HUSH, BOY!
YOU MAKE IT SEEM LIKE I DID SOMETHING TO MAKE YOU CRY!
B-BUT...
IT'S MY FAULT...
SNIFL
IT'S ALL MY FAULT THAT ROI...
SNIFL
SNIFL
I'M SORRY...
I'M SORRY...
SNIFL

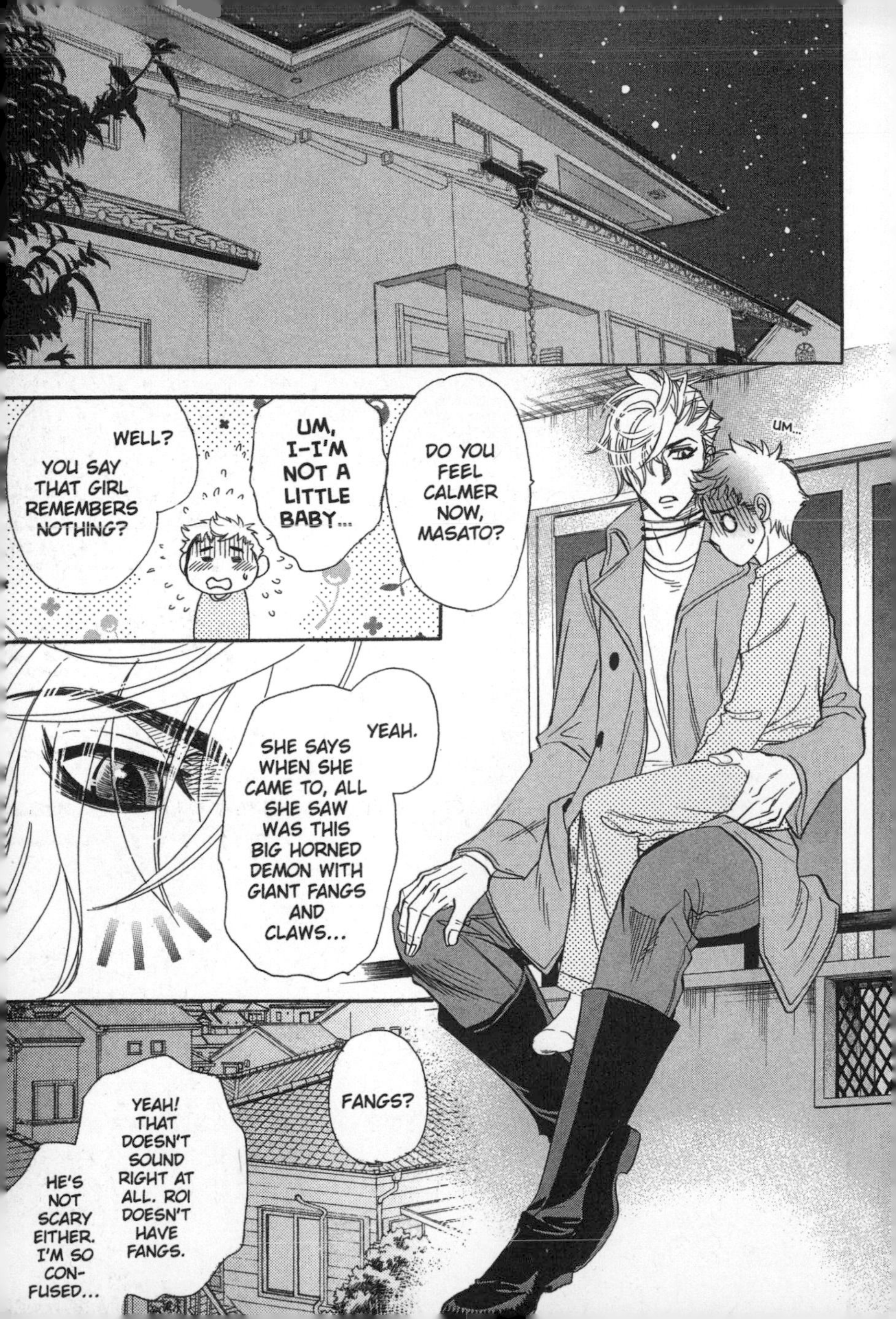
DO YOU FEEL CALMER NOW, MASATO?
UM...
UM, I-I'M NOT A LITTLE BABY...
WELL? YOU SAY THAT GIRL REMEMBERS NOTHING?
YEAH. SHE SAYS WHEN SHE CAME TO, ALL SHE SAW WAS THIS BIG HORNED DEMON WITH GIANT FANGS AND CLAWS...
FANGS?
YEAH! THAT DOESN'T SOUND RIGHT AT ALL. ROI DOESN'T HAVE FANGS.
HE'S NOT SCARY EITHER. I'M SO CON-FUSED...

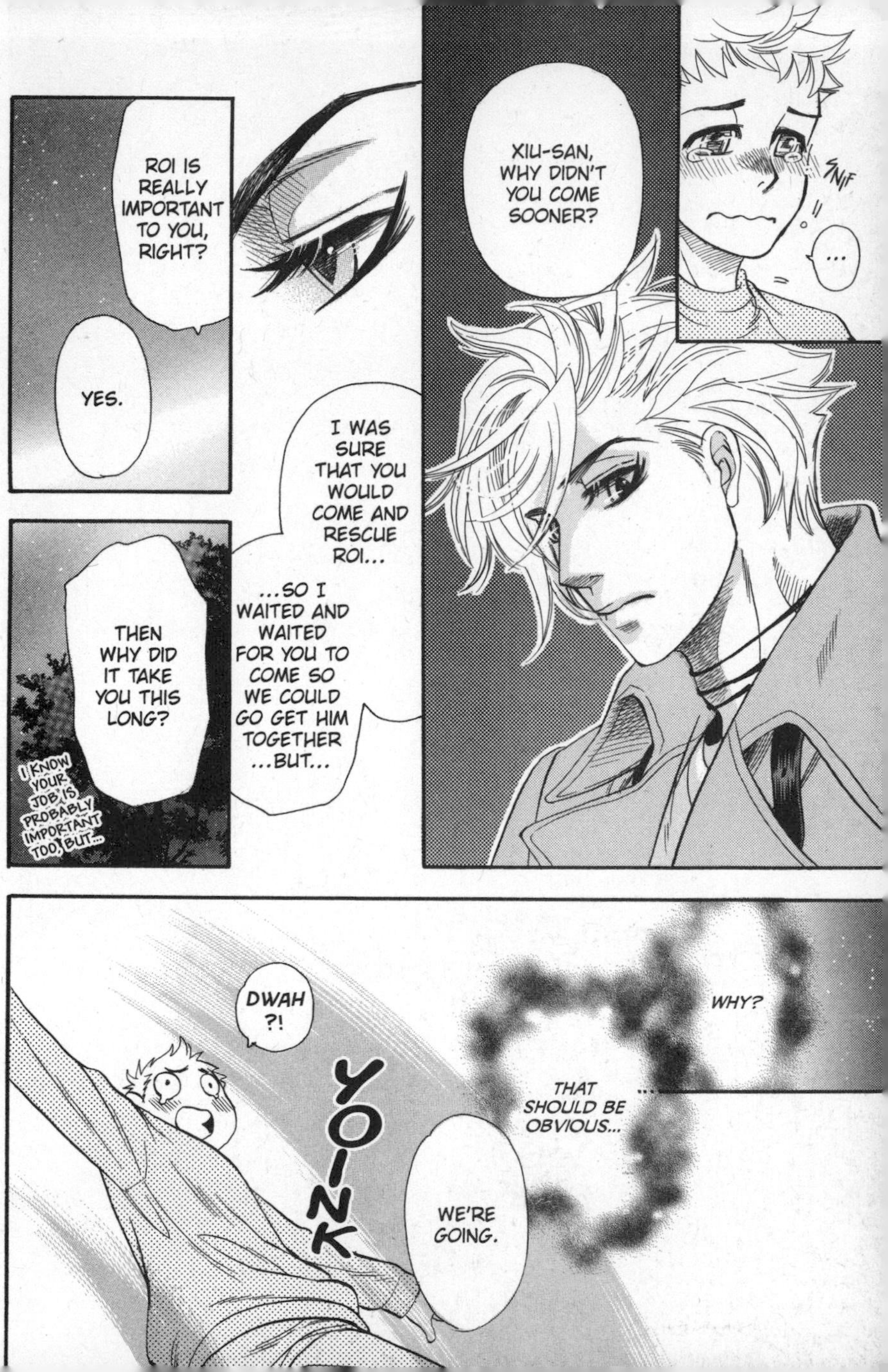

XIU-SAN, WHY DIDN'T YOU COME SOONER?
SNIF
...
I WAS SURE THAT YOU WOULD COME AND RESCUE ROI...
...SO I WAITED AND WAITED FOR YOU TO COME SO WE COULD GO GET HIM TOGETHER ...BUT...
ROI IS REALLY IMPORTANT TO YOU, RIGHT?
YES.
THEN WHY DID IT TAKE YOU THIS LONG?
I KNOW YOUR JOB IS PROBABLY IMPORTANT TOO, BUT...
WHY?
...THAT SHOULD BE OBVIOUS...
WE'RE GOING.
YOINK
DWAH ?!

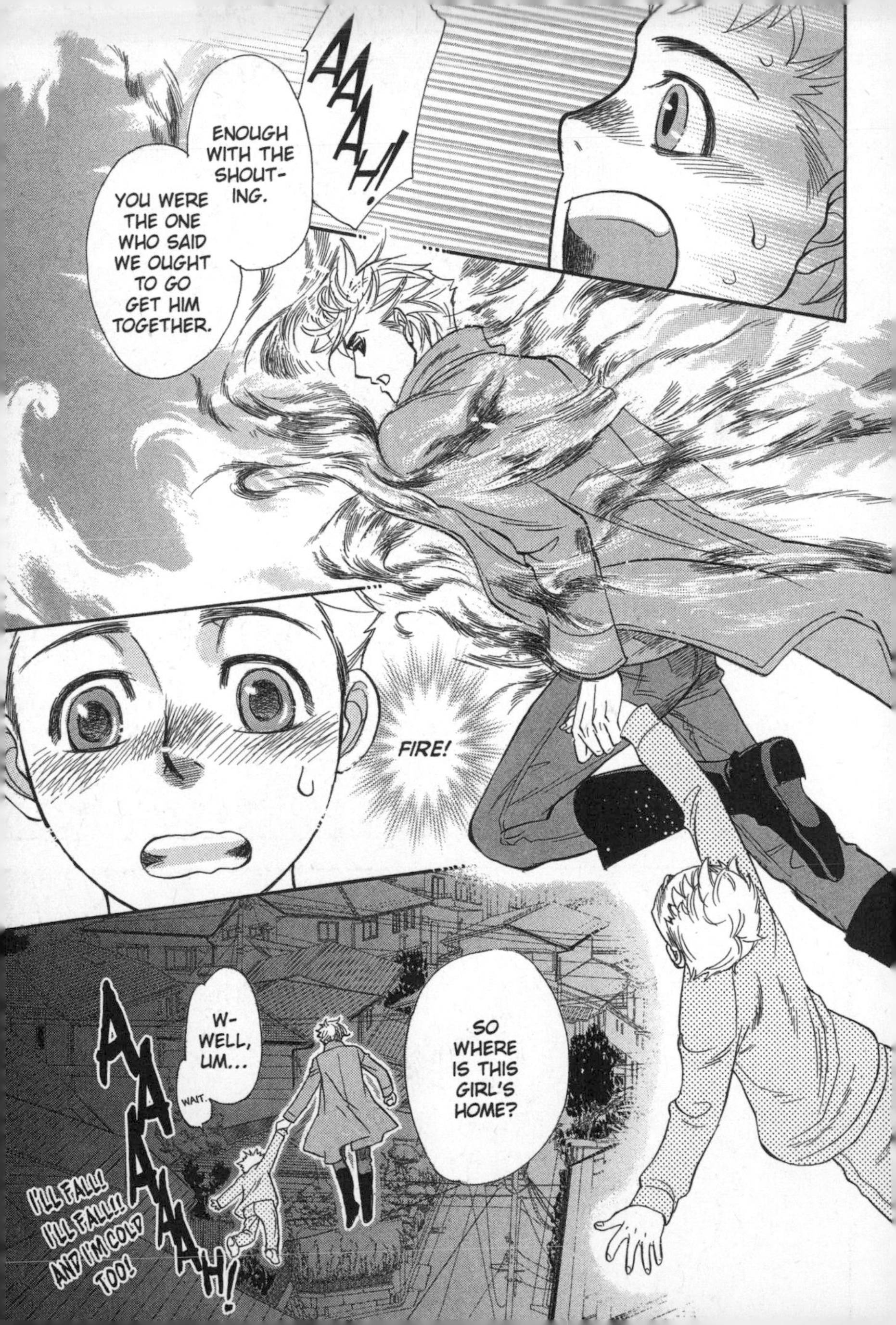
AAAAH!
ENOUGH WITH THE SHOUTING.
YOU WERE THE ONE WHO SAID WE OUGHT TO GO GET HIM TOGETHER.
FIRE!
SO WHERE IS THIS GIRL'S HOME?
W-WELL, UM...
WAIT.
AAAAAAH!
I'LL FALL! I'LL FALL!! AND I'M COLD TOO!

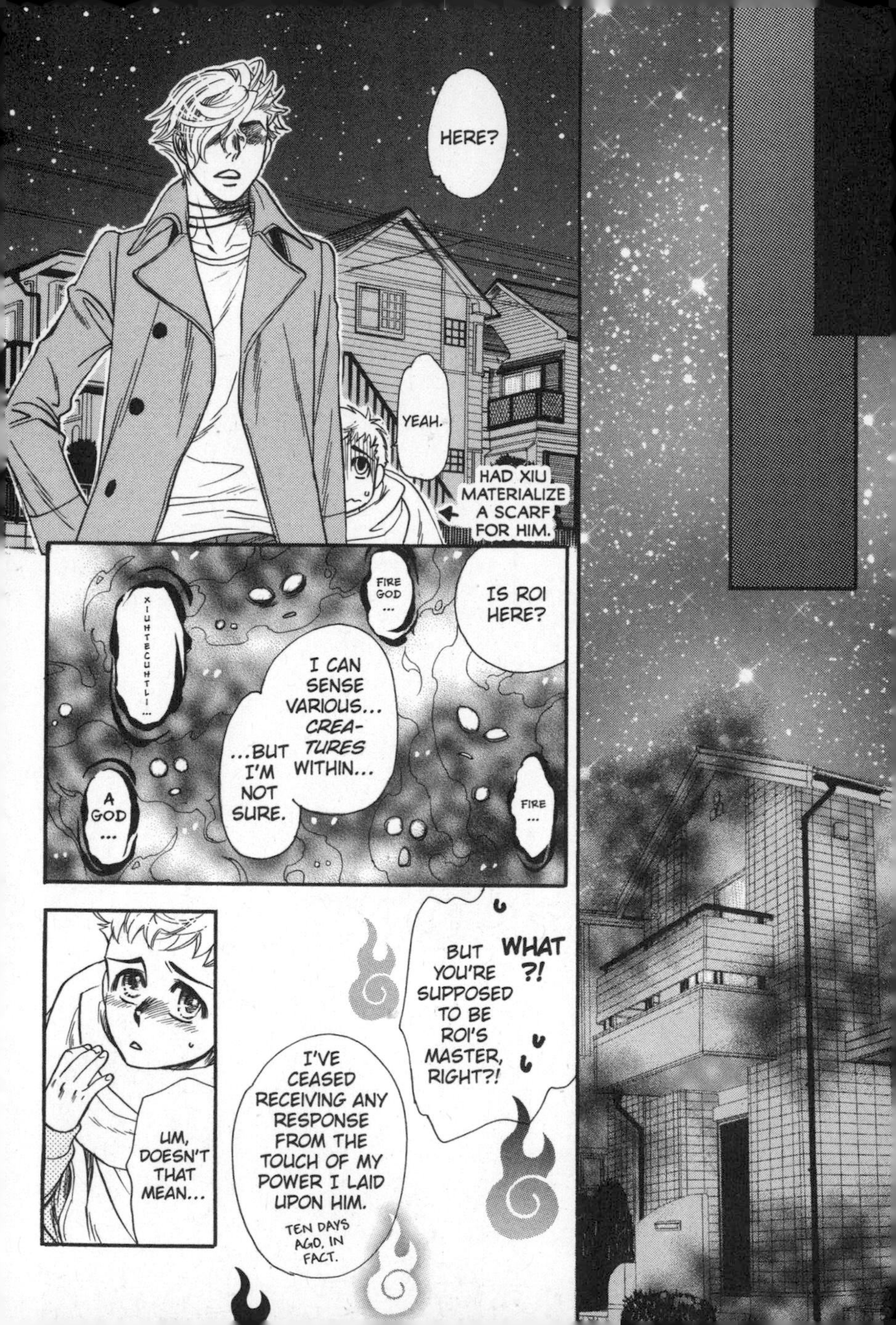
HERE?
YEAH.
HAD XIU MATERIALIZE A SCARF FOR HIM.
IS ROI HERE?
FIRE GOD ...
I CAN SENSE VARIOUS... CREATURES WITHIN...
XIUHTECUHTLI...
...BUT I'M NOT SURE.
FIRE ...
A GOD ...
WHAT?!
BUT YOU'RE SUPPOSED TO BE ROI'S MASTER, RIGHT?!
I'VE CEASED RECEIVING ANY RESPONSE FROM THE TOUCH OF MY POWER I LAID UPON HIM.
TEN DAYS AGO, IN FACT.
UM, DOESN'T THAT MEAN...

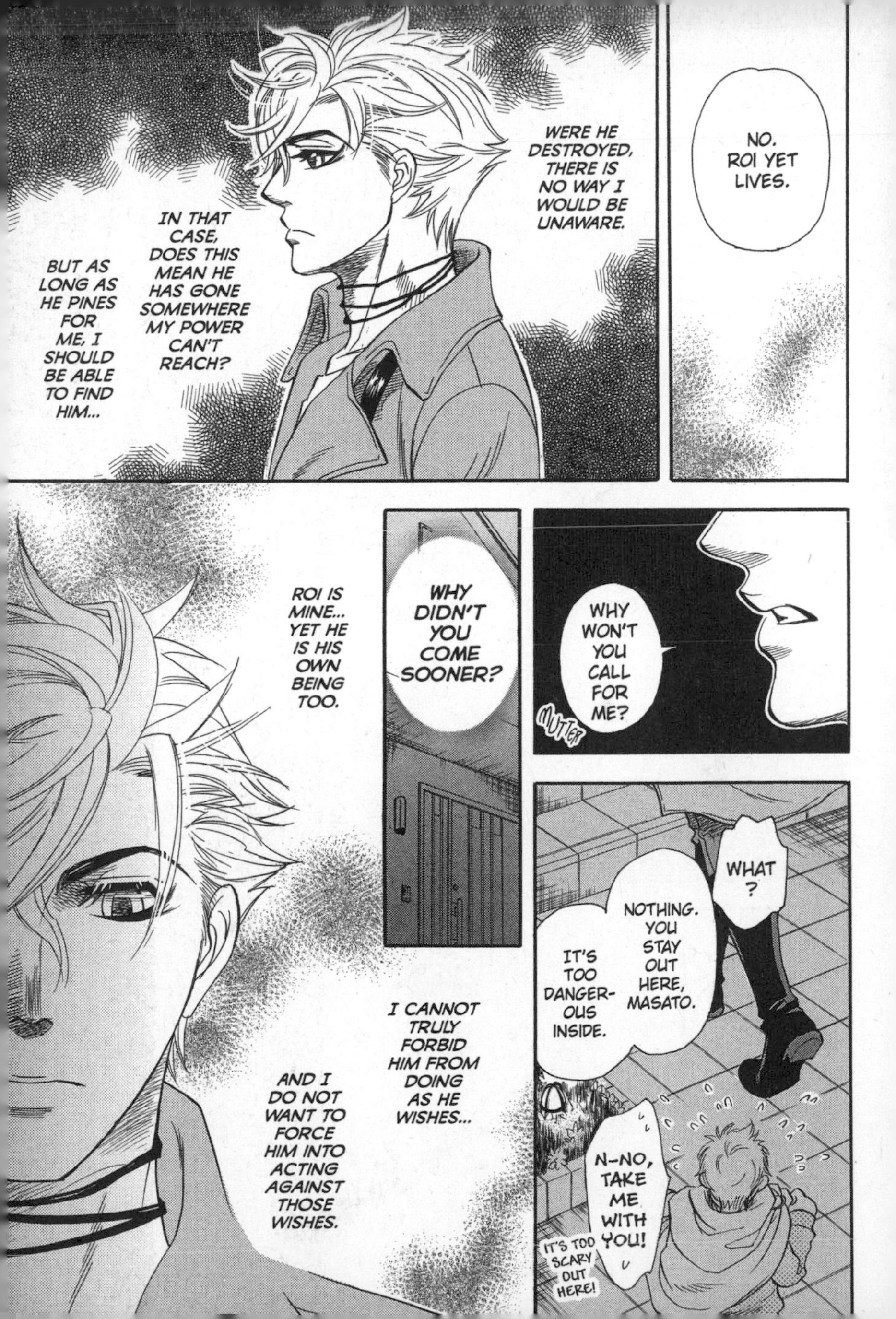
NO. ROI YET LIVES.
WERE HE DESTROYED, THERE IS NO WAY I WOULD BE UNAWARE.
IN THAT CASE, DOES THIS MEAN HE HAS GONE SOMEWHERE MY POWER CAN'T REACH?
BUT AS LONG AS HE PINES FOR ME, I SHOULD BE ABLE TO FIND HIM...
WHY WON'T YOU CALL FOR ME?
MUTTER
WHAT?
NOTHING. YOU STAY OUT HERE, MASATO.
IT'S TOO DANGER-OUS INSIDE.
N-NO, TAKE ME WITH YOU!
IT'S TOO SCARY OUT HERE!
WHY DIDN'T YOU COME SOONER?
ROI IS MINE... YET HE IS HIS OWN BEING TOO.
I CANNOT TRULY FORBID HIM FROM DOING AS HE WISHES...
AND I DO NOT WANT TO FORCE HIM INTO ACTING AGAINST THOSE WISHES.

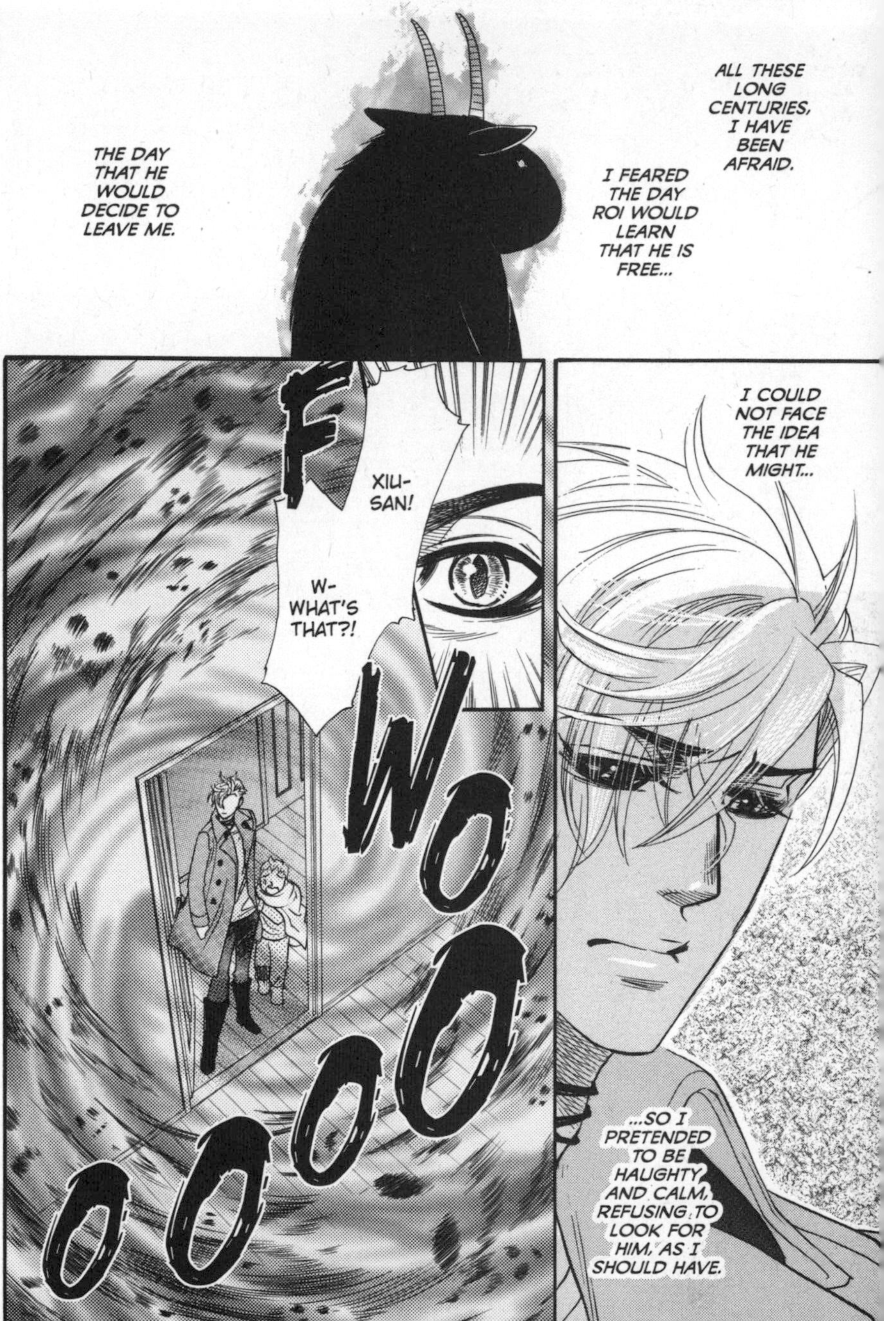
ALL THESE LONG CENTURIES, I HAVE BEEN AFRAID.
I FEARED THE DAY ROI WOULD LEARN THAT HE IS FREE...
THE DAY THAT HE WOULD DECIDE TO LEAVE ME.
I COULD NOT FACE THE IDEA THAT HE MIGHT...
...SO I PRETENDED TO BE HAUGHTY AND CALM, REFUSING TO LOOK FOR HIM, AS I SHOULD HAVE.
FWOOOOOOO
XIU-SAN!
W-WHAT'S THAT?!

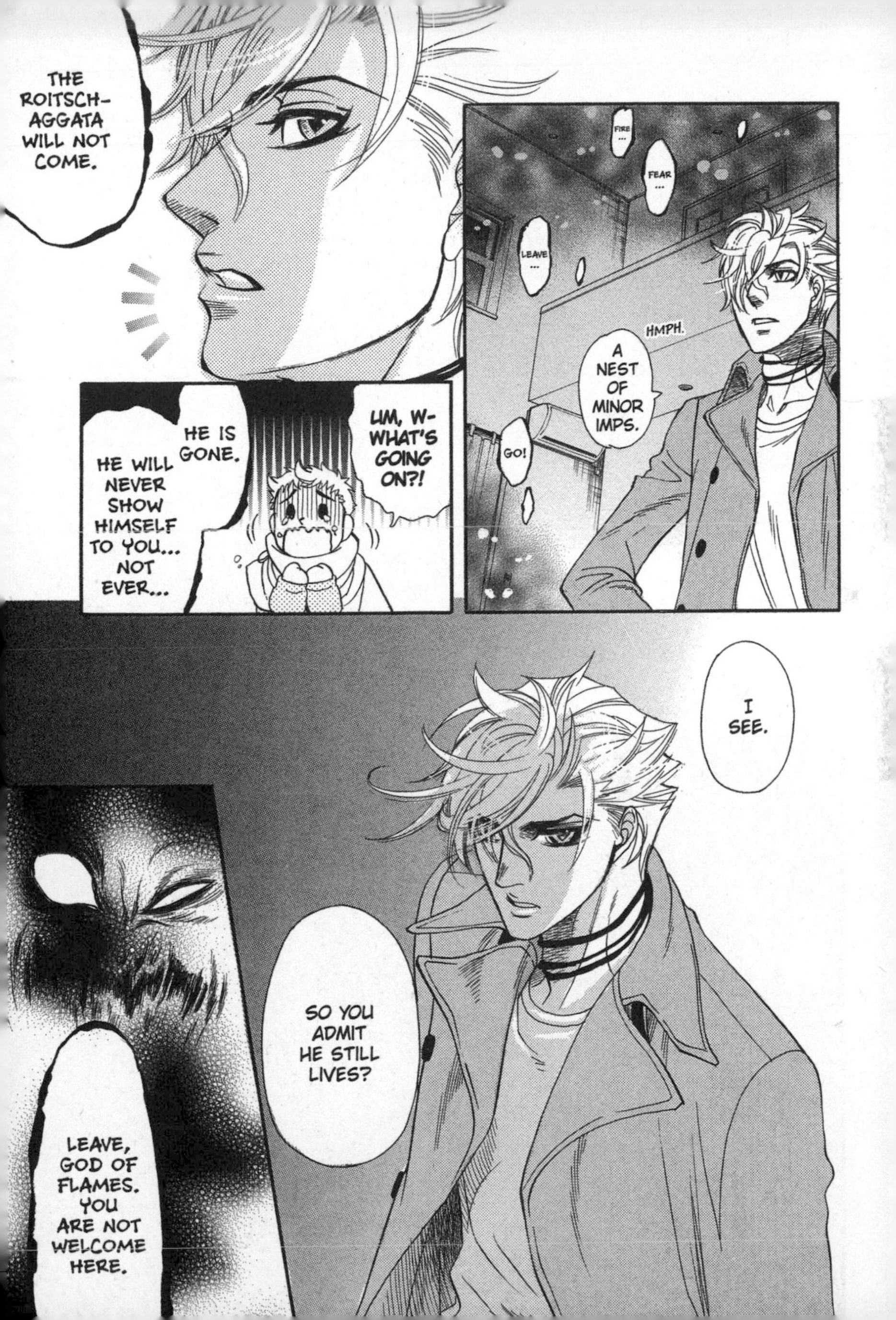
FEAR...
FIRE...
LEAVE...
HMPH.
A NEST OF MINOR IMPS.
GO!
THE ROITSCH-AGGATA WILL NOT COME.
UM, W-WHAT'S GOING ON?!
HE IS GONE.
HE WILL NEVER SHOW HIMSELF TO YOU... NOT EVER...
I SEE.
SO YOU ADMIT HE STILL LIVES?
LEAVE, GOD OF FLAMES. YOU ARE NOT WELCOME HERE.

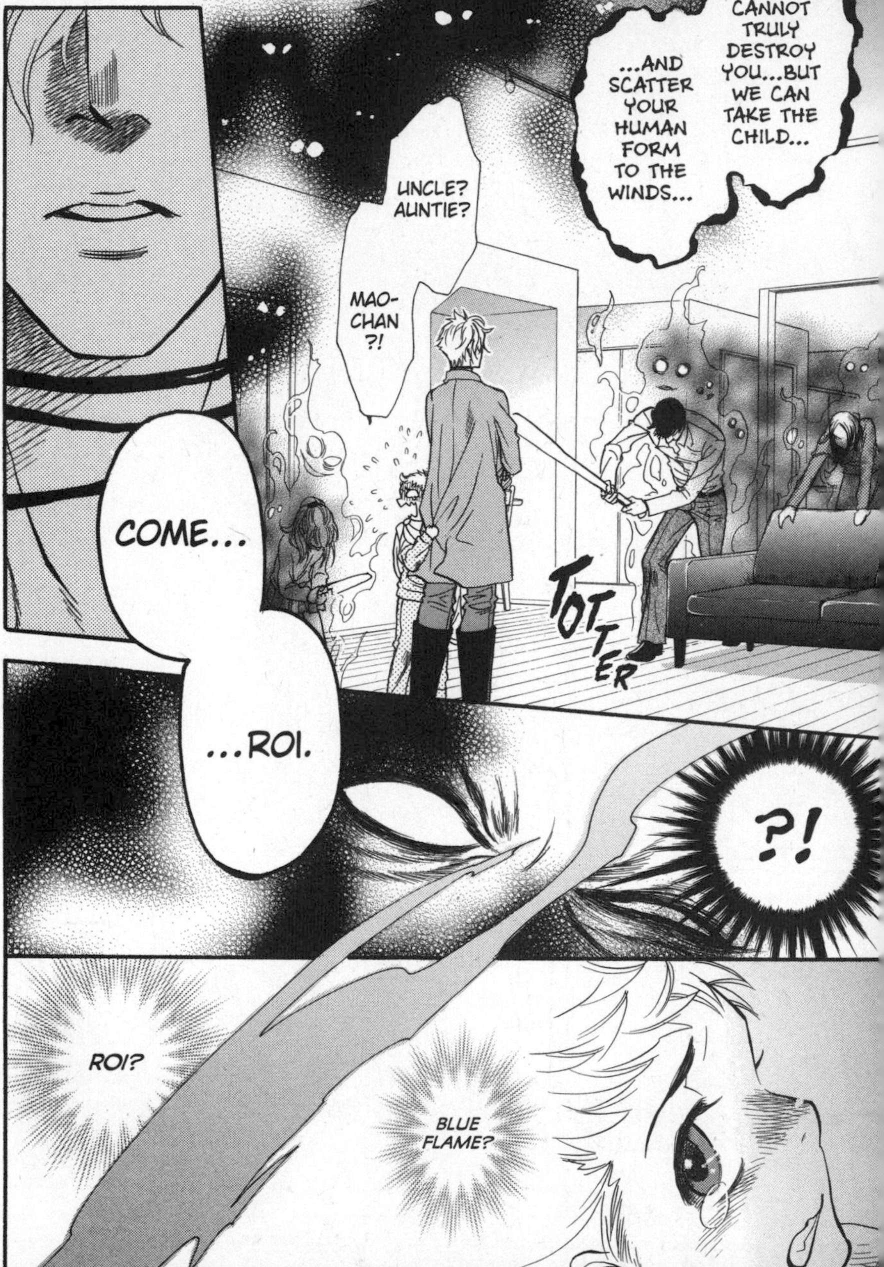
WE CANNOT TRULY DESTROY YOU...BUT WE CAN TAKE THE CHILD...
...AND SCATTER YOUR HUMAN FORM TO THE WINDS...
UNCLE? AUNTIE?
MAO-CHAN?!
TOTTER
COME...
...ROI.
?!
ROI?
BLUE FLAME?

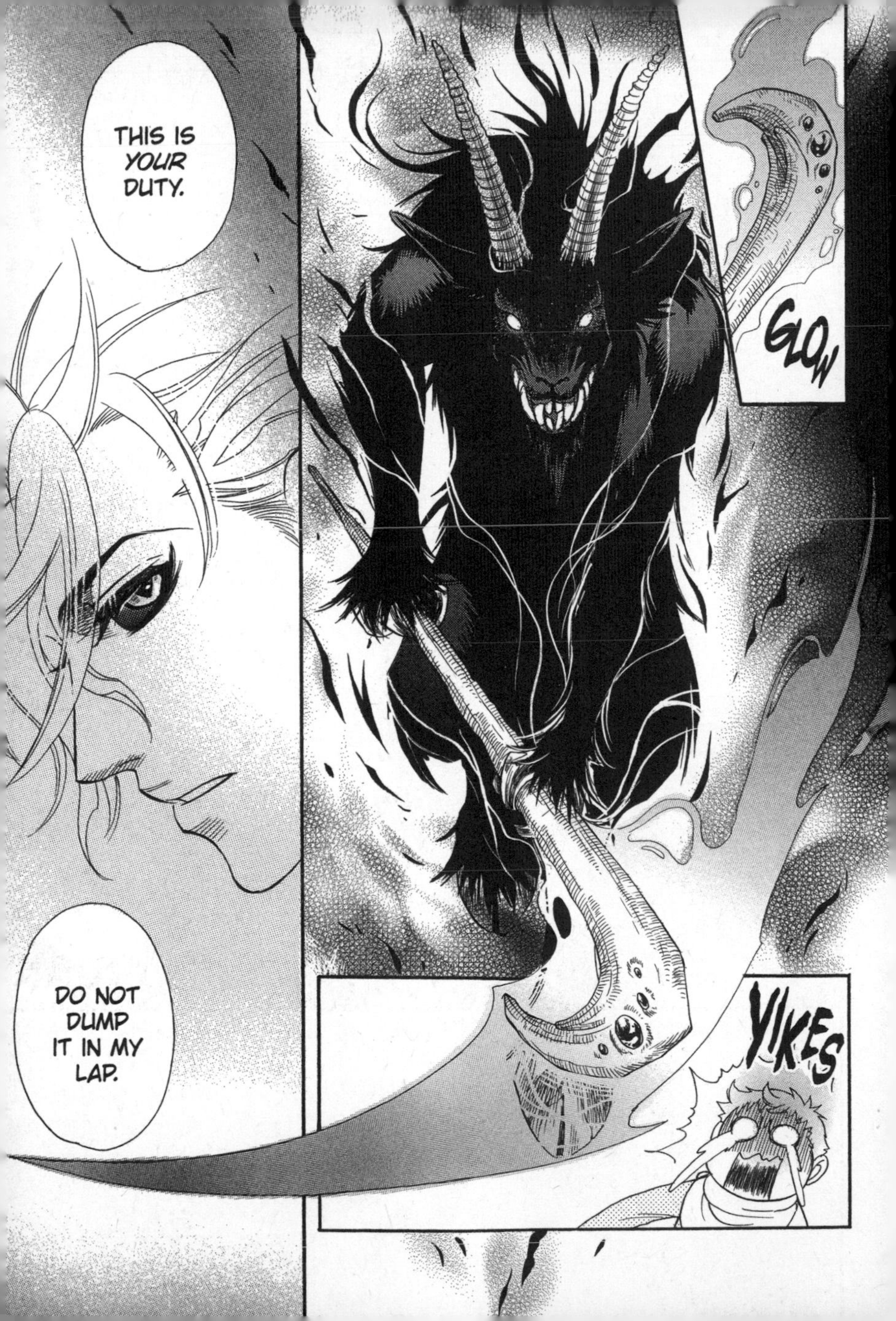
GLOW
YIKES
THIS IS YOUR DUTY.
DO NOT DUMP IT IN MY LAP.

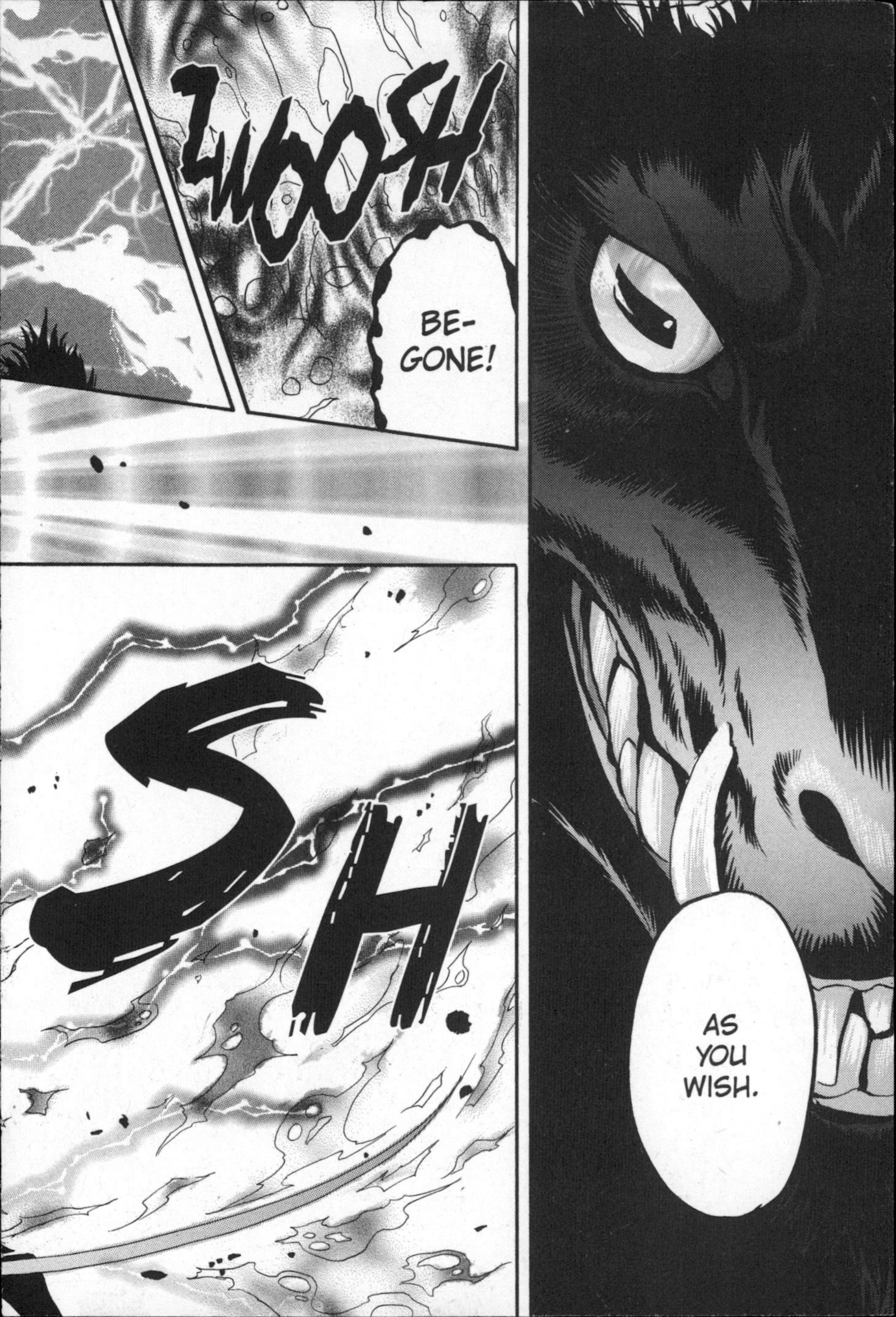
AS YOU WISH.
WHOOSH
BE-GONE!
SH

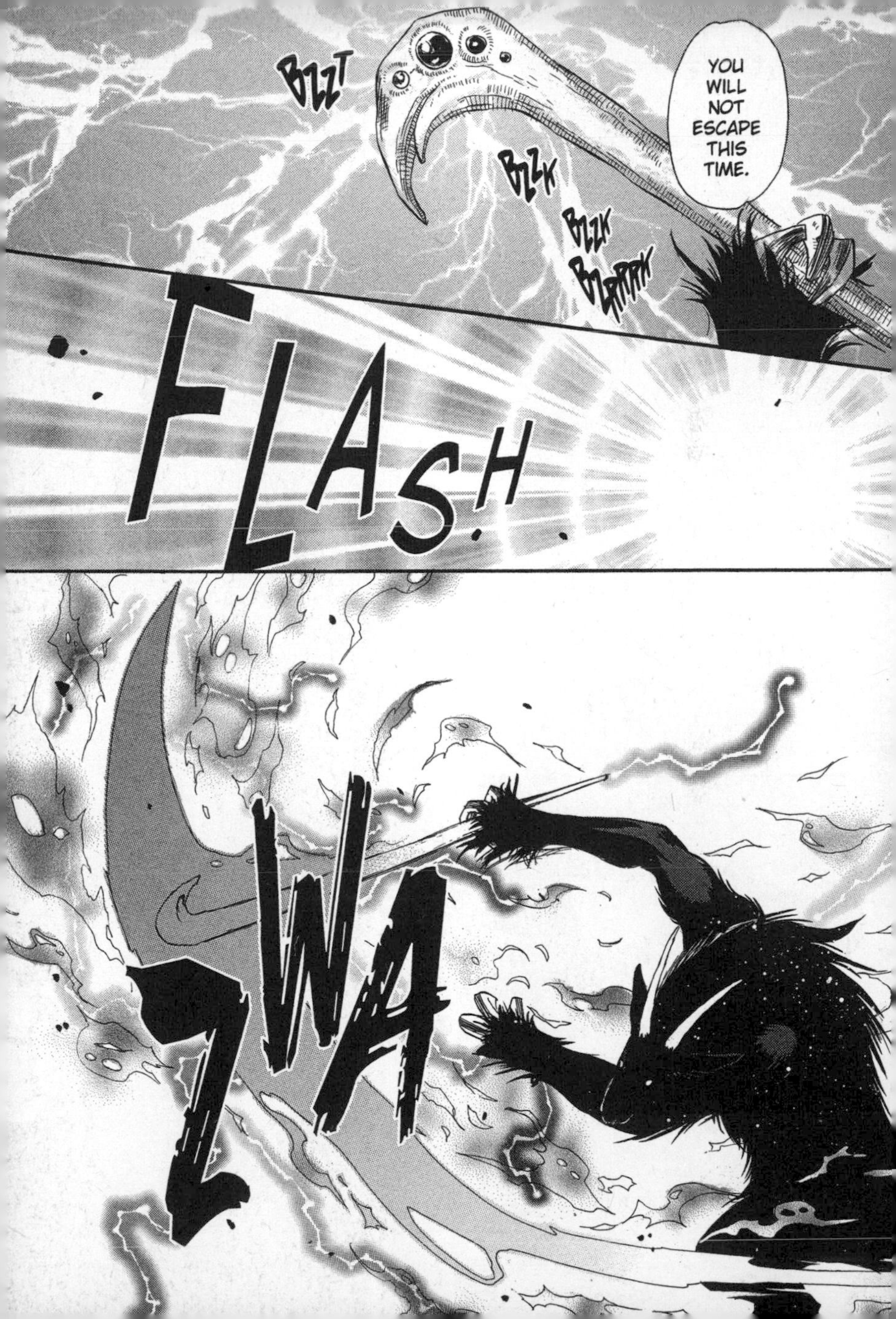
YOU WILL NOT ESCAPE THIS TIME.
BZZK
BZZK
BZZRRRRK
BZZT
FLASH!
ZWA

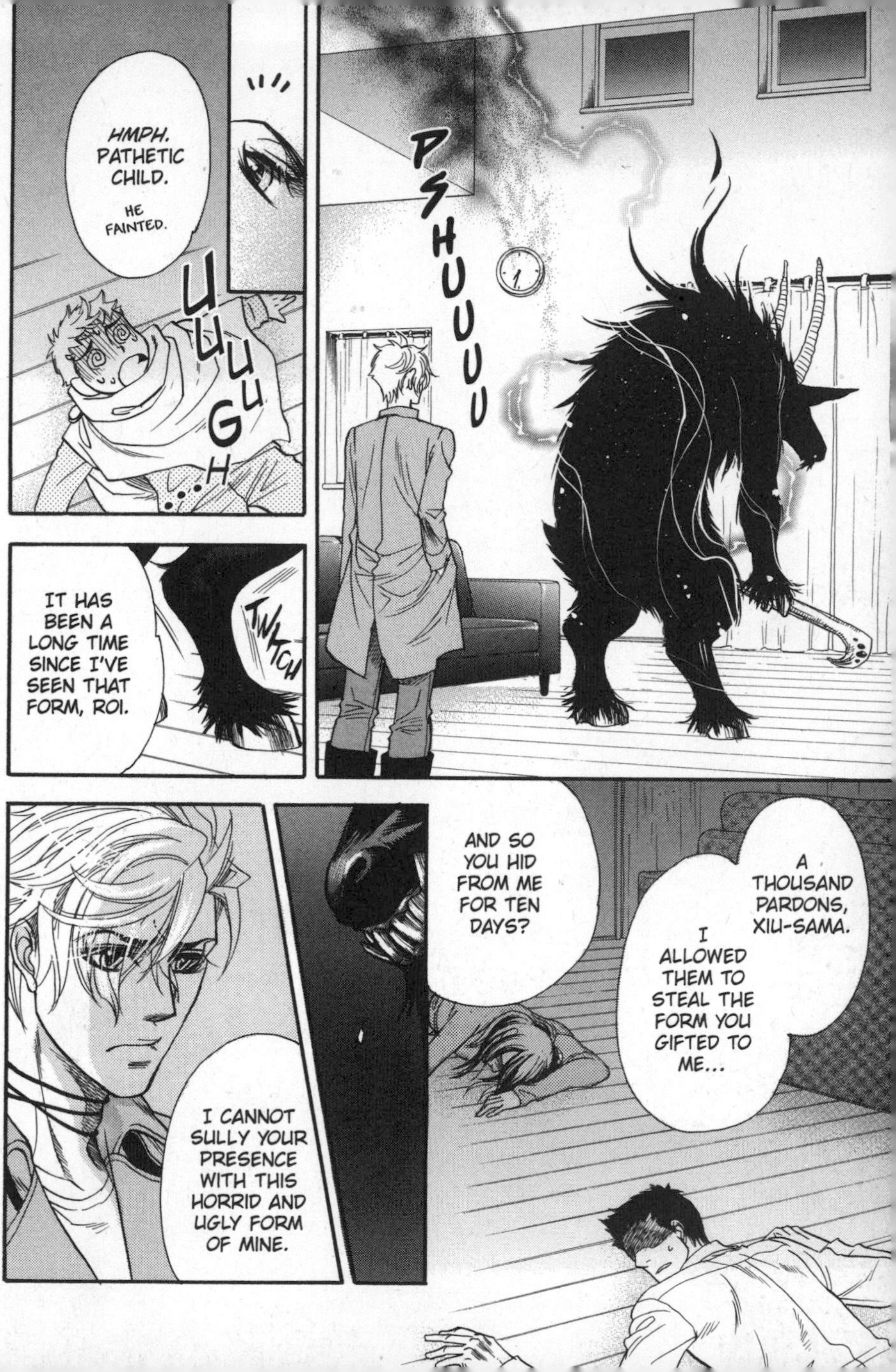
PSHUUUUU
HMPH. PATHETIC CHILD.
HE FAINTED.
UUUUGH
...
IT HAS BEEN A LONG TIME SINCE I'VE SEEN THAT FORM, ROI.
TWKCH
A THOUSAND PARDONS, XIU-SAMA.
I ALLOWED THEM TO STEAL THE FORM YOU GIFTED TO ME...
AND SO YOU HID FROM ME FOR TEN DAYS?
I CANNOT SULLY YOUR PRESENCE WITH THIS HORRID AND UGLY FORM OF MINE.

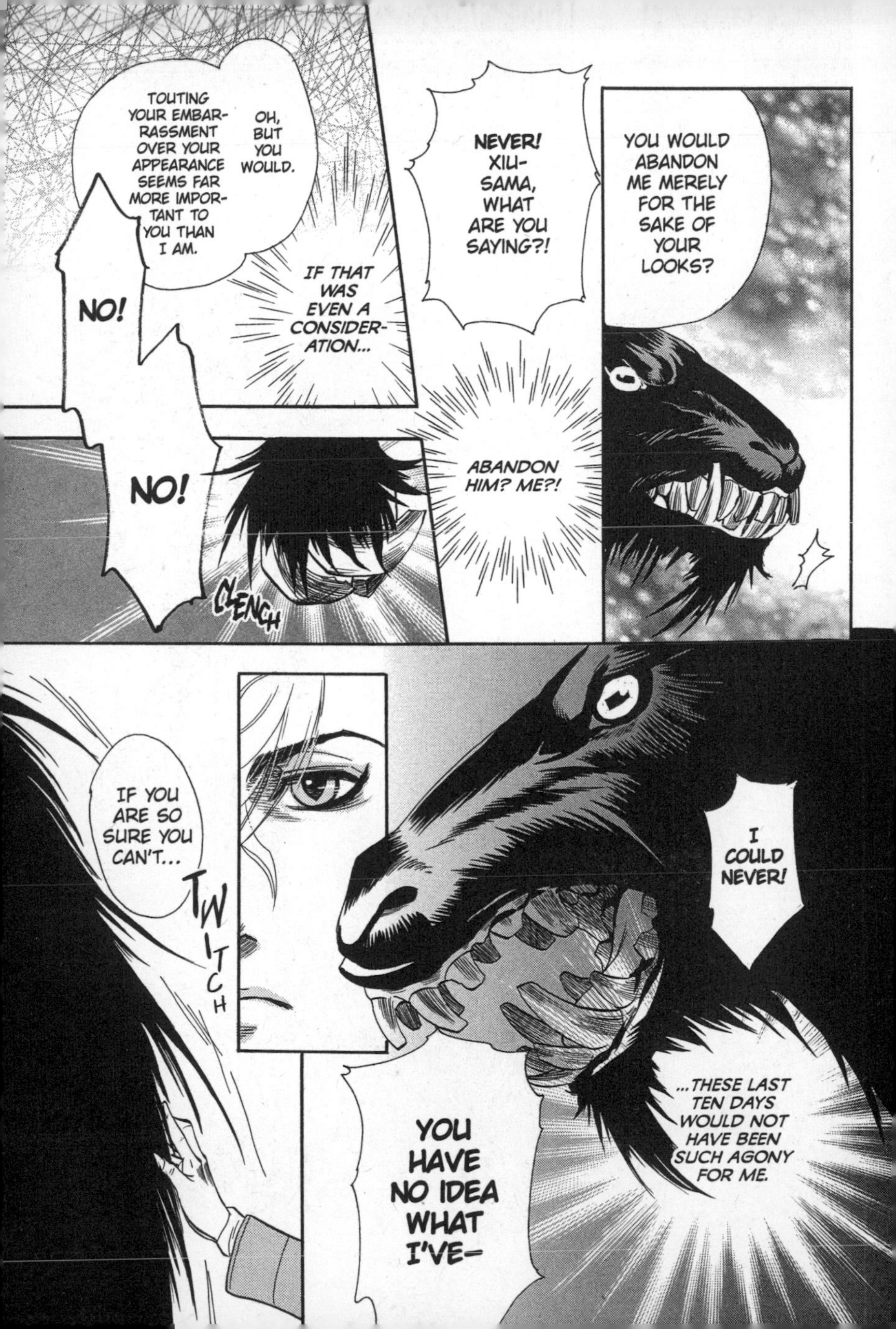
YOU WOULD ABANDON ME MERELY FOR THE SAKE OF YOUR LOOKS?
NEVER! XIU-SAMA, WHAT ARE YOU SAYING?!
OH, BUT YOU WOULD.
TOUTING YOUR EMBARRASSMENT OVER YOUR APPEARANCE SEEMS FAR MORE IMPORTANT TO YOU THAN I AM.
IF THAT WAS EVEN A CONSIDERATION...
NO!
ABANDON HIM? ME?!
NO!
CLENCH
I COULD NEVER!
IF YOU ARE SO SURE YOU CAN'T...
TWITCH
...THESE LAST TEN DAYS WOULD NOT HAVE BEEN SUCH AGONY FOR ME.
YOU HAVE NO IDEA WHAT I'VE—

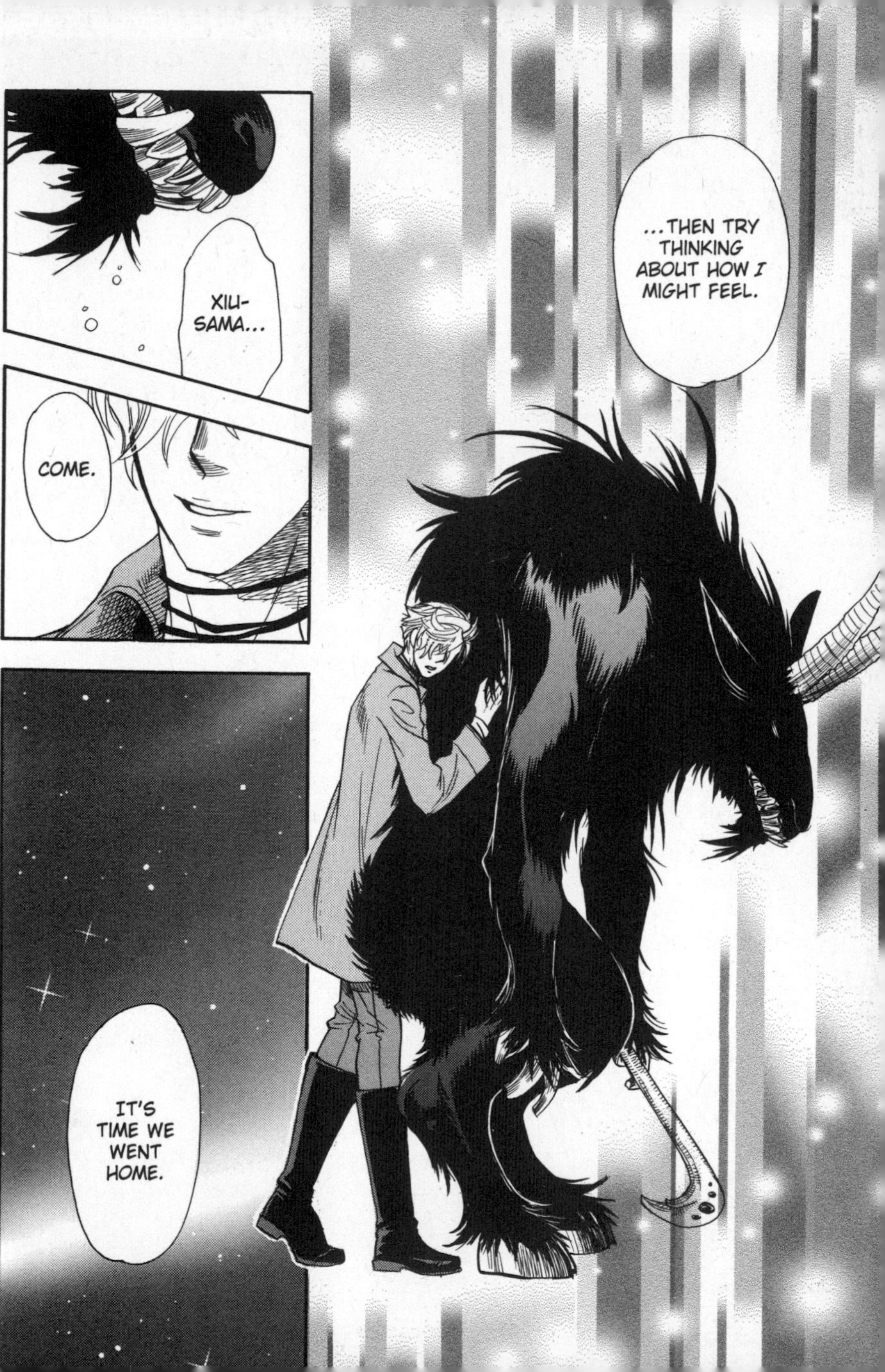
...THEN TRY THINKING ABOUT HOW I MIGHT FEEL.
XIU-SAMA...
COME.
IT'S TIME WE WENT HOME.

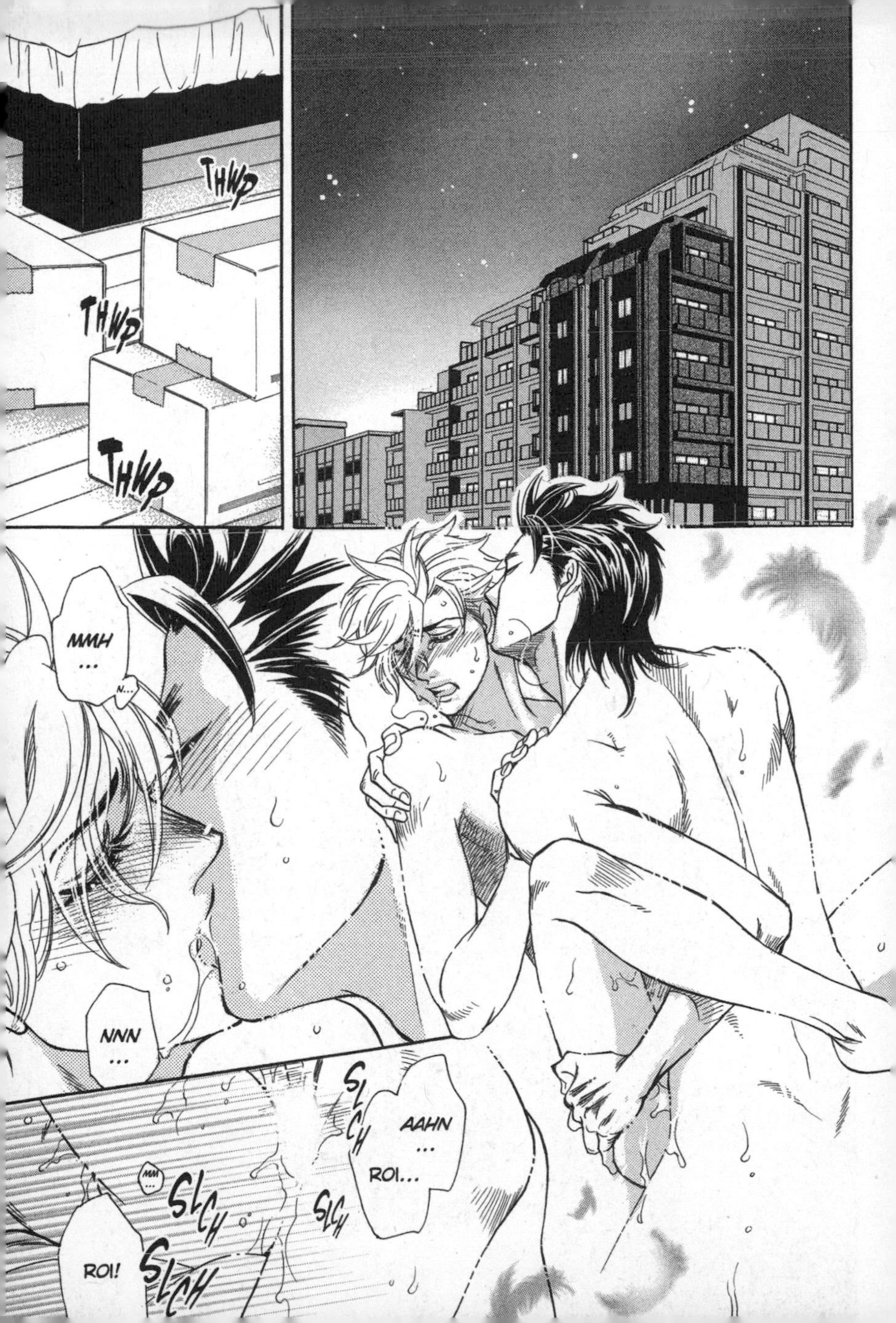
THWP
THWP
THWP
MMH ...
N...
NNN ...
SLCH
AAHN ... ROI...
SLCH
MM...
SLCH
ROI!
SLCH

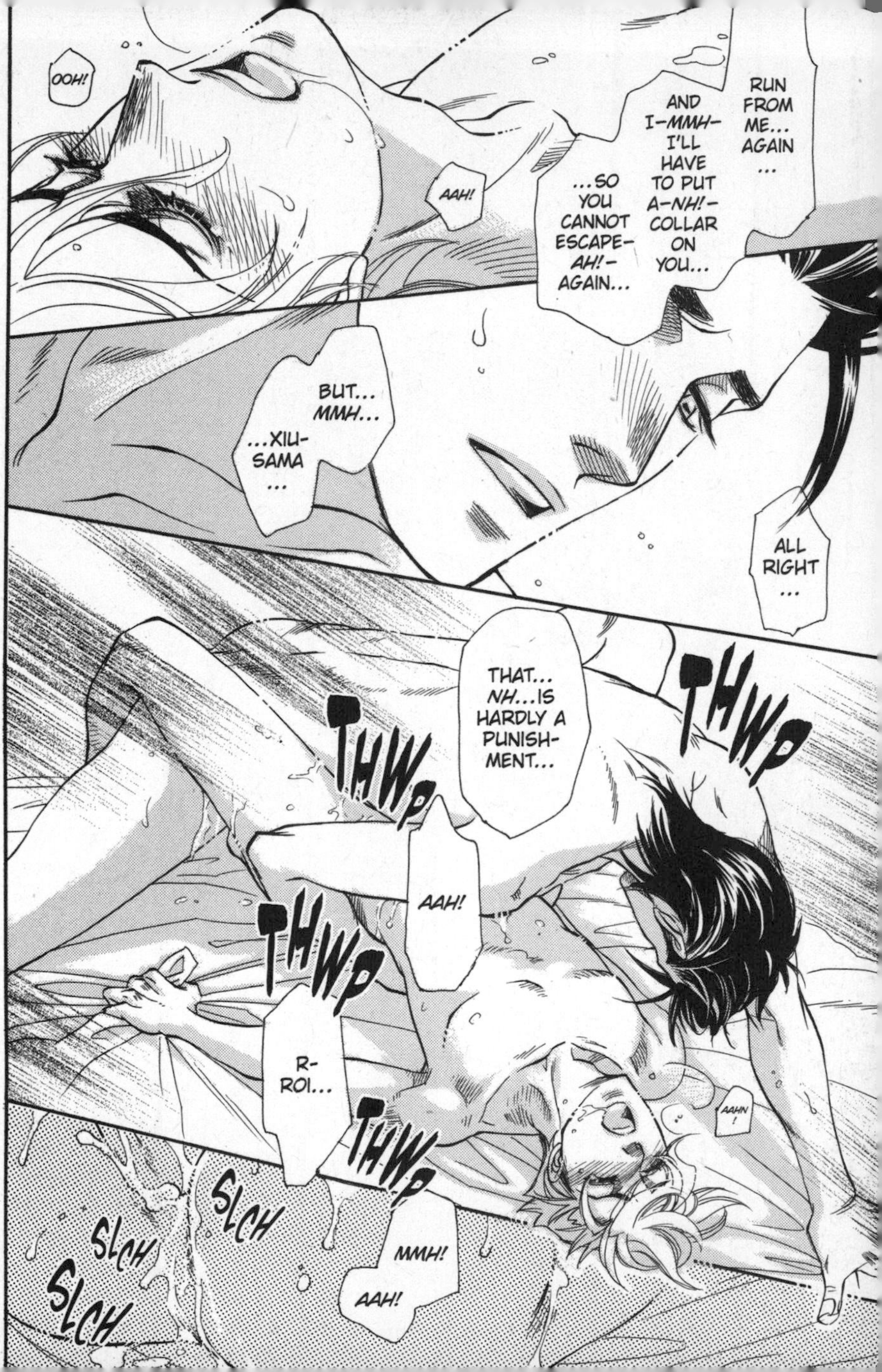
RUN FROM ME... AGAIN...
AND I—MMH— I'LL HAVE TO PUT A—NH!— COLLAR ON YOU...
...SO YOU CANNOT ESCAPE—AH!— AGAIN...
AAH!
OOH!
ALL RIGHT...
BUT... MMH...
...XIU-SAMA...
THWP
THAT... NH...IS HARDLY A PUNISHMENT...
THWP
AAH!
THWP
R-ROI...
AAHN!
THWP
SLCH
MMH!
AAH!
SLCH
SLCH

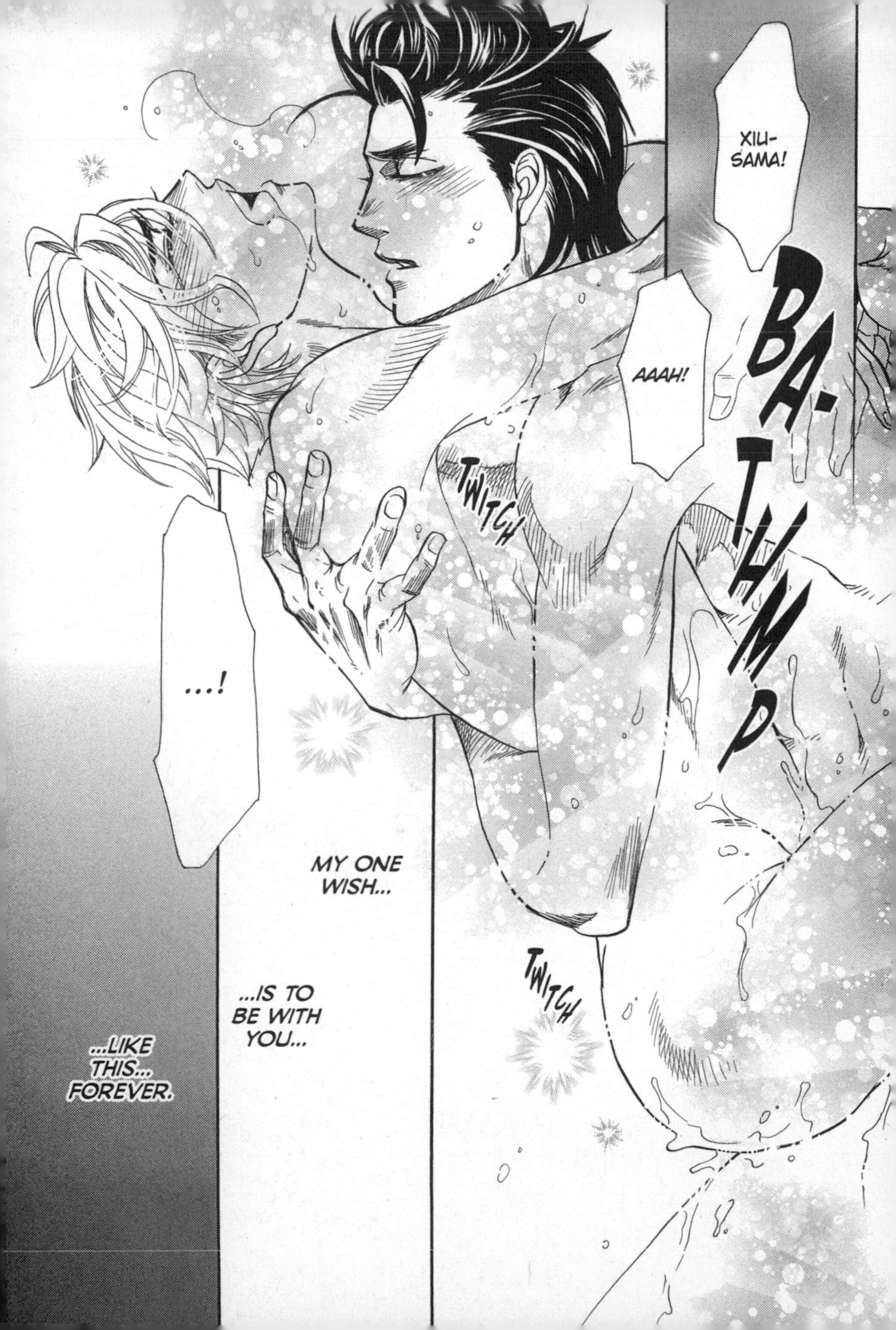
XIU-SAMA!
AAAH!
BA-THMP
TWITCH
TWITCH
MY ONE WISH...
...IS TO BE WITH YOU...
...!
...LIKE THIS... FOREVER.

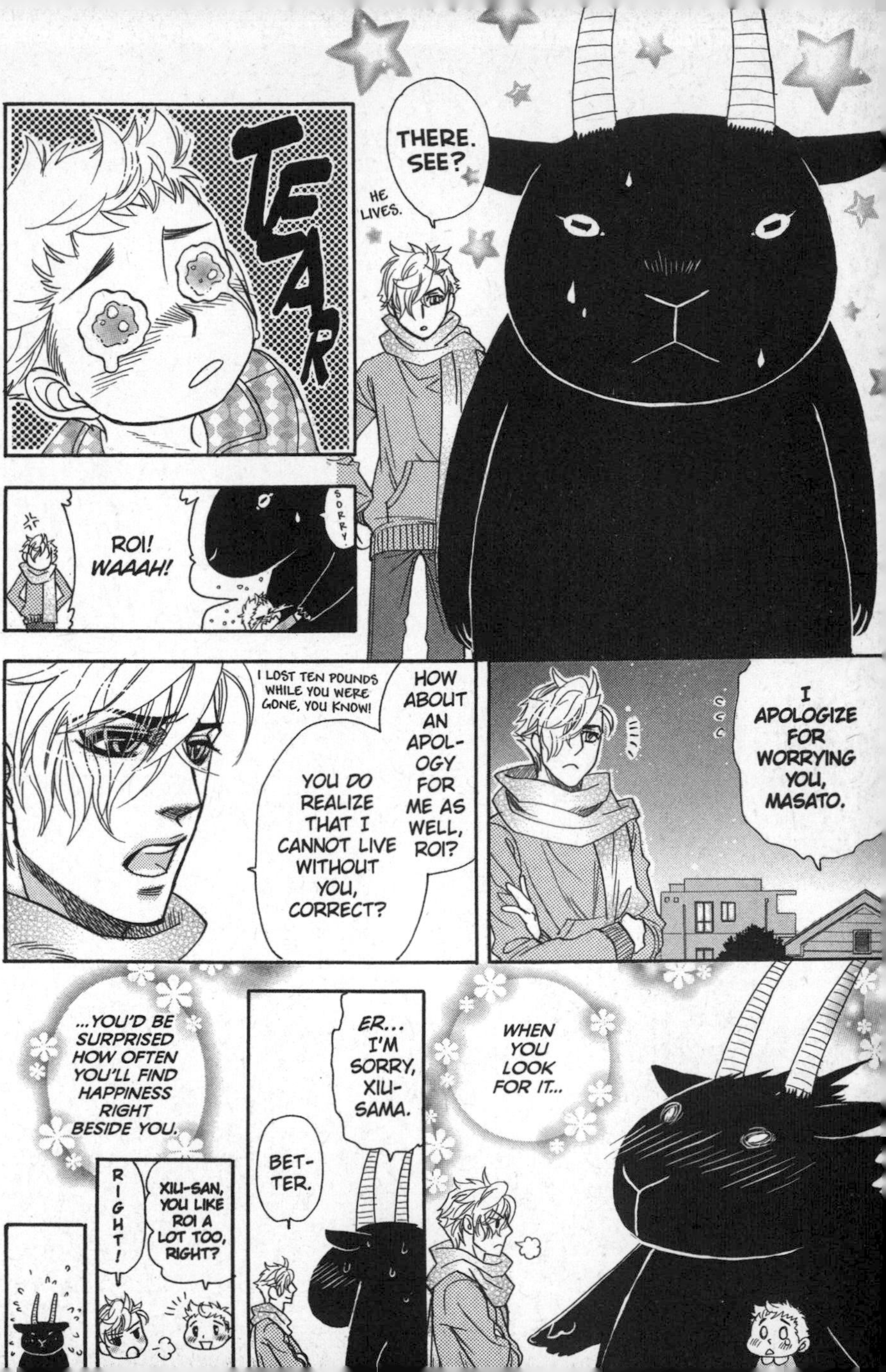
THERE. SEE?
HE LIVES.
TEAR
ROI! WAAAH!
SORRY.
I APOLOGIZE FOR WORRYING YOU, MASATO.
HOW ABOUT AN APOLOGY FOR ME AS WELL, ROI?
I LOST TEN POUNDS WHILE YOU WERE GONE, YOU KNOW!
YOU DO REALIZE THAT I CANNOT LIVE WITHOUT YOU, CORRECT?
WHEN YOU LOOK FOR IT...
ER... I'M SORRY, XIU-SAMA.
BETTER.
...YOU'D BE SURPRISED HOW OFTEN YOU'LL FIND HAPPINESS RIGHT BESIDE YOU.
XIU-SAN, YOU LIKE ROI A LOT TOO, RIGHT?
RIGHT!

END

Bohra Naono Presents

THANKS, ROI!

彼方者の
困惑
あっちものこんわく

Midnight Stranger

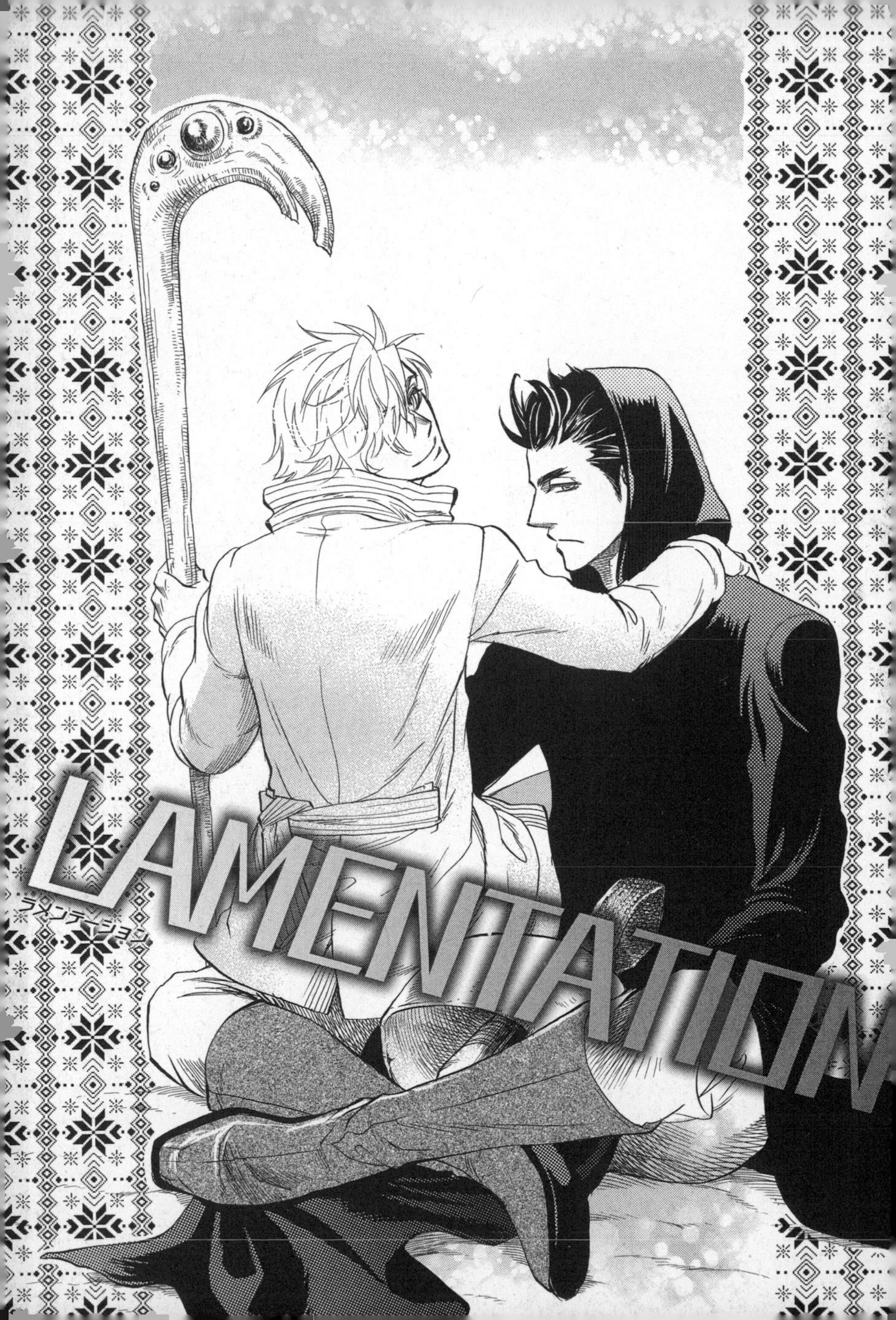
LAMENTATION
ラメンテーション

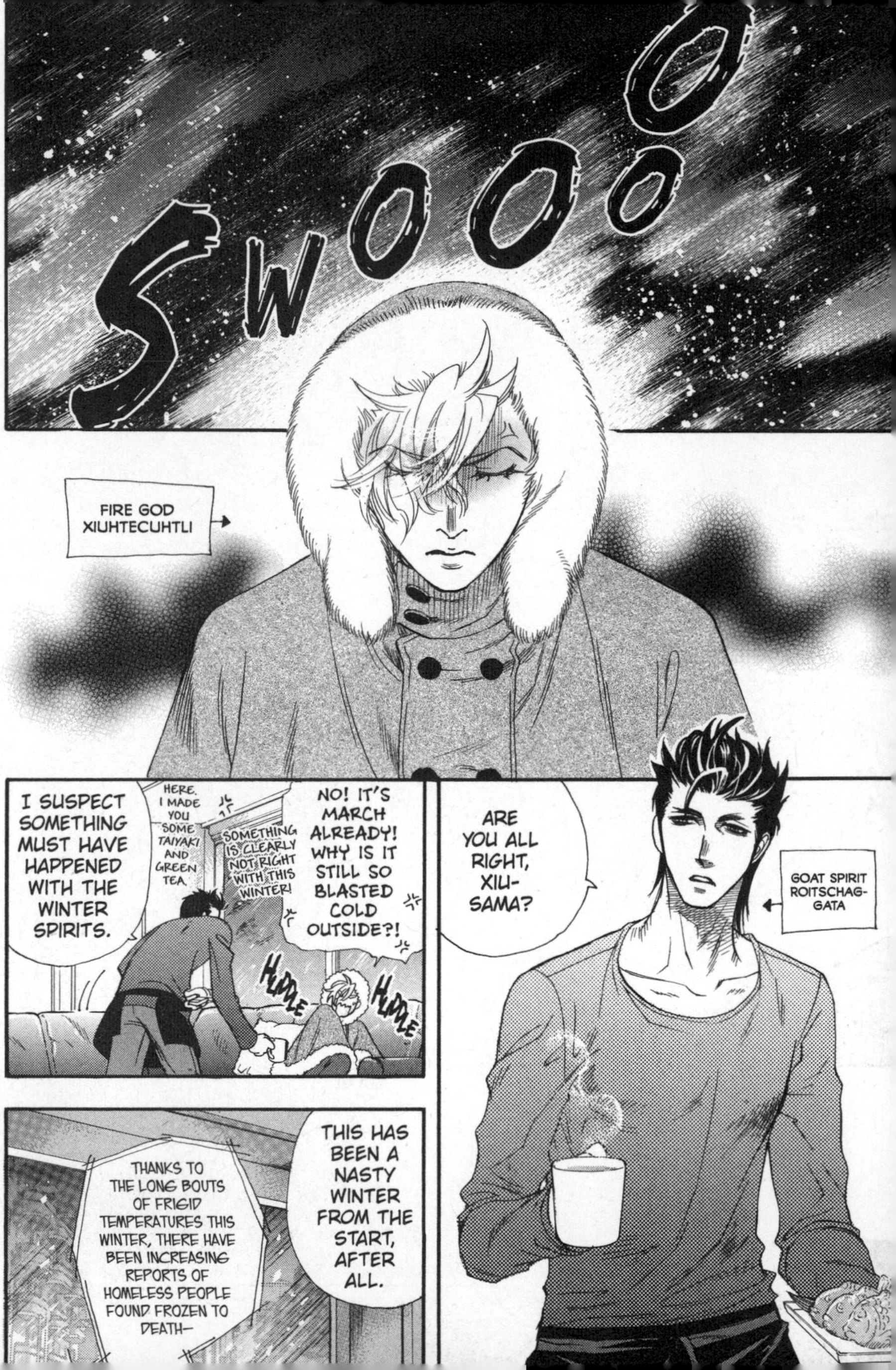
SWOOOOO
FIRE GOD XIUHTECUHTLI
ARE YOU ALL RIGHT, XIU-SAMA?
GOAT SPIRIT ROITSCHAGGATA
NO! IT'S MARCH ALREADY! WHY IS IT STILL SO BLASTED COLD OUTSIDE?!
SOMETHING IS CLEARLY NOT RIGHT WITH THIS WINTER!
HERE. I MADE YOU SOME TAIYAKI AND GREEN TEA.
I SUSPECT SOMETHING MUST HAVE HAPPENED WITH THE WINTER SPIRITS.
HUDDLE
HUDDLE
THIS HAS BEEN A NASTY WINTER FROM THE START, AFTER ALL.
THANKS TO THE LONG BOUTS OF FRIGID TEMPERATURES THIS WINTER, THERE HAVE BEEN INCREASING REPORTS OF HOMELESS PEOPLE FOUND FROZEN TO DEATH—

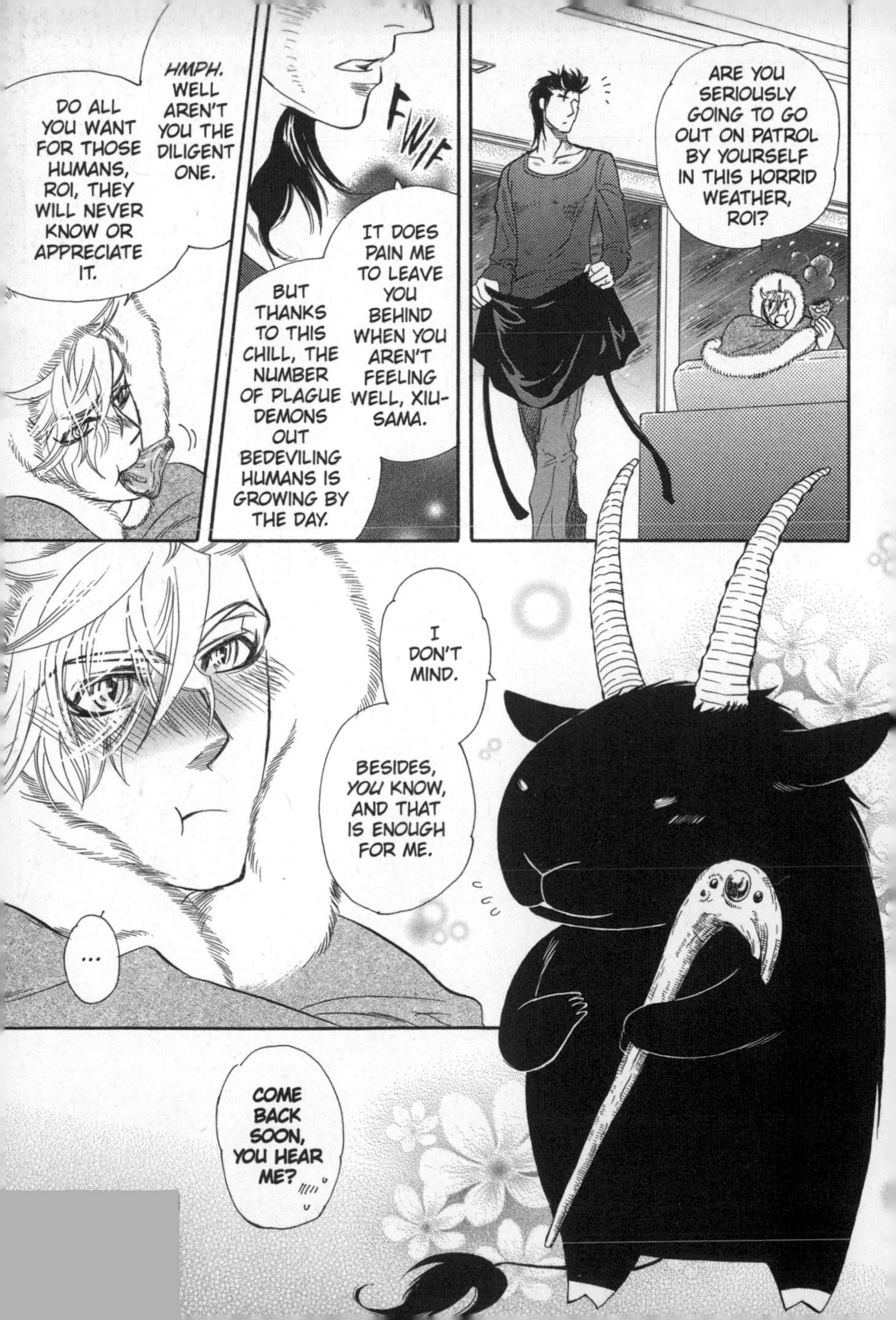

ARE YOU SERIOUSLY GOING TO GO OUT ON PATROL BY YOURSELF IN THIS HORRID WEATHER, ROI?
FWIF
IT DOES PAIN ME TO LEAVE YOU BEHIND WHEN YOU AREN'T FEELING WELL, XIU-SAMA.
BUT THANKS TO THIS CHILL, THE NUMBER OF PLAGUE DEMONS OUT BEDEVILING HUMANS IS GROWING BY THE DAY.
HMPH. WELL AREN'T YOU THE DILIGENT ONE.
DO ALL YOU WANT FOR THOSE HUMANS, ROI, THEY WILL NEVER KNOW OR APPRECIATE IT.
I DON'T MIND.
BESIDES, YOU KNOW, AND THAT IS ENOUGH FOR ME.
...
COME BACK SOON, YOU HEAR ME?

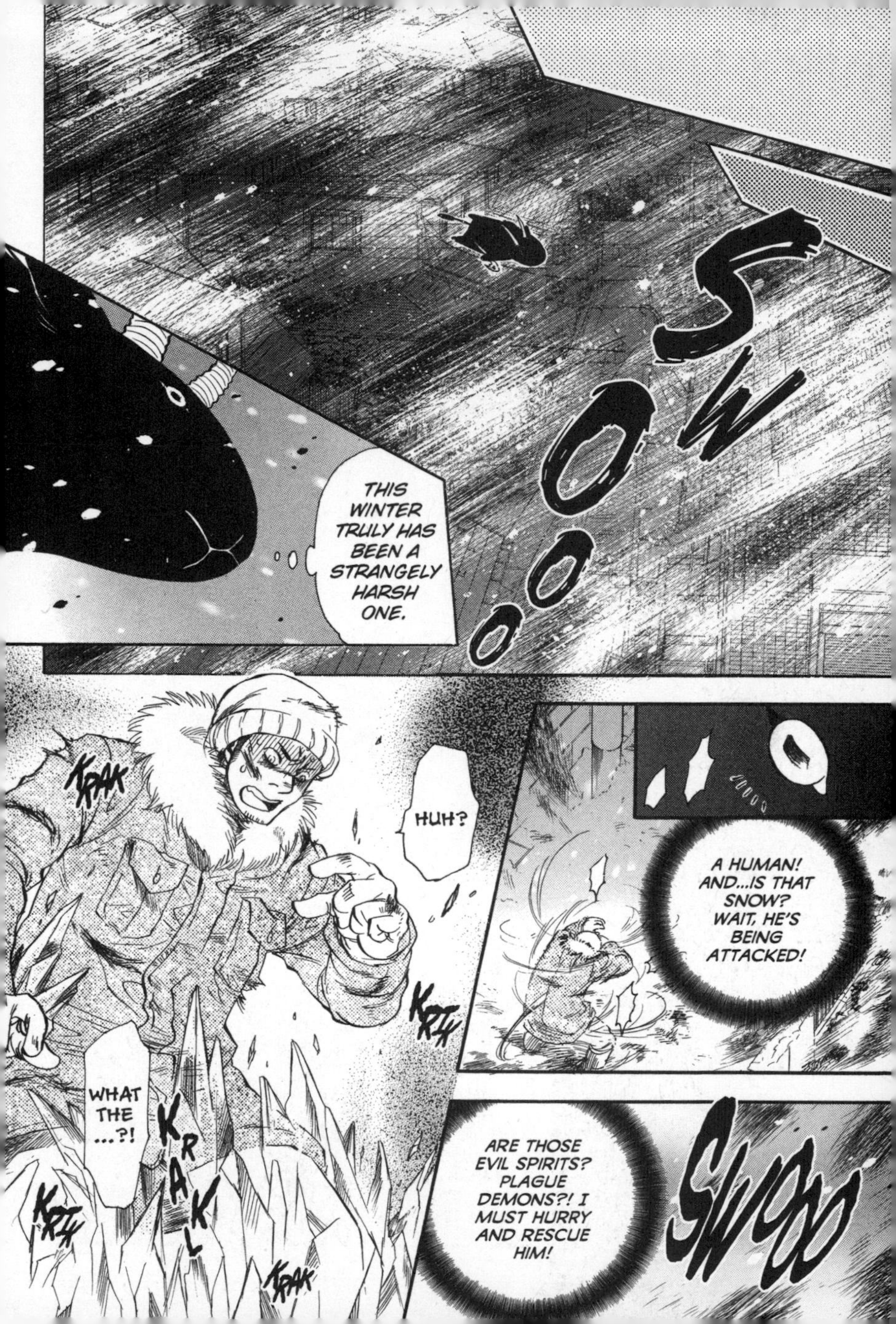
SWOOOO
THIS WINTER TRULY HAS BEEN A STRANGELY HARSH ONE.
A HUMAN! AND...IS THAT SNOW? WAIT, HE'S BEING ATTACKED!
ARE THOSE EVIL SPIRITS? PLAGUE DEMONS?! I MUST HURRY AND RESCUE HIM!
SWOO
HUH?
KRAK
KRIK
WHAT THE ...?!
KRAKL
KRIK
KRAK

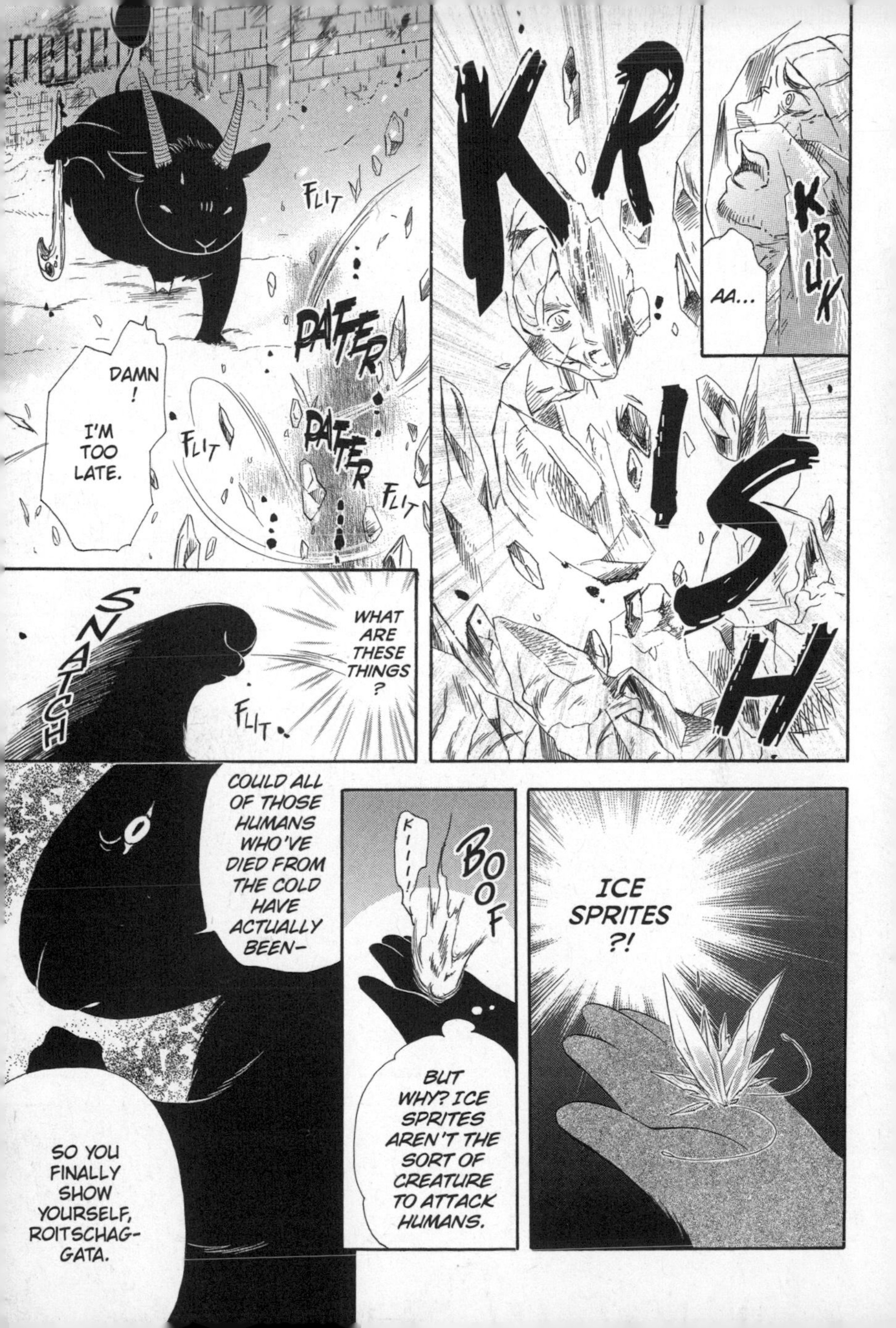

KRUK
AA...
KRISH
DAMN!
I'M TOO LATE.
FLIT
PATTER
PATTER
FLIT
FLIT
SNATCH
WHAT ARE THESE THINGS?
FLIT
ICE SPRITES?!
K!!!!
BOOF
BUT WHY? ICE SPRITES AREN'T THE SORT OF CREATURE TO ATTACK HUMANS.
COULD ALL OF THOSE HUMANS WHO'VE DIED FROM THE COLD HAVE ACTUALLY BEEN-
SO YOU FINALLY SHOW YOURSELF, ROITSCHAGGATA.

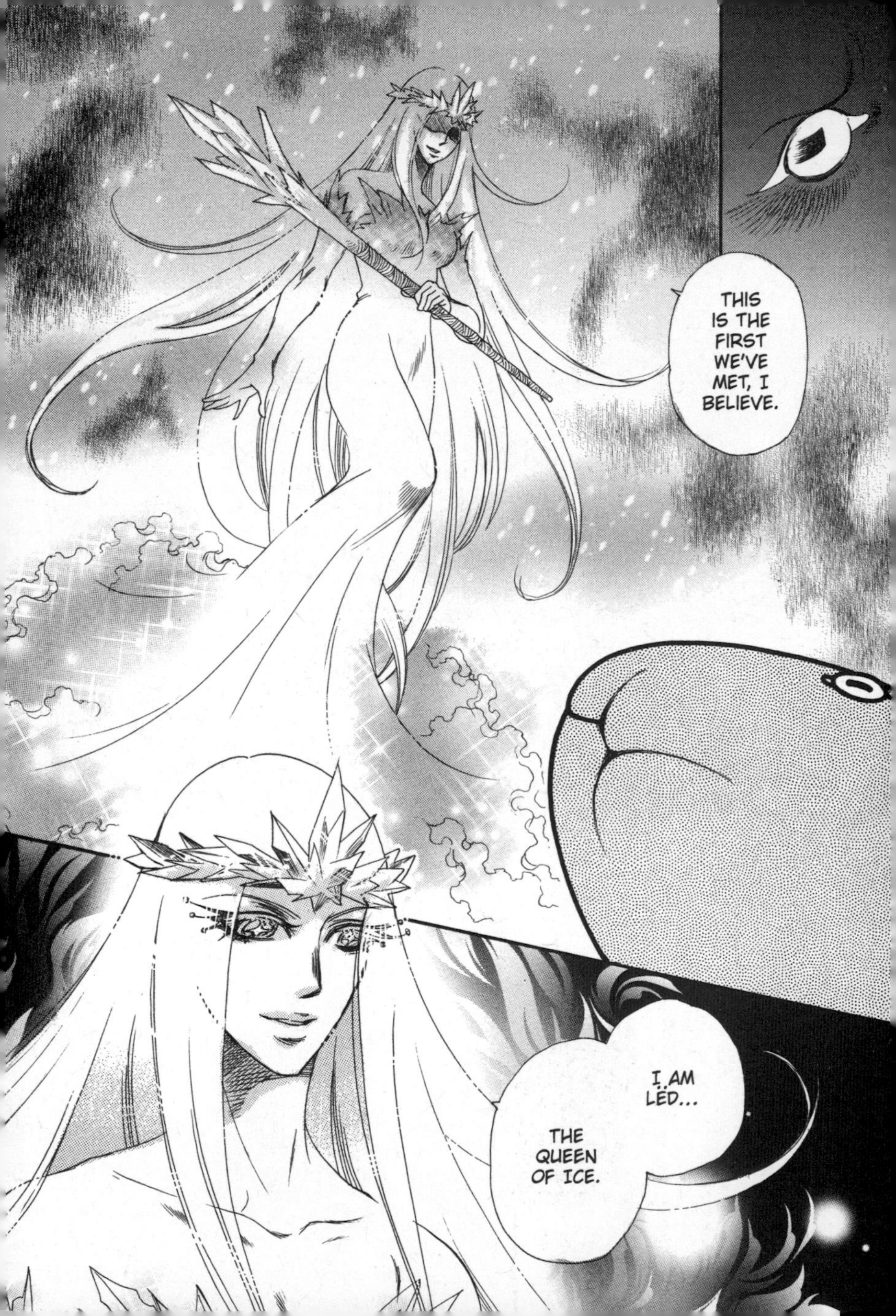
THIS IS THE FIRST WE'VE MET, I BELIEVE.
I AM LÉD...
THE QUEEN OF ICE.

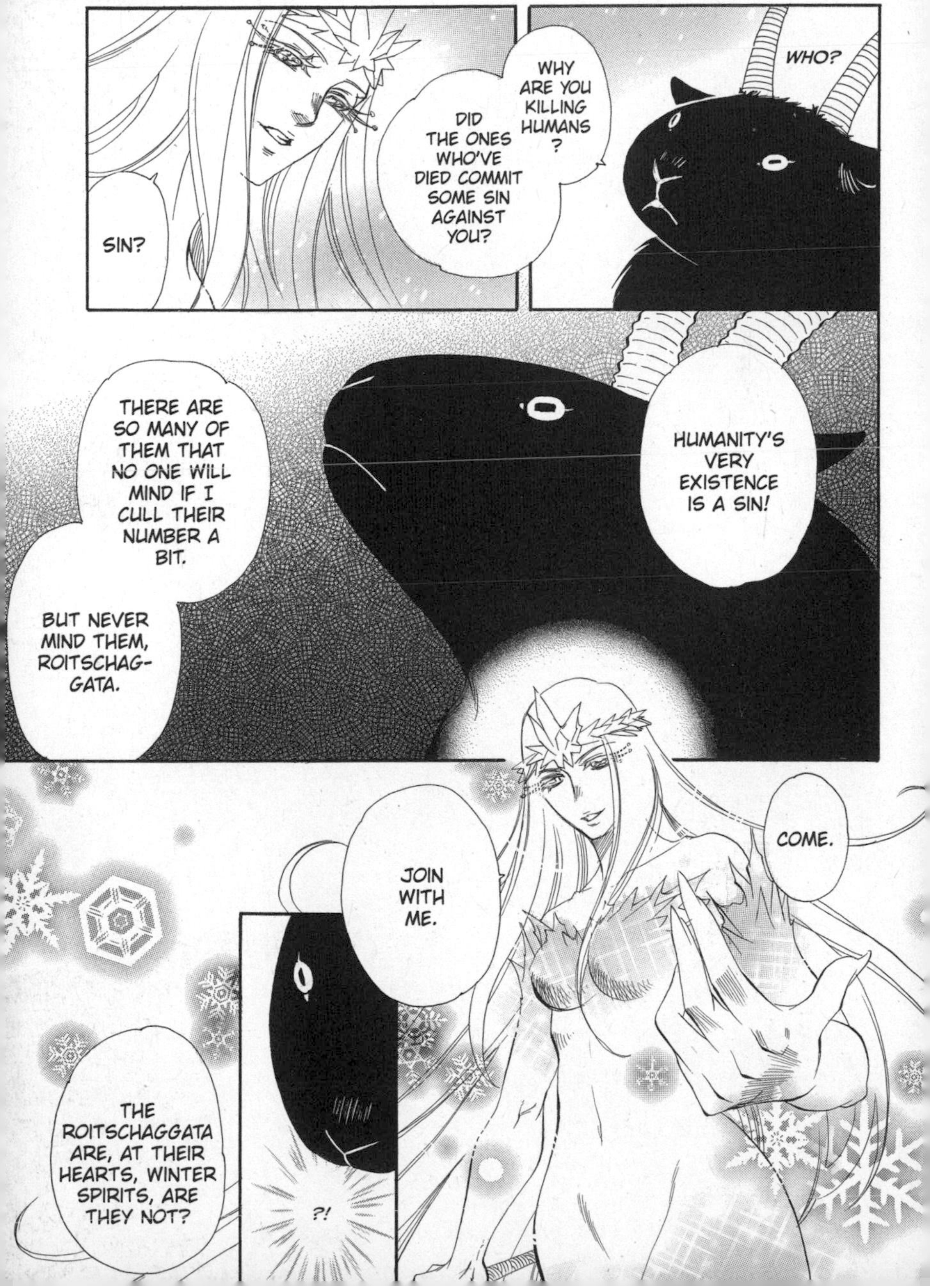
WHO?
WHY ARE YOU KILLING HUMANS?
DID THE ONES WHO'VE DIED COMMIT SOME SIN AGAINST YOU?
SIN?
HUMANITY'S VERY EXISTENCE IS A SIN!
THERE ARE SO MANY OF THEM THAT NO ONE WILL MIND IF I CULL THEIR NUMBER A BIT.
BUT NEVER MIND THEM, ROITSCHAGGATA.
COME.
JOIN WITH ME.
THE ROITSCHAGGATA ARE, AT THEIR HEARTS, WINTER SPIRITS, ARE THEY NOT?
?!

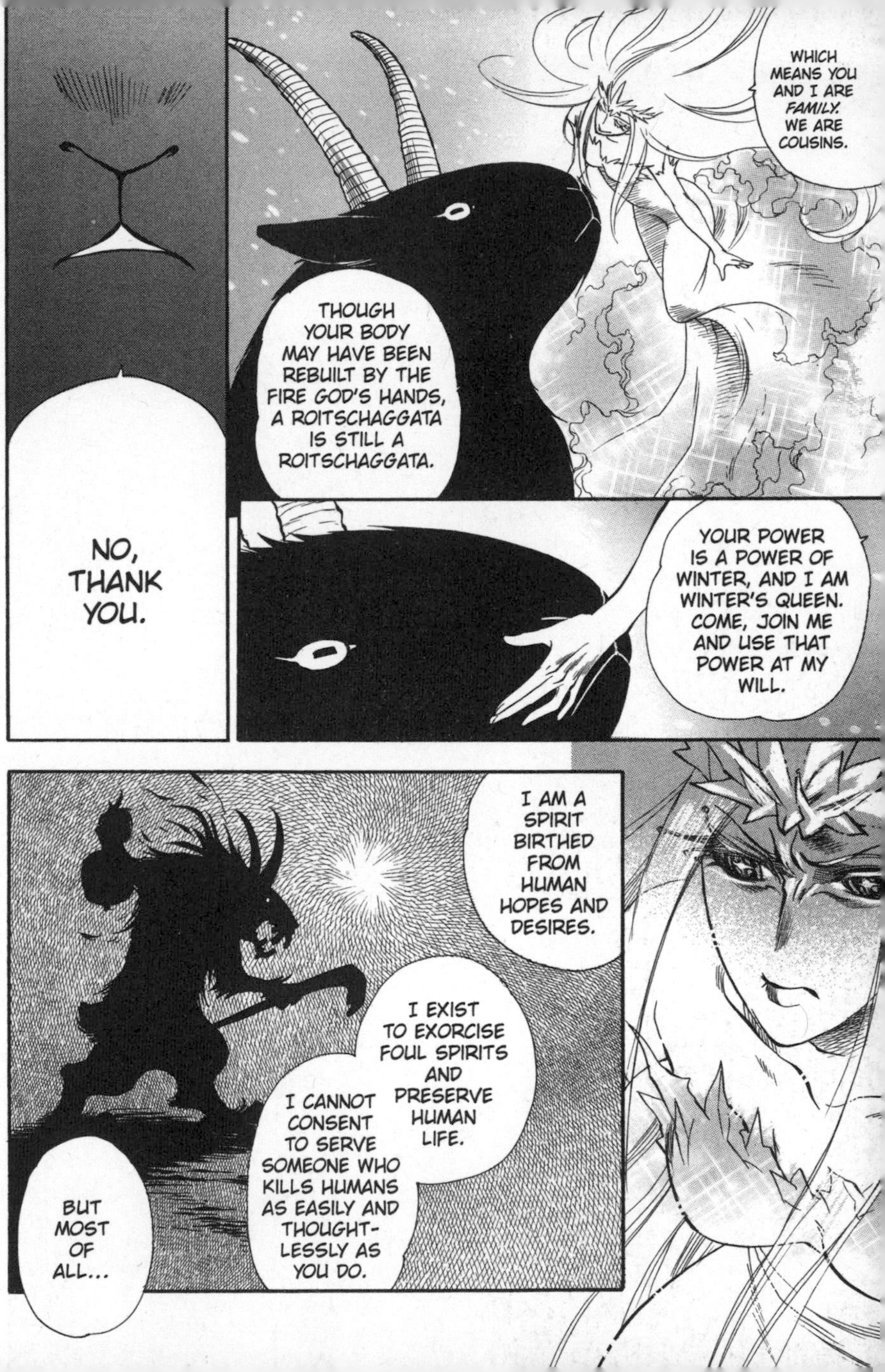
WHICH MEANS YOU AND I ARE *FAMILY.* WE ARE COUSINS.
THOUGH YOUR BODY MAY HAVE BEEN REBUILT BY THE FIRE GOD'S HANDS, A ROITSCHAGGATA IS STILL A ROITSCHAGGATA.
YOUR POWER IS A POWER OF WINTER, AND I AM WINTER'S QUEEN. COME, JOIN ME AND USE THAT POWER AT MY WILL.
NO, THANK YOU.
I AM A SPIRIT BIRTHED FROM HUMAN HOPES AND DESIRES.
I EXIST TO EXORCISE FOUL SPIRITS AND PRESERVE HUMAN LIFE.
I CANNOT CONSENT TO SERVE SOMEONE WHO KILLS HUMANS AS EASILY AND THOUGHT-LESSLY AS YOU DO.
BUT MOST OF ALL...

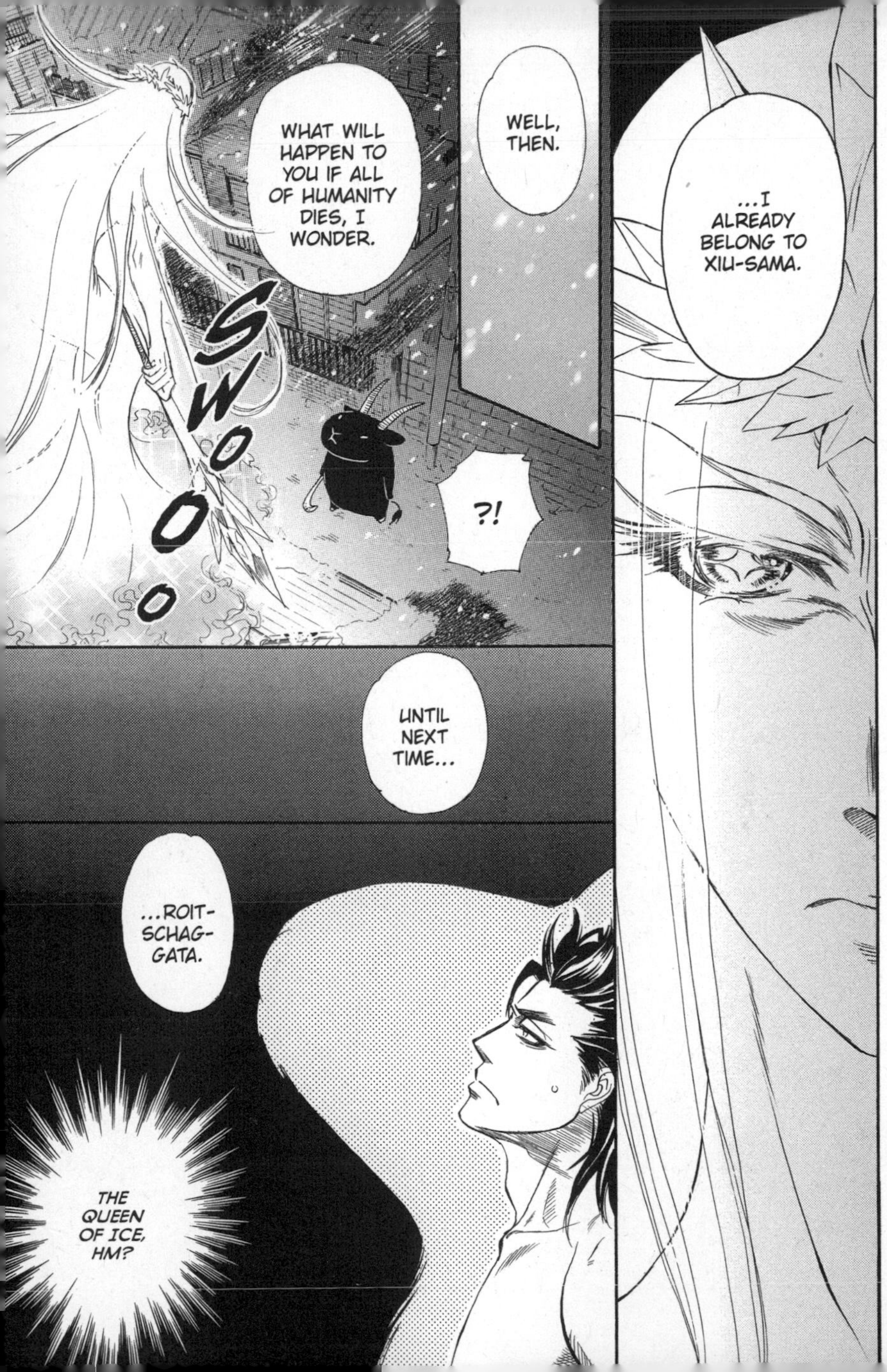
...I ALREADY BELONG TO XIU-SAMA.
WELL, THEN.
WHAT WILL HAPPEN TO YOU IF ALL OF HUMANITY DIES, I WONDER.
SWOOOO
?!
UNTIL NEXT TIME...
...ROIT-SCHAG-GATA.
THE QUEEN OF ICE, HM?

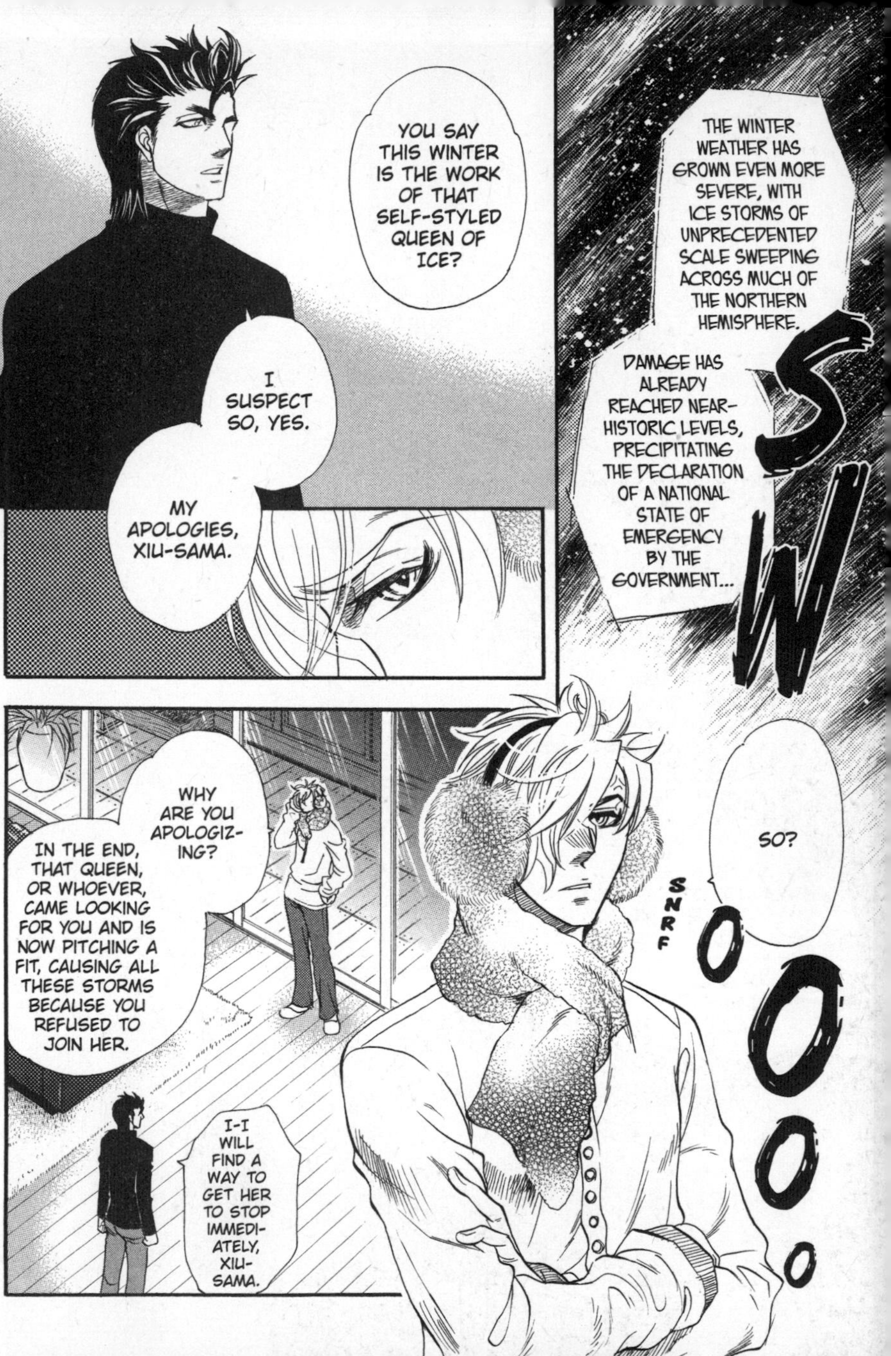
THE WINTER WEATHER HAS GROWN EVEN MORE SEVERE, WITH ICE STORMS OF UNPRECEDENTED SCALE SWEEPING ACROSS MUCH OF THE NORTHERN HEMISPHERE.
DAMAGE HAS ALREADY REACHED NEAR-HISTORIC LEVELS, PRECIPITATING THE DECLARATION OF A NATIONAL STATE OF EMERGENCY BY THE GOVERNMENT...
SWOOOOO
YOU SAY THIS WINTER IS THE WORK OF THAT SELF-STYLED QUEEN OF ICE?
I SUSPECT SO, YES.
MY APOLOGIES, XIU-SAMA.
SO?
SNRF
WHY ARE YOU APOLOGIZING?
IN THE END, THAT QUEEN, OR WHOEVER, CAME LOOKING FOR YOU AND IS NOW PITCHING A FIT, CAUSING ALL THESE STORMS BECAUSE YOU REFUSED TO JOIN HER.
I-I WILL FIND A WAY TO GET HER TO STOP IMMEDIATELY, XIU-SAMA.

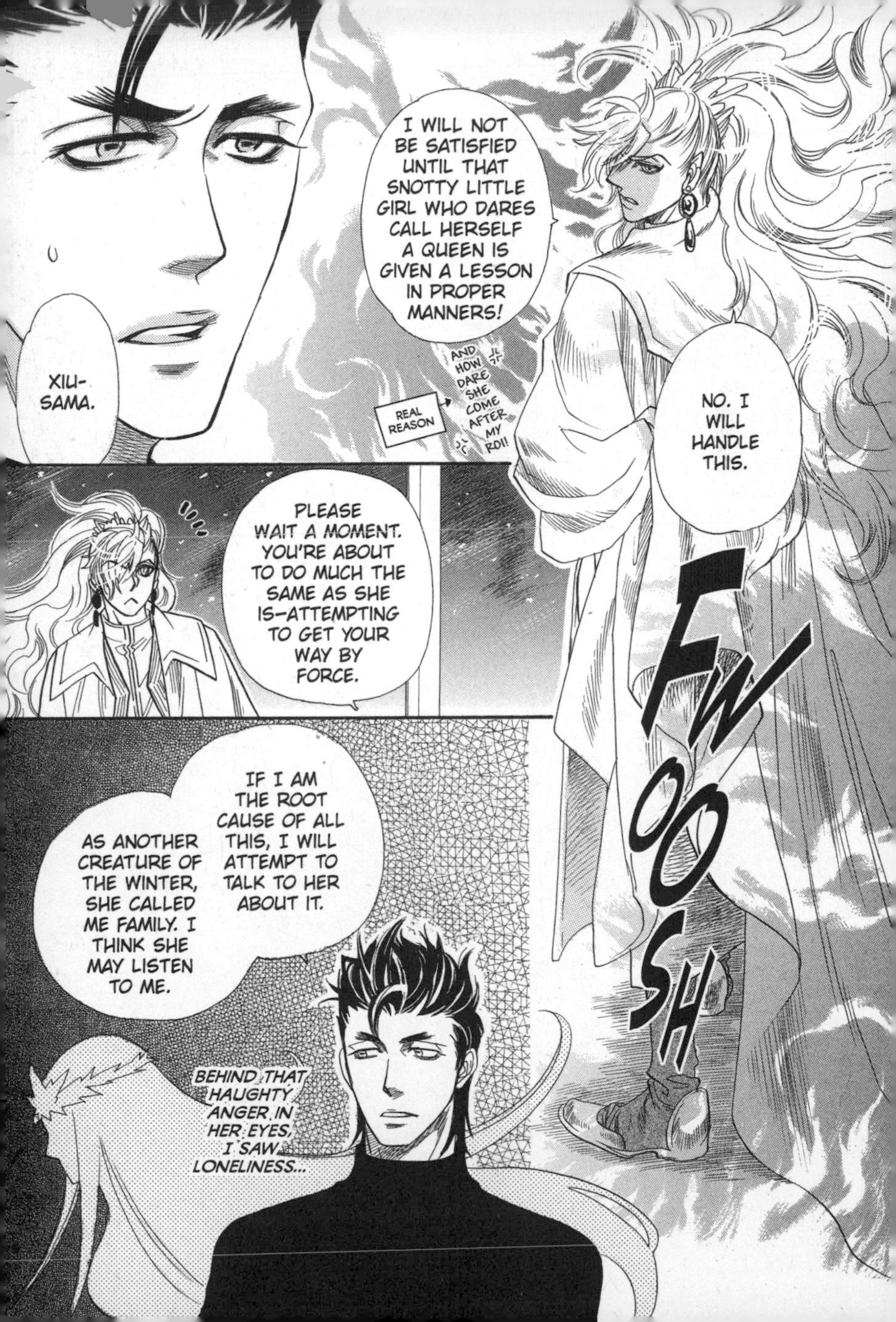
I WILL NOT BE SATISFIED UNTIL THAT SNOTTY LITTLE GIRL WHO DARES CALL HERSELF A QUEEN IS GIVEN A LESSON IN PROPER MANNERS!
AND HOW DARE SHE COME AFTER MY RDI!
REAL REASON
NO. I WILL HANDLE THIS.
FWOOSH
XIU-SAMA.
PLEASE WAIT A MOMENT. YOU'RE ABOUT TO DO MUCH THE SAME AS SHE IS—ATTEMPTING TO GET YOUR WAY BY FORCE.
IF I AM THE ROOT CAUSE OF ALL THIS, I WILL ATTEMPT TO TALK TO HER ABOUT IT.
AS ANOTHER CREATURE OF THE WINTER, SHE CALLED ME FAMILY. I THINK SHE MAY LISTEN TO ME.
BEHIND THAT HAUGHTY ANGER IN HER EYES, I SAW LONELINESS...

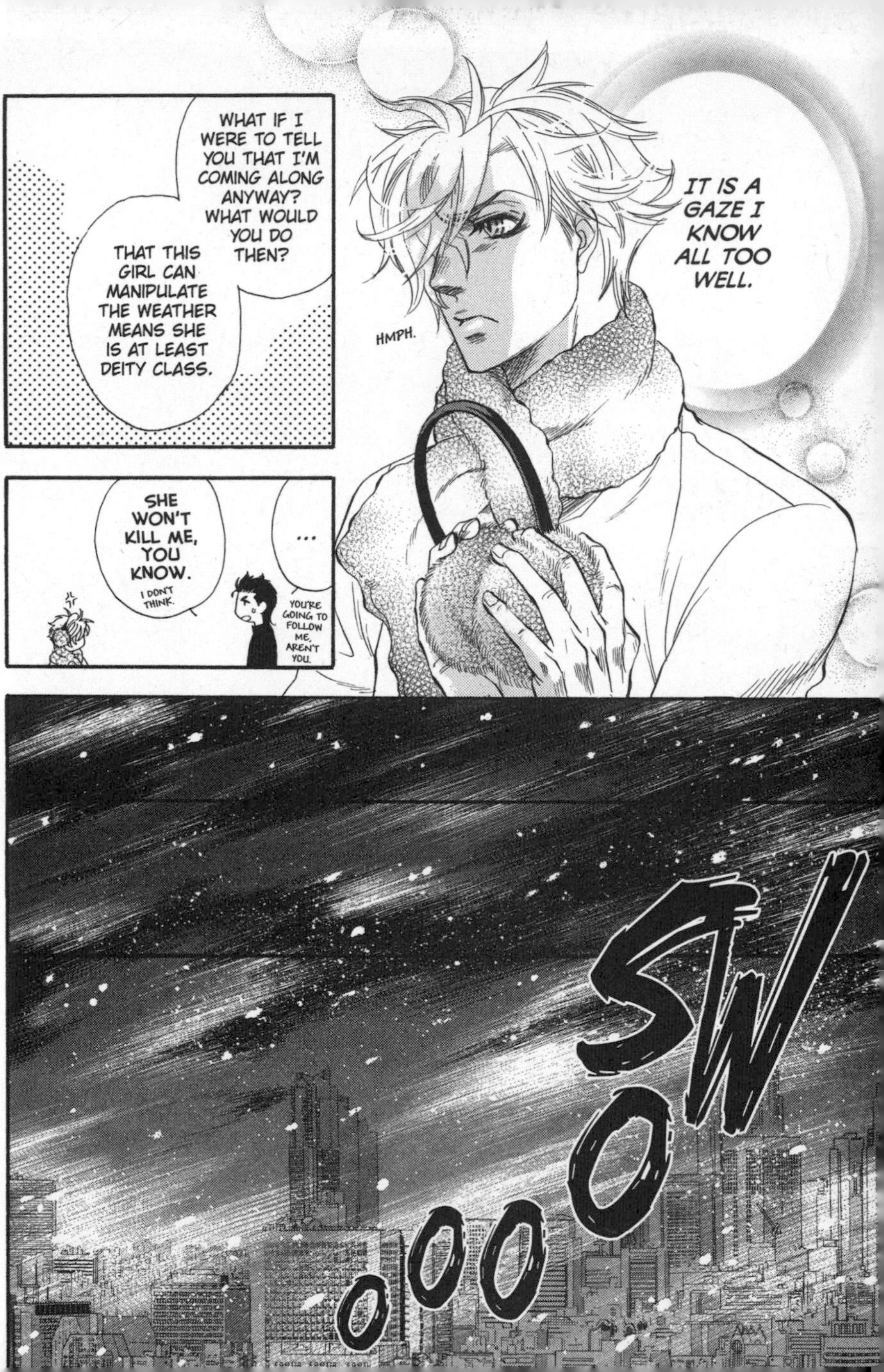
IT IS A GAZE I KNOW ALL TOO WELL.
HMPH.
WHAT IF I WERE TO TELL YOU THAT I'M COMING ALONG ANYWAY? WHAT WOULD YOU DO THEN?
THAT THIS GIRL CAN MANIPULATE THE WEATHER MEANS SHE IS AT LEAST DEITY CLASS.
...
YOU'RE GOING TO FOLLOW ME, AREN'T YOU.
SHE WON'T KILL ME, YOU KNOW.
I DON'T THINK.
SWOOOOO

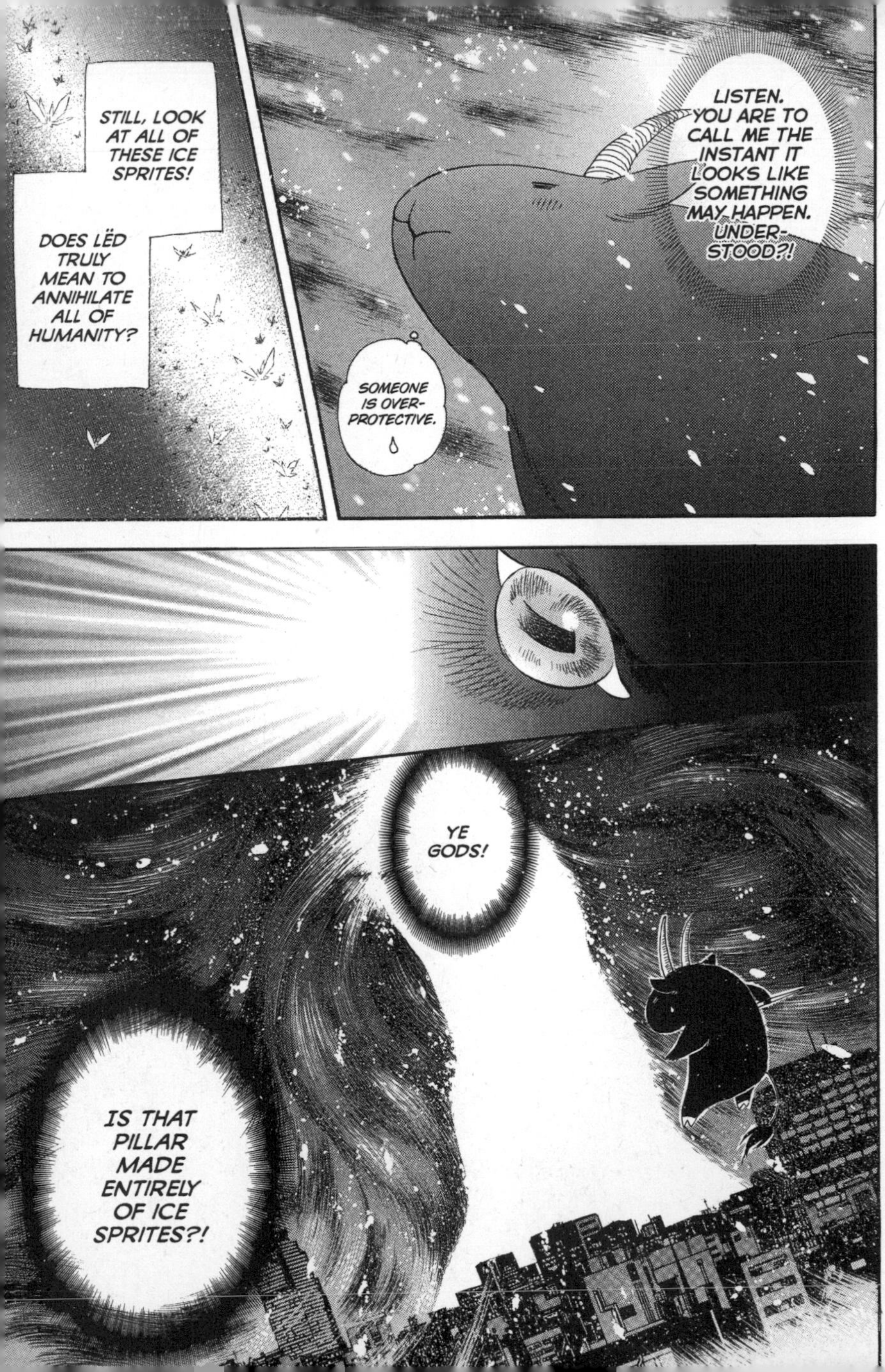
LISTEN. YOU ARE TO CALL ME THE INSTANT IT LOOKS LIKE SOMETHING MAY HAPPEN. UNDER-STOOD?!
SOMEONE IS OVER-PROTECTIVE.
STILL, LOOK AT ALL OF THESE ICE SPRITES!
DOES LËD TRULY MEAN TO ANNIHILATE ALL OF HUMANITY?
YE GODS!
IS THAT PILLAR MADE ENTIRELY OF ICE SPRITES?!

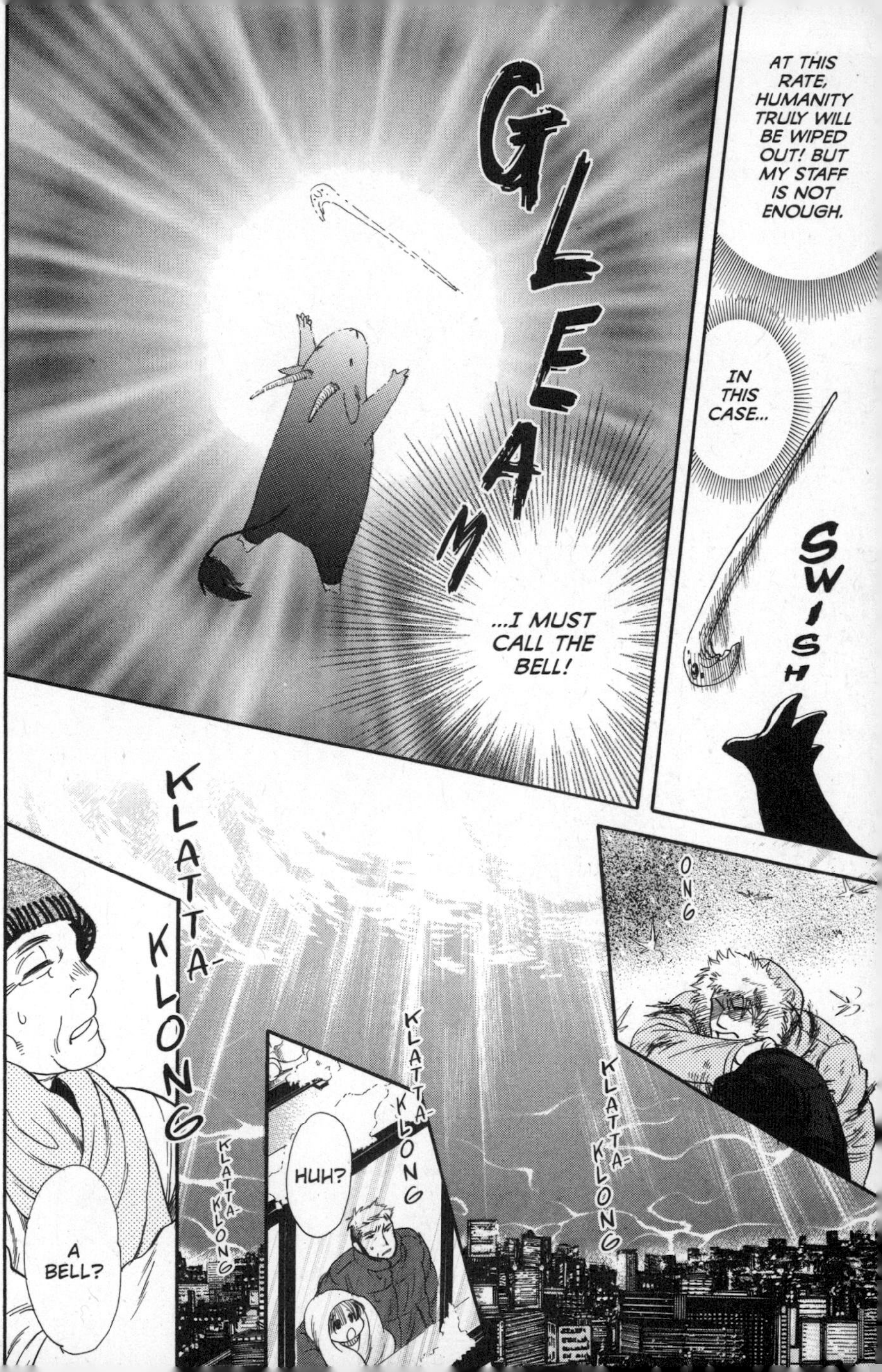
AT THIS RATE, HUMANITY TRULY WILL BE WIPED OUT! BUT MY STAFF IS NOT ENOUGH.
IN THIS CASE...
SWISH
GLEAM
...I MUST CALL THE BELL!
ONG
KLATTA-KLONG
KLATTA-KLONG
HUH?
KLATTA-KLONG
KLATTA-KLONG
A BELL?

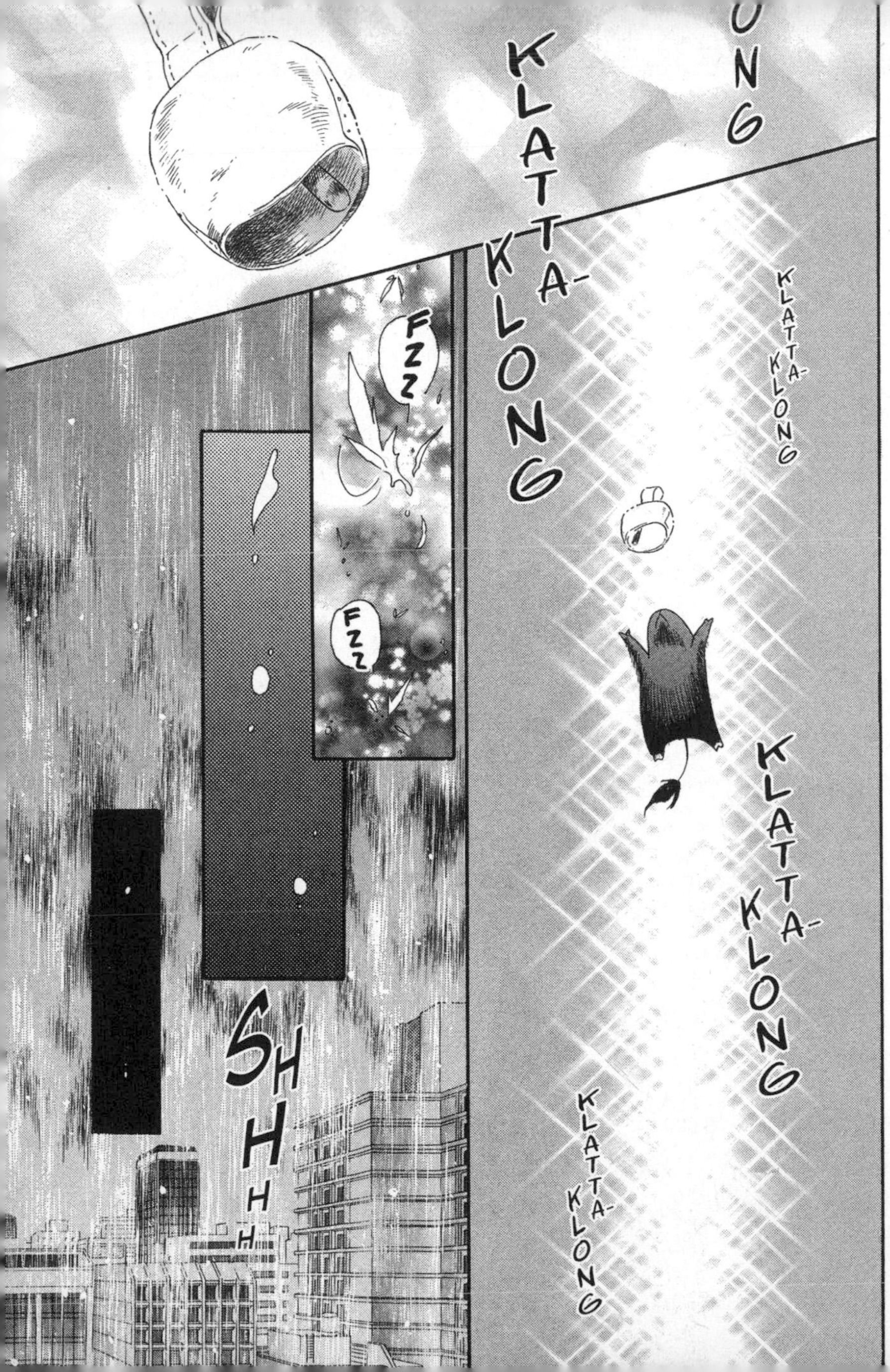
KLATTA-KLONG
KLATTA-KLONG
KLATTA-KLONG
KLATTA-KLONG
FZZ
FZZ
SHHHH

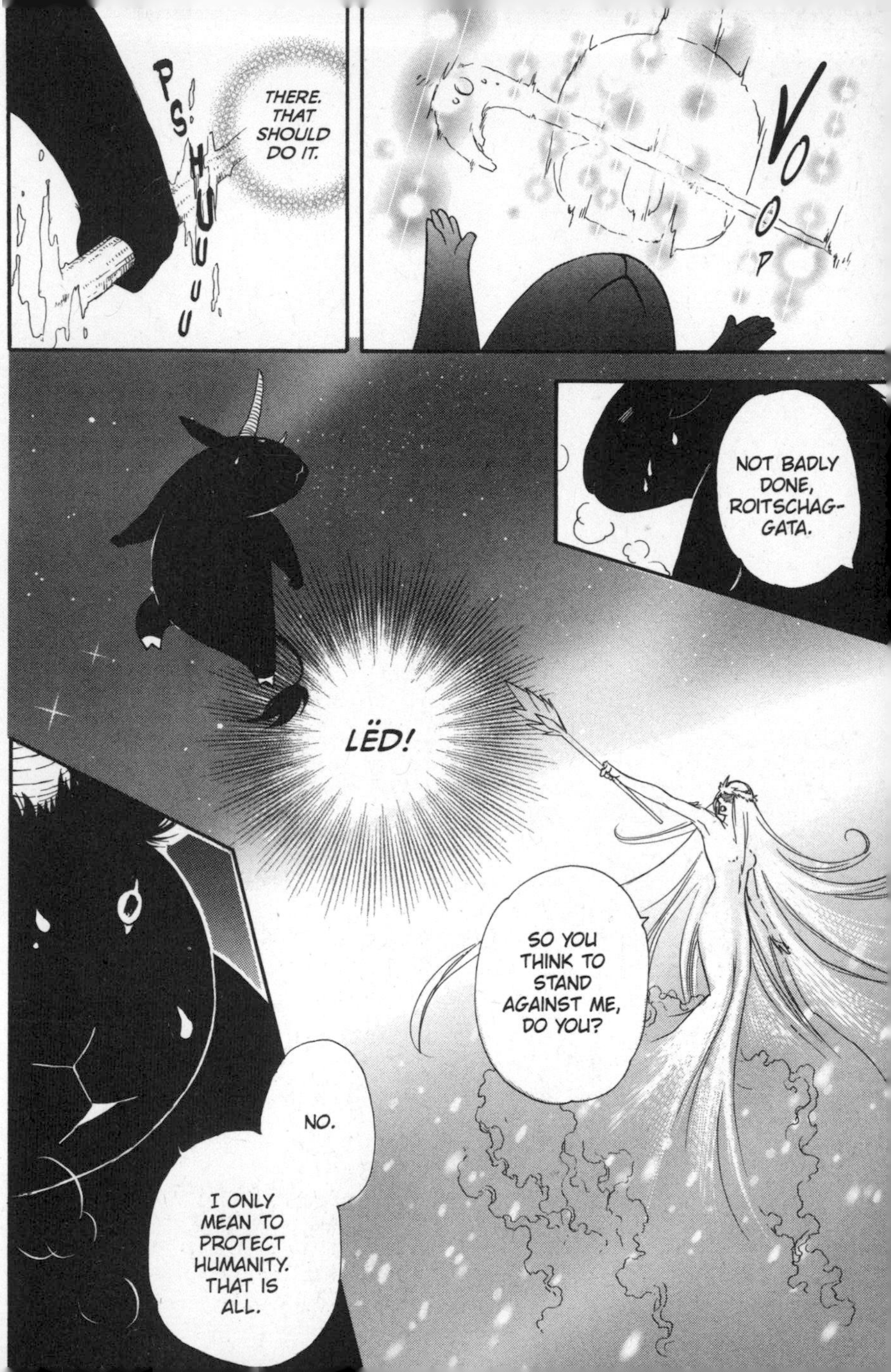
VOOP
PS! HUUUUU
THERE. THAT SHOULD DO IT.
NOT BADLY DONE, ROITSCHAG-GATA.
LËD!
SO YOU THINK TO STAND AGAINST ME, DO YOU?
NO.
I ONLY MEAN TO PROTECT HUMANITY. THAT IS ALL.

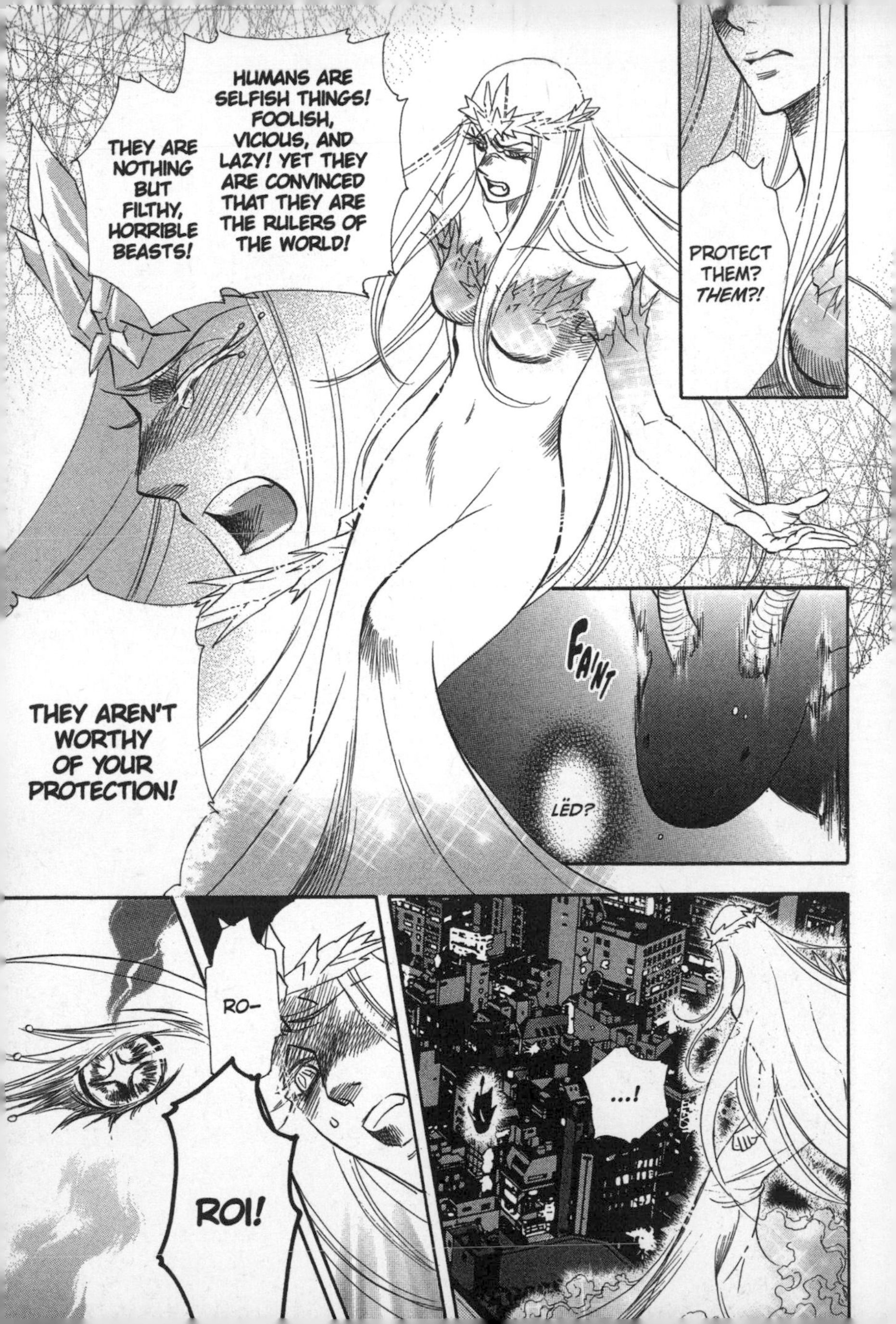
PROTECT THEM? *THEM?!*
HUMANS ARE SELFISH THINGS! FOOLISH, VICIOUS, AND LAZY! YET THEY ARE CONVINCED THAT THEY ARE THE RULERS OF THE WORLD!
THEY ARE NOTHING BUT FILTHY, HORRIBLE BEASTS!
THEY AREN'T WORTHY OF YOUR PROTECTION!
FAINT
LËD?
...!
RO-
ROI!

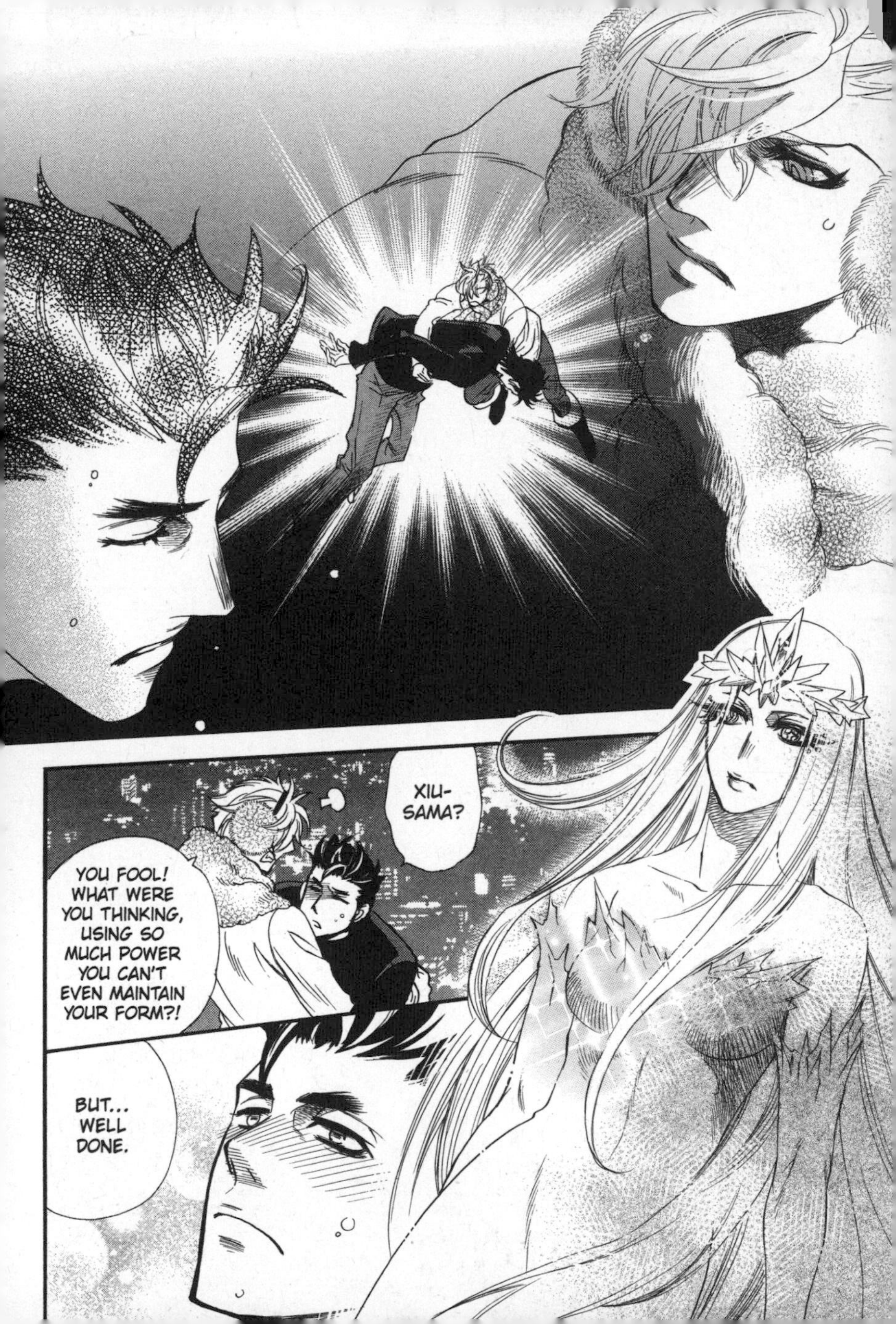
XIU-SAMA?
YOU FOOL! WHAT WERE YOU THINKING, USING SO MUCH POWER YOU CAN'T EVEN MAINTAIN YOUR FORM?!
BUT... WELL DONE.

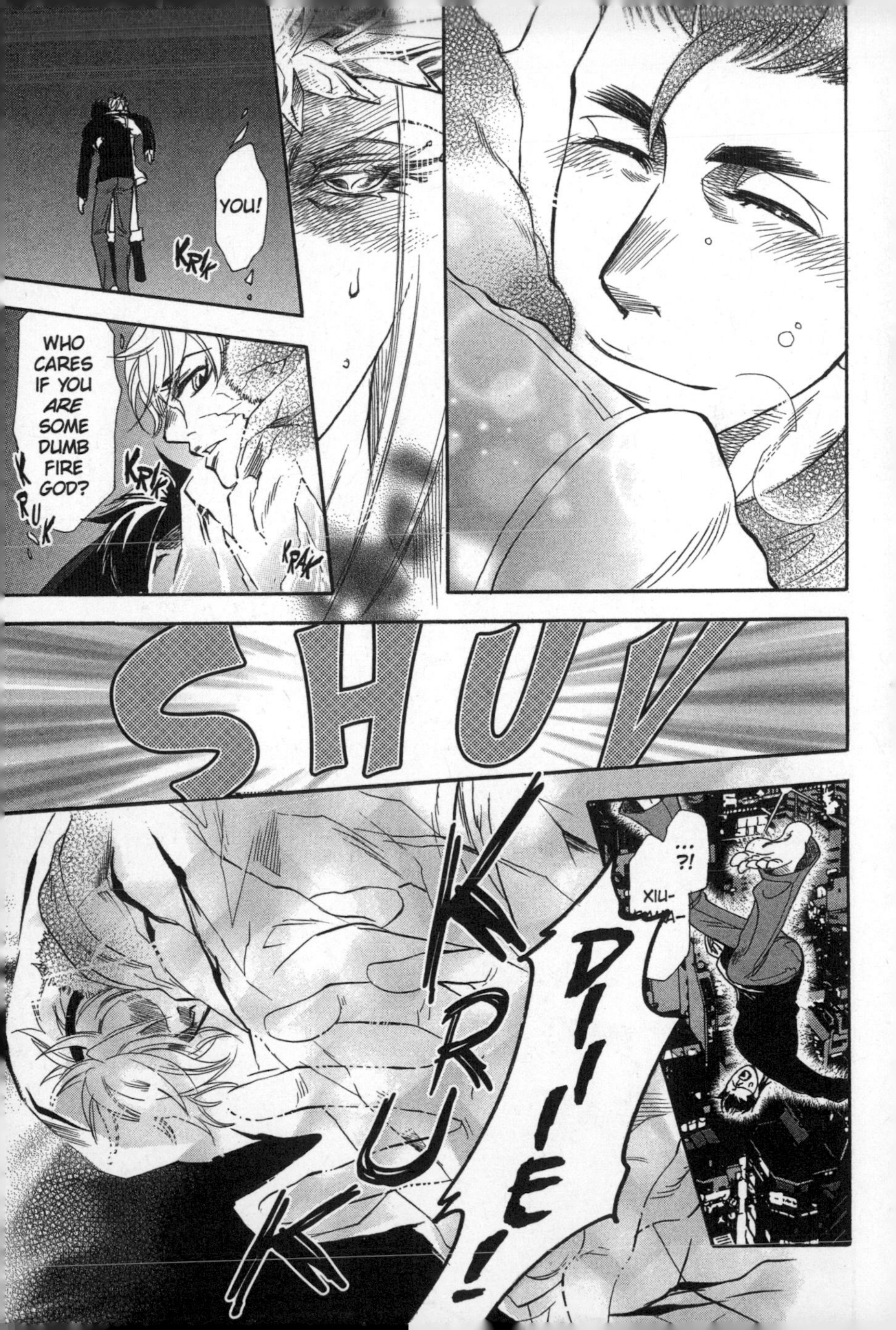
YOU!
KRIK
WHO CARES IF YOU ARE SOME DUMB FIRE GOD?
KRIK
KRUK
KRAK
SHUV
...?!
XIU-
KRUK
DIIIIE!

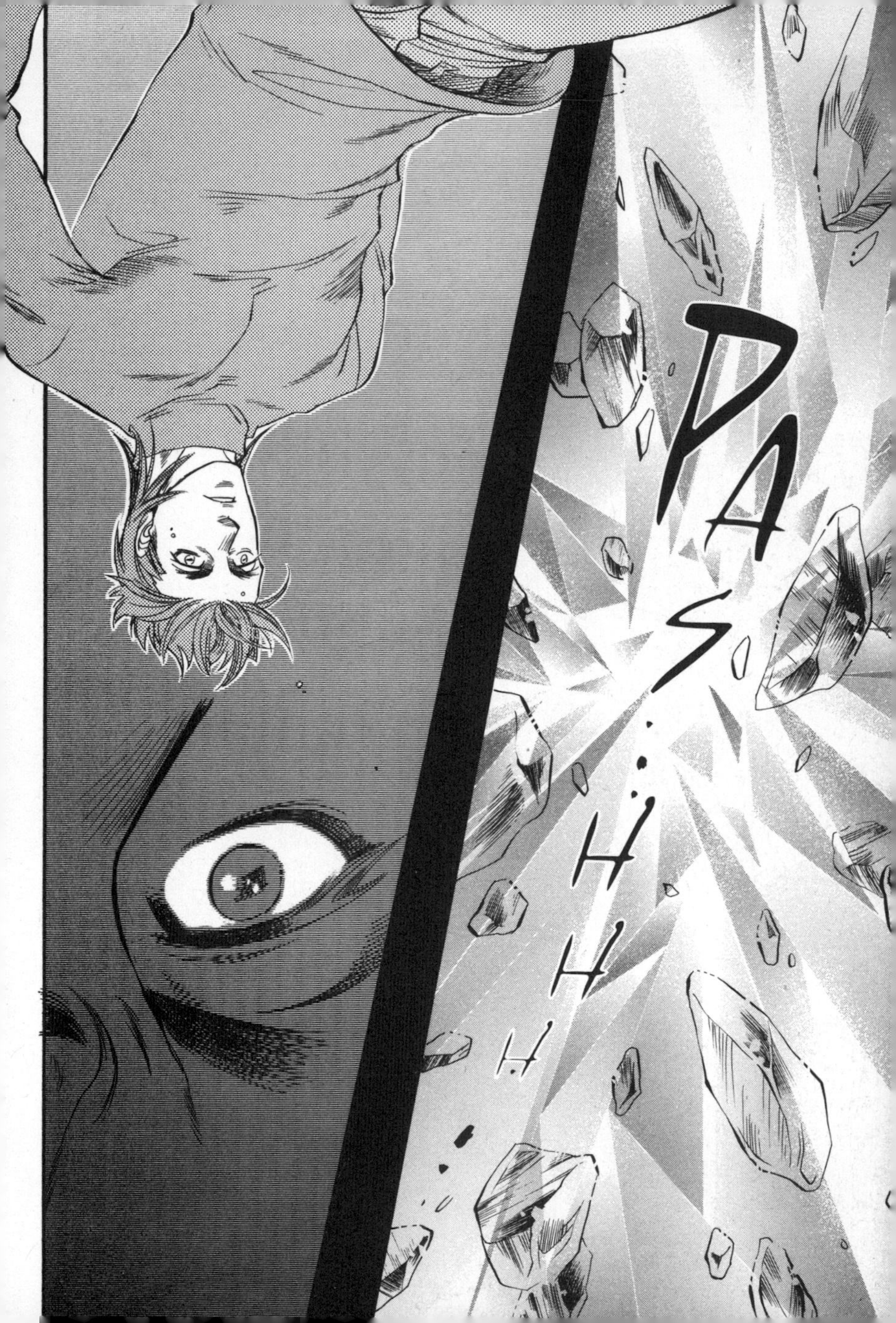
PASHHH

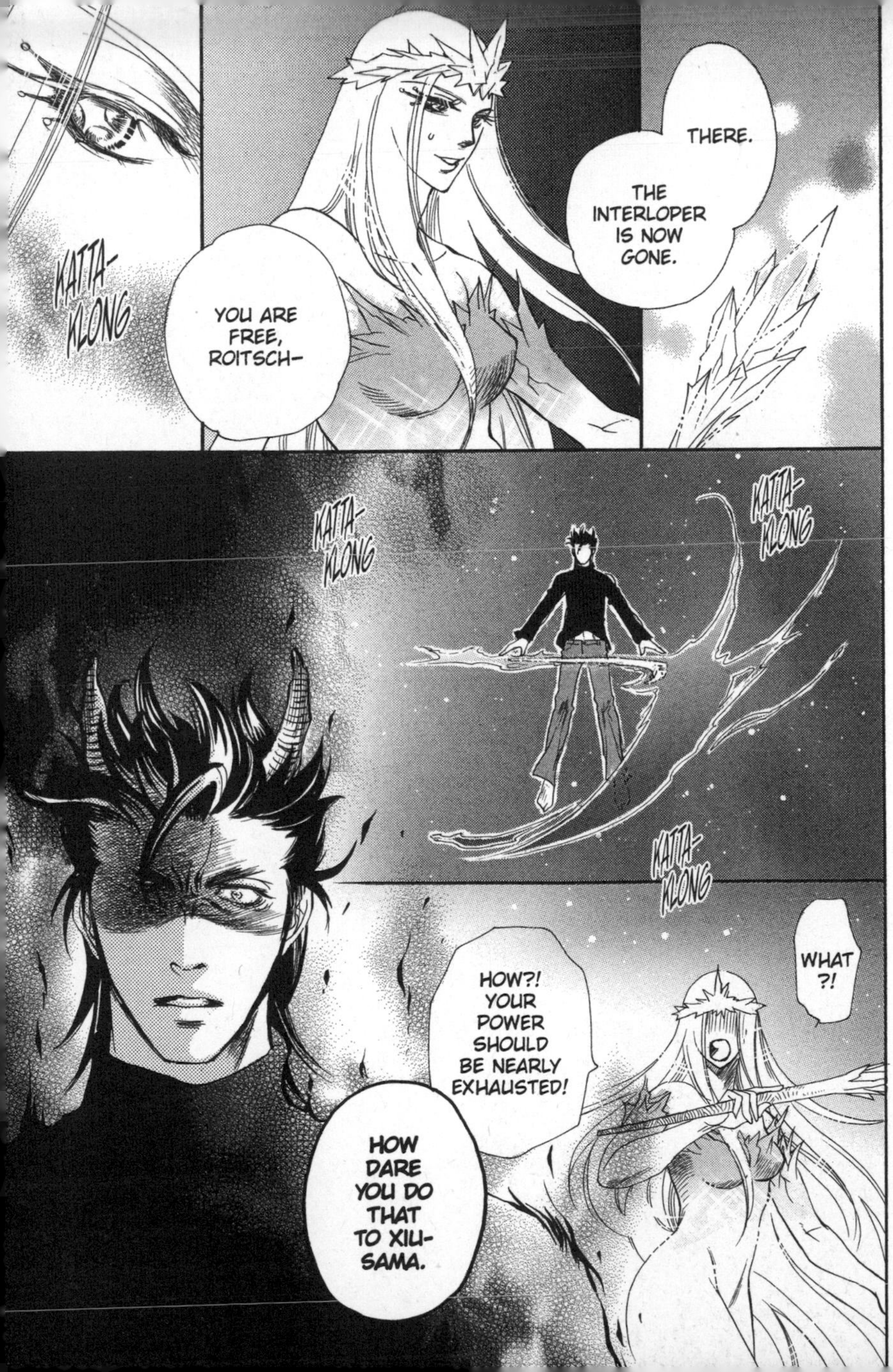
THERE.
THE INTERLOPER IS NOW GONE.
YOU ARE FREE, ROITSCH-
KATTA-KLONG
KATTA-KLONG
KATTA-KLONG
KATTA-KLONG
WHAT?!
HOW?! YOUR POWER SHOULD BE NEARLY EXHAUSTED!
HOW DARE YOU DO THAT TO XIU-SAMA.

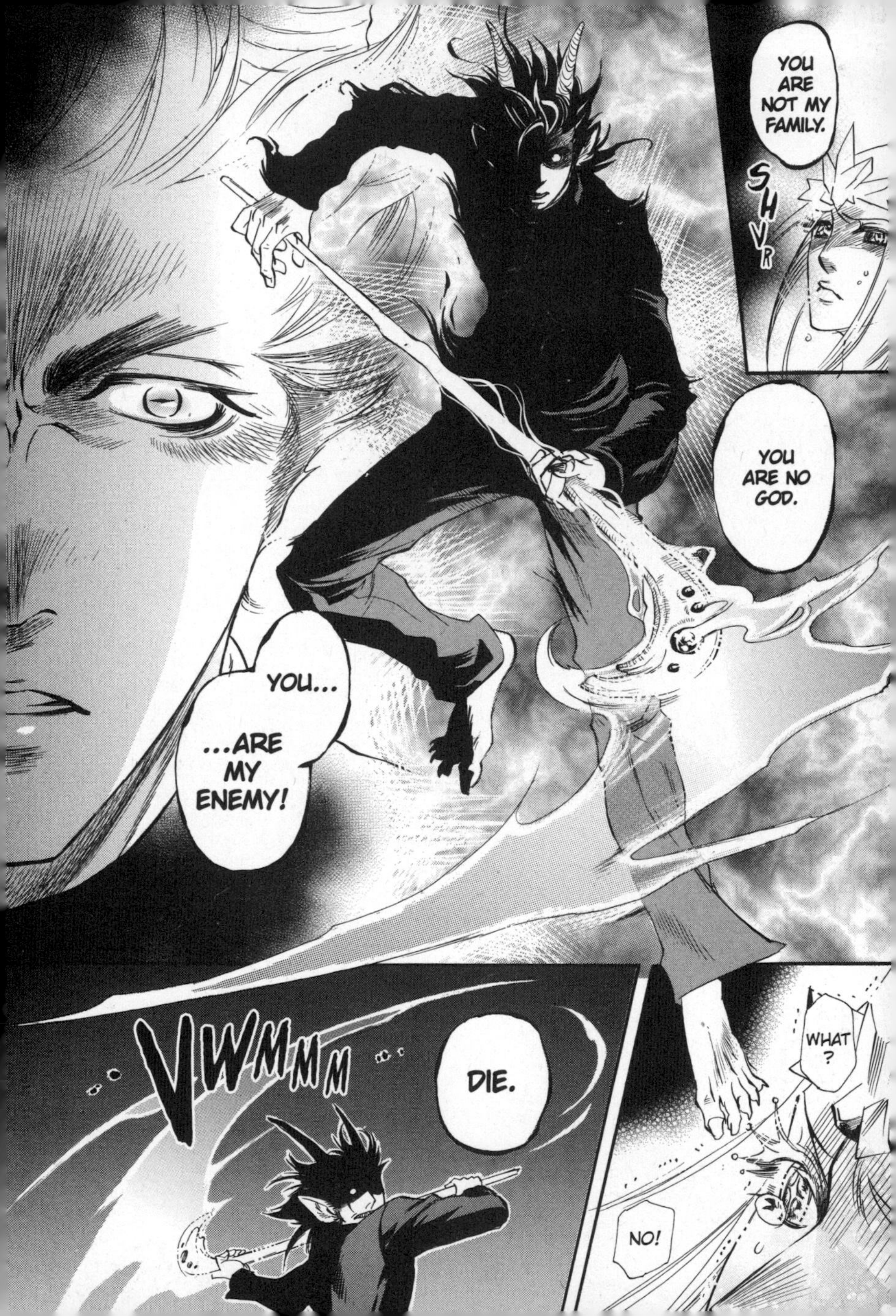
YOU ARE NOT MY FAMILY.
SHVR
YOU ARE NO GOD.
YOU...
...ARE MY ENEMY!
WHAT?
NO!
DIE.
VWMMM

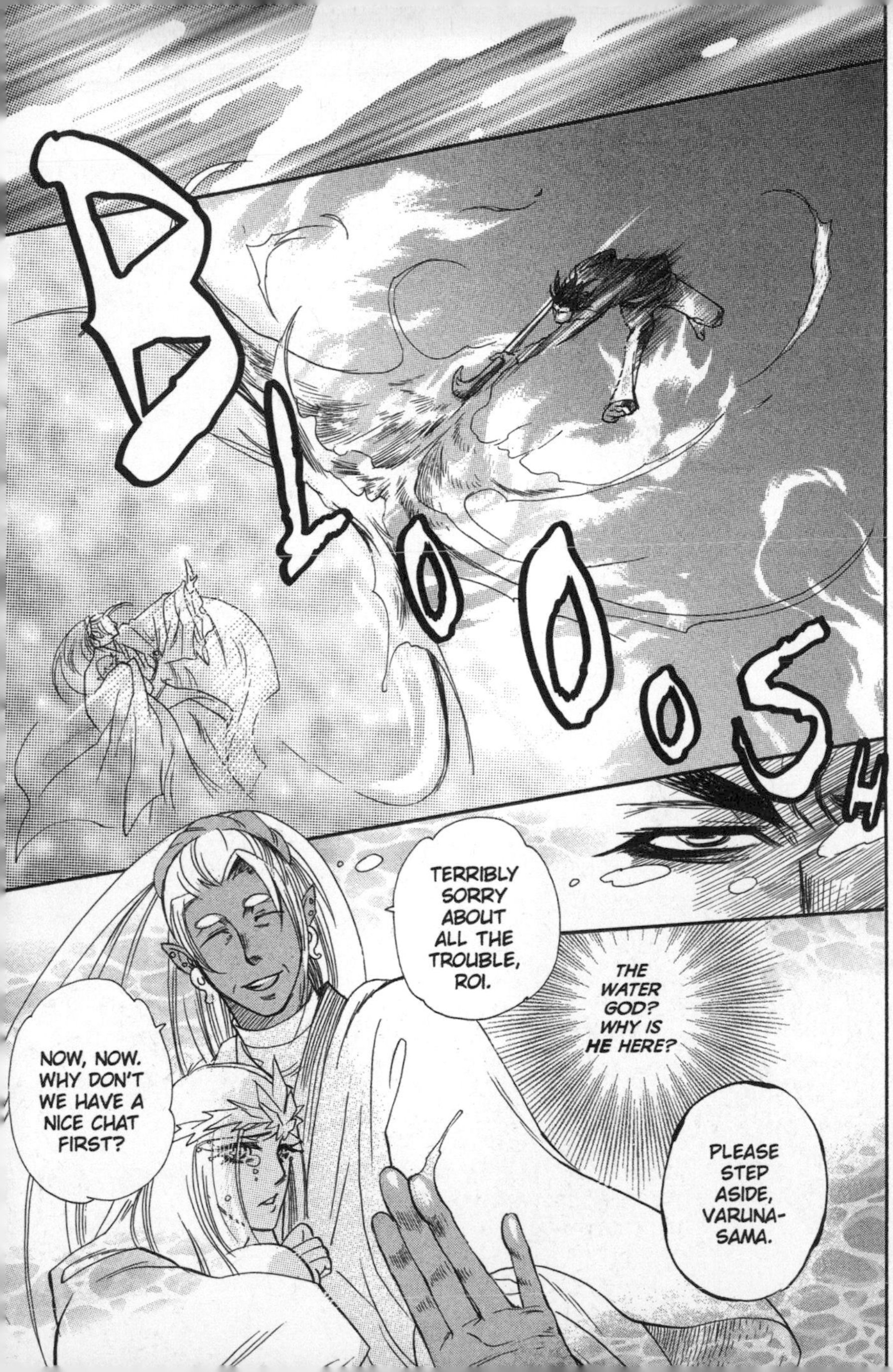
BLOOOOSH
THE WATER GOD? WHY IS HE HERE?
TERRIBLY SORRY ABOUT ALL THE TROUBLE, ROI.
PLEASE STEP ASIDE, VARUNA-SAMA.
NOW, NOW. WHY DON'T WE HAVE A NICE CHAT FIRST?

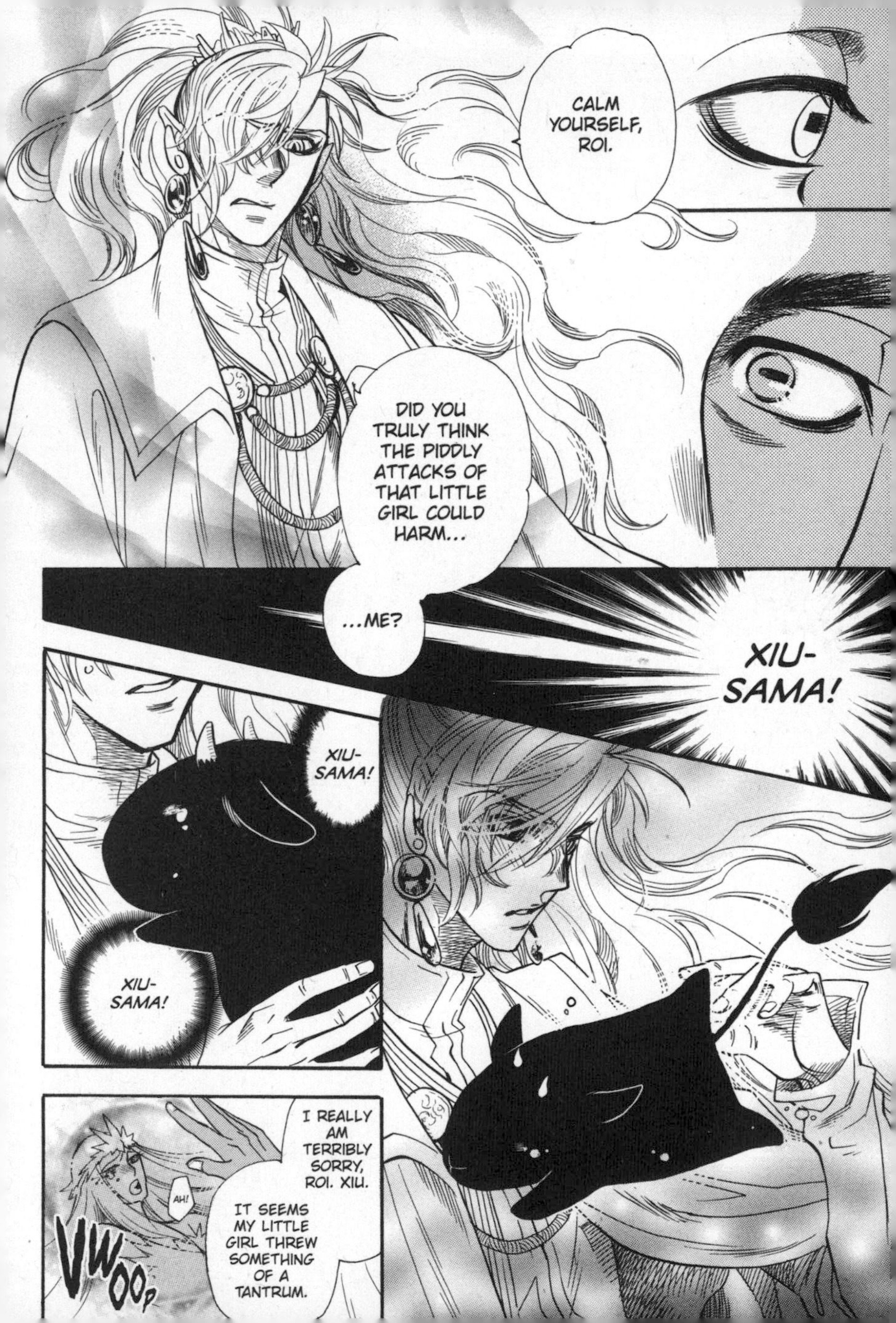
CALM YOURSELF, ROI.
DID YOU TRULY THINK THE PIDDLY ATTACKS OF THAT LITTLE GIRL COULD HARM...
...ME?
XIU-SAMA!
XIU-SAMA!
XIU-SAMA!
I REALLY AM TERRIBLY SORRY, ROI. XIU.
IT SEEMS MY LITTLE GIRL THREW SOMETHING OF A TANTRUM.
AH!
VWOOP

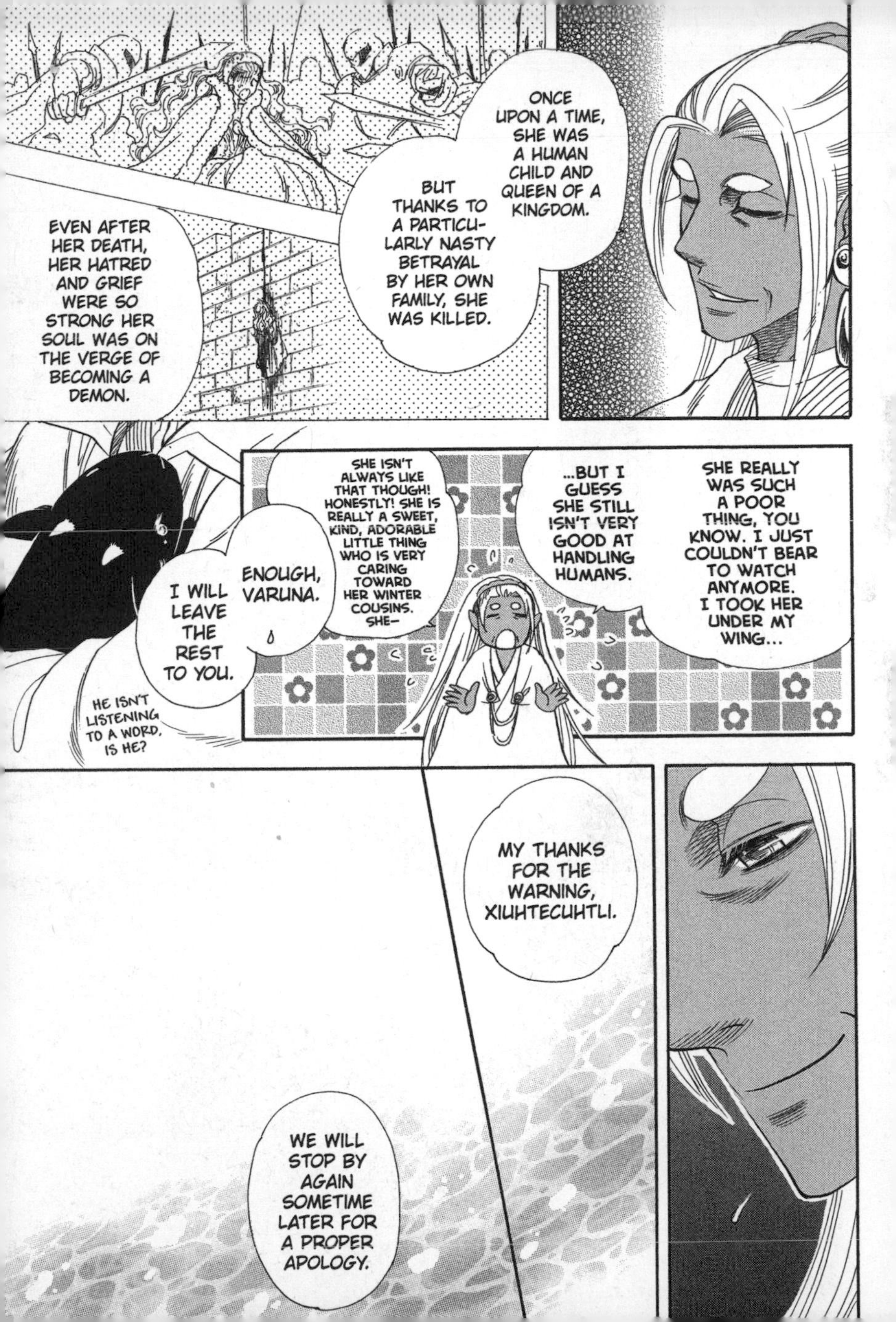
ONCE UPON A TIME, SHE WAS A HUMAN CHILD AND QUEEN OF A KINGDOM.
BUT THANKS TO A PARTICULARLY NASTY BETRAYAL BY HER OWN FAMILY, SHE WAS KILLED.
EVEN AFTER HER DEATH, HER HATRED AND GRIEF WERE SO STRONG HER SOUL WAS ON THE VERGE OF BECOMING A DEMON.
SHE REALLY WAS SUCH A POOR THING, YOU KNOW. I JUST COULDN'T BEAR TO WATCH ANYMORE. I TOOK HER UNDER MY WING...
...BUT I GUESS SHE STILL ISN'T VERY GOOD AT HANDLING HUMANS.
SHE ISN'T ALWAYS LIKE THAT THOUGH! HONESTLY! SHE IS REALLY A SWEET, KIND, ADORABLE LITTLE THING WHO IS VERY CARING TOWARD HER WINTER COUSINS. SHE—
ENOUGH, VARUNA.
I WILL LEAVE THE REST TO YOU.
HE ISN'T LISTENING TO A WORD, IS HE?
MY THANKS FOR THE WARNING, XIUHTECUHTLI.
WE WILL STOP BY AGAIN SOMETIME LATER FOR A PROPER APOLOGY.

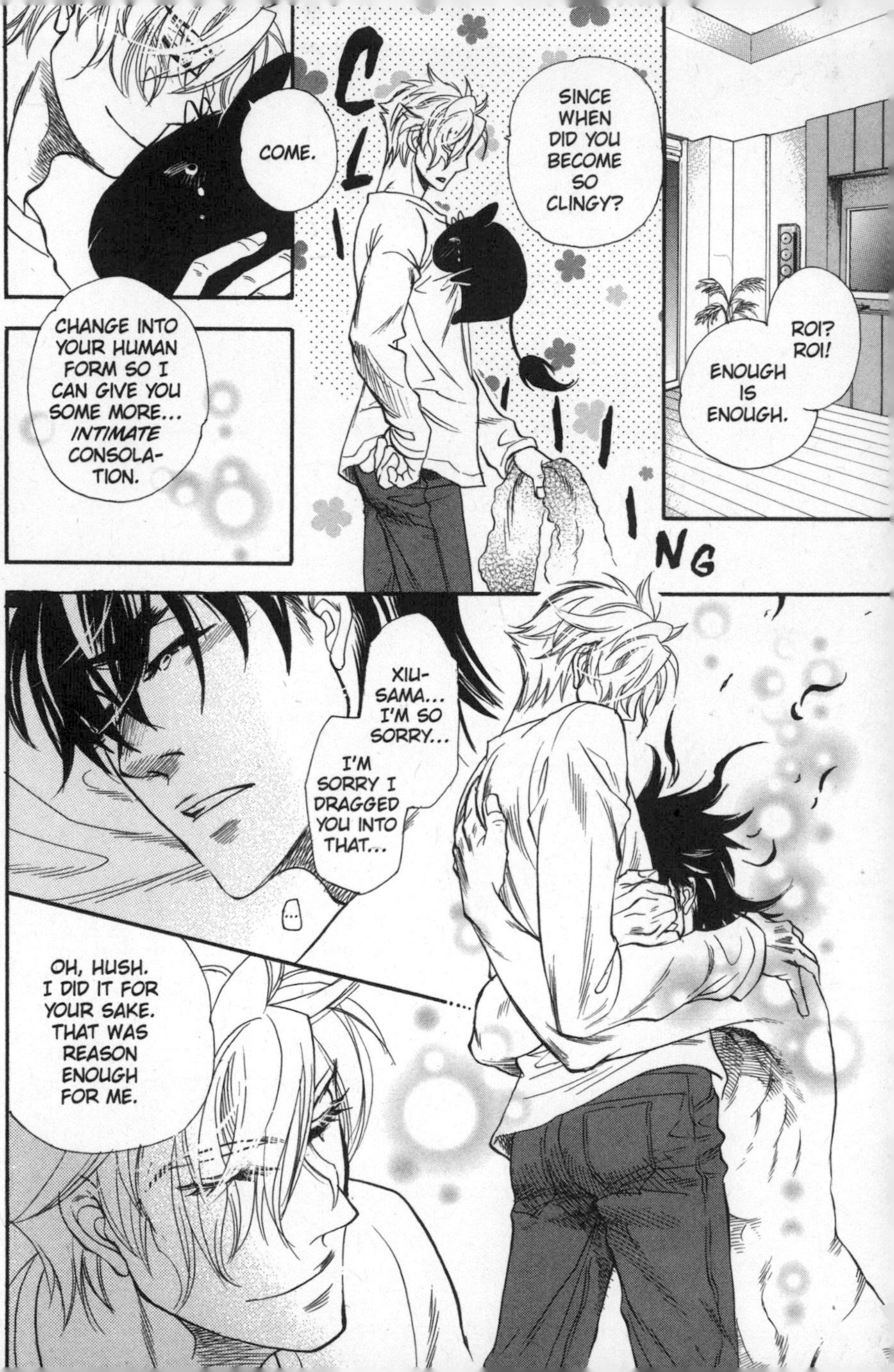
ROI? ROI! ENOUGH IS ENOUGH.
SINCE WHEN DID YOU BECOME SO CLINGY?
CLIIIIING
COME.
CHANGE INTO YOUR HUMAN FORM SO I CAN GIVE YOU SOME MORE... *INTIMATE* CONSOLATION.
XIU-SAMA... I'M SO SORRY...
I'M SORRY I DRAGGED YOU INTO THAT...
...
...
OH, HUSH. I DID IT FOR YOUR SAKE. THAT WAS REASON ENOUGH FOR ME.

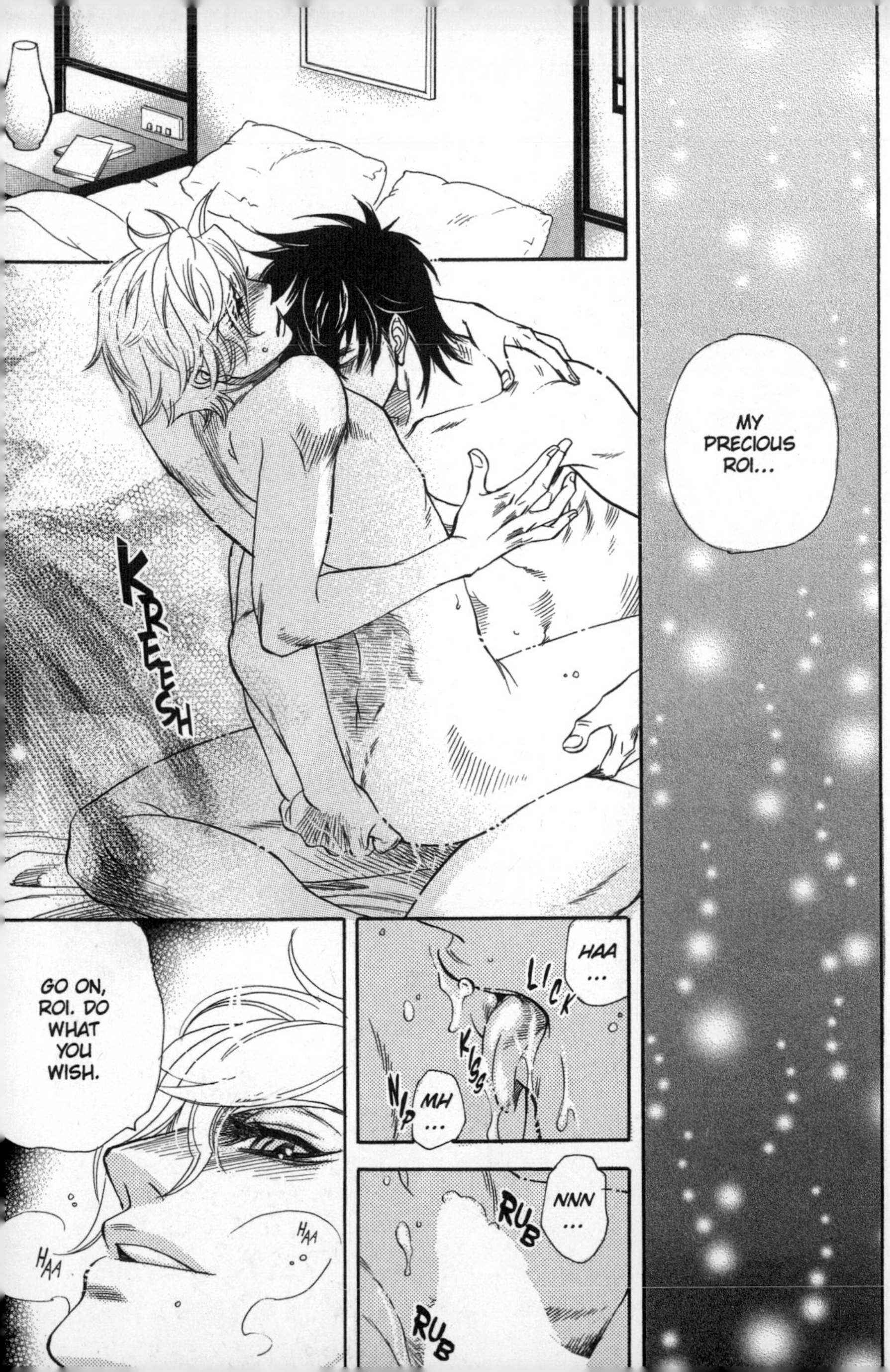
MY PRECIOUS ROI...
KREESH
HAA ...
LICK
KISS
NIP
MH ...
NNN ...
RUB
RUB
GO ON, ROI. DO WHAT YOU WISH.
HAA
HAA

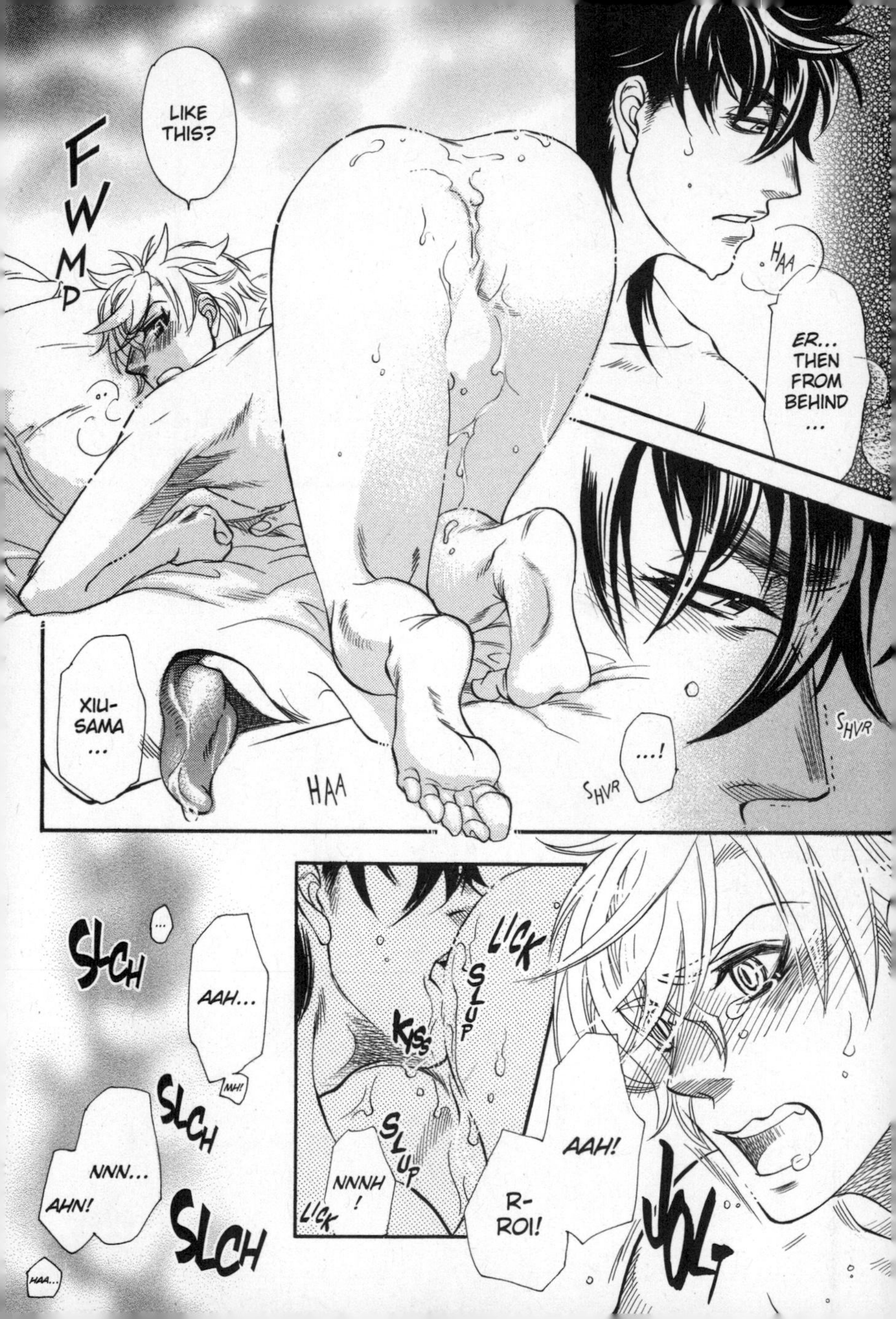
HAA
ER... THEN FROM BEHIND ...
SHVR
...!
SHVR
LIKE THIS?
FWMP
XIU-SAMA ...
HAA
AAH!
R-ROI!
JOLT
LICK
SLUP
KYSS
SLUP
NNNH!
LICK
...
AAH...
MH!
NNN...
AHN!
SLCH
SLCH
SLCH
HAA...

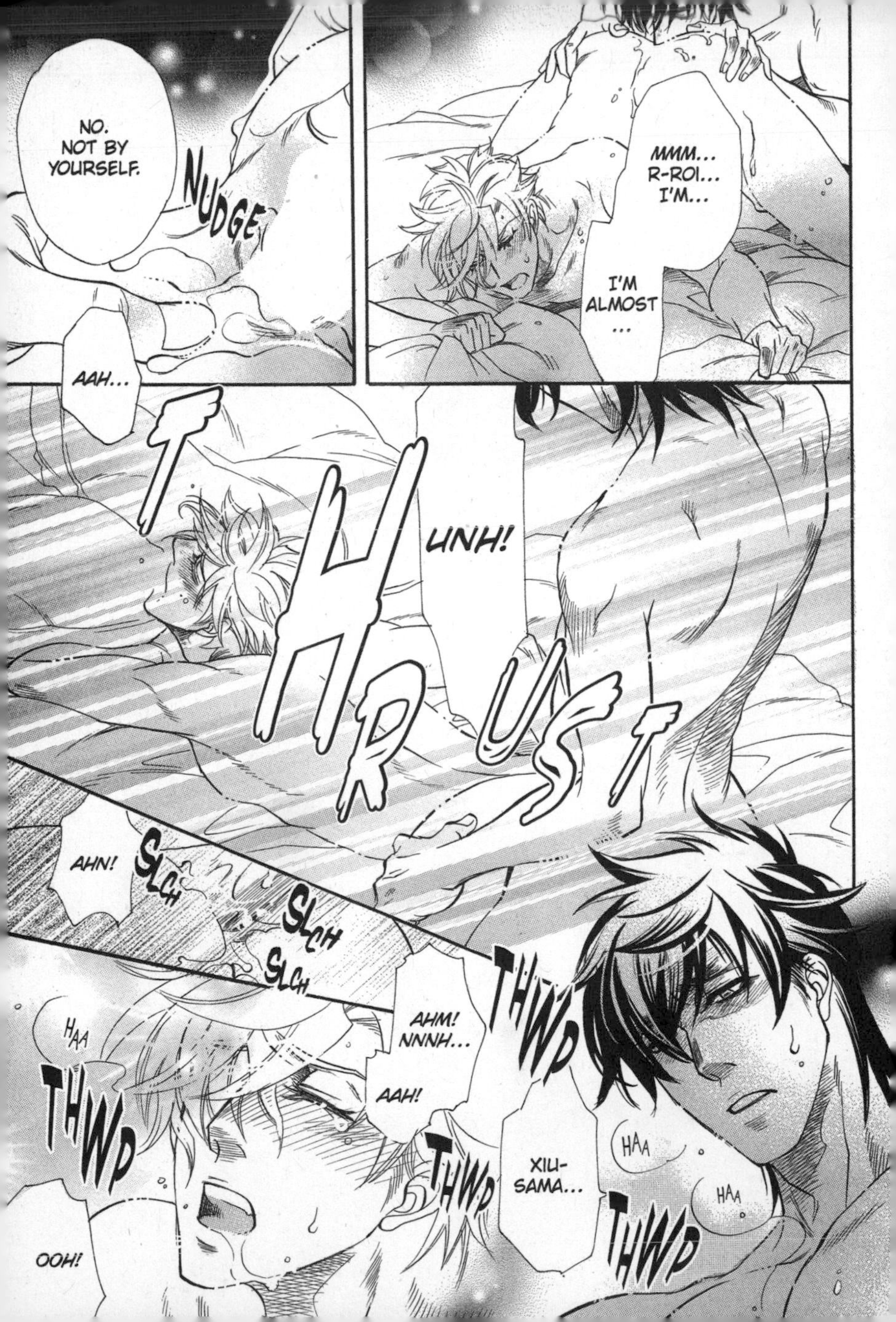
MMM... R-ROI... I'M...
I'M ALMOST ...
NO. NOT BY YOURSELF.
NUDGE
AAH...
UNH!
THRUST
AHN!
SLCH
SLCH
SLCH
THWP
AHM! NNNH...
AAH!
HAA
HAA
HAA
XIU-SAMA...
THWP
THWP
HAA
THWP
OOH!

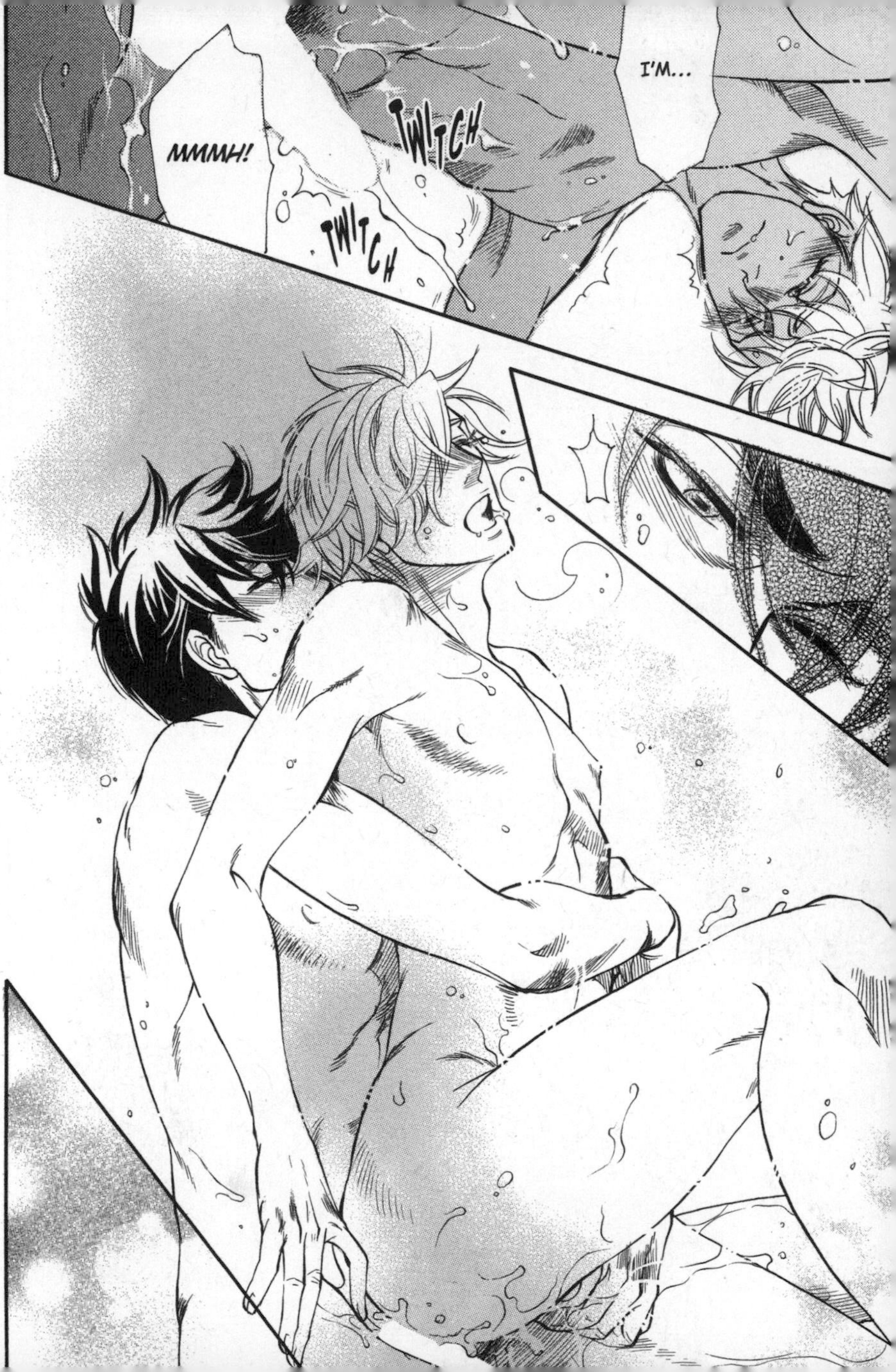
I'M...
TWITCH
MMMH!
TWITCH

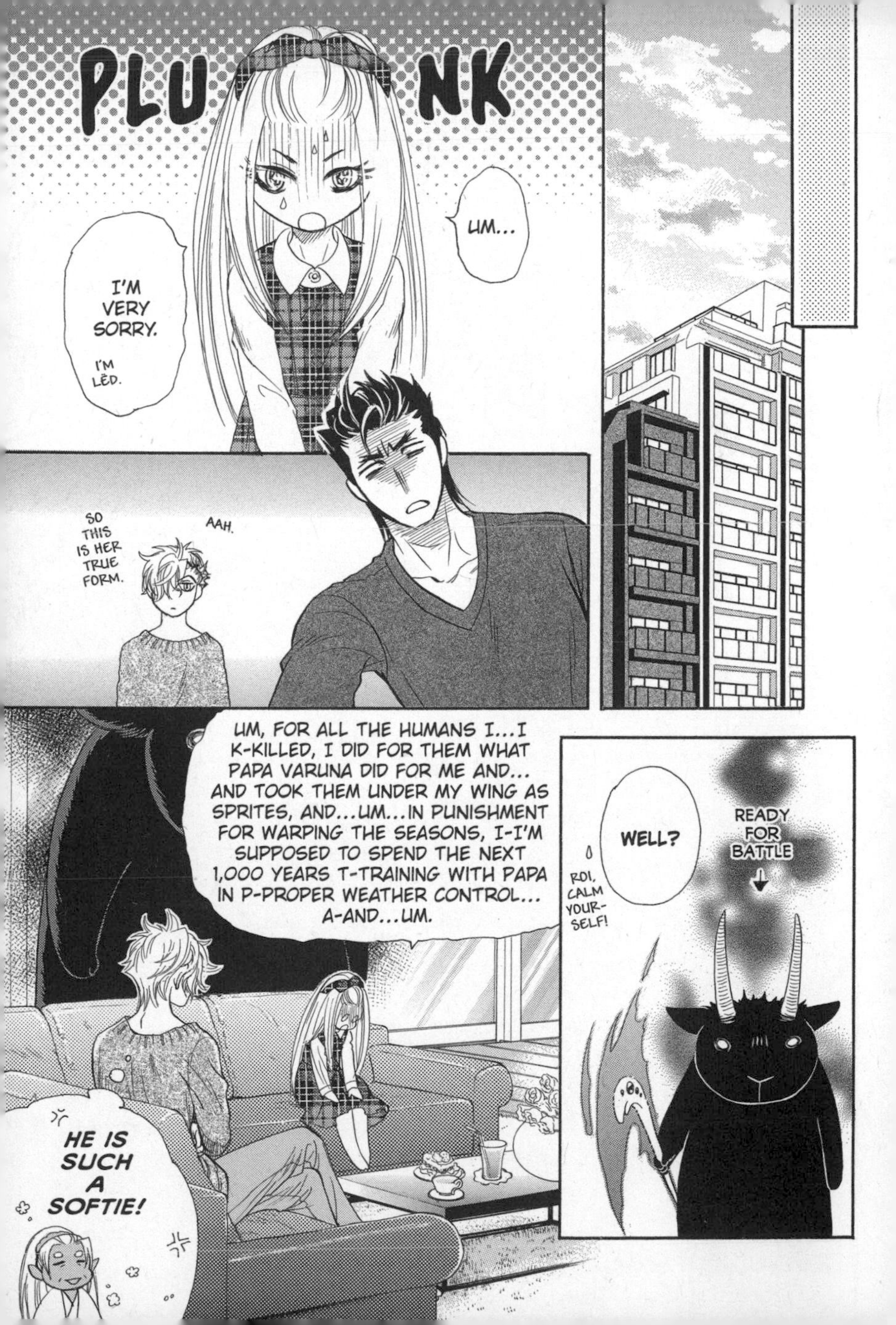
PLU NK
UM...
I'M VERY SORRY.
I'M LËD.
AAH.
SO THIS IS HER TRUE FORM.
READY FOR BATTLE
WELL?
RDI, CALM YOUR-SELF!
UM, FOR ALL THE HUMANS I...I K-KILLED, I DID FOR THEM WHAT PAPA VARUNA DID FOR ME AND... AND TOOK THEM UNDER MY WING AS SPRITES, AND...UM...IN PUNISHMENT FOR WARPING THE SEASONS, I-I'M SUPPOSED TO SPEND THE NEXT 1,000 YEARS T-TRAINING WITH PAPA IN P-PROPER WEATHER CONTROL... A-AND...UM.
HE IS SUCH A SOFTIE!

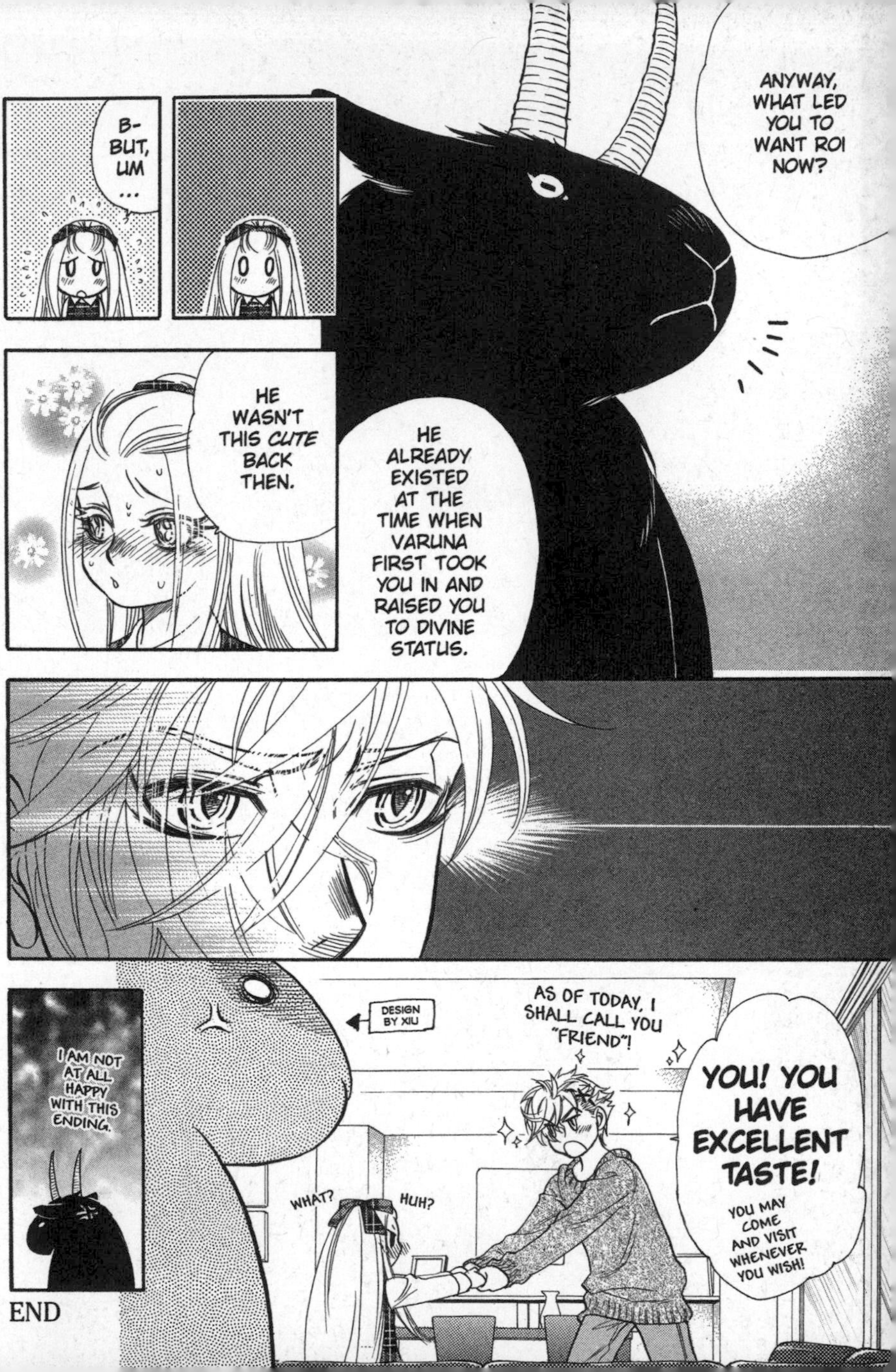
ANYWAY, WHAT LED YOU TO WANT ROI NOW?
HE ALREADY EXISTED AT THE TIME WHEN VARUNA FIRST TOOK YOU IN AND RAISED YOU TO DIVINE STATUS.
B-BUT, UM ...
HE WASN'T THIS *CUTE* BACK THEN.
YOU! YOU HAVE EXCELLENT TASTE!
AS OF TODAY, I SHALL CALL YOU "FRIEND"!
YOU MAY COME AND VISIT WHENEVER YOU WISH!
HUH?
WHAT?
DESIGN BY XIU
I AM NOT AT ALL HAPPY WITH THIS ENDING.
END

Bohra Naono Presents

彼方者の
困惑

Midnight Stranger

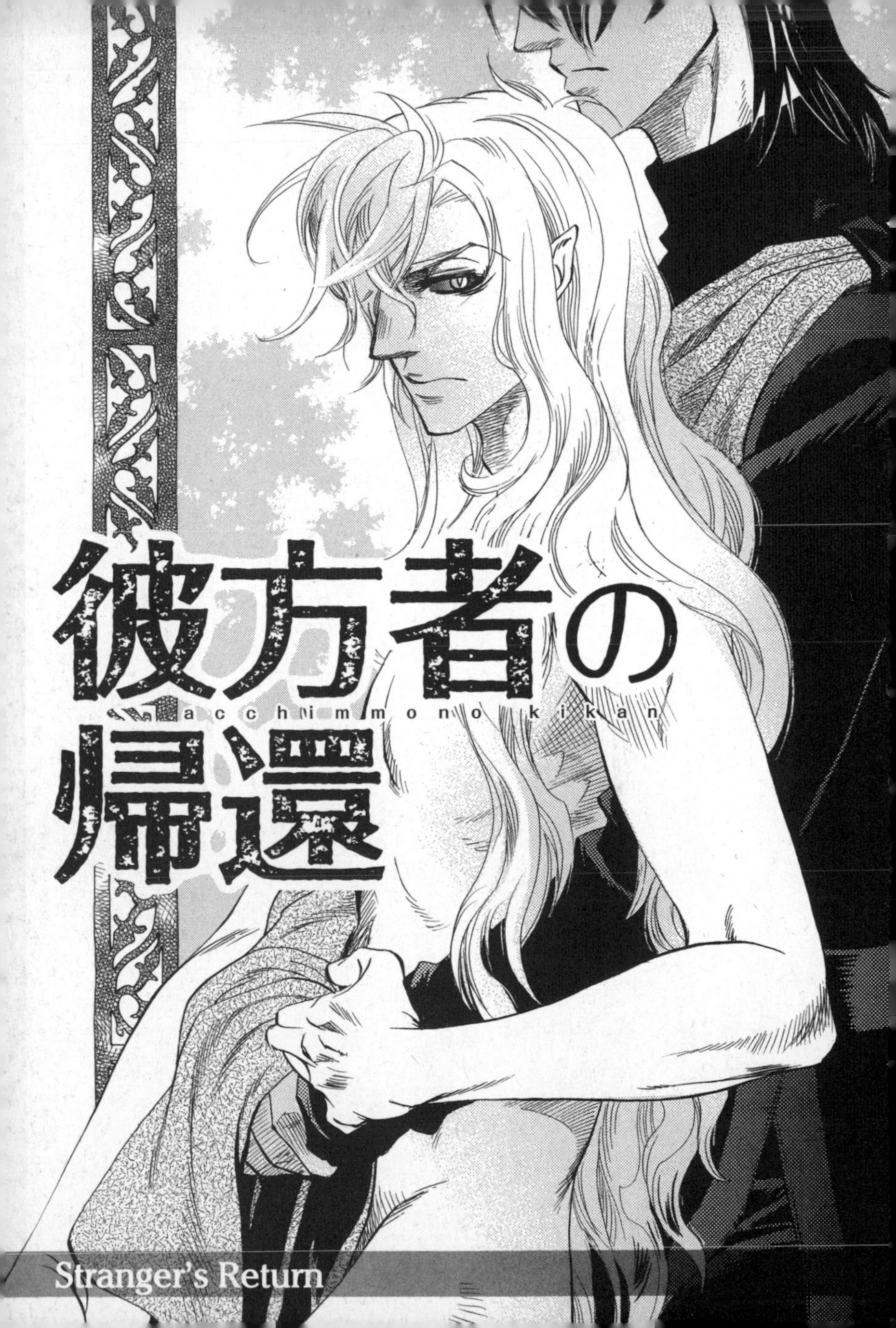
彼方者の帰還
acchimmono kikan
Stranger's Return

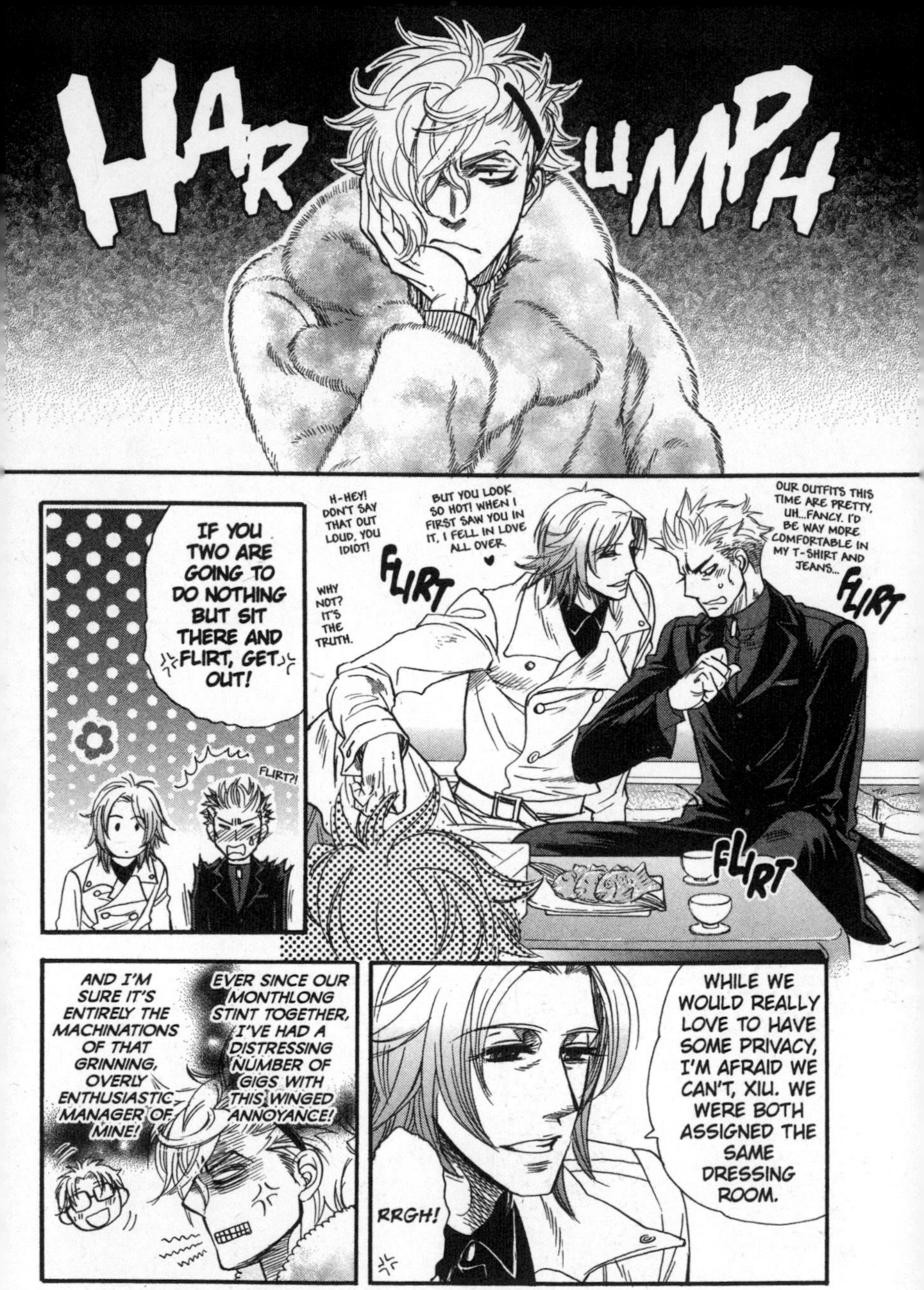
HARUMPH
OUR OUTFITS THIS TIME ARE PRETTY, UH...FANCY. I'D BE WAY MORE COMFORTABLE IN MY T-SHIRT AND JEANS...
FLIRT
BUT YOU LOOK SO HOT! WHEN I FIRST SAW YOU IN IT, I FELL IN LOVE ALL OVER.
H-HEY! DON'T SAY THAT OUT LOUD, YOU IDIOT!
FLIRT
WHY NOT? IT'S THE TRUTH.
FLIRT
IF YOU TWO ARE GOING TO DO NOTHING BUT SIT THERE AND FLIRT, GET OUT!
FLIRT?!
WHILE WE WOULD REALLY LOVE TO HAVE SOME PRIVACY, I'M AFRAID WE CAN'T, XIU. WE WERE BOTH ASSIGNED THE SAME DRESSING ROOM.
RRGH!
EVER SINCE OUR MONTHLONG STINT TOGETHER, I'VE HAD A DISTRESSING NUMBER OF GIGS WITH THIS WINGED ANNOYANCE!
AND I'M SURE IT'S ENTIRELY THE MACHINATIONS OF THAT GRINNING, OVERLY ENTHUSIASTIC MANAGER OF MINE!

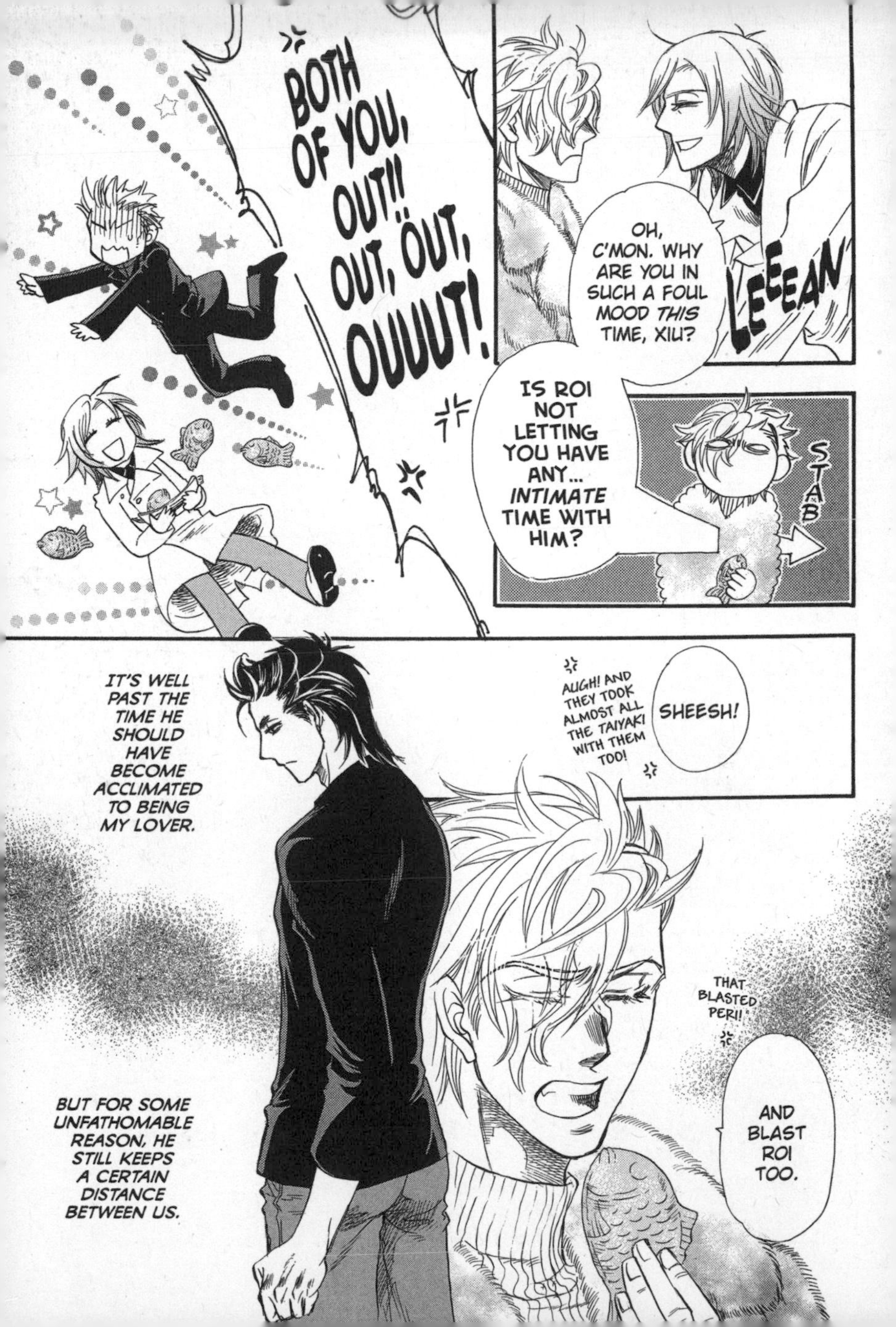
OH, C'MON. WHY ARE YOU IN SUCH A FOUL MOOD *THIS* TIME, XIU?
LEEEAN
IS ROI NOT LETTING YOU HAVE ANY... *INTIMATE* TIME WITH HIM?
STAB
BOTH OF YOU, OUT!! OUT, OUT, OUUUT!
SHEESH!
AUGH! AND THEY TOOK ALMOST ALL THE TAIYAKI WITH THEM TOO!
IT'S WELL PAST THE TIME HE SHOULD HAVE BECOME ACCLIMATED TO BEING MY LOVER.
THAT BLASTED PERI!
AND BLAST ROI TOO.
BUT FOR SOME UNFATHOMABLE REASON, HE STILL KEEPS A CERTAIN DISTANCE BETWEEN US.

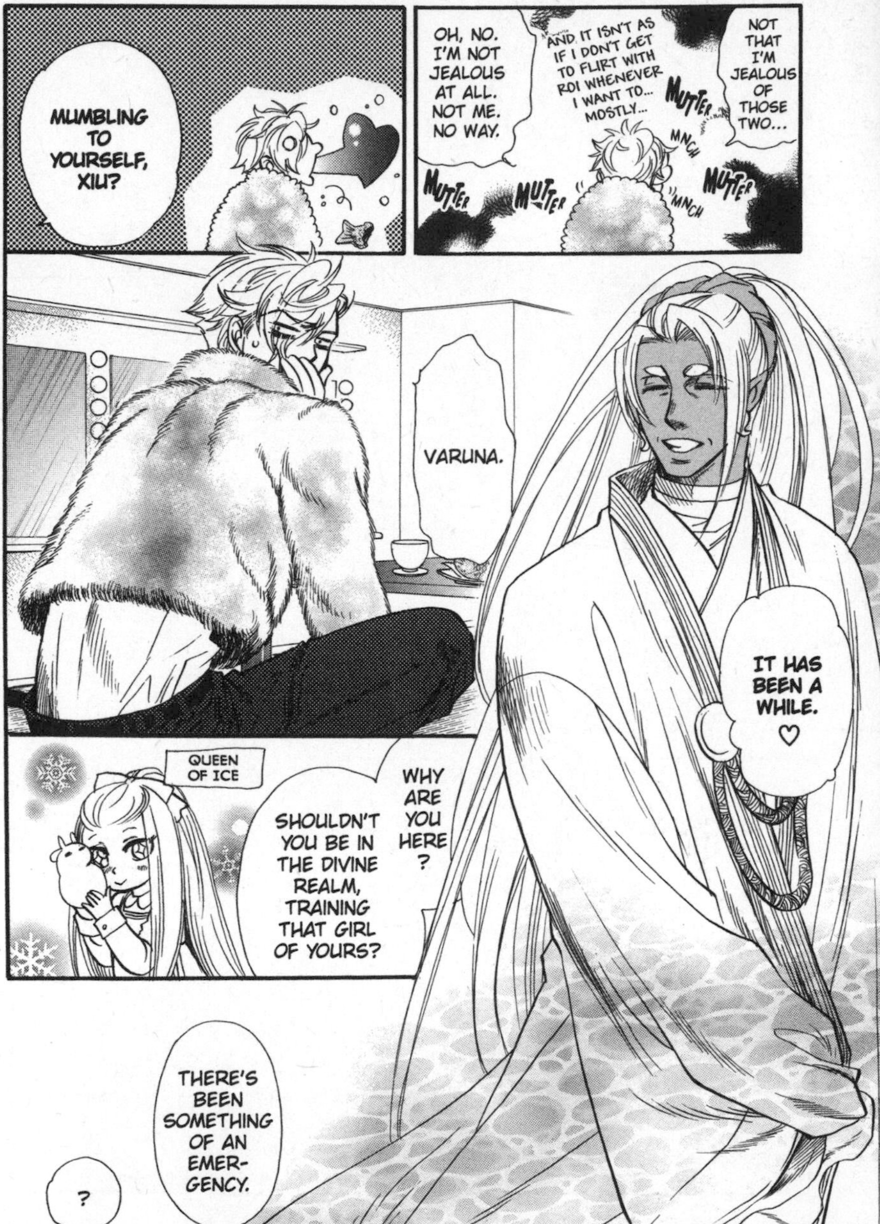
NOT THAT I'M JEALOUS OF THOSE TWO...
AND IT ISN'T AS IF I DON'T GET TO FLIRT WITH RDI WHENEVER I WANT TO... MOSTLY...
OH, NO. I'M NOT JEALOUS AT ALL. NOT ME. NO WAY.
MUTTER
MNCH
MNCH
MUTTER
MUTTER
MUTTER
MUMBLING TO YOURSELF, XIU?
VARUNA.
IT HAS BEEN A WHILE. ♡
QUEEN OF ICE
WHY ARE YOU HERE?
SHOULDN'T YOU BE IN THE DIVINE REALM, TRAINING THAT GIRL OF YOURS?
THERE'S BEEN SOMETHING OF AN EMERGENCY.
?

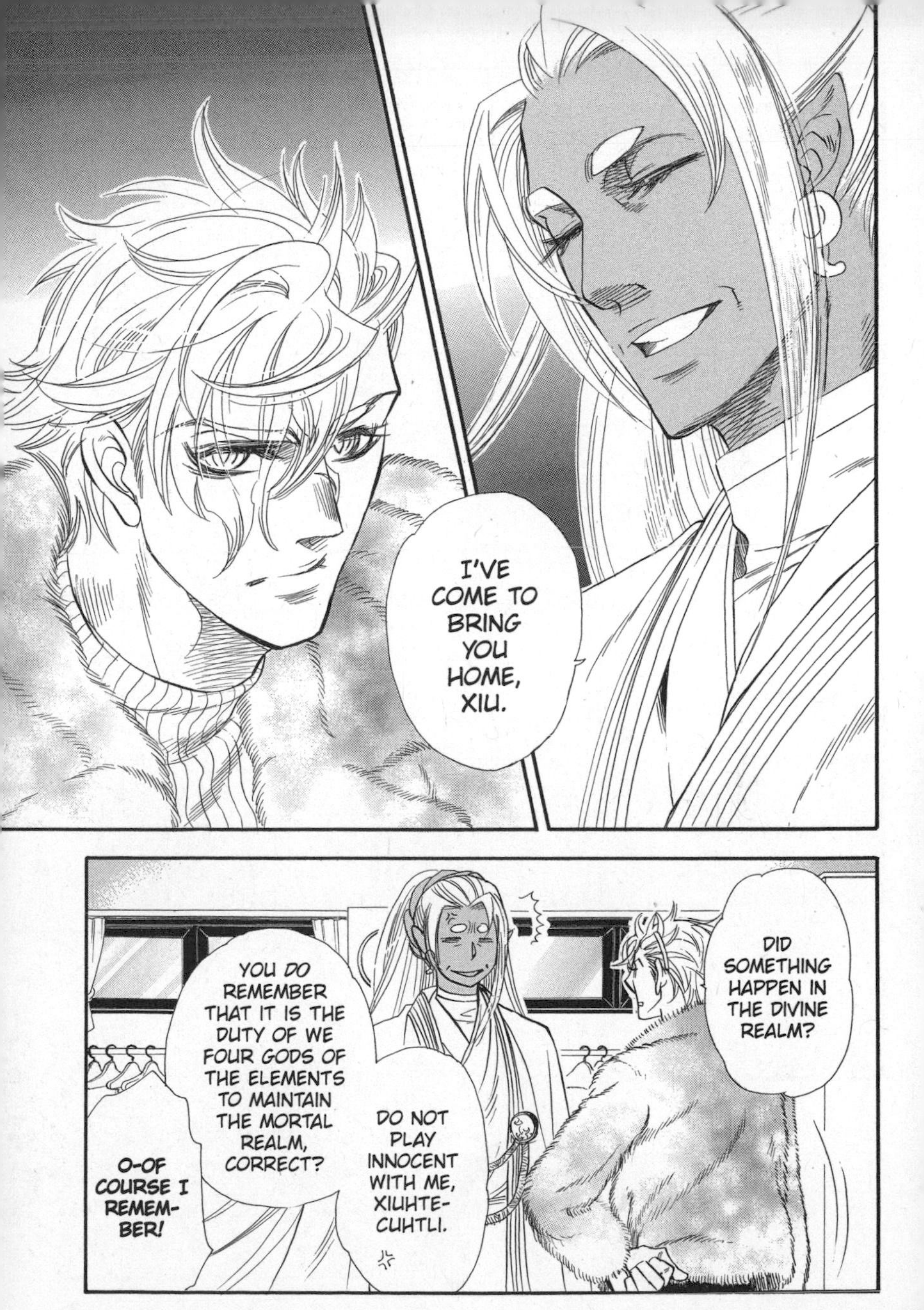
I'VE COME TO BRING YOU HOME, XIU.
DID SOMETHING HAPPEN IN THE DIVINE REALM?
DO NOT PLAY INNOCENT WITH ME, XIUHTE-CUHTLI.
YOU *DO* REMEMBER THAT IT IS THE DUTY OF WE FOUR GODS OF THE ELEMENTS TO MAINTAIN THE MORTAL REALM, CORRECT?
O-OF COURSE I REMEMBER!

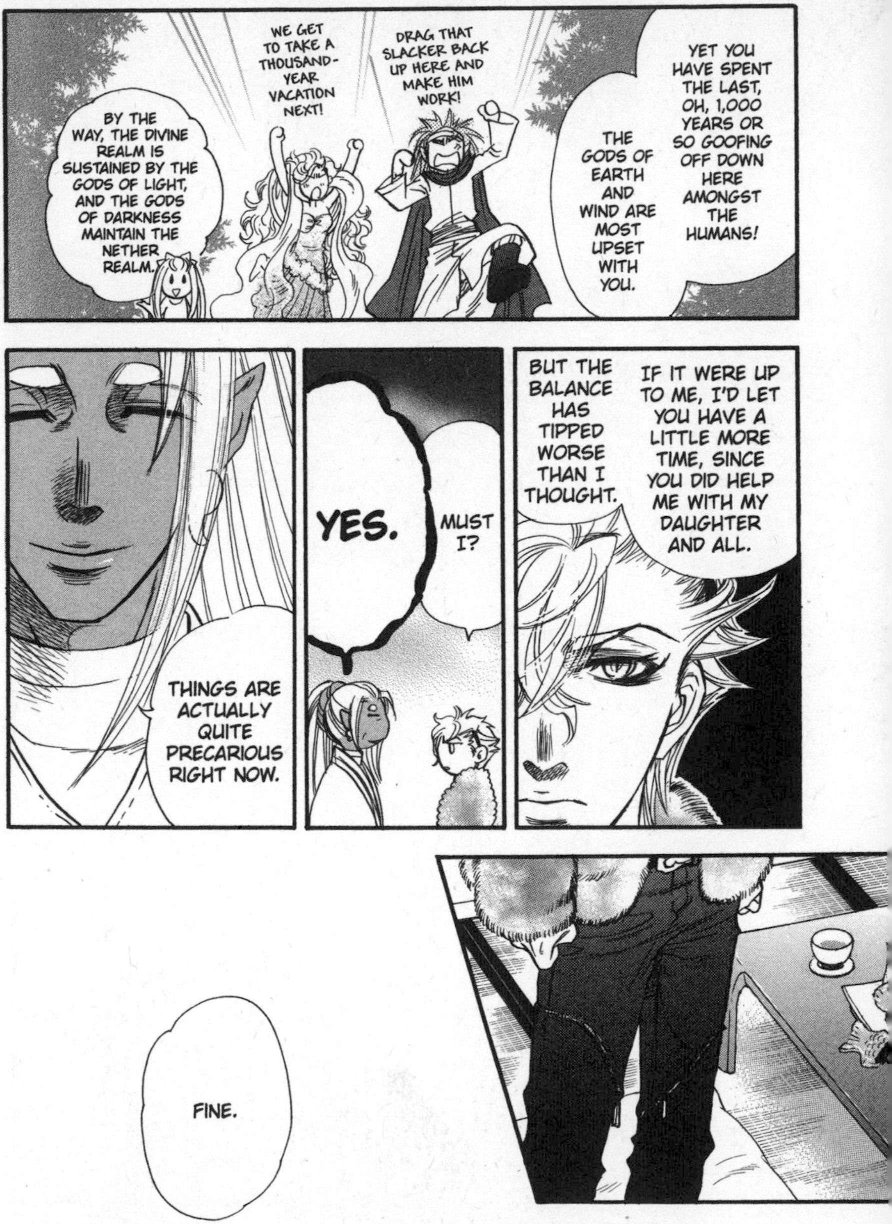
YET YOU HAVE SPENT THE LAST, OH, 1,000 YEARS OR SO GOOFING OFF DOWN HERE AMONGST THE HUMANS!
THE GODS OF EARTH AND WIND ARE MOST UPSET WITH YOU.
DRAG THAT SLACKER BACK UP HERE AND MAKE HIM WORK!
WE GET TO TAKE A THOUSAND-YEAR VACATION NEXT!
BY THE WAY, THE DIVINE REALM IS SUSTAINED BY THE GODS OF LIGHT, AND THE GODS OF DARKNESS MAINTAIN THE NETHER REALM.
IF IT WERE UP TO ME, I'D LET YOU HAVE A LITTLE MORE TIME, SINCE YOU DID HELP ME WITH MY DAUGHTER AND ALL.
BUT THE BALANCE HAS TIPPED WORSE THAN I THOUGHT.
MUST I?
YES.
THINGS ARE ACTUALLY QUITE PRECARIOUS RIGHT NOW.
FINE.

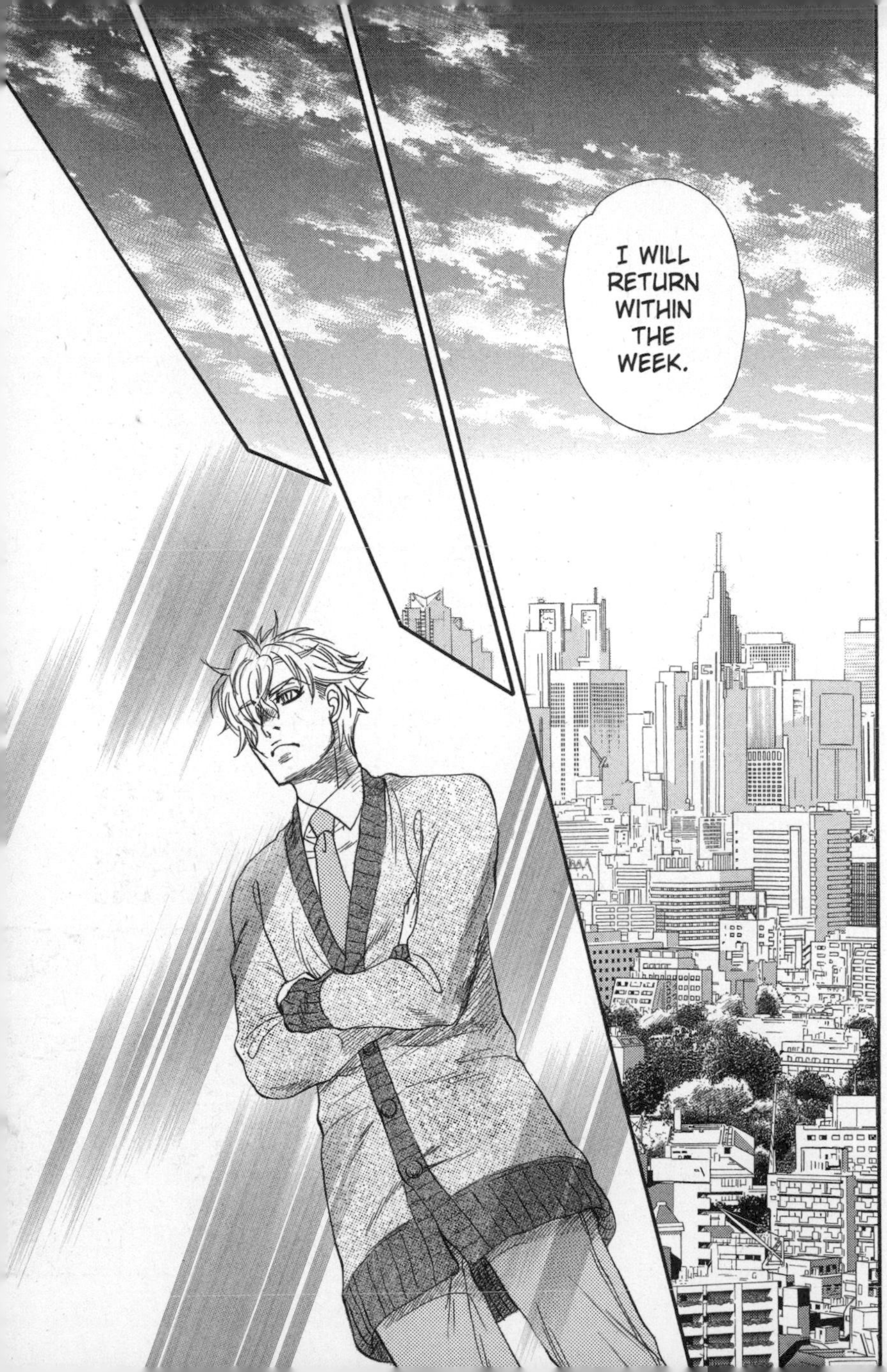
I WILL RETURN WITHIN THE WEEK.

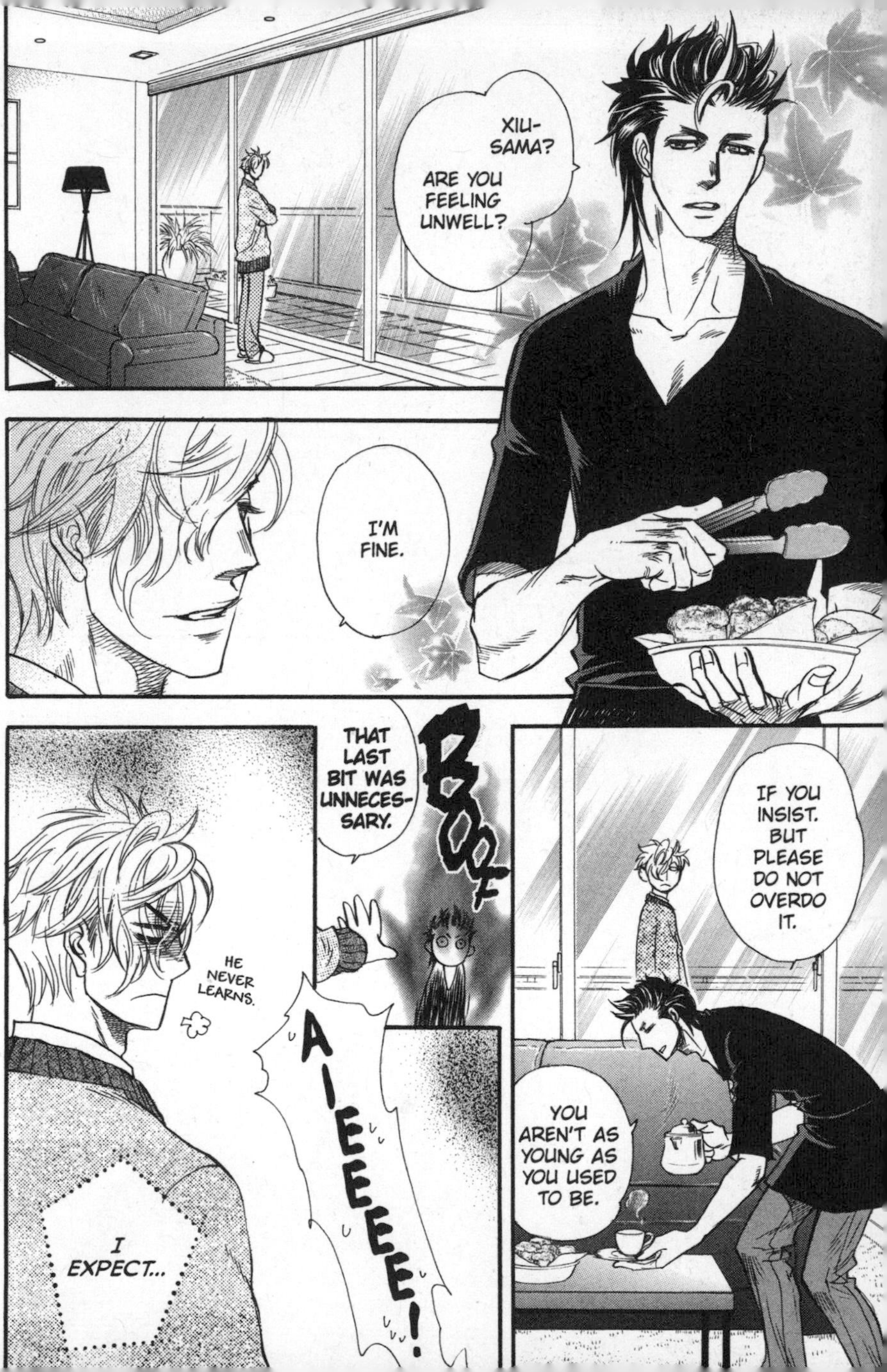
XIU-SAMA?
ARE YOU FEELING UNWELL?
I'M FINE.
IF YOU INSIST. BUT PLEASE DO NOT OVERDO IT.
YOU AREN'T AS YOUNG AS YOU USED TO BE.
THAT LAST BIT WAS UNNECES-SARY.
BOOF
AIEEEEE!
HE NEVER LEARNS.
I EXPECT...

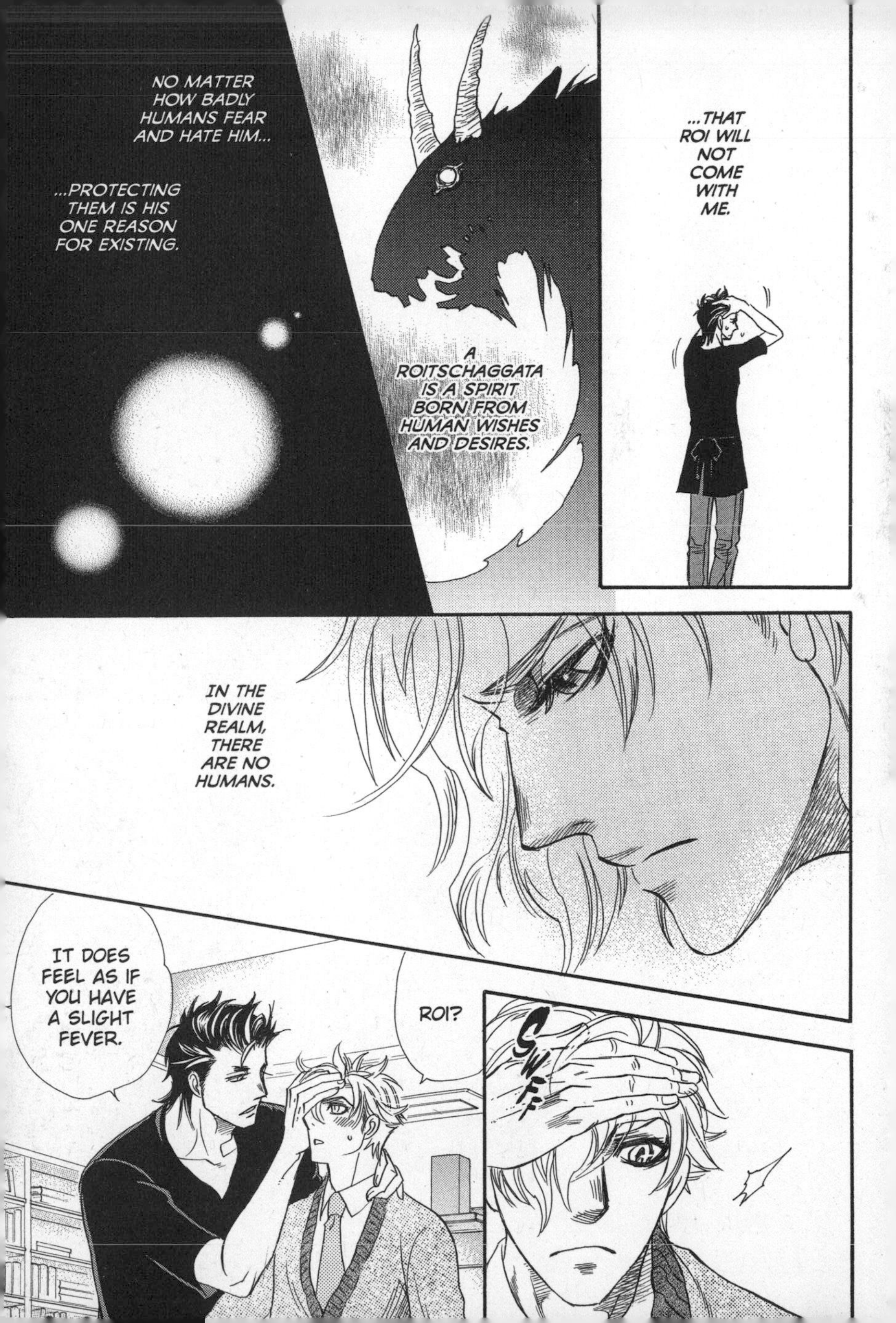
...THAT ROI WILL NOT COME WITH ME.
A ROITSCHAGGATA IS A SPIRIT BORN FROM HUMAN WISHES AND DESIRES.
NO MATTER HOW BADLY HUMANS FEAR AND HATE HIM...
...PROTECTING THEM IS HIS ONE REASON FOR EXISTING.
IN THE DIVINE REALM, THERE ARE NO HUMANS.
SWFF
ROI?
IT DOES FEEL AS IF YOU HAVE A SLIGHT FEVER.

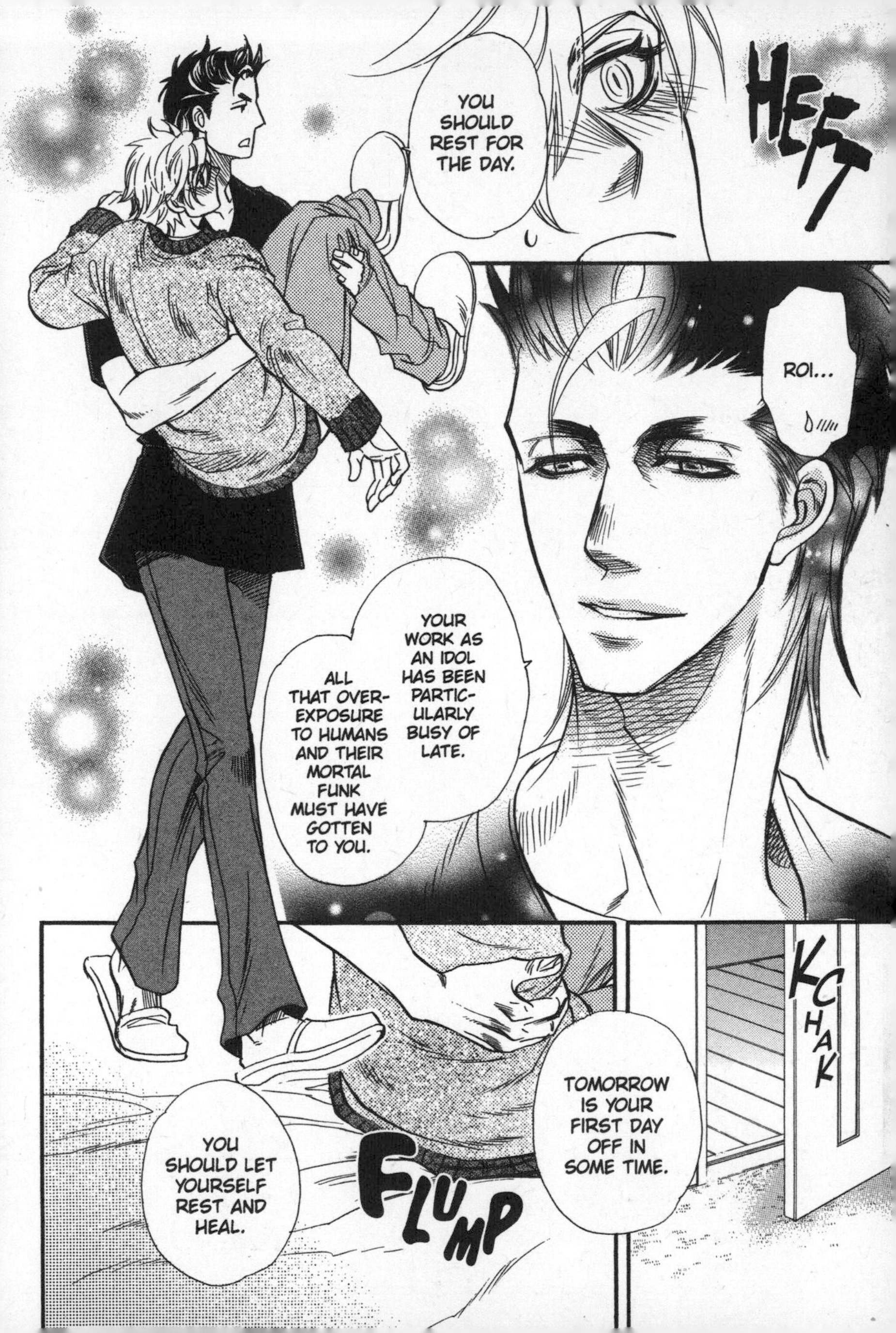
HEFT
YOU SHOULD REST FOR THE DAY.
ROI...
YOUR WORK AS AN IDOL HAS BEEN PARTIC-ULARLY BUSY OF LATE.
ALL THAT OVER-EXPOSURE TO HUMANS AND THEIR MORTAL FUNK MUST HAVE GOTTEN TO YOU.
KCHAK
TOMORROW IS YOUR FIRST DAY OFF IN SOME TIME.
FLUMP
YOU SHOULD LET YOURSELF REST AND HEAL.

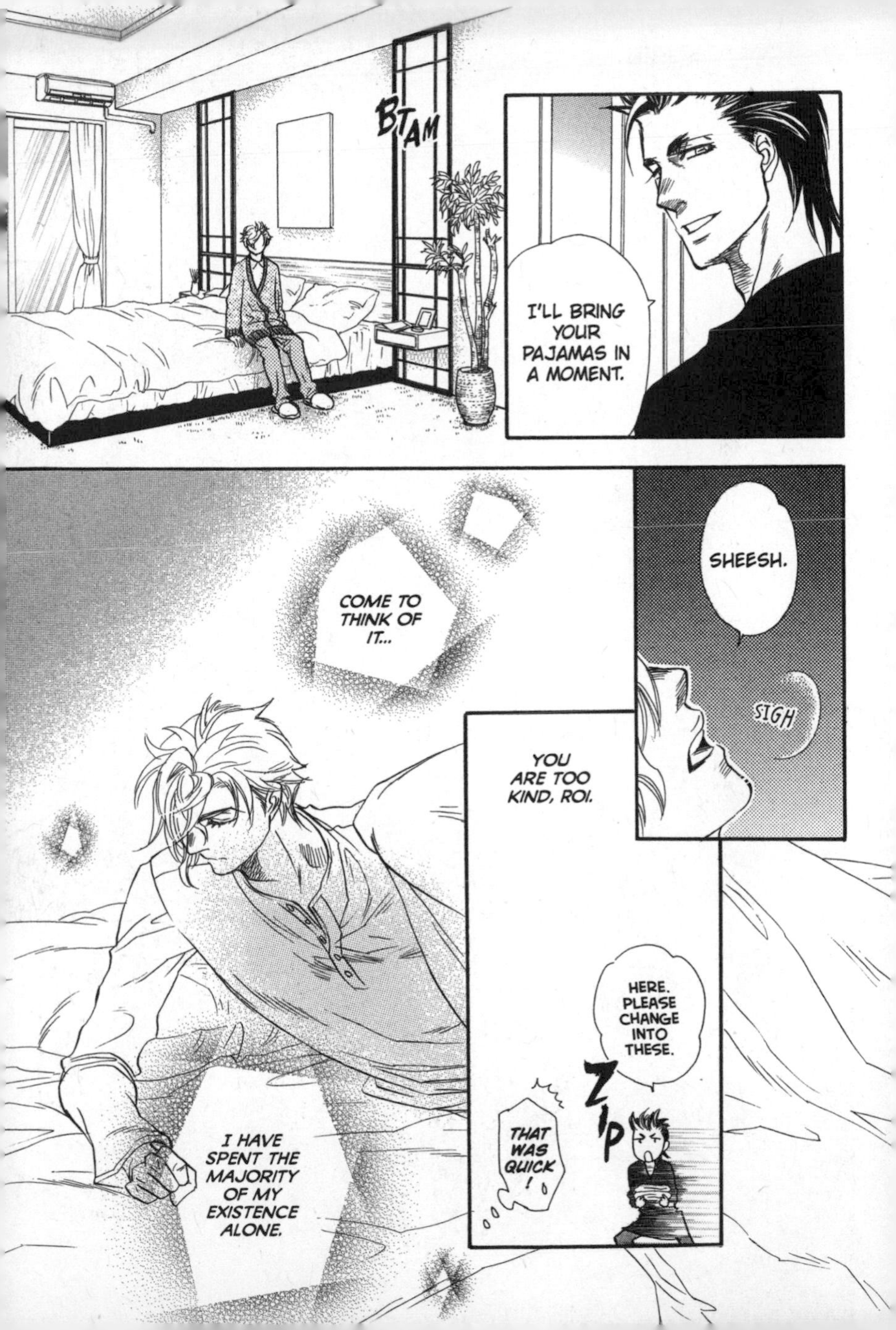
I'LL BRING YOUR PAJAMAS IN A MOMENT.
BTAM
SHEESH.
SIGH
YOU ARE TOO KIND, ROI.
HERE. PLEASE CHANGE INTO THESE.
ZIP
THAT WAS QUICK!
COME TO THINK OF IT...
I HAVE SPENT THE MAJORITY OF MY EXISTENCE ALONE.

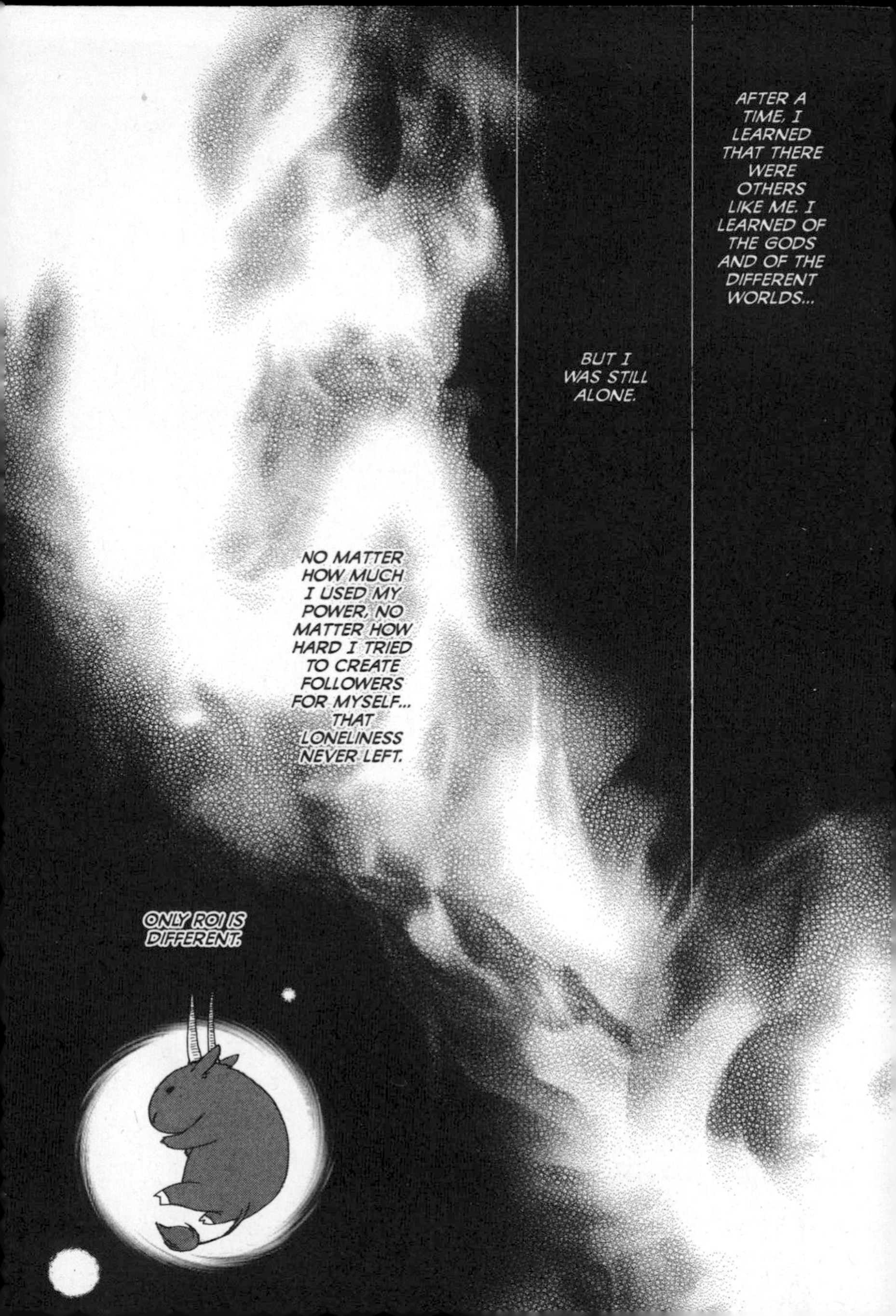
AFTER A TIME, I LEARNED THAT THERE WERE OTHERS LIKE ME. I LEARNED OF THE GODS AND OF THE DIFFERENT WORLDS...
BUT I WAS STILL ALONE.
NO MATTER HOW MUCH I USED MY POWER, NO MATTER HOW HARD I TRIED TO CREATE FOLLOWERS FOR MYSELF... THAT LONELINESS NEVER LEFT.
ONLY ROI IS DIFFERENT.

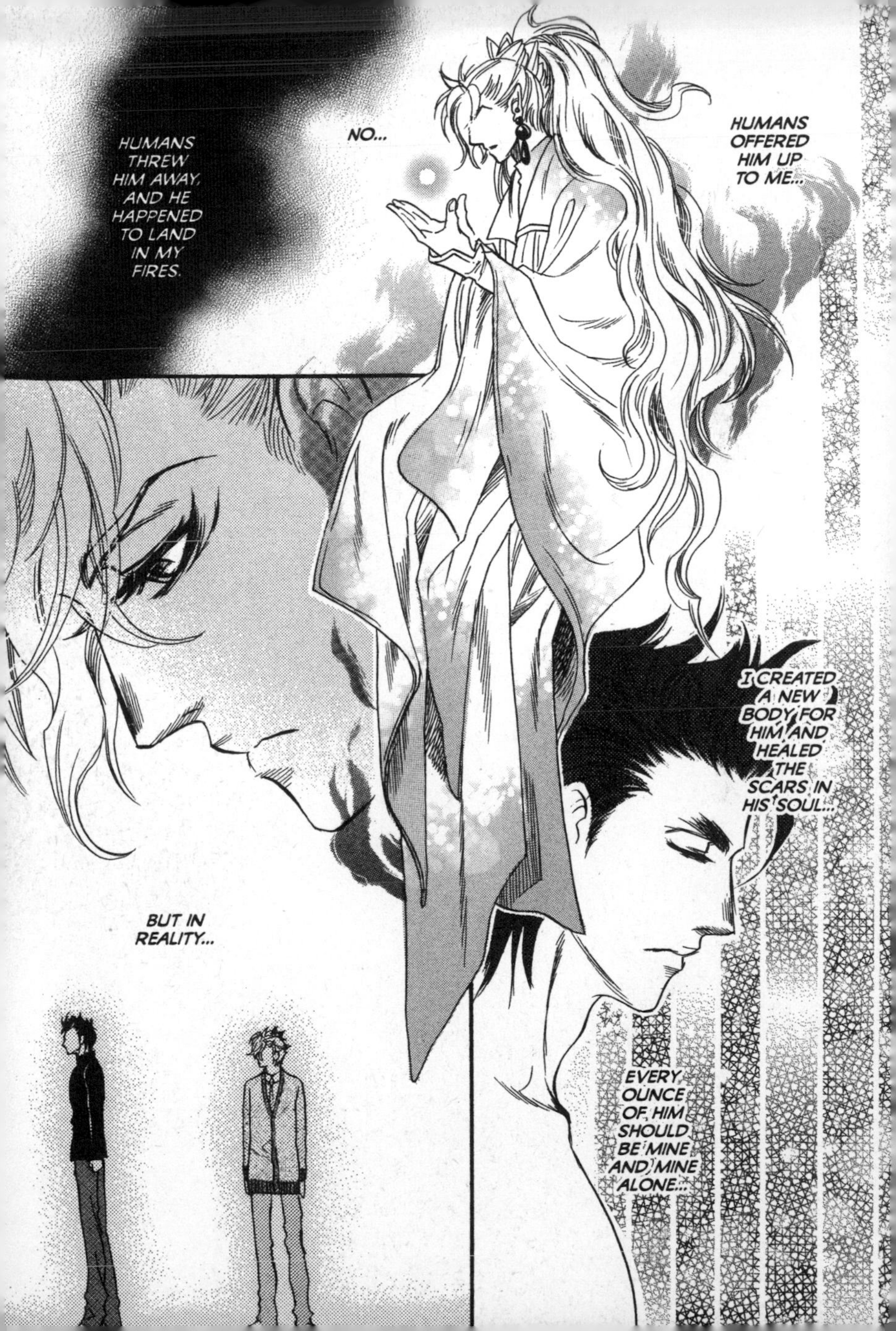
HUMANS OFFERED HIM UP TO ME...
NO...
HUMANS THREW HIM AWAY, AND HE HAPPENED TO LAND IN MY FIRES.
I CREATED A NEW BODY FOR HIM AND HEALED THE SCARS IN HIS SOUL...
EVERY OUNCE OF HIM SHOULD BE MINE AND MINE ALONE...
BUT IN REALITY...

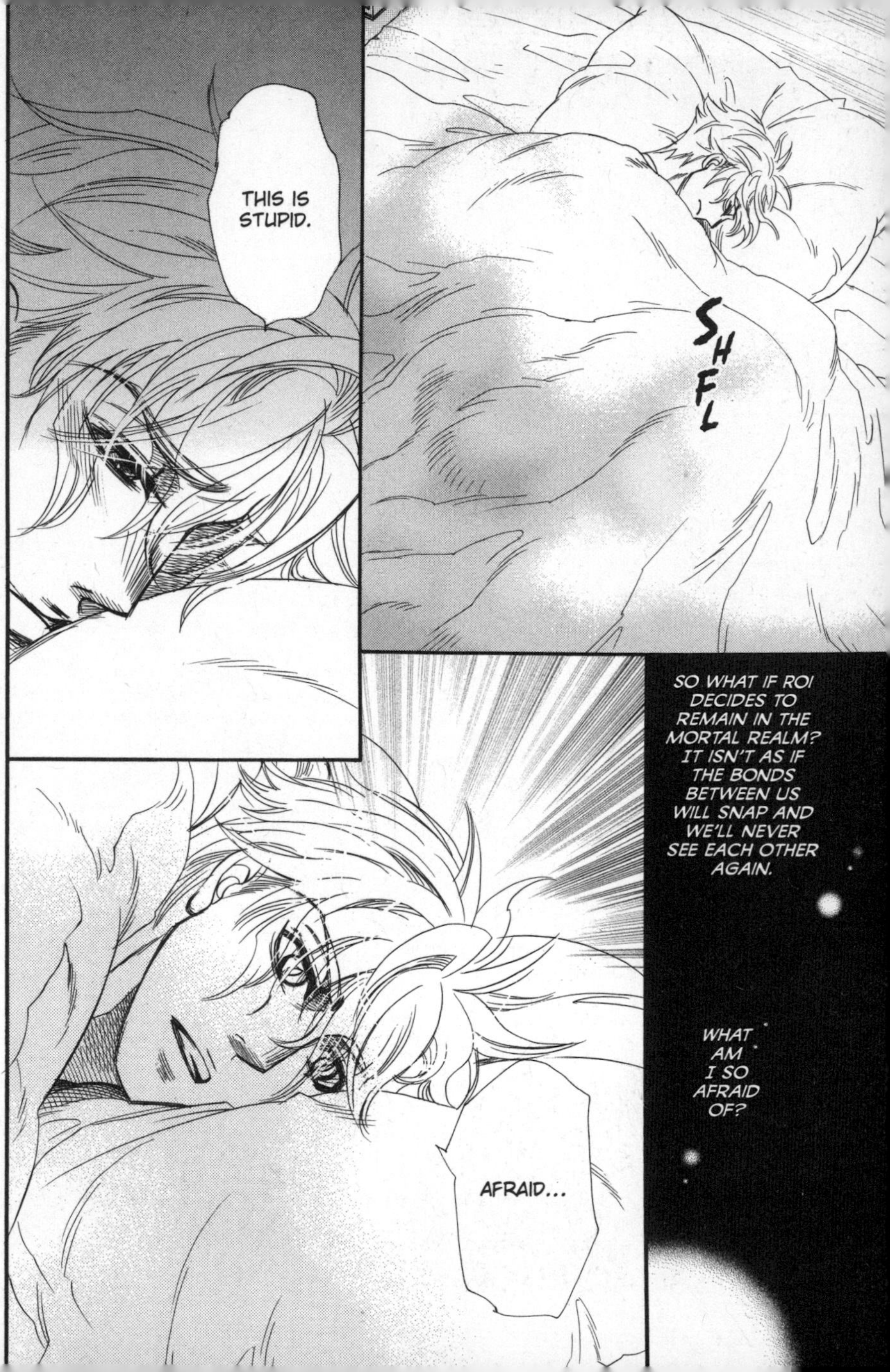
SHFL
THIS IS STUPID.
SO WHAT IF ROI DECIDES TO REMAIN IN THE MORTAL REALM? IT ISN'T AS IF THE BONDS BETWEEN US WILL SNAP AND WE'LL NEVER SEE EACH OTHER AGAIN.
WHAT AM I SO AFRAID OF?
AFRAID...

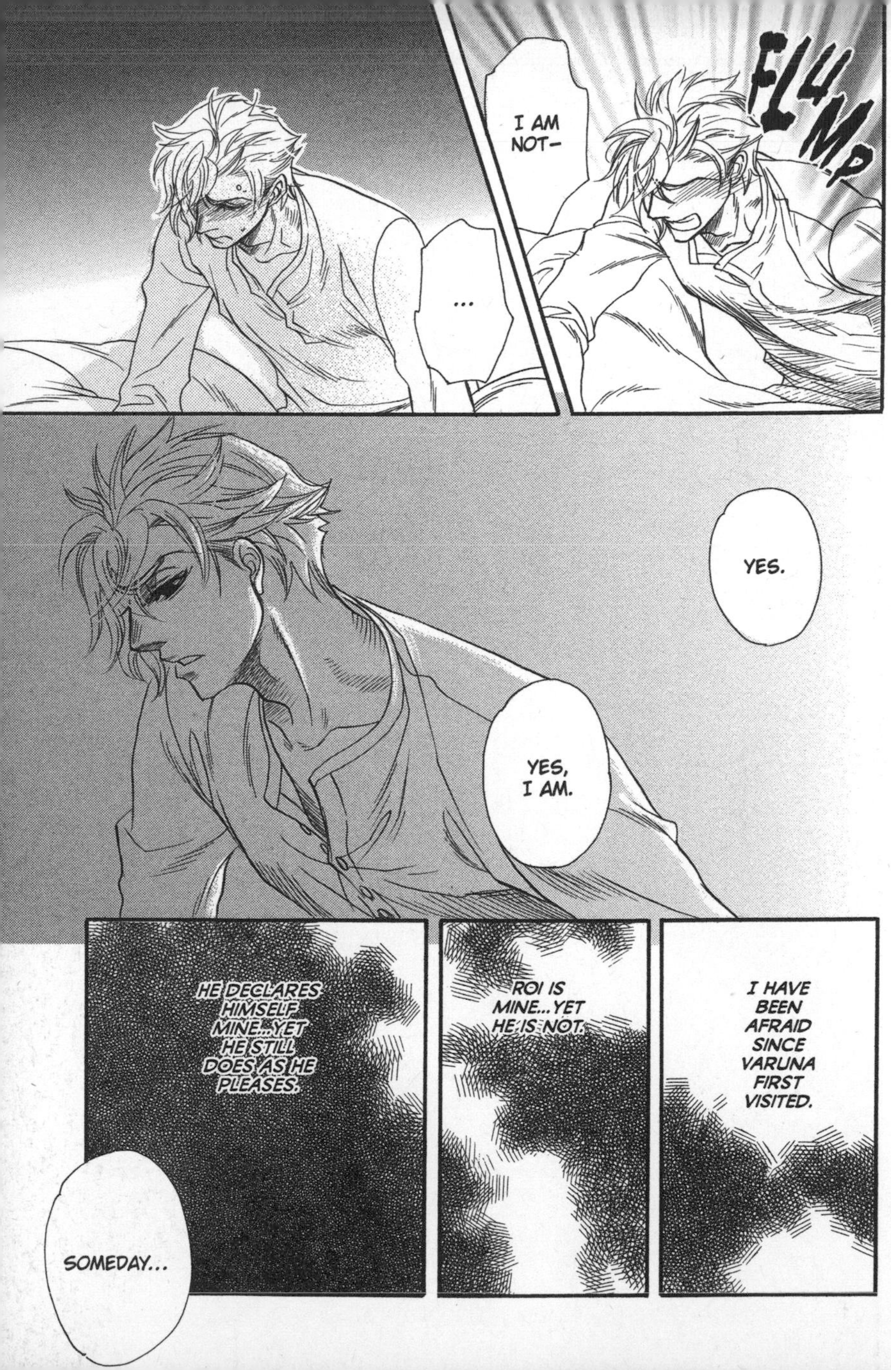
I AM NOT–
FLUMP
...
YES.
YES, I AM.
I HAVE BEEN AFRAID SINCE VARUNA FIRST VISITED.
ROI IS MINE...YET HE IS NOT.
HE DECLARES HIMSELF MINE...YET HE STILL DOES AS HE PLEASES.
SOMEDAY...

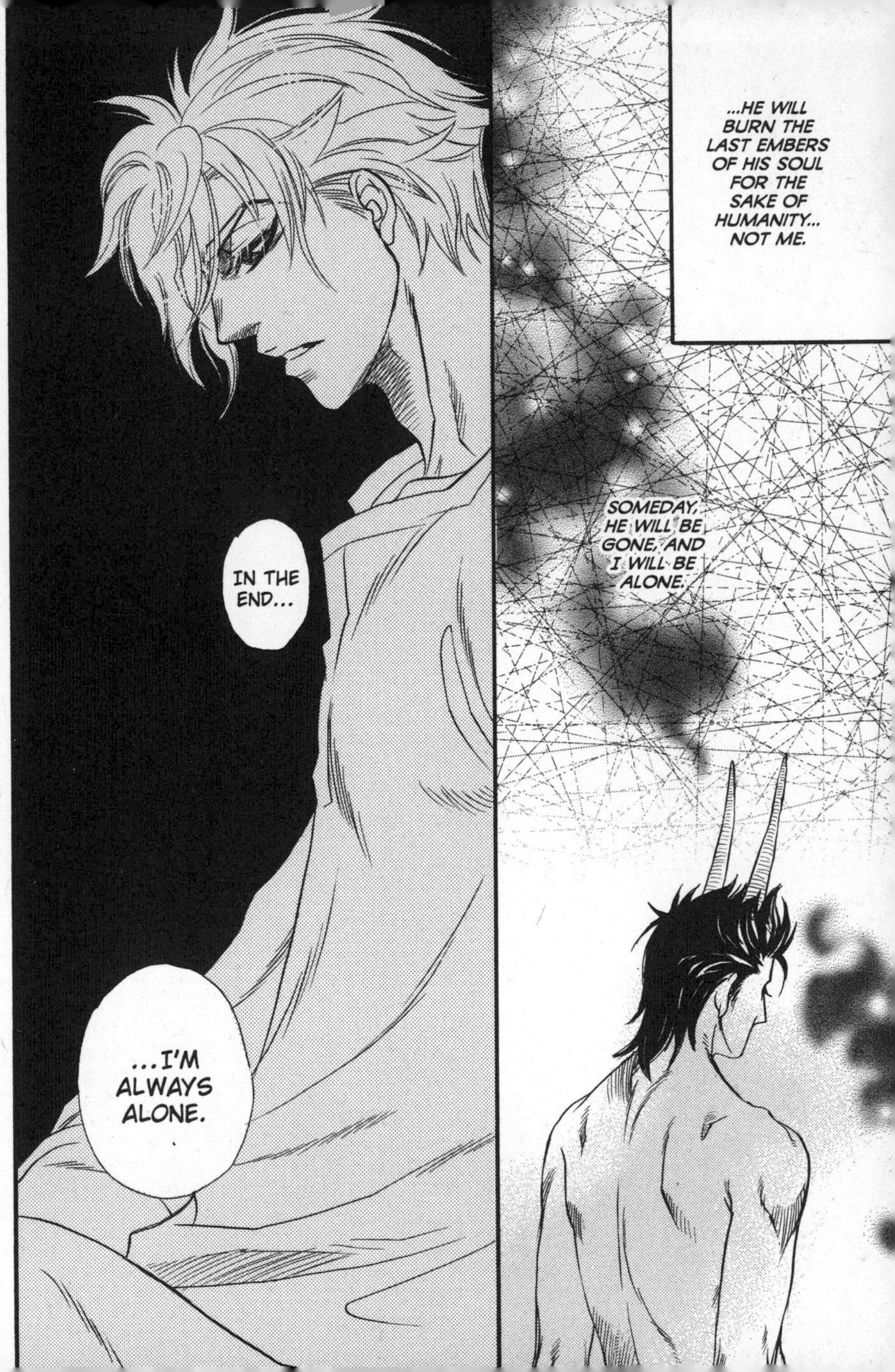
...HE WILL BURN THE LAST EMBERS OF HIS SOUL FOR THE SAKE OF HUMANITY... NOT ME.
SOMEDAY, HE WILL BE GONE, AND I WILL BE ALONE.
IN THE END...
...I'M ALWAYS ALONE.

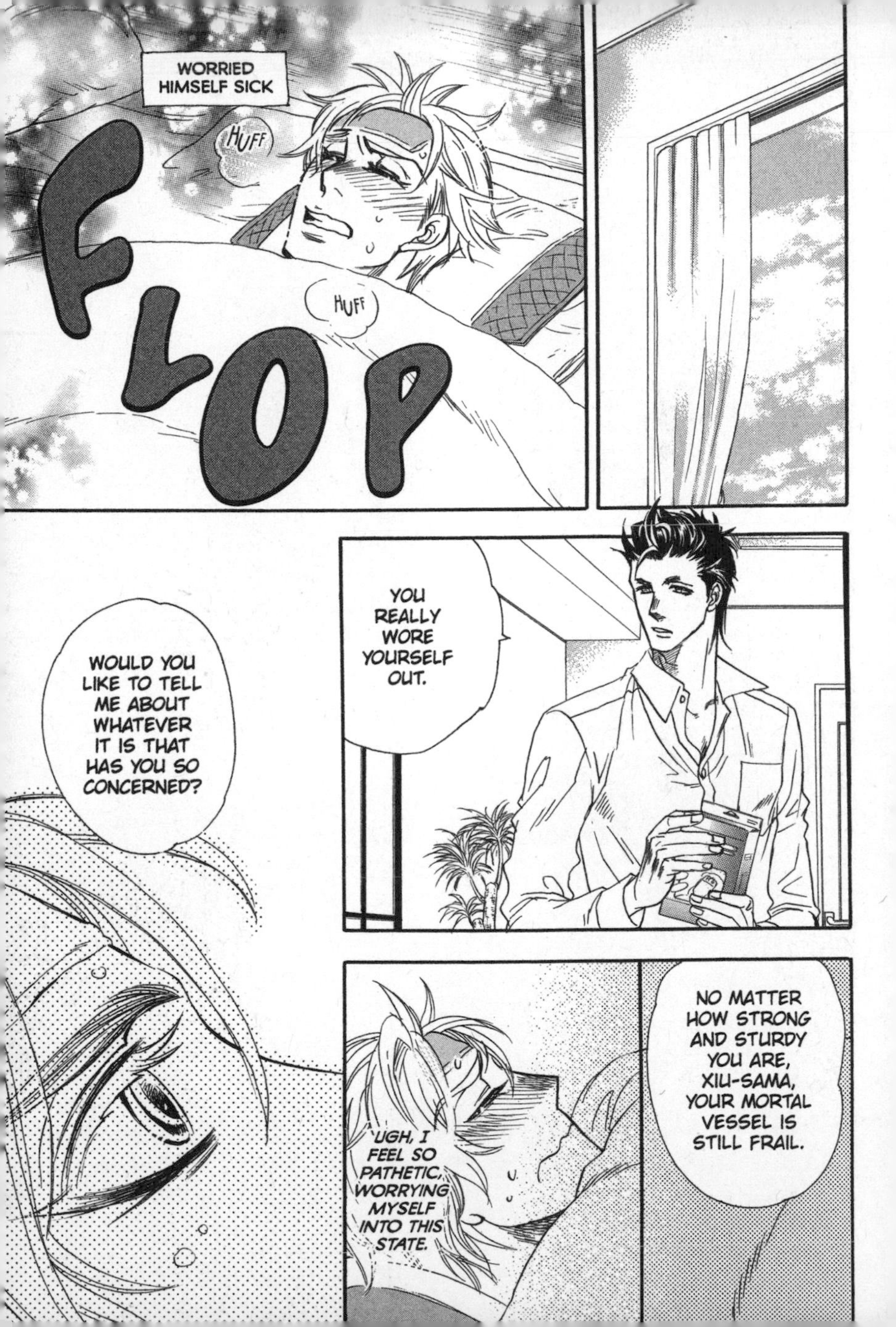
WORRIED HIMSELF SICK
HUFF
FLOP
HUFF
YOU REALLY WORE YOURSELF OUT.
NO MATTER HOW STRONG AND STURDY YOU ARE, XIU-SAMA, YOUR MORTAL VESSEL IS STILL FRAIL.
UGH, I FEEL SO PATHETIC, WORRYING MYSELF INTO THIS STATE.
WOULD YOU LIKE TO TELL ME ABOUT WHATEVER IT IS THAT HAS YOU SO CONCERNED?

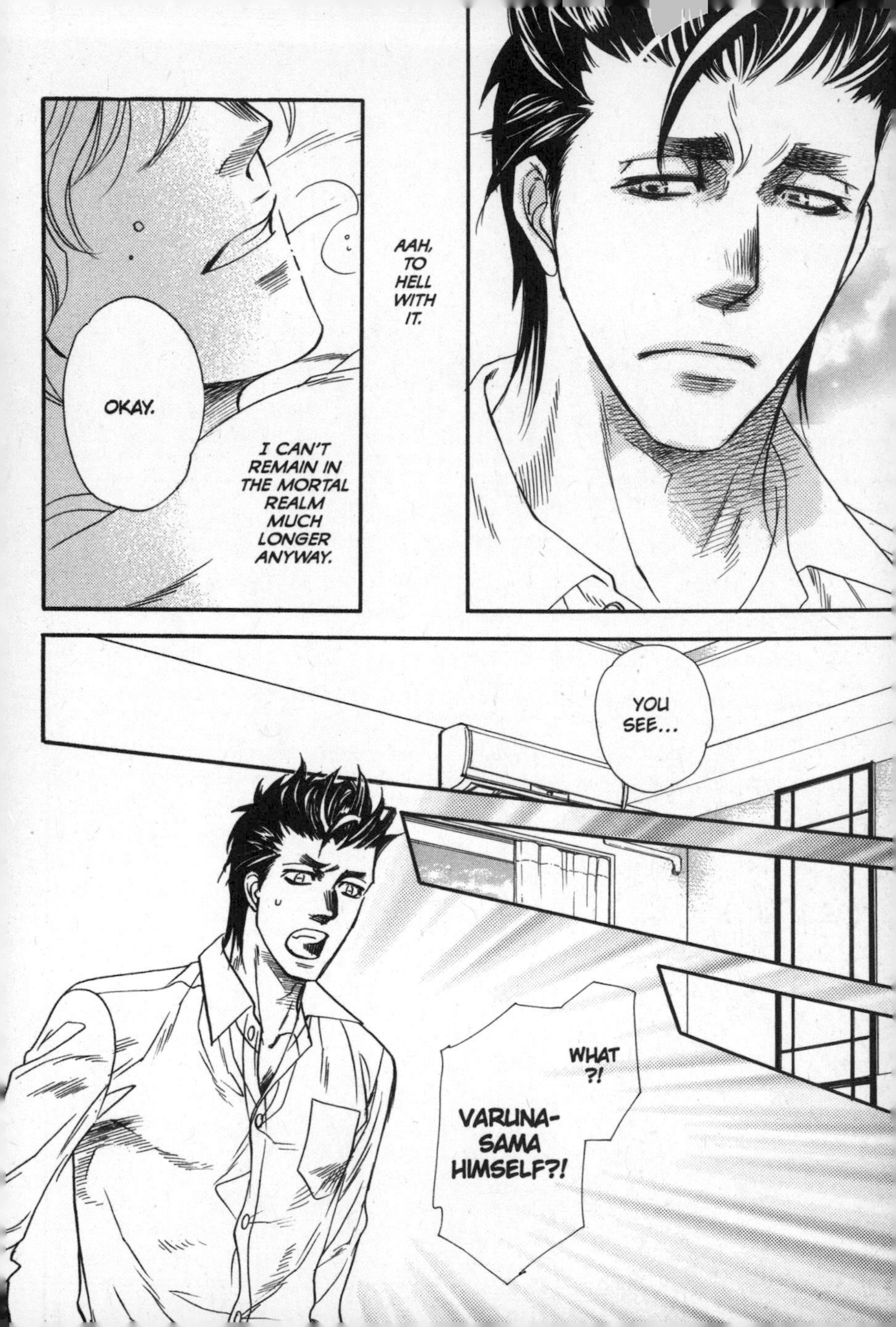
AAH, TO HELL WITH IT.
OKAY.
I CAN'T REMAIN IN THE MORTAL REALM MUCH LONGER ANYWAY.
YOU SEE...
WHAT?!
VARUNA-SAMA HIMSELF?!

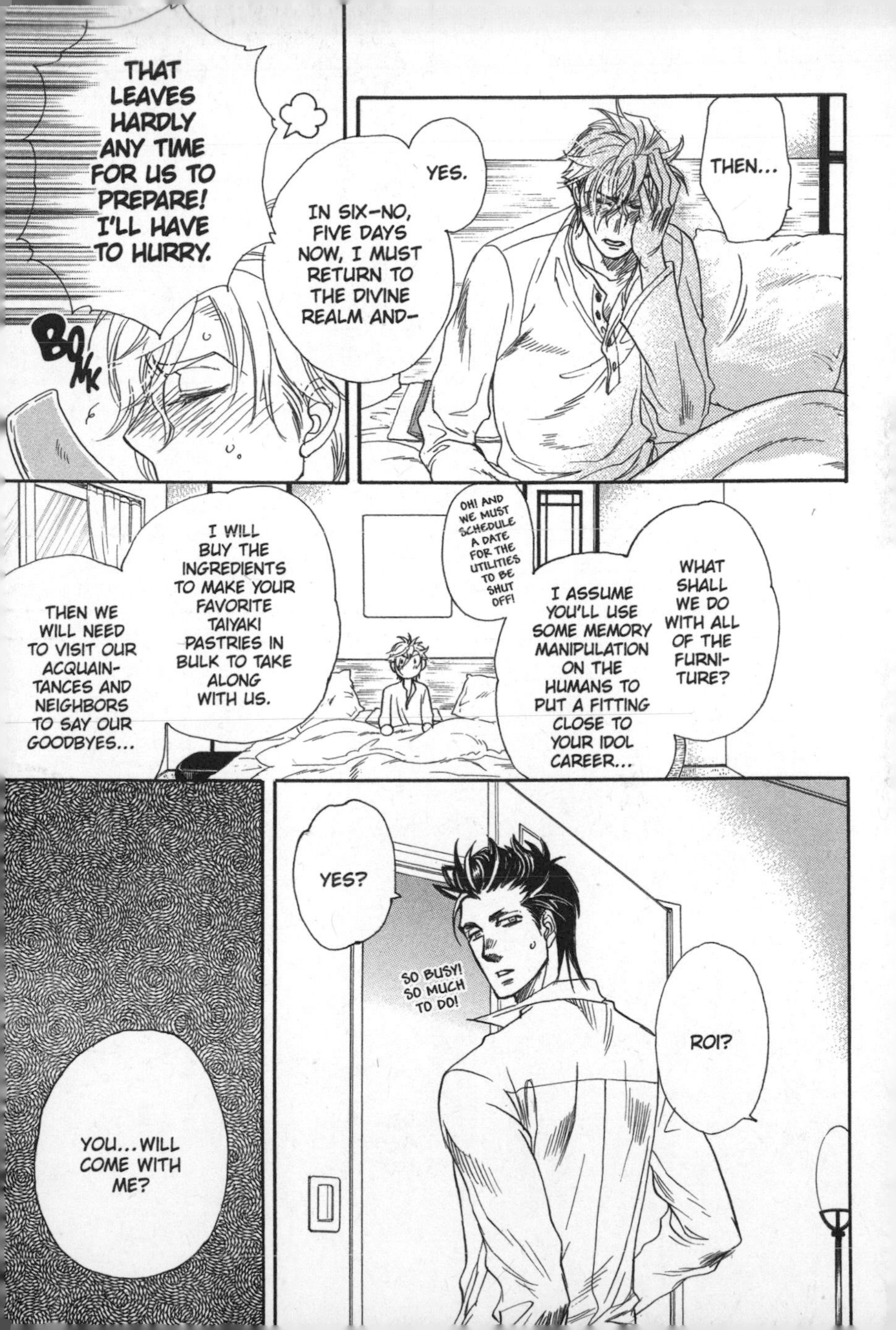
THEN...
YES.
IN SIX—NO, FIVE DAYS NOW, I MUST RETURN TO THE DIVINE REALM AND—
THAT LEAVES HARDLY ANY TIME FOR US TO PREPARE! I'LL HAVE TO HURRY.
BONK
WHAT SHALL WE DO WITH ALL OF THE FURNI-TURE?
I ASSUME YOU'LL USE SOME MEMORY MANIPULATION ON THE HUMANS TO PUT A FITTING CLOSE TO YOUR IDOL CAREER...
OH! AND WE MUST SCHEDULE A DATE FOR THE UTILITIES TO BE SHUT OFF!
I WILL BUY THE INGREDIENTS TO MAKE YOUR FAVORITE TAIYAKI PASTRIES IN BULK TO TAKE ALONG WITH US.
THEN WE WILL NEED TO VISIT OUR ACQUAIN-TANCES AND NEIGHBORS TO SAY OUR GOODBYES...
ROI?
YES?
SO BUSY! SO MUCH TO DO!
YOU...WILL COME WITH ME?

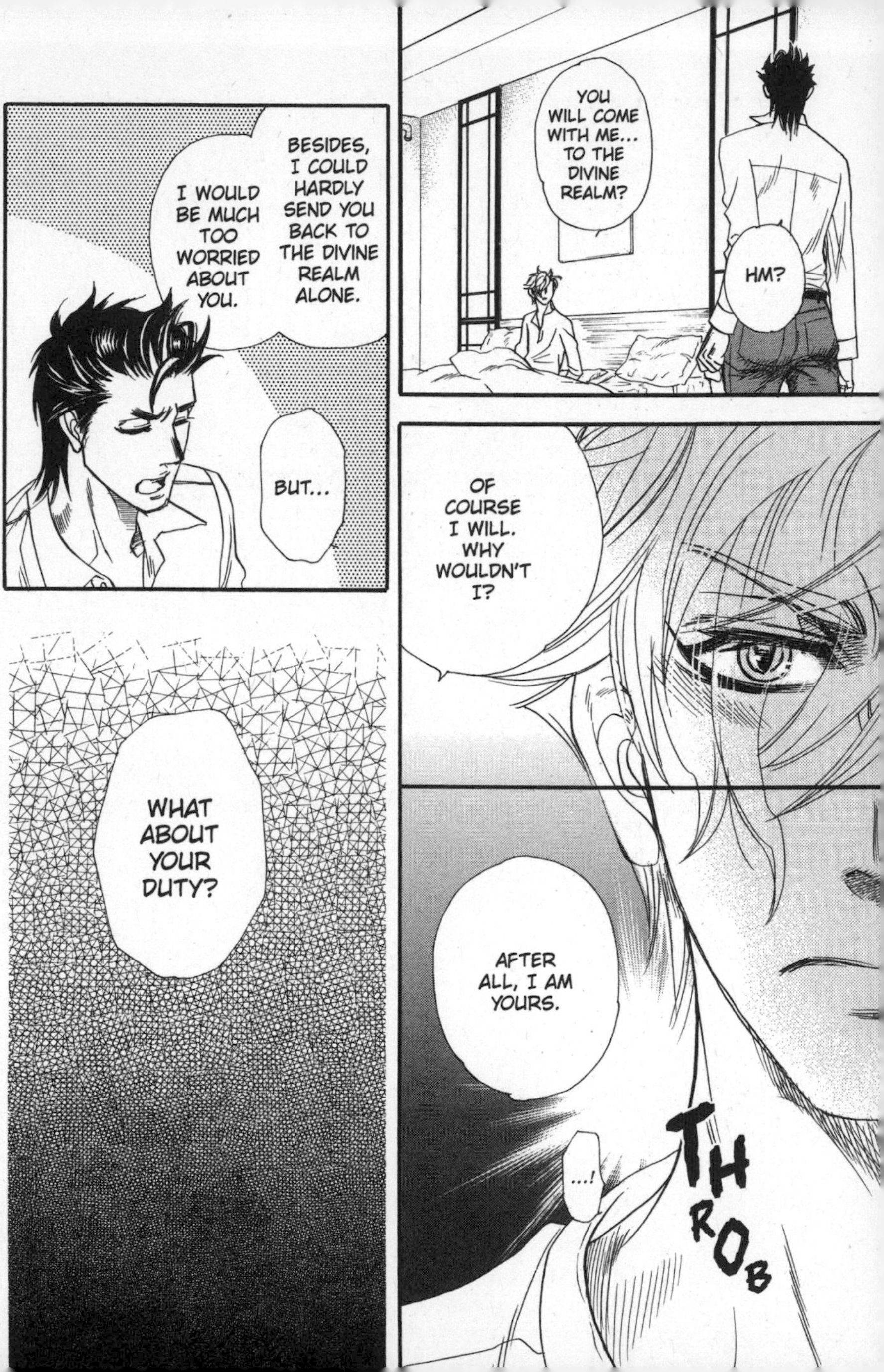
YOU WILL COME WITH ME... TO THE DIVINE REALM?
HM?
OF COURSE I WILL. WHY WOULDN'T I?
BESIDES, I COULD HARDLY SEND YOU BACK TO THE DIVINE REALM ALONE.
I WOULD BE MUCH TOO WORRIED ABOUT YOU.
BUT...
WHAT ABOUT YOUR DUTY?
AFTER ALL, I AM YOURS.
...!
THROB

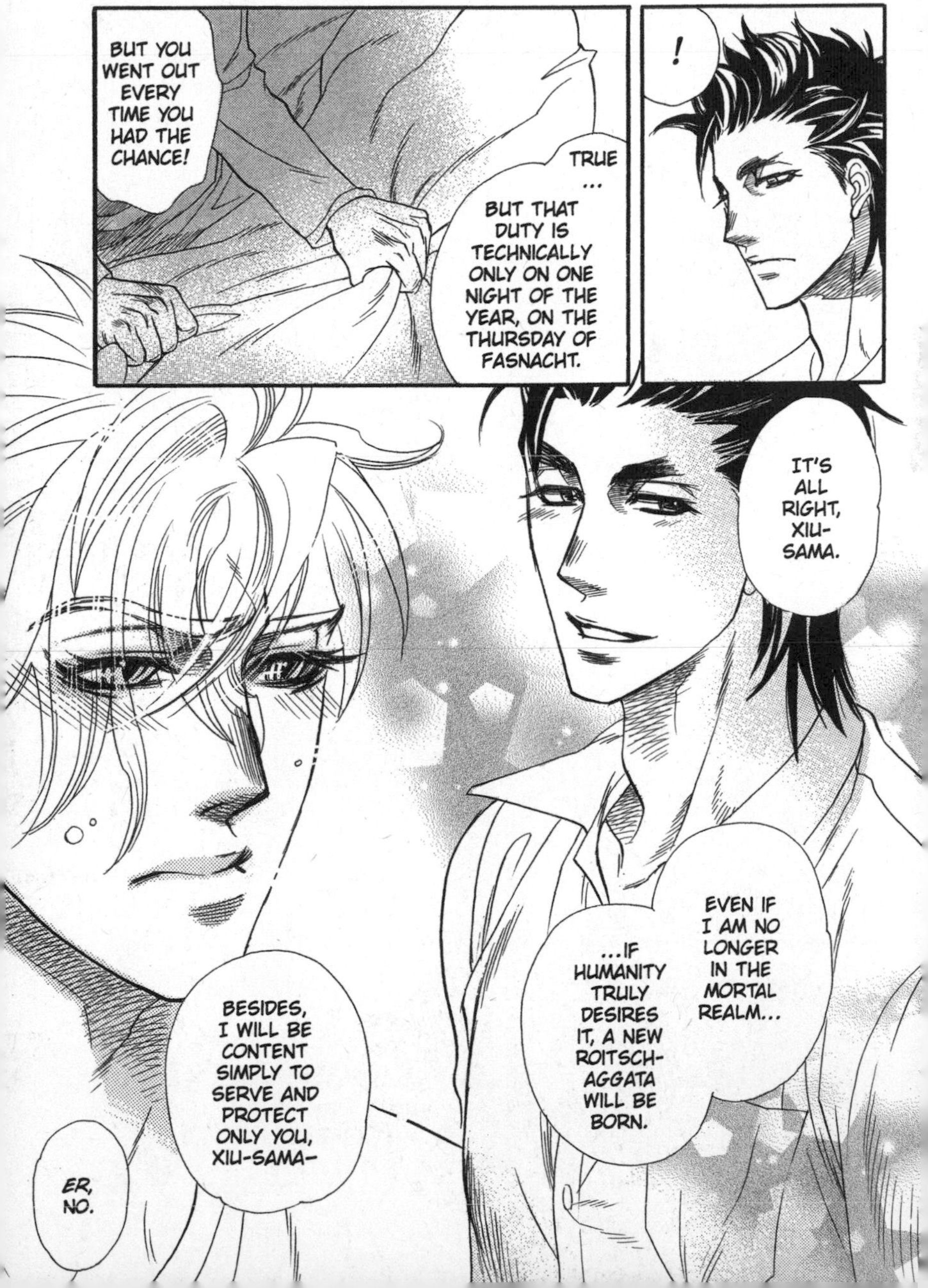
!
BUT YOU WENT OUT EVERY TIME YOU HAD THE CHANCE!
TRUE...
BUT THAT DUTY IS TECHNICALLY ONLY ON ONE NIGHT OF THE YEAR, ON THE THURSDAY OF FASNACHT.
IT'S ALL RIGHT, XIU-SAMA.
EVEN IF I AM NO LONGER IN THE MORTAL REALM...
...IF HUMANITY TRULY DESIRES IT, A NEW ROITSCH-AGGATA WILL BE BORN.
BESIDES, I WILL BE CONTENT SIMPLY TO SERVE AND PROTECT ONLY YOU, XIU-SAMA-
ER, NO.

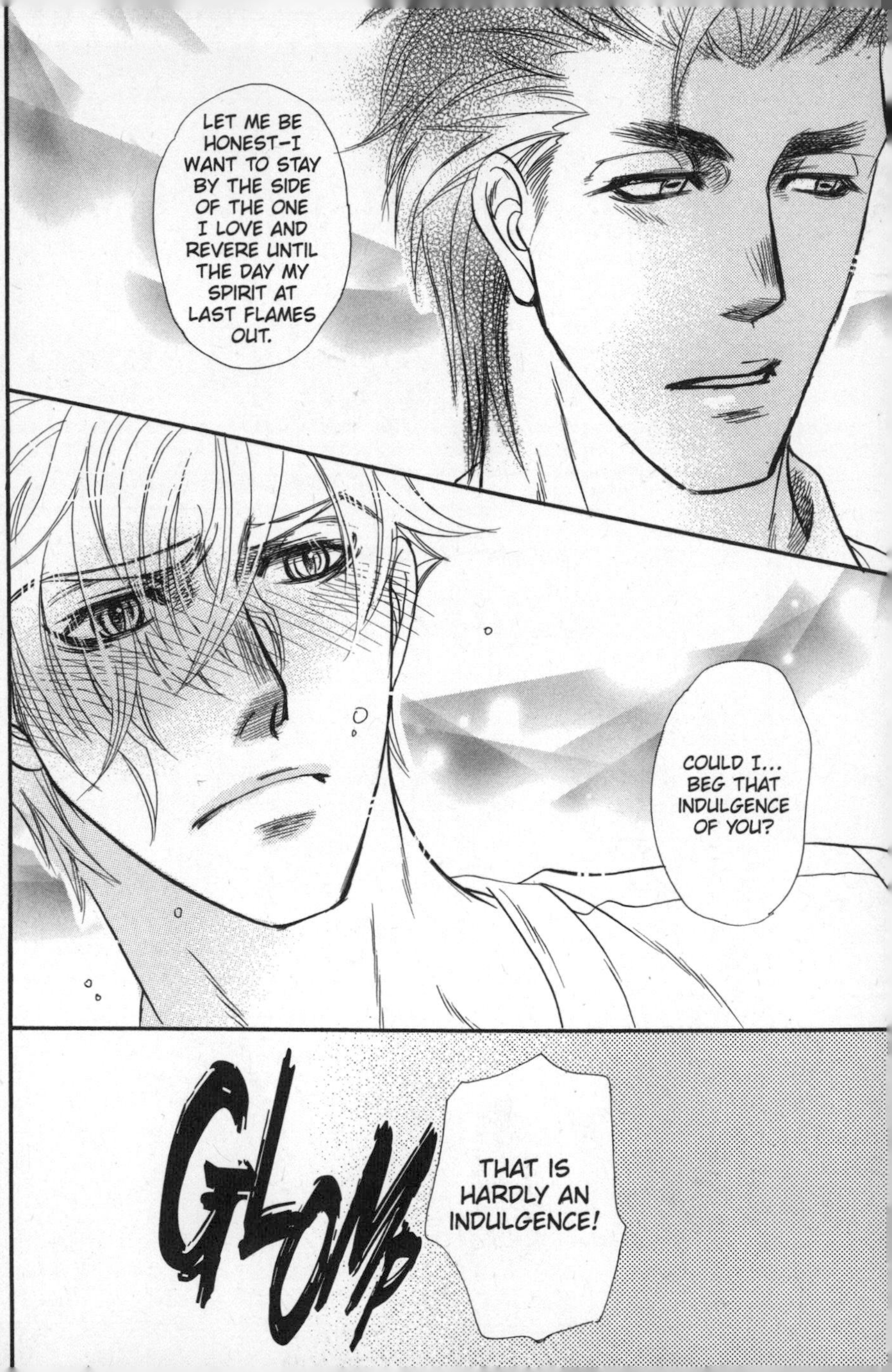
LET ME BE HONEST—I WANT TO STAY BY THE SIDE OF THE ONE I LOVE AND REVERE UNTIL THE DAY MY SPIRIT AT LAST FLAMES OUT.
COULD I... BEG THAT INDULGENCE OF YOU?
THAT IS HARDLY AN INDULGENCE!
GLOM

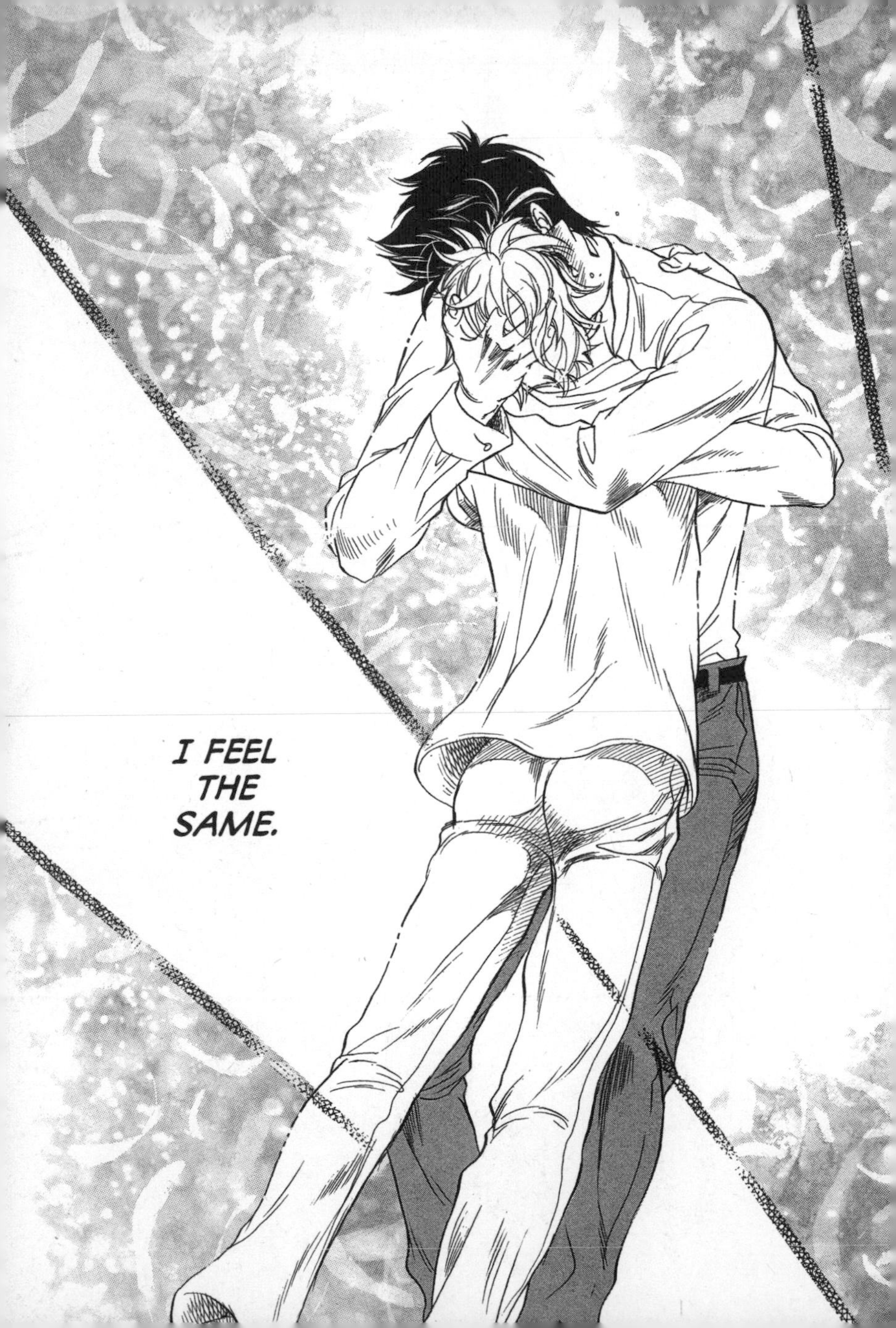
I FEEL THE SAME.

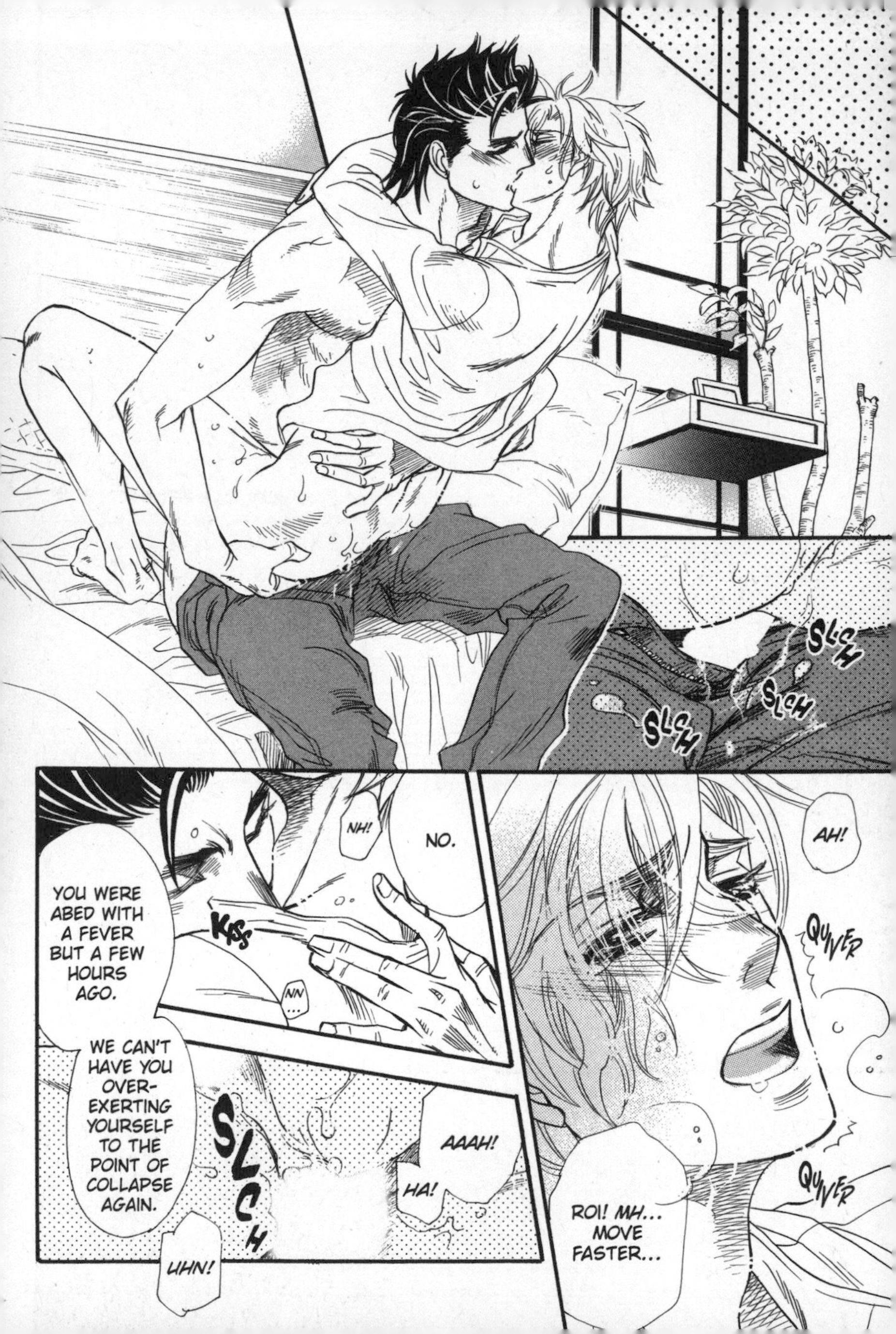
SLCH
SLCH
SLCH
AH!
QUIVER
QUIVER
ROI! MH... MOVE FASTER...
NO.
NH!
KISS
NN...
YOU WERE ABED WITH A FEVER BUT A FEW HOURS AGO.
WE CAN'T HAVE YOU OVER-EXERTING YOURSELF TO THE POINT OF COLLAPSE AGAIN.
SLCH
AAAH!
HA!
UHN!

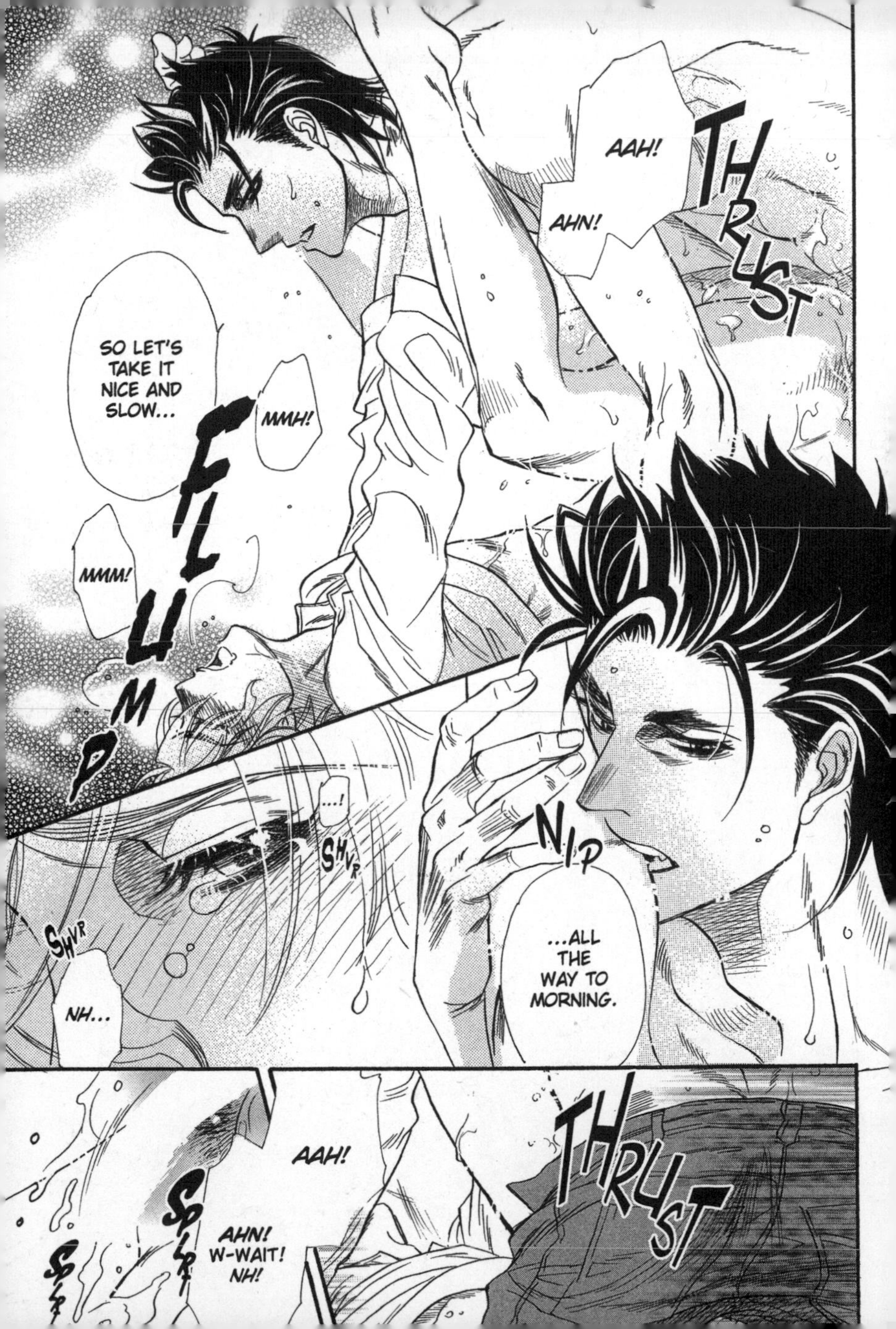
THRUST
AAH!
AHN!
SO LET'S TAKE IT NICE AND SLOW...
MMH!
FLUMP
MMM!
NIP
...ALL THE WAY TO MORNING.
...!
SHVR
SHVR
NH...
THRUST
AAH!
AHN! W-WAIT! NH!
SPLRT
SPLRT

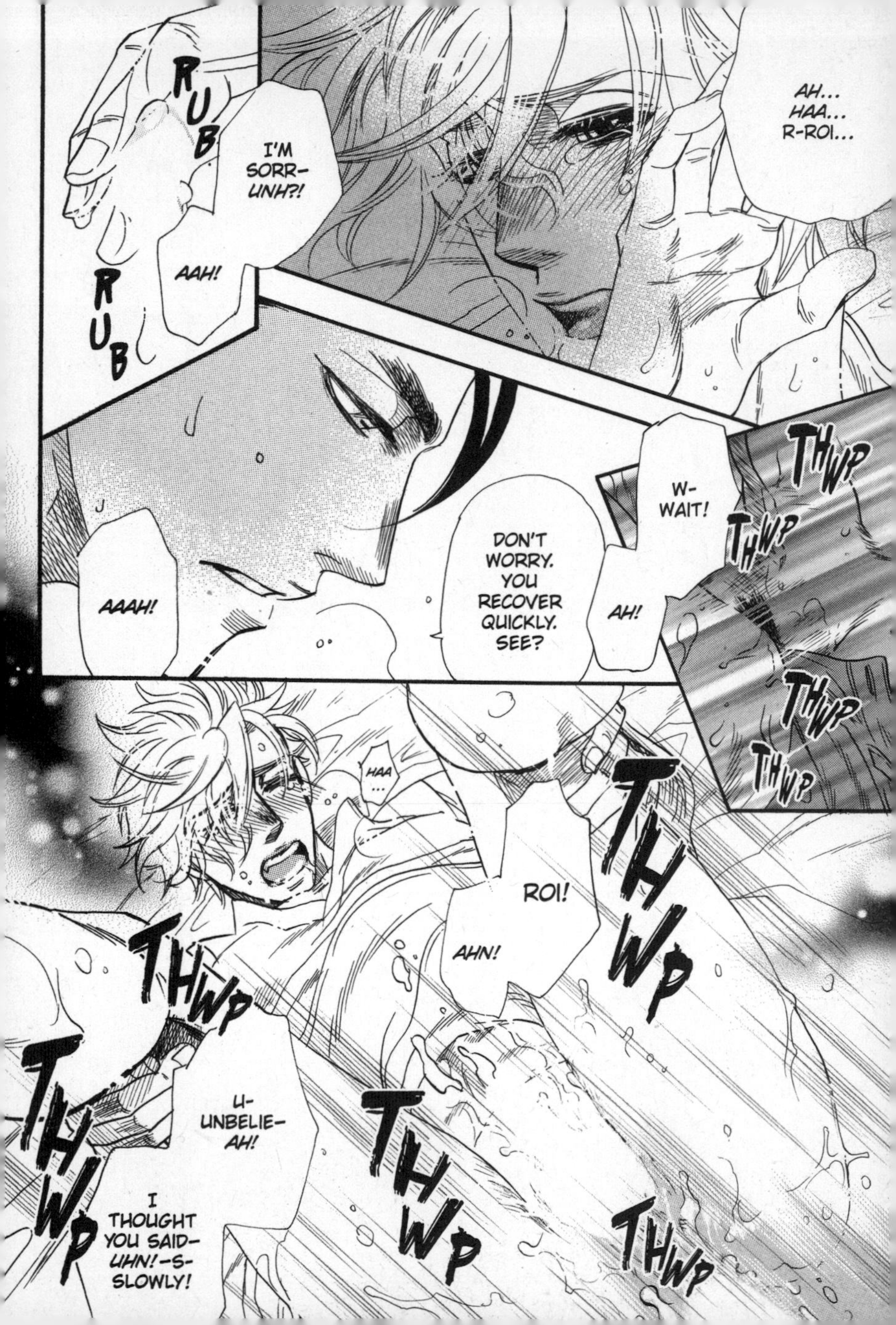
AH... HAA... R-ROI...
I'M SORR-UNH?!
AAH!
RUB
RUB
THWP
THWP
THWP
THWP
W-WAIT!
AH!
DON'T WORRY. YOU RECOVER QUICKLY. SEE?
AAAH!
HAA...
THWP
ROI!
AHN!
THWP
THWP
THWP
U-UNBELIE-AH!
I THOUGHT YOU SAID-UHN!-S-SLOWLY!
THWP

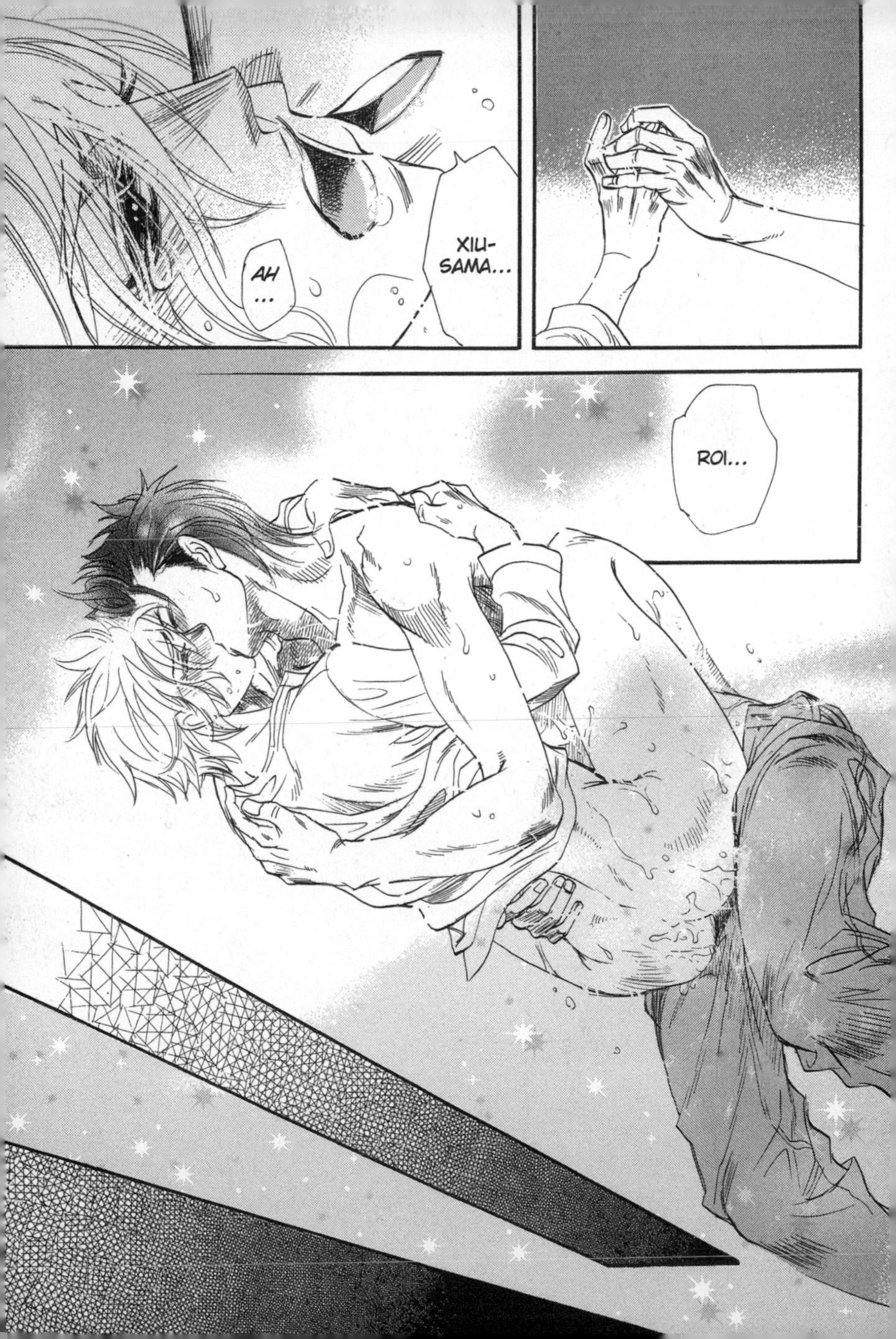
XIU-SAMA...
AH ...
ROI...

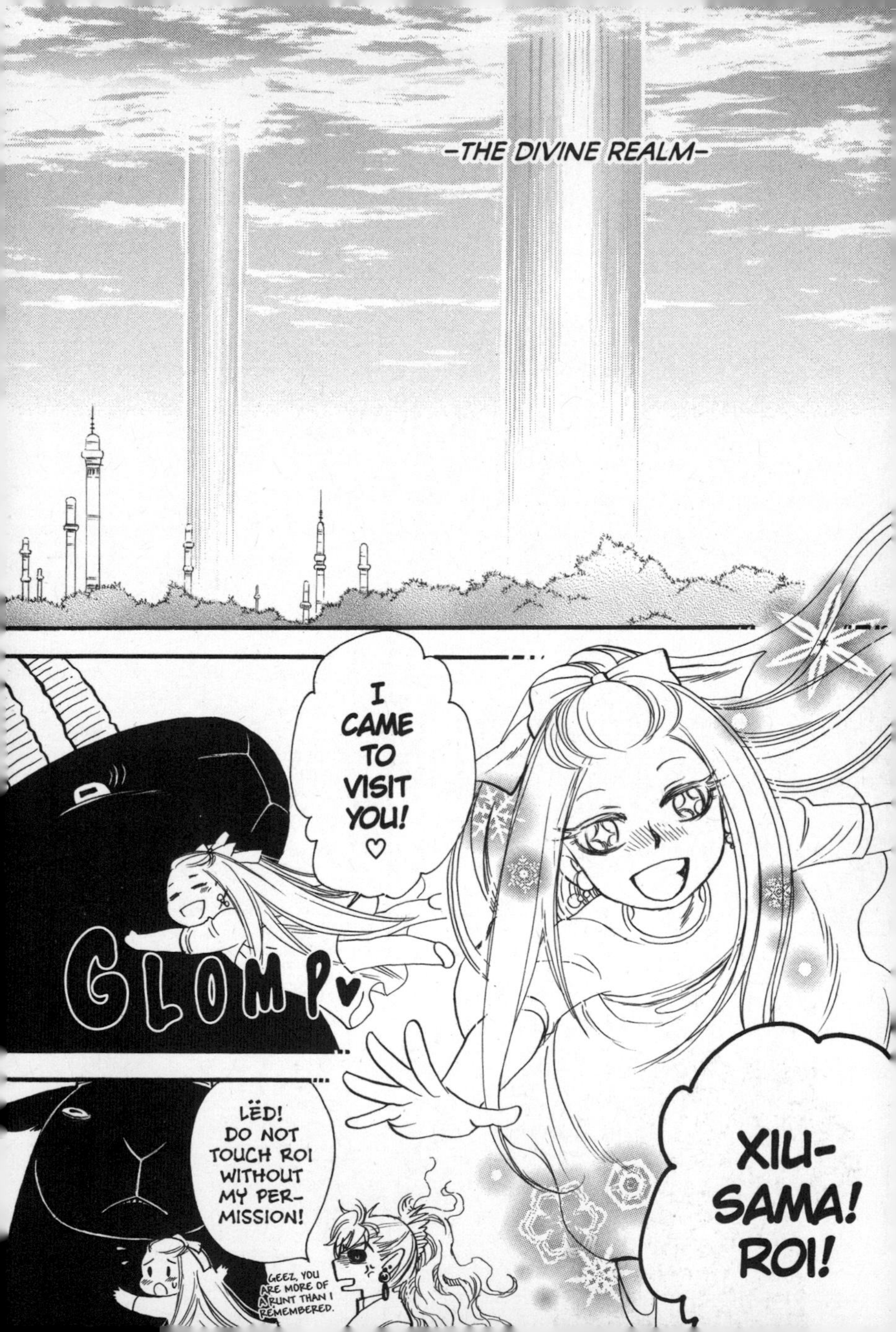
-THE DIVINE REALM-
XIU-SAMA! ROI!
I CAME TO VISIT YOU! ♡
GLOMP ♥
LËD! DO NOT TOUCH ROI WITHOUT MY PER-MISSION!
GEEZ, YOU ARE MORE OF A RUNT THAN I REMEMBERED.

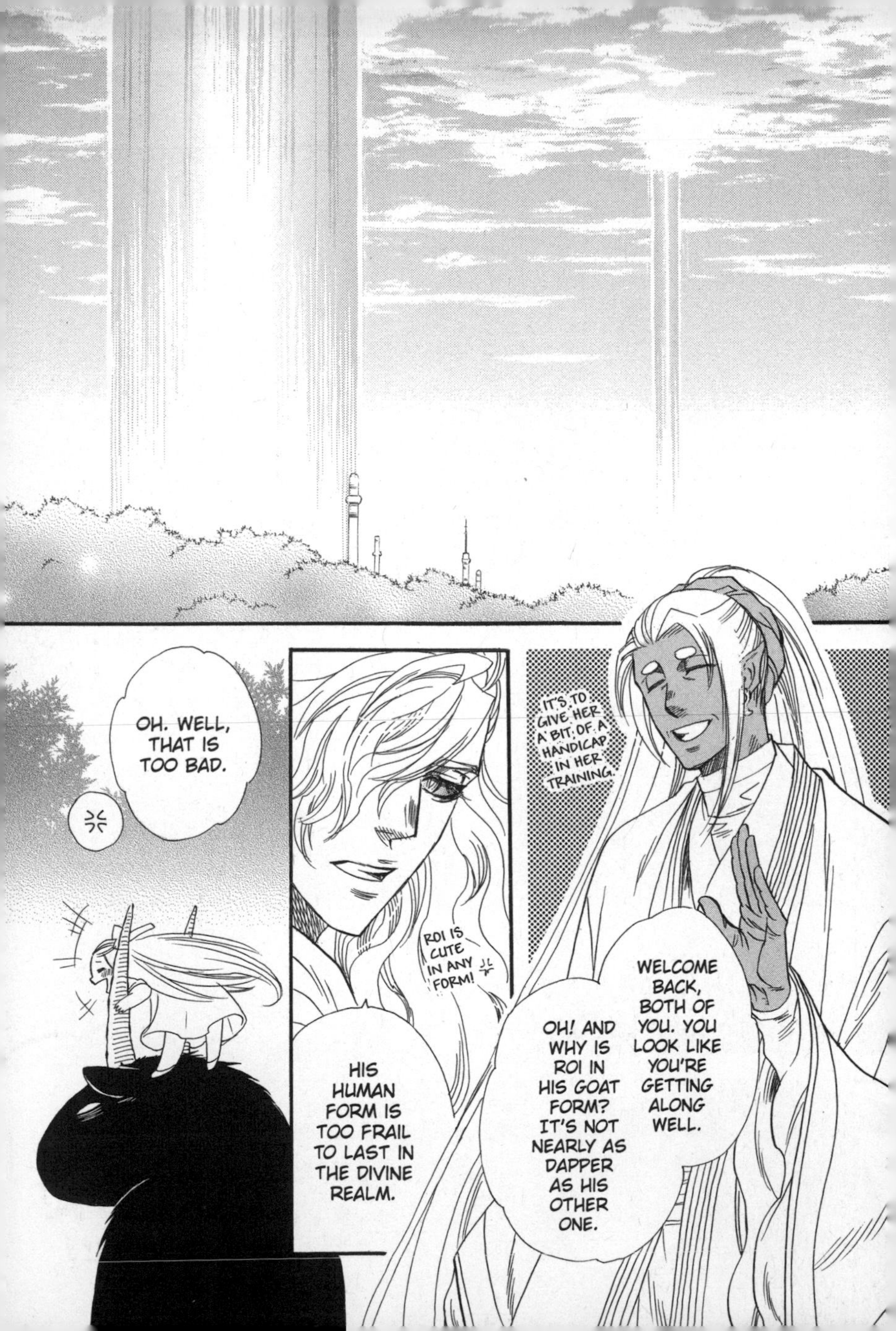
WELCOME BACK, BOTH OF YOU. YOU LOOK LIKE YOU'RE GETTING ALONG WELL.
OH! AND WHY IS ROI IN HIS GOAT FORM? IT'S NOT NEARLY AS DAPPER AS HIS OTHER ONE.
HIS HUMAN FORM IS TOO FRAIL TO LAST IN THE DIVINE REALM.
ROI IS CUTE IN ANY FORM!
IT'S TO GIVE HER A BIT OF A HANDICAP IN HER TRAINING.
OH. WELL, THAT IS TOO BAD.

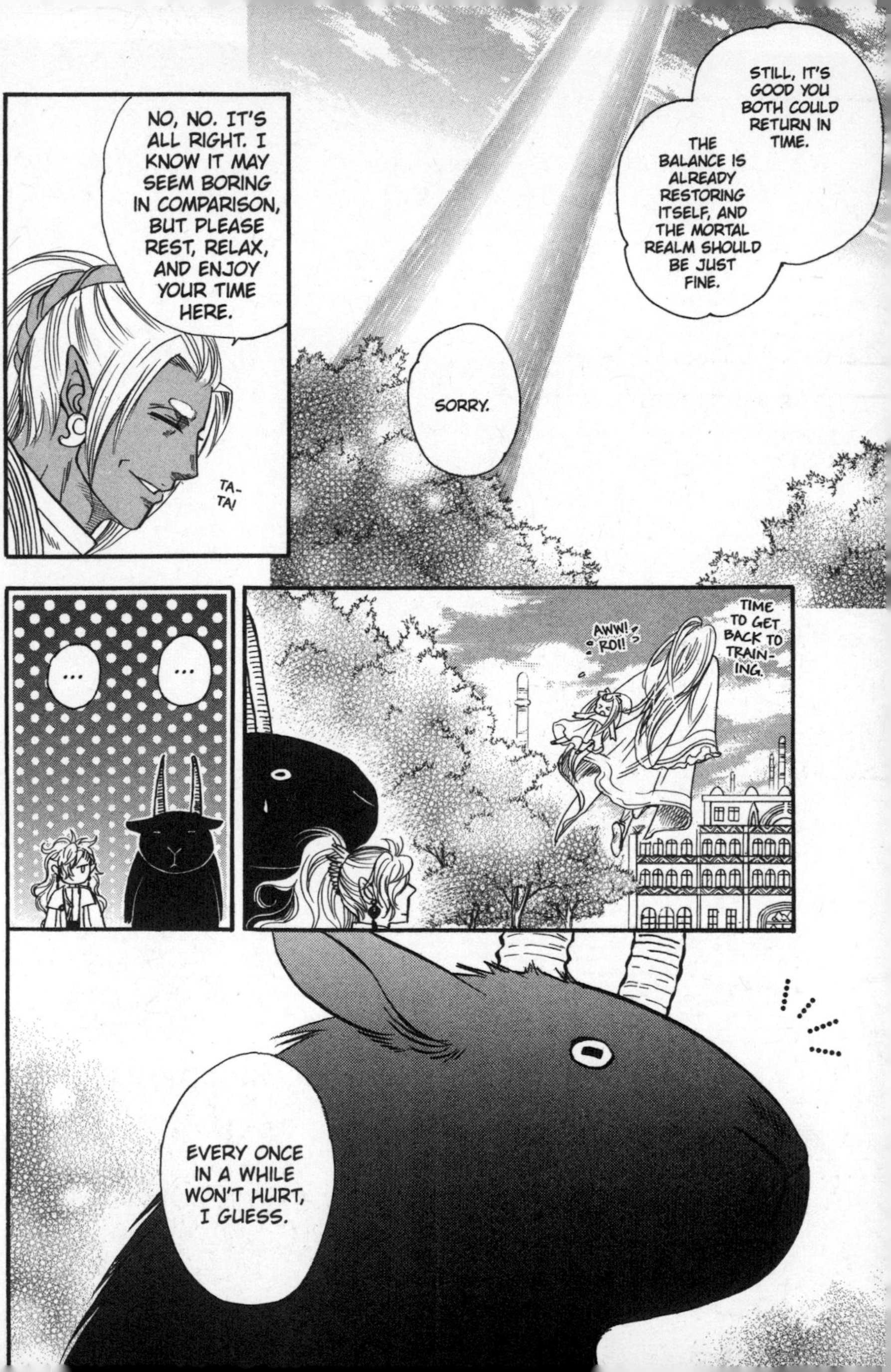
STILL, IT'S GOOD YOU BOTH COULD RETURN IN TIME.
THE BALANCE IS ALREADY RESTORING ITSELF, AND THE MORTAL REALM SHOULD BE JUST FINE.
SORRY.
NO, NO. IT'S ALL RIGHT. I KNOW IT MAY SEEM BORING IN COMPARISON, BUT PLEASE REST, RELAX, AND ENJOY YOUR TIME HERE.
TA-TA!
TIME TO GET BACK TO TRAIN-ING.
AWW! ROI!
...
...
EVERY ONCE IN A WHILE WON'T HURT, I GUESS.

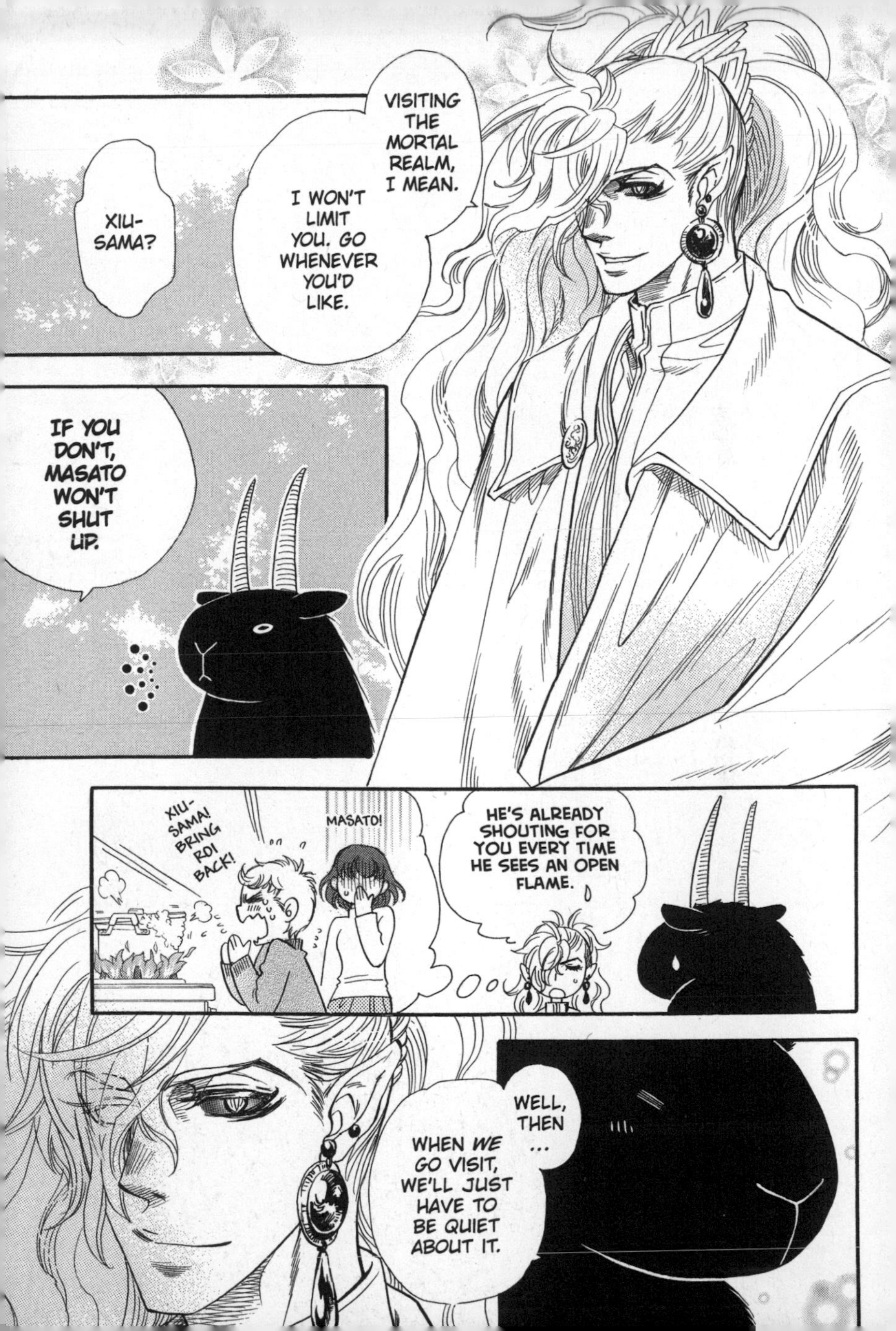
VISITING THE MORTAL REALM, I MEAN.
I WON'T LIMIT YOU. GO WHENEVER YOU'D LIKE.
XIU-SAMA?
IF YOU DON'T, MASATO WON'T SHUT UP.
HE'S ALREADY SHOUTING FOR YOU EVERY TIME HE SEES AN OPEN FLAME.
MASATO!
XIU-SAMA! BRING RDI BACK!
WELL, THEN ...
WHEN *WE* GO VISIT, WE'LL JUST HAVE TO BE QUIET ABOUT IT.

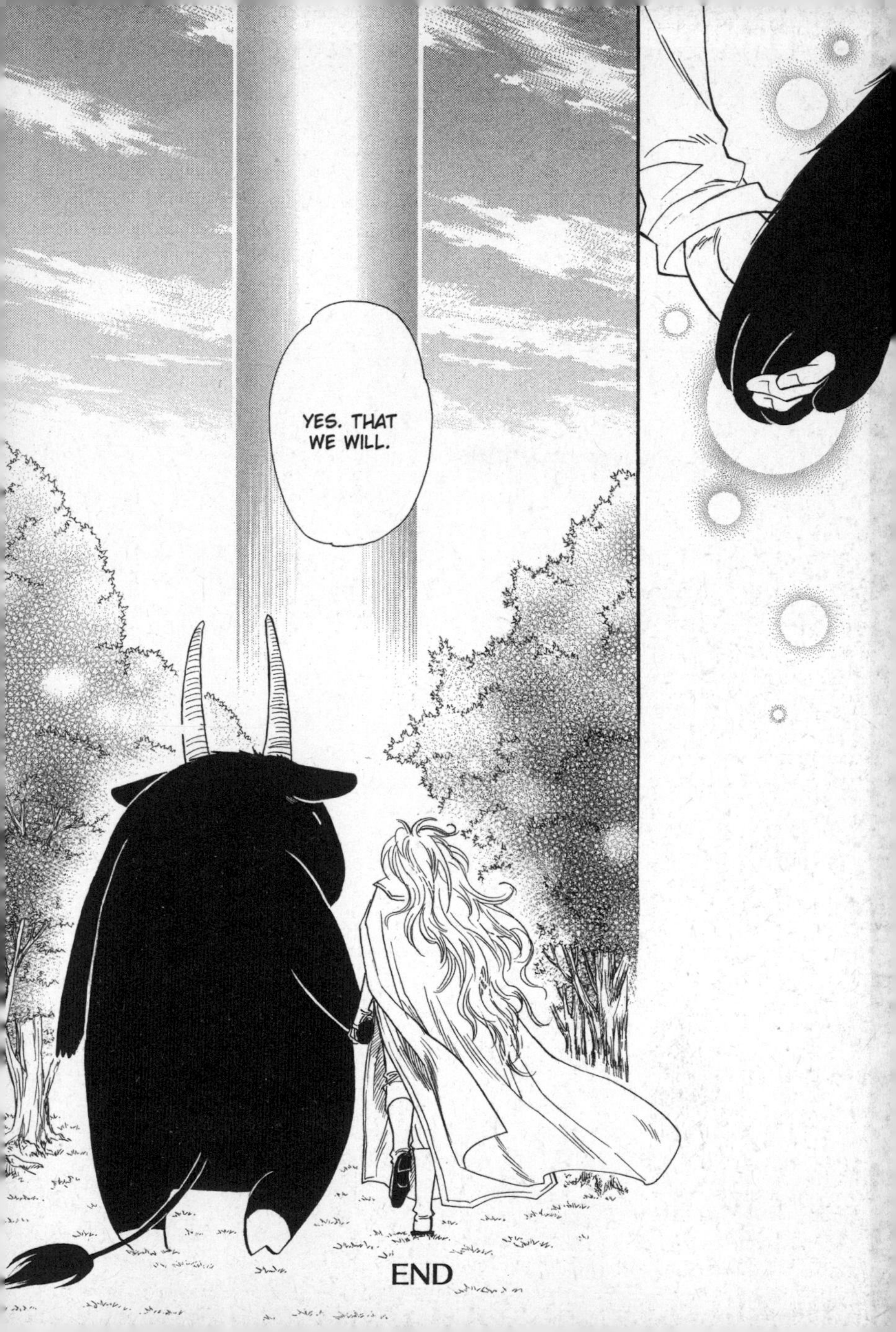
YES. THAT WE WILL.
END

Bohra Naono Presents

彼方者の
困惑
あっちものこんわく

Midnight Stranger

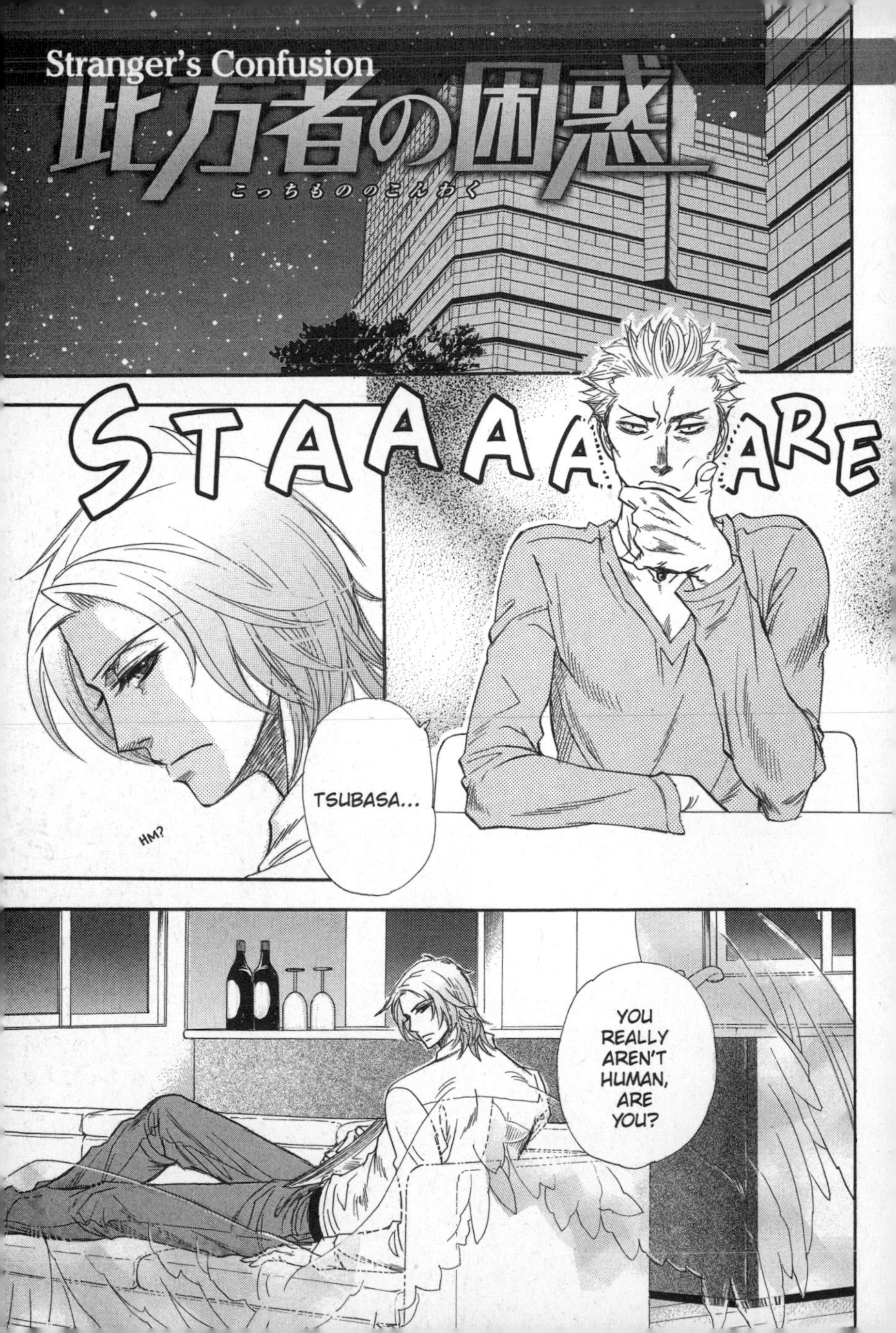
Stranger's Confusion
此方者の困惑
こっちもののこんわく
STAAAAARE
TSUBASA...
HM?
YOU REALLY AREN'T HUMAN, ARE YOU?

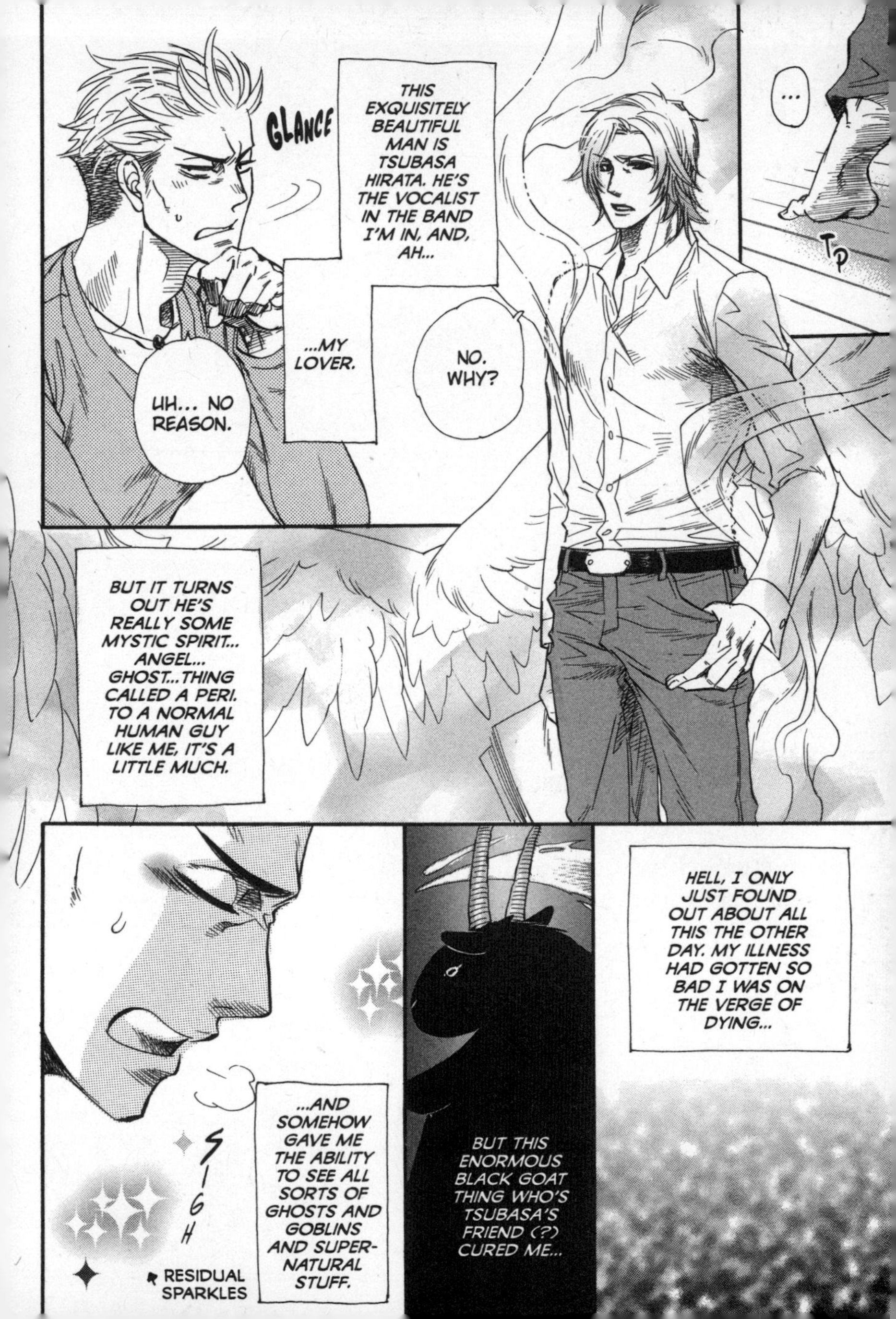
...
TP
GLANCE
THIS EXQUISITELY BEAUTIFUL MAN IS TSUBASA HIRATA. HE'S THE VOCALIST IN THE BAND I'M IN, AND, AH...
...MY LOVER.
NO. WHY?
UH... NO REASON.
BUT IT TURNS OUT HE'S REALLY SOME MYSTIC SPIRIT... ANGEL... GHOST...THING CALLED A PERI. TO A NORMAL HUMAN GUY LIKE ME, IT'S A LITTLE MUCH.
HELL, I ONLY JUST FOUND OUT ABOUT ALL THIS THE OTHER DAY. MY ILLNESS HAD GOTTEN SO BAD I WAS ON THE VERGE OF DYING...
BUT THIS ENORMOUS BLACK GOAT THING WHO'S TSUBASA'S FRIEND (?) CURED ME...
...AND SOMEHOW GAVE ME THE ABILITY TO SEE ALL SORTS OF GHOSTS AND GOBLINS AND SUPER-NATURAL STUFF.
SIGH
RESIDUAL SPARKLES

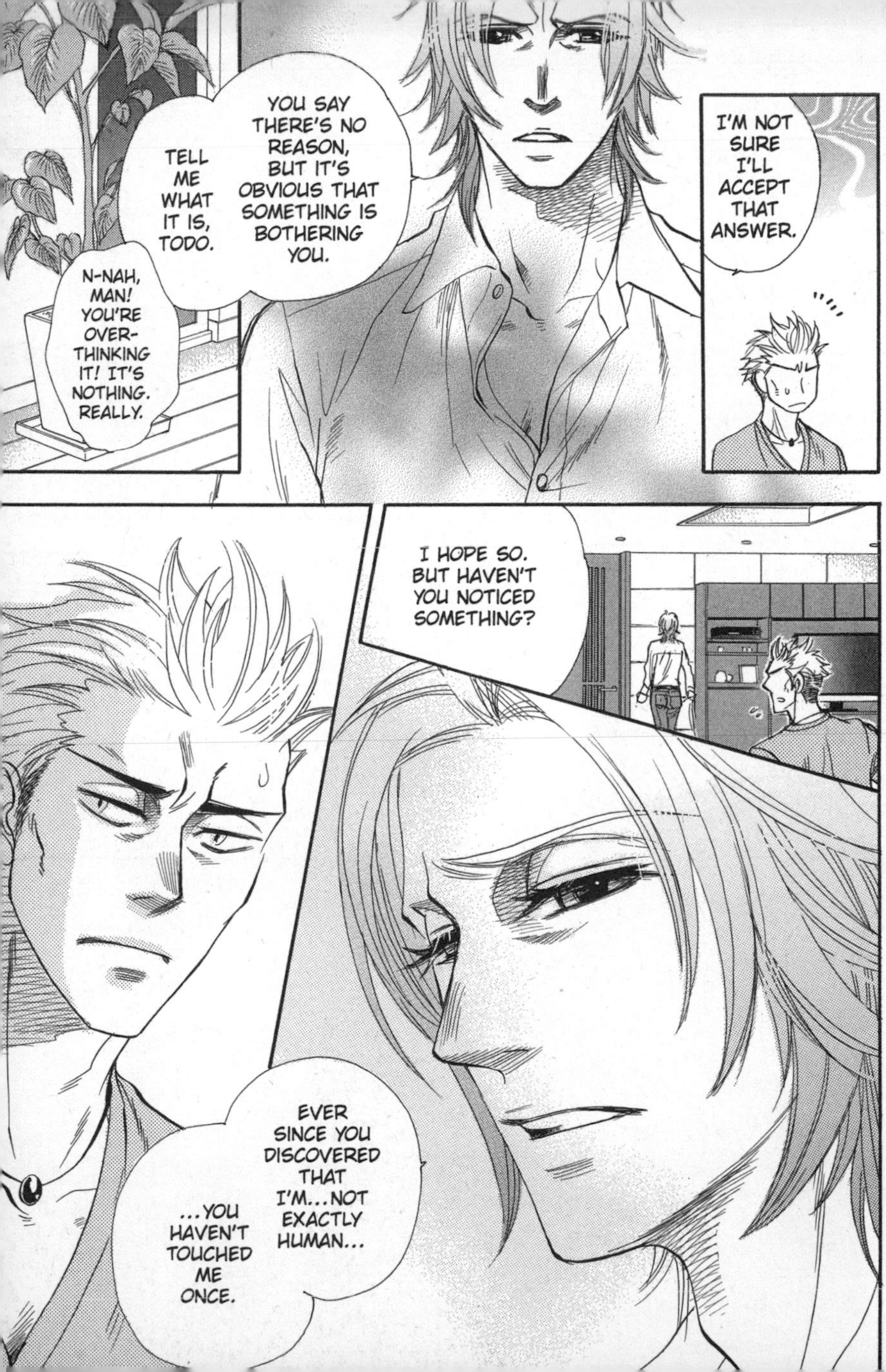
I'M NOT SURE I'LL ACCEPT THAT ANSWER.
YOU SAY THERE'S NO REASON, BUT IT'S OBVIOUS THAT SOMETHING IS BOTHERING YOU.
TELL ME WHAT IT IS, TODO.
N-NAH, MAN! YOU'RE OVER-THINKING IT! IT'S NOTHING. REALLY.
I HOPE SO. BUT HAVEN'T YOU NOTICED SOMETHING?
EVER SINCE YOU DISCOVERED THAT I'M...NOT EXACTLY HUMAN...
...YOU HAVEN'T TOUCHED ME ONCE.

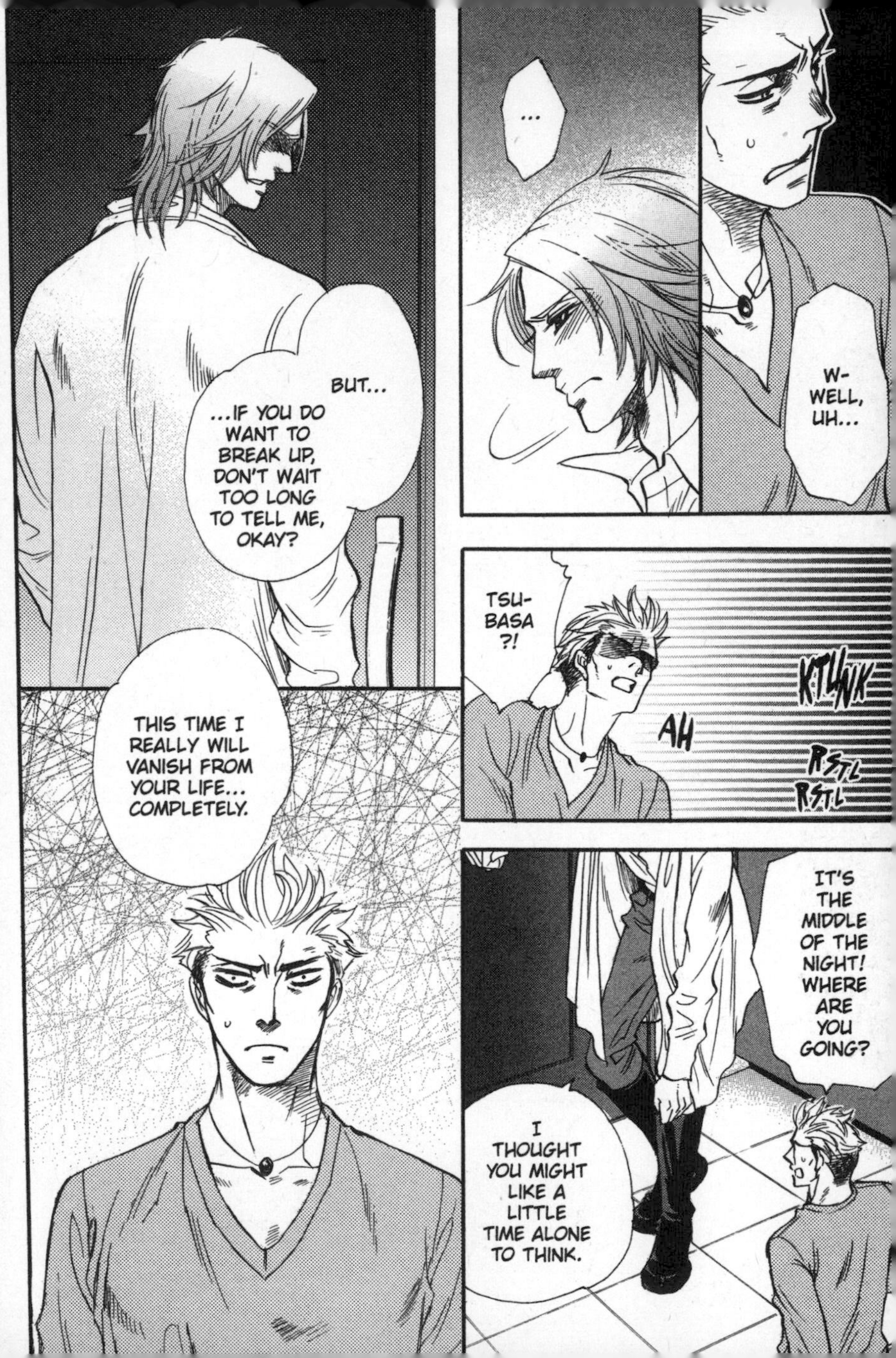
BUT...
...IF YOU DO WANT TO BREAK UP, DON'T WAIT TOO LONG TO TELL ME, OKAY?
THIS TIME I REALLY WILL VANISH FROM YOUR LIFE... COMPLETELY.
...
W-WELL, UH...
KTUNK
AH
TSU-BASA?!
RSTL RSTL
IT'S THE MIDDLE OF THE NIGHT! WHERE ARE YOU GOING?
I THOUGHT YOU MIGHT LIKE A LITTLE TIME ALONE TO THINK.

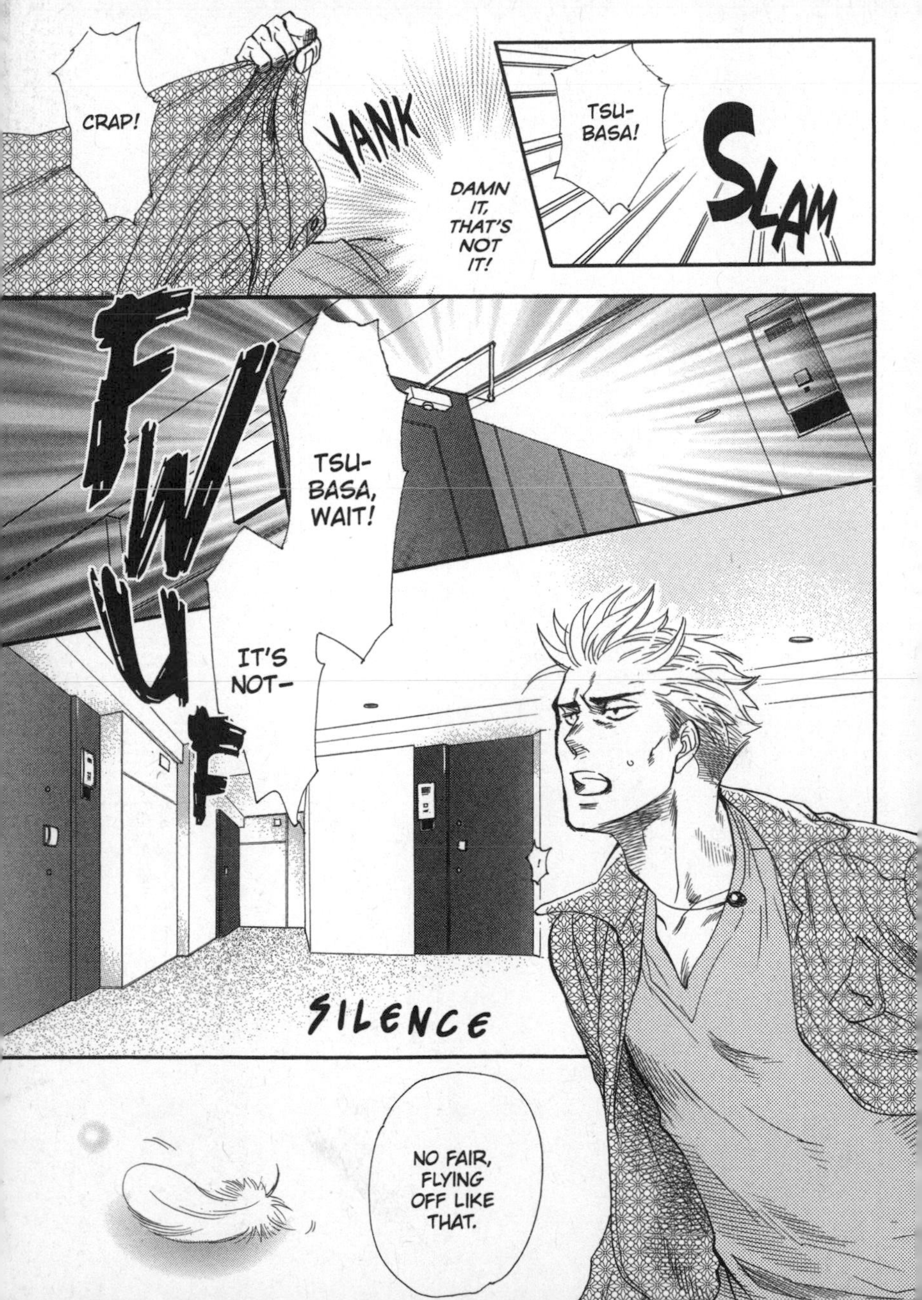
TSU-BASA!
SLAM
DAMN IT, THAT'S NOT IT!
YANK
CRAP!
FWUF
TSU-BASA, WAIT!
IT'S NOT-
SILENCE
NO FAIR, FLYING OFF LIKE THAT.

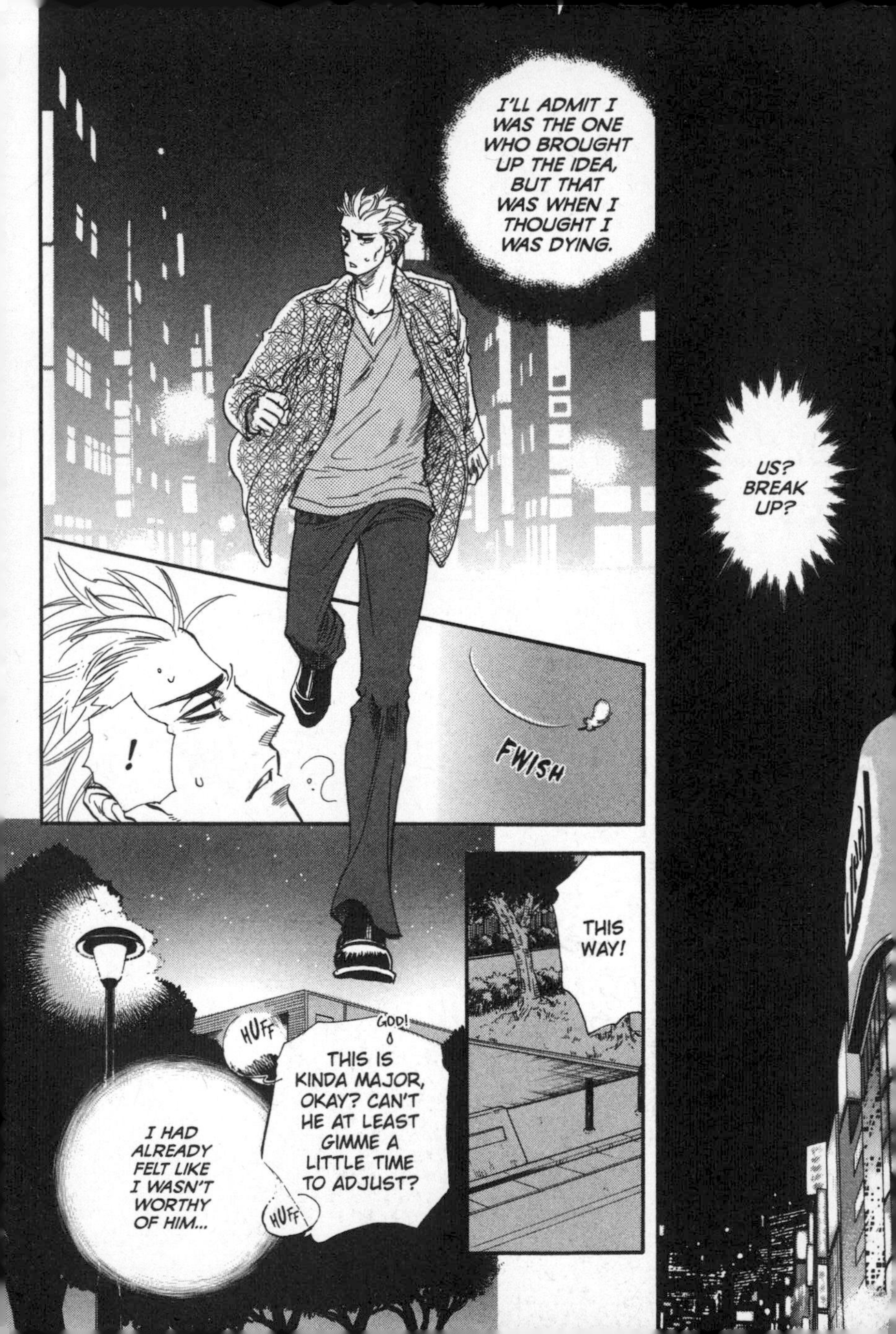
US? BREAK UP?
I'LL ADMIT I WAS THE ONE WHO BROUGHT UP THE IDEA, BUT THAT WAS WHEN I THOUGHT I WAS DYING.
FWISH
THIS WAY!
HUFF
GOD!
THIS IS KINDA MAJOR, OKAY? CAN'T HE AT LEAST GIMME A LITTLE TIME TO ADJUST?
HUFF
I HAD ALREADY FELT LIKE I WASN'T WORTHY OF HIM...

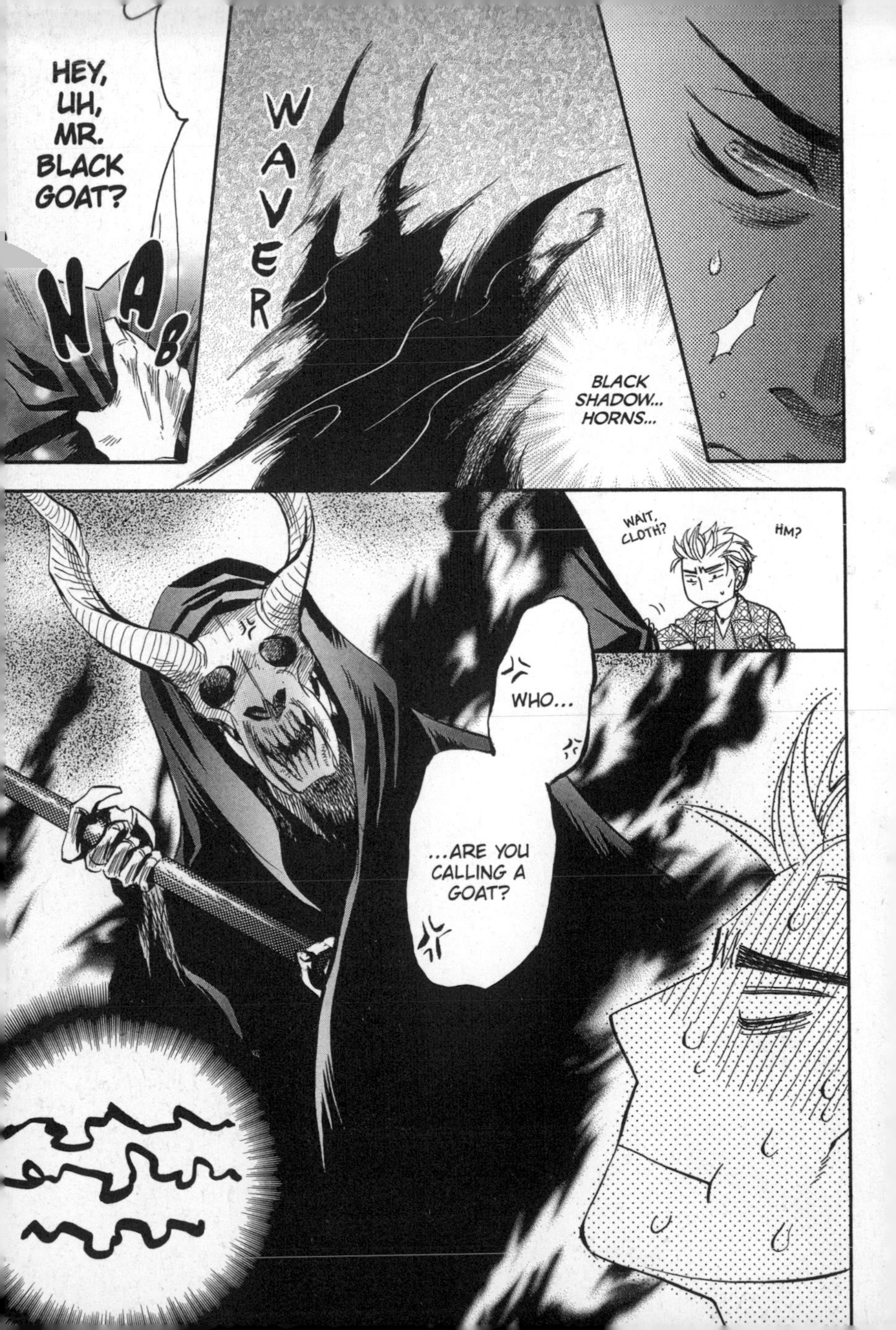
BLACK SHADOW... HORNS...
WAVER
HEY, UH, MR. BLACK GOAT?
NAB
HM?
WAIT, CLOTH?
WHO...
...ARE YOU CALLING A GOAT?

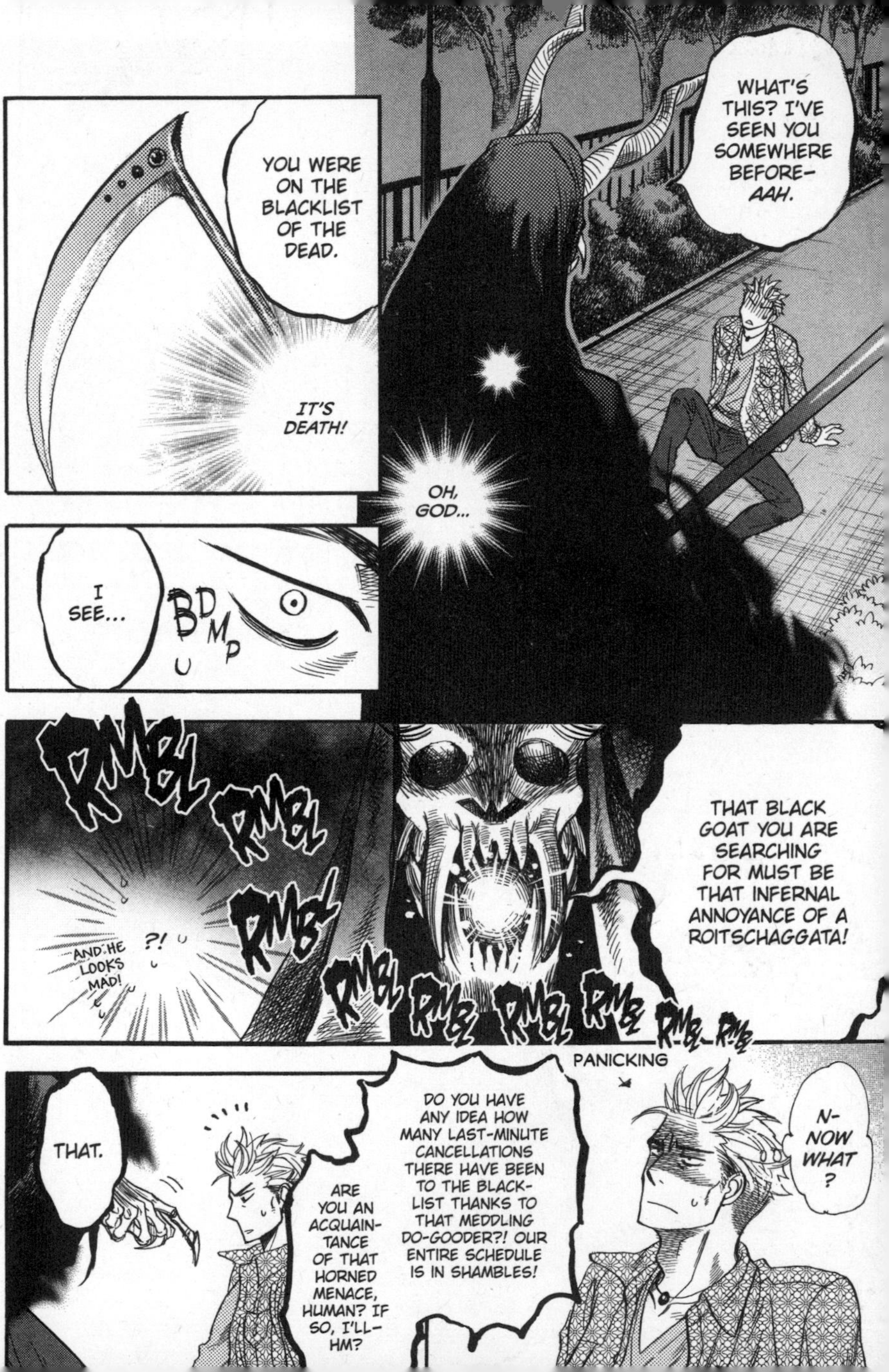
WHAT'S THIS? I'VE SEEN YOU SOMEWHERE BEFORE— AAH.
OH, GOD...
YOU WERE ON THE BLACKLIST OF THE DEAD.
IT'S DEATH!
I SEE...
BDUMP
THAT BLACK GOAT YOU ARE SEARCHING FOR MUST BE THAT INFERNAL ANNOYANCE OF A ROITSCHAGGATA!
RMBL RMBL RMBL RMBL RMBL RMBL RMBL RMBL RMBL
?!
AND HE LOOKS MAD!
PANICKING
N-NOW WHAT?
DO YOU HAVE ANY IDEA HOW MANY LAST-MINUTE CANCELLATIONS THERE HAVE BEEN TO THE BLACKLIST THANKS TO THAT MEDDLING DO-GOODER?! OUR ENTIRE SCHEDULE IS IN SHAMBLES!
ARE YOU AN ACQUAINTANCE OF THAT HORNED MENACE, HUMAN? IF SO, I'LL— HM?
THAT.

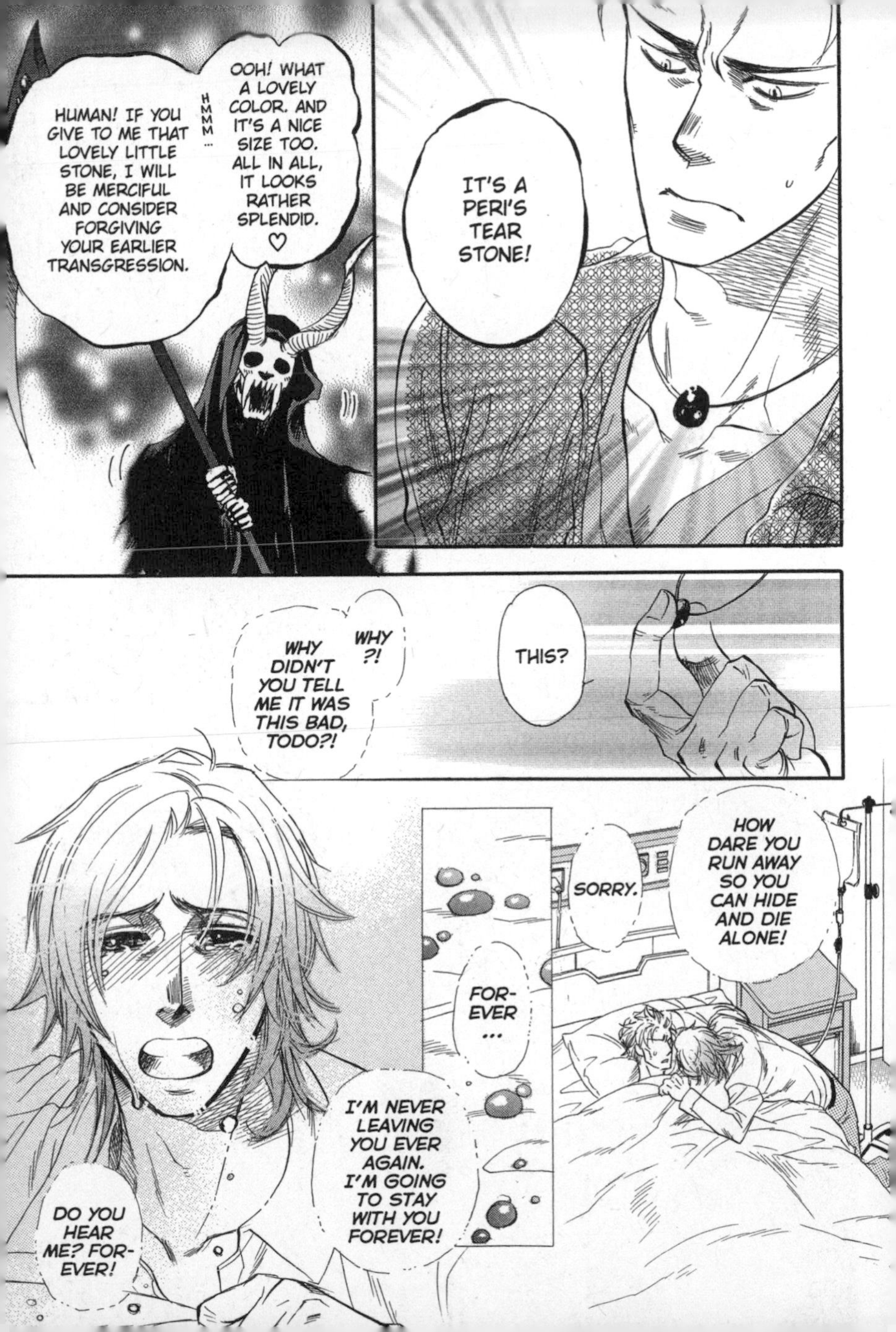
IT'S A PERI'S TEAR STONE!
OOH! WHAT A LOVELY COLOR. AND IT'S A NICE SIZE TOO. ALL IN ALL, IT LOOKS RATHER SPLENDID. ♡
HMMM...
HUMAN! IF YOU GIVE TO ME THAT LOVELY LITTLE STONE, I WILL BE MERCIFUL AND CONSIDER FORGIVING YOUR EARLIER TRANSGRESSION.
THIS?
WHY?!
WHY DIDN'T YOU TELL ME IT WAS THIS BAD, TODO?!
HOW DARE YOU RUN AWAY SO YOU CAN HIDE AND DIE ALONE!
SORRY.
FOR-EVER...
I'M NEVER LEAVING YOU EVER AGAIN. I'M GOING TO STAY WITH YOU FOREVER!
DO YOU HEAR ME? FOR-EVER!

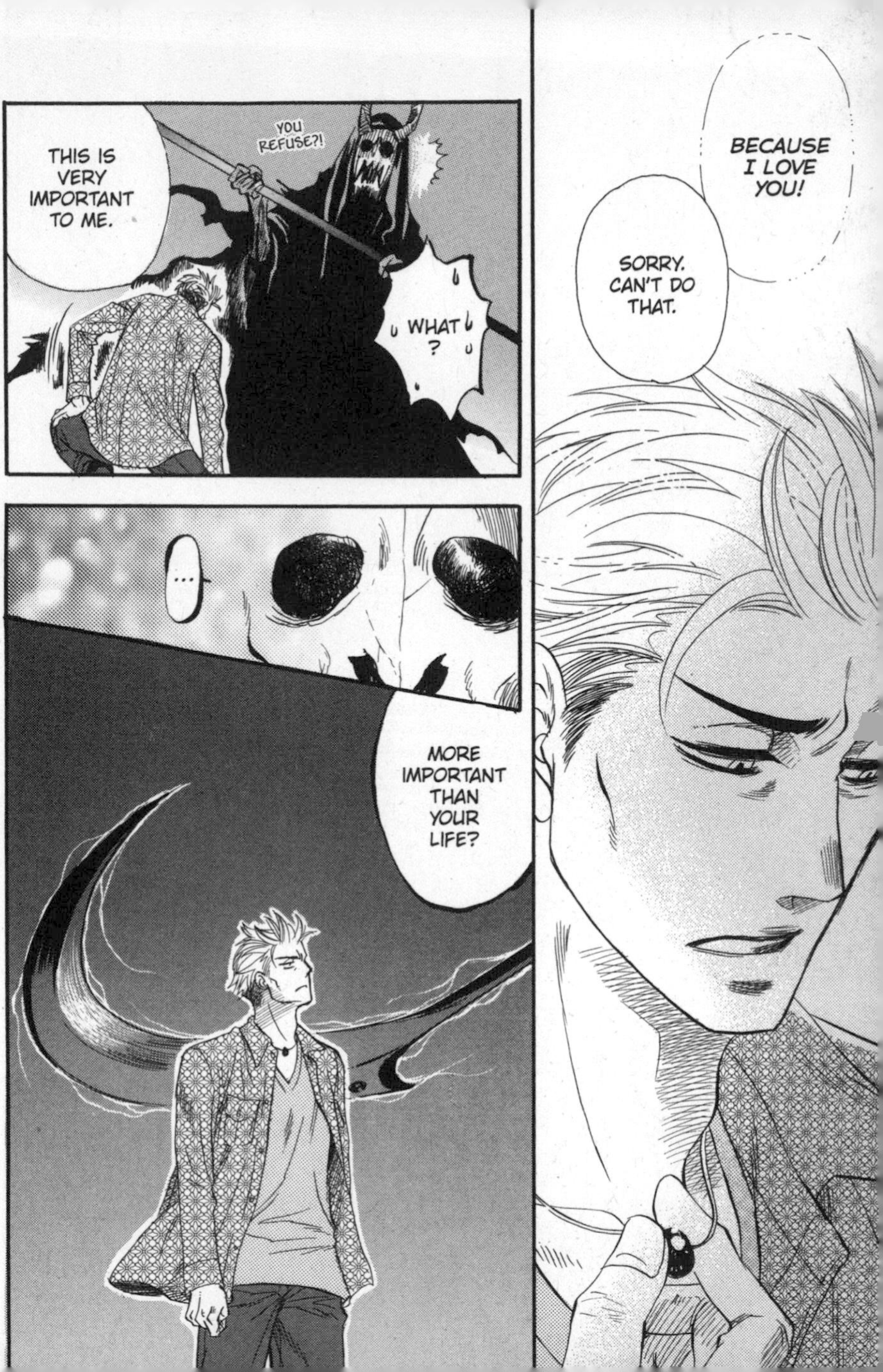
BECAUSE I LOVE YOU!
SORRY. CAN'T DO THAT.
YOU REFUSE?!
THIS IS VERY IMPORTANT TO ME.
WHAT?
...
MORE IMPORTANT THAN YOUR LIFE?

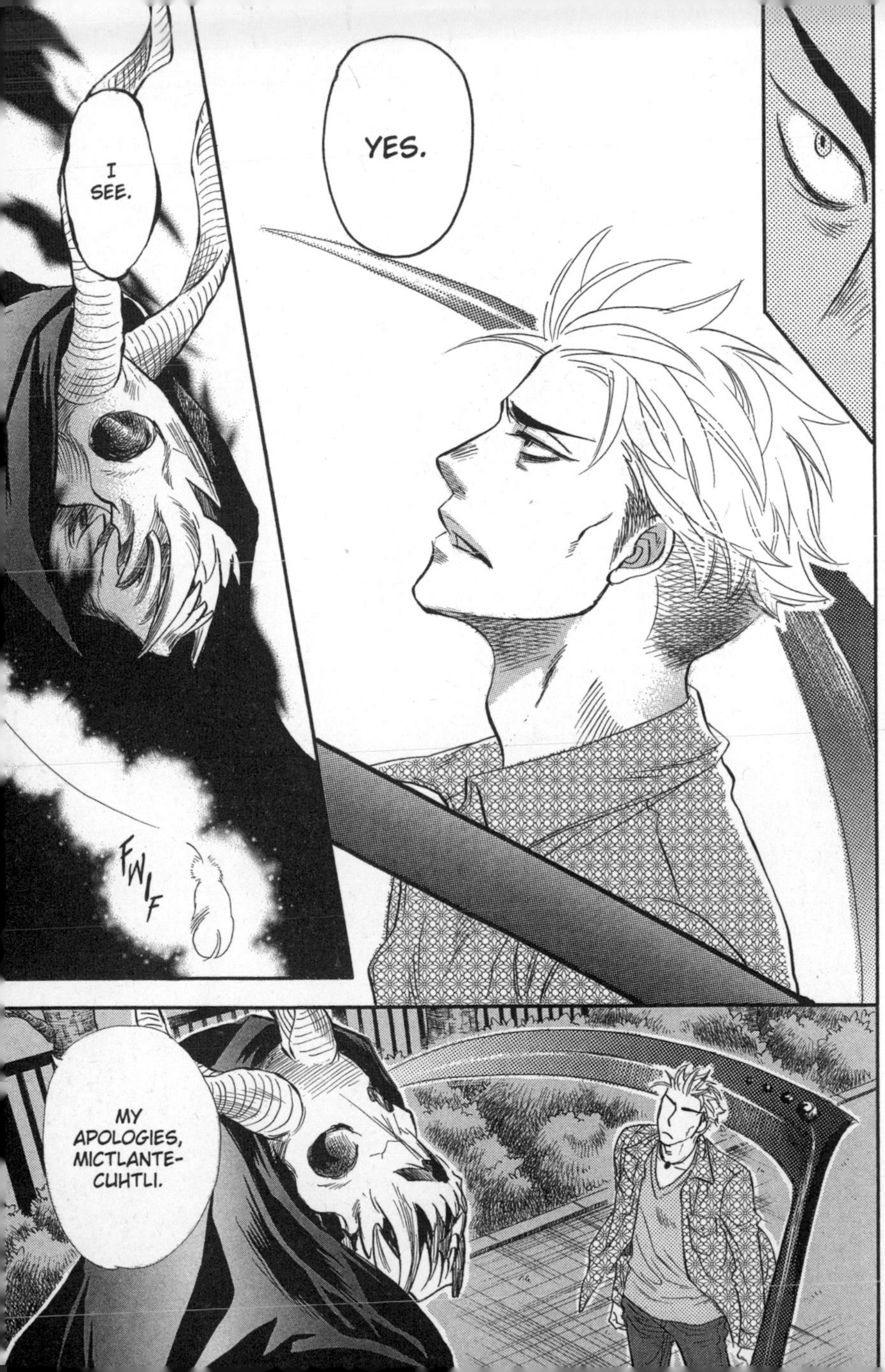
YES.
I SEE.
FWIF
MY APOLOGIES, MICTLANTE-CUHTLI.

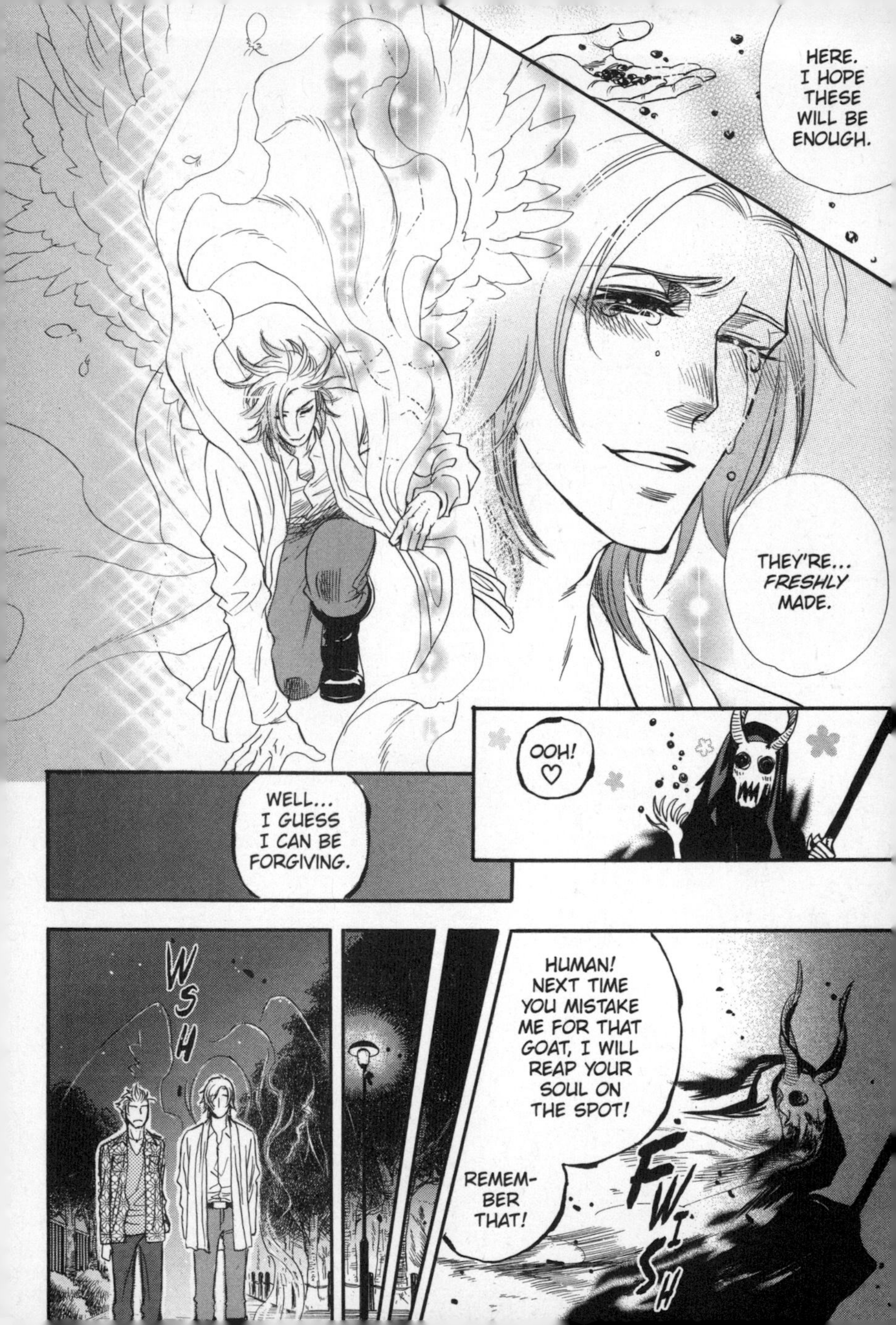
HERE. I HOPE THESE WILL BE ENOUGH.
THEY'RE... FRESHLY MADE.
OOH! ♡
WELL... I GUESS I CAN BE FORGIVING.
HUMAN! NEXT TIME YOU MISTAKE ME FOR THAT GOAT, I WILL REAP YOUR SOUL ON THE SPOT!
REMEM-BER THAT!
FWISH
WSH

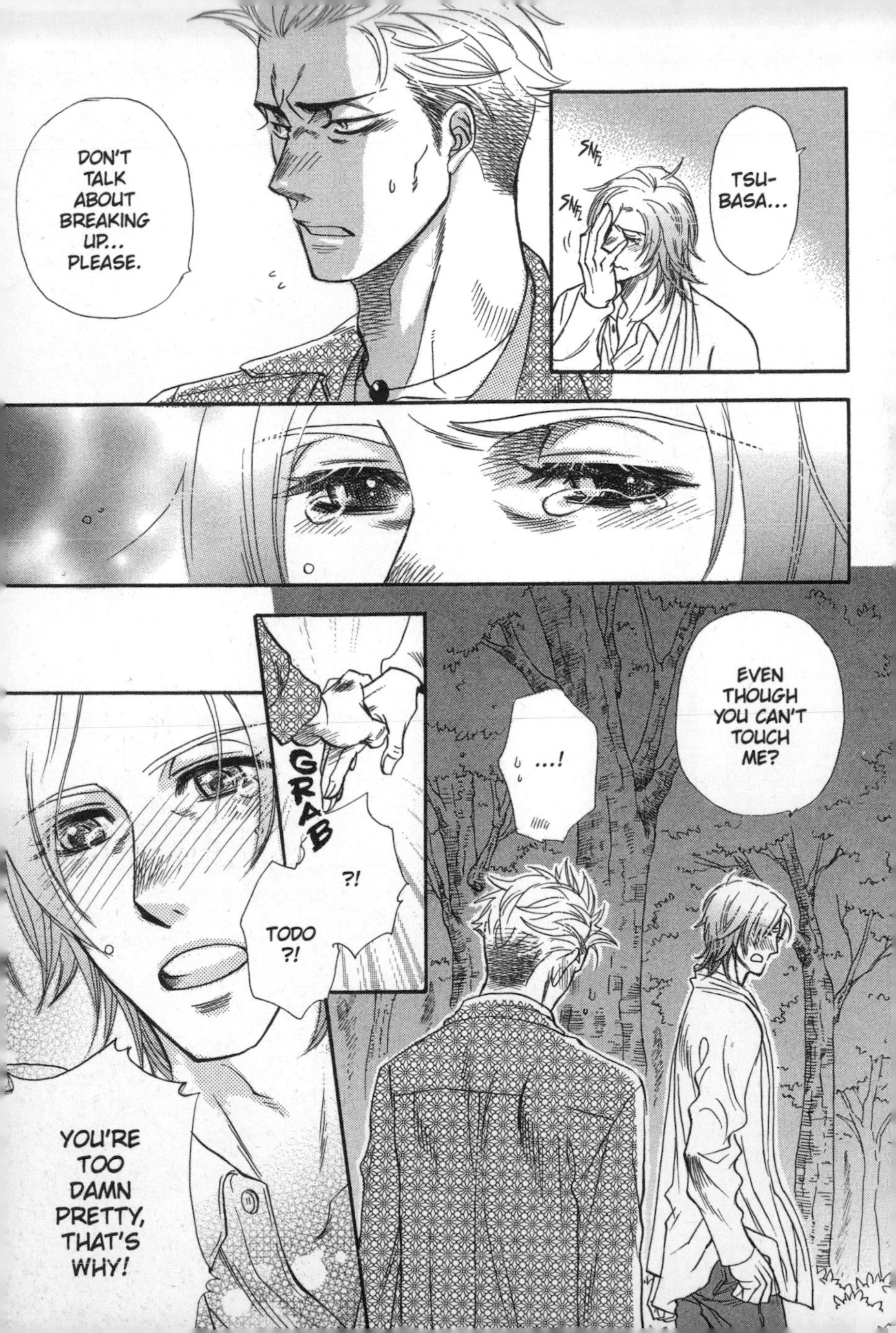
SNFL
SNFL
TSU-BASA...
DON'T TALK ABOUT BREAKING UP... PLEASE.
EVEN THOUGH YOU CAN'T TOUCH ME?
...!
GRAB
?!
TODO ?!
YOU'RE TOO DAMN PRETTY, THAT'S WHY!

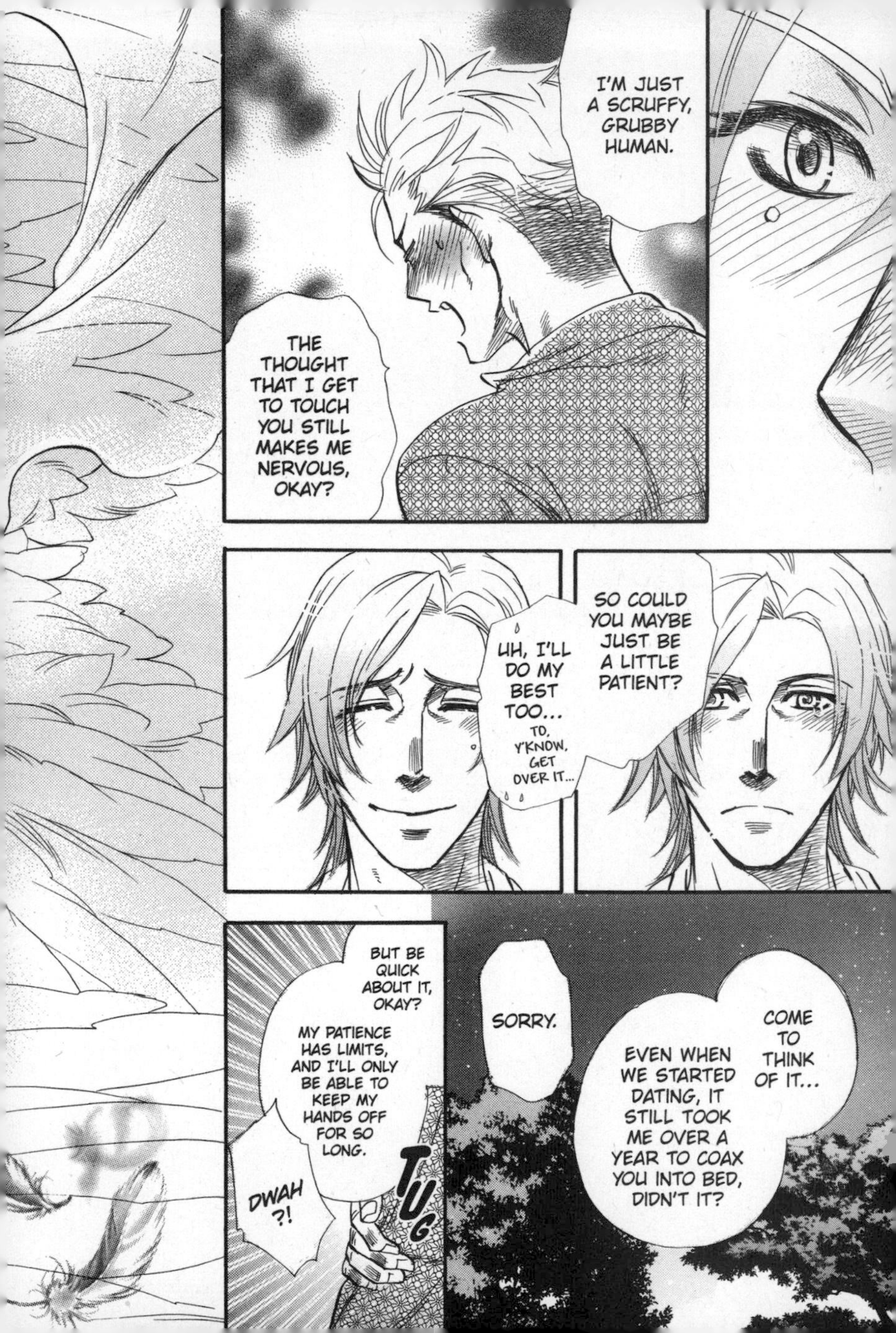
I'M JUST A SCRUFFY, GRUBBY HUMAN.
THE THOUGHT THAT I GET TO TOUCH YOU STILL MAKES ME NERVOUS, OKAY?
SO COULD YOU MAYBE JUST BE A LITTLE PATIENT?
UH, I'LL DO MY BEST TOO...
TO, Y'KNOW, GET OVER IT...
COME TO THINK OF IT...
EVEN WHEN WE STARTED DATING, IT STILL TOOK ME OVER A YEAR TO COAX YOU INTO BED, DIDN'T IT?
SORRY.
BUT BE QUICK ABOUT IT, OKAY?
MY PATIENCE HAS LIMITS, AND I'LL ONLY BE ABLE TO KEEP MY HANDS OFF FOR SO LONG.
TUG
DWAH ?!

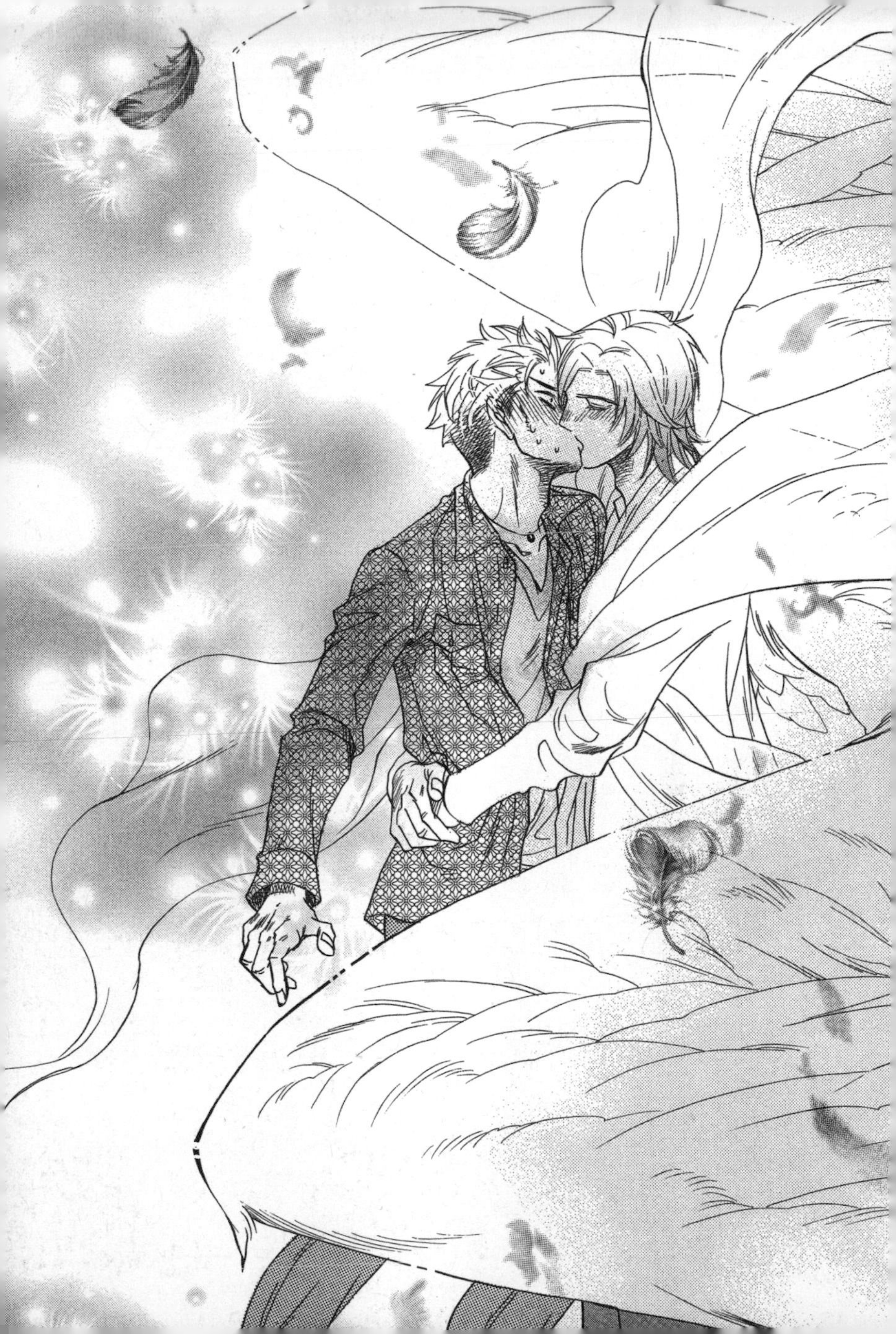

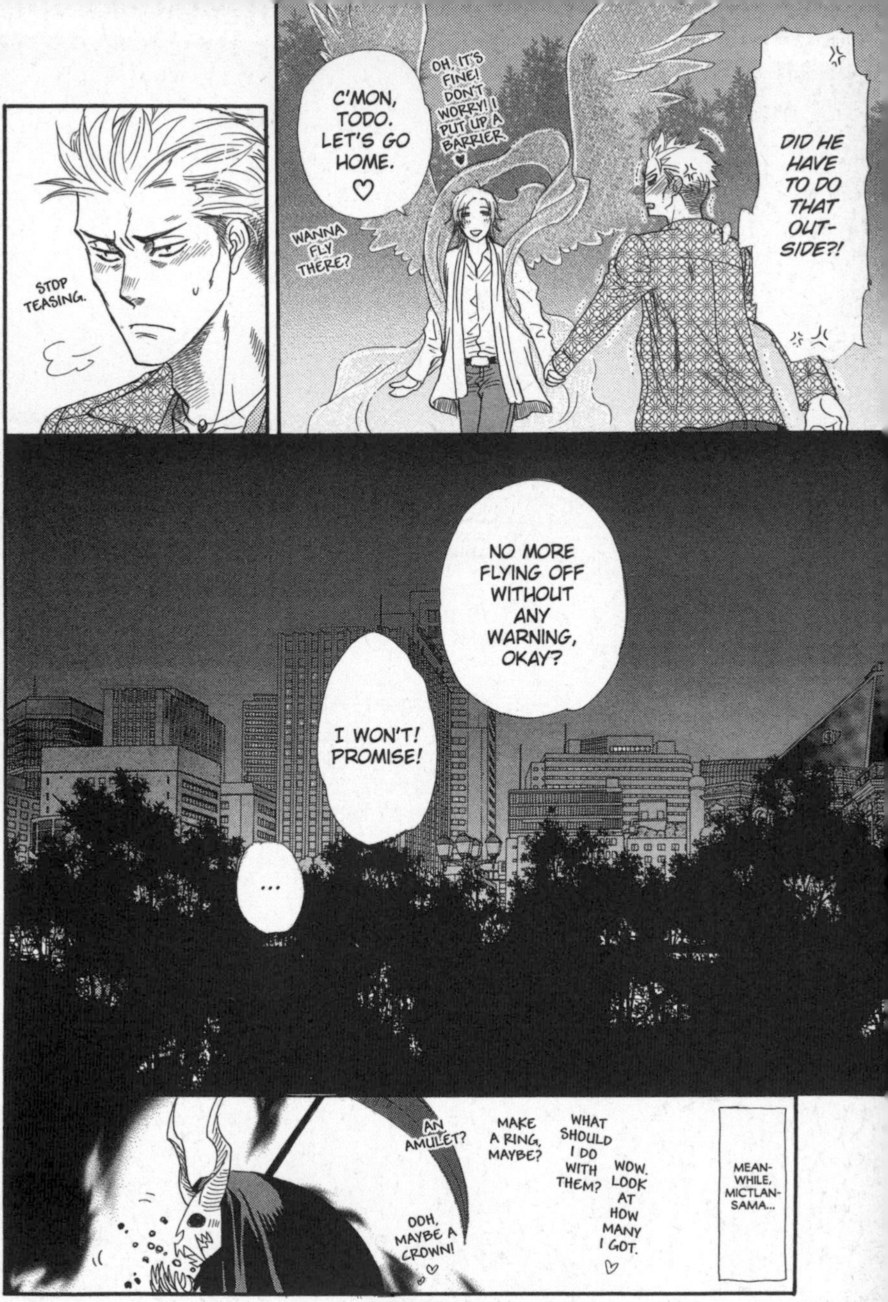
DID HE HAVE TO DO THAT OUT-SIDE?!
OH, IT'S FINE! DON'T WORRY! I PUT UP A BARRIER ♥
C'MON, TODO. LET'S GO HOME. ♡
WANNA FLY THERE?
STOP TEASING.
NO MORE FLYING OFF WITHOUT ANY WARNING, OKAY?
I WON'T! PROMISE!
...
MEAN-WHILE, MICTLAN-SAMA...
WOW. LOOK AT HOW MANY I GOT. ♡
WHAT SHOULD I DO WITH THEM?
MAKE A RING, MAYBE?
AN AMULET?
OOH, MAYBE A CROWN! ♡

END

Bohra Naono Presents

彼方者の
困惑
あっちもののこんわく

Midnight Stranger

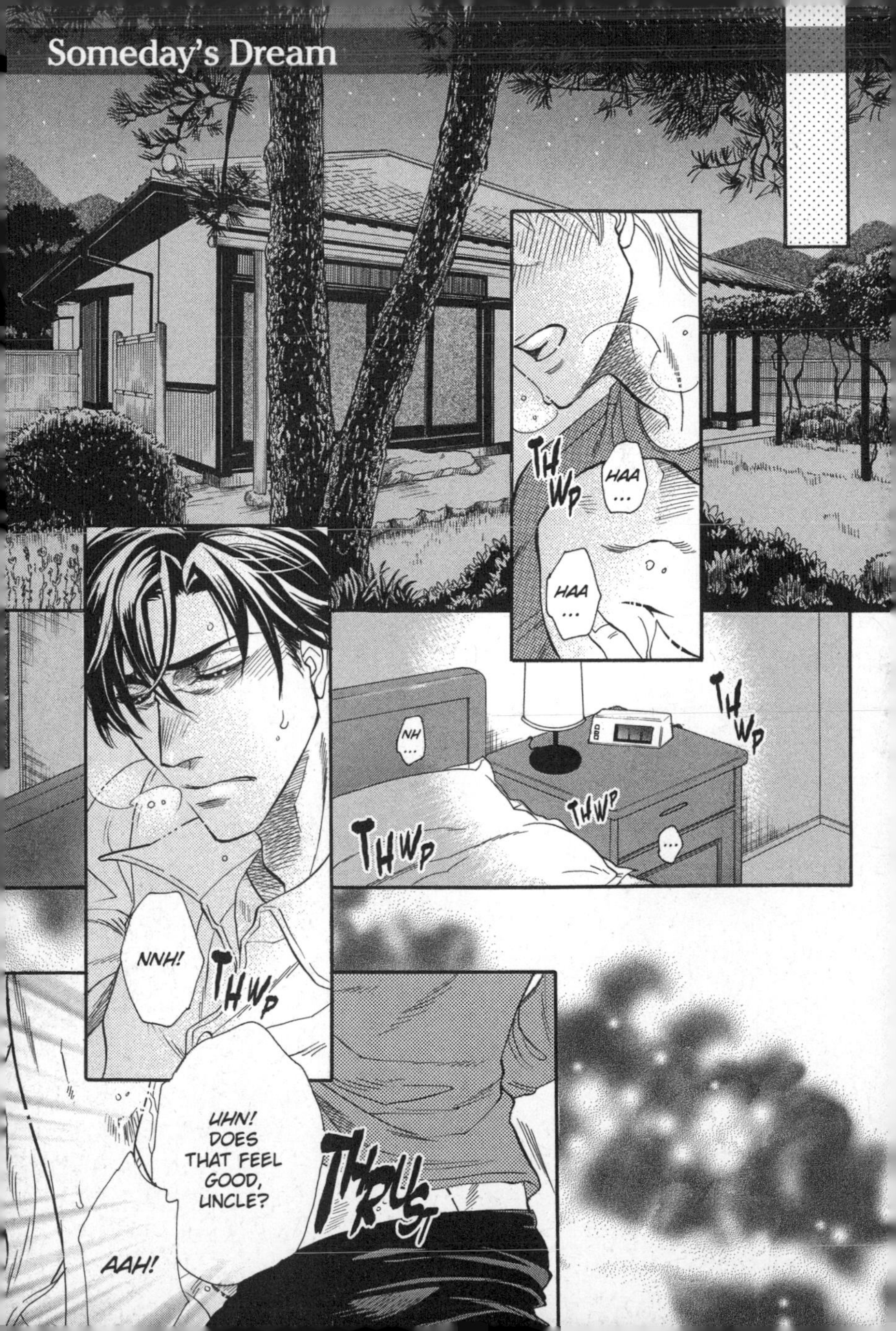
THWP
HAA...
HAA...
THWP
NH...
THWP
THWP
...
NNH!
THWP
UHN! DOES THAT FEEL GOOD, UNCLE?
THRUST
AAH!

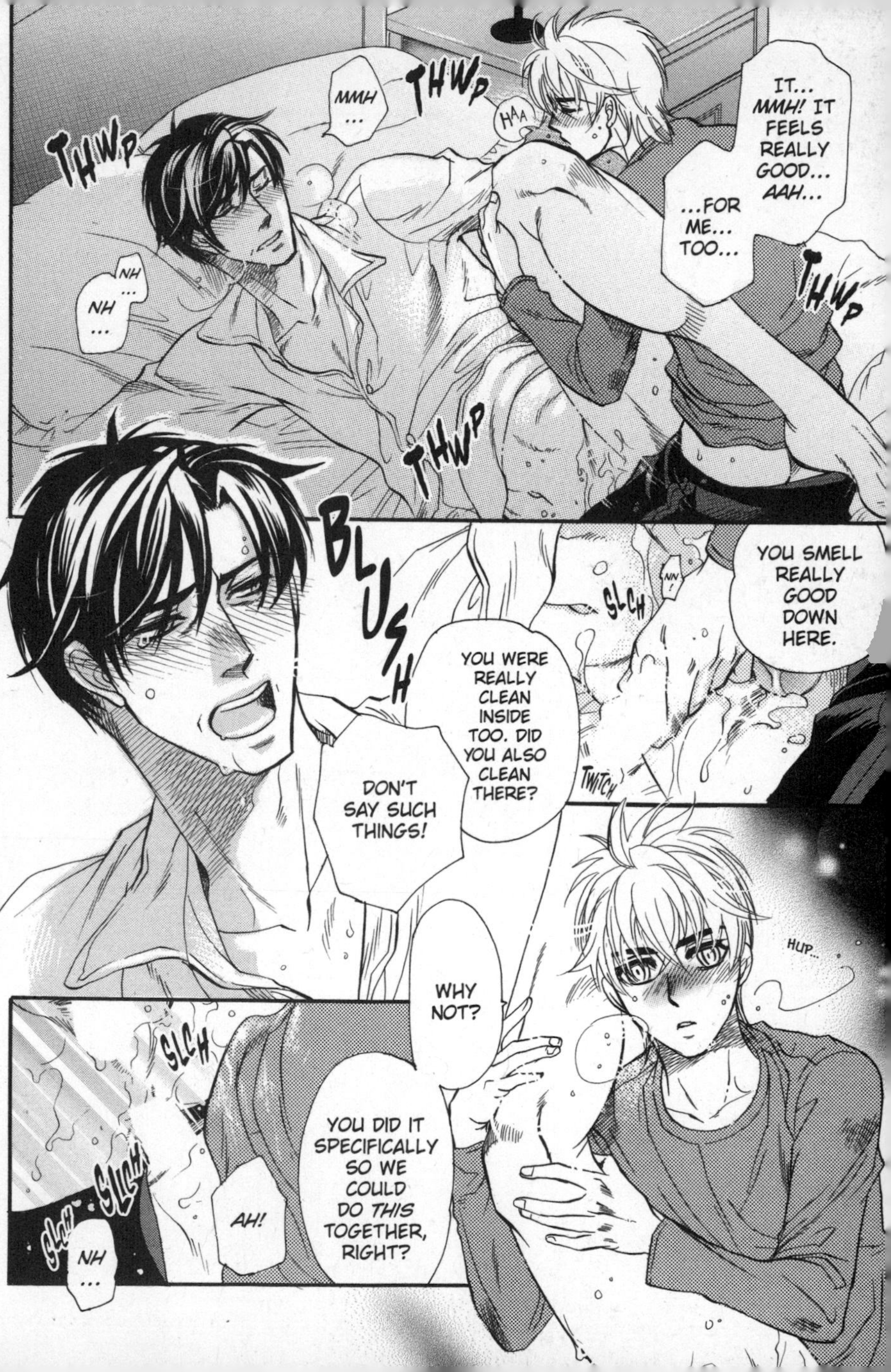
IT... MMH! IT FEELS REALLY GOOD... AAH...
...FOR ME... TOO...
THWP
HAA
THWP
MMH...
THWP
NH... NH...
THWP
YOU SMELL REALLY GOOD DOWN HERE.
NN!
SLCH
TWITCH
BLUSH
YOU WERE REALLY CLEAN INSIDE TOO. DID YOU ALSO CLEAN THERE?
DON'T SAY SUCH THINGS!
HUP...
WHY NOT?
YOU DID IT SPECIFICALLY SO WE COULD DO *THIS* TOGETHER, RIGHT?
SLCH
AH!
SLICH
SLCH
NH...

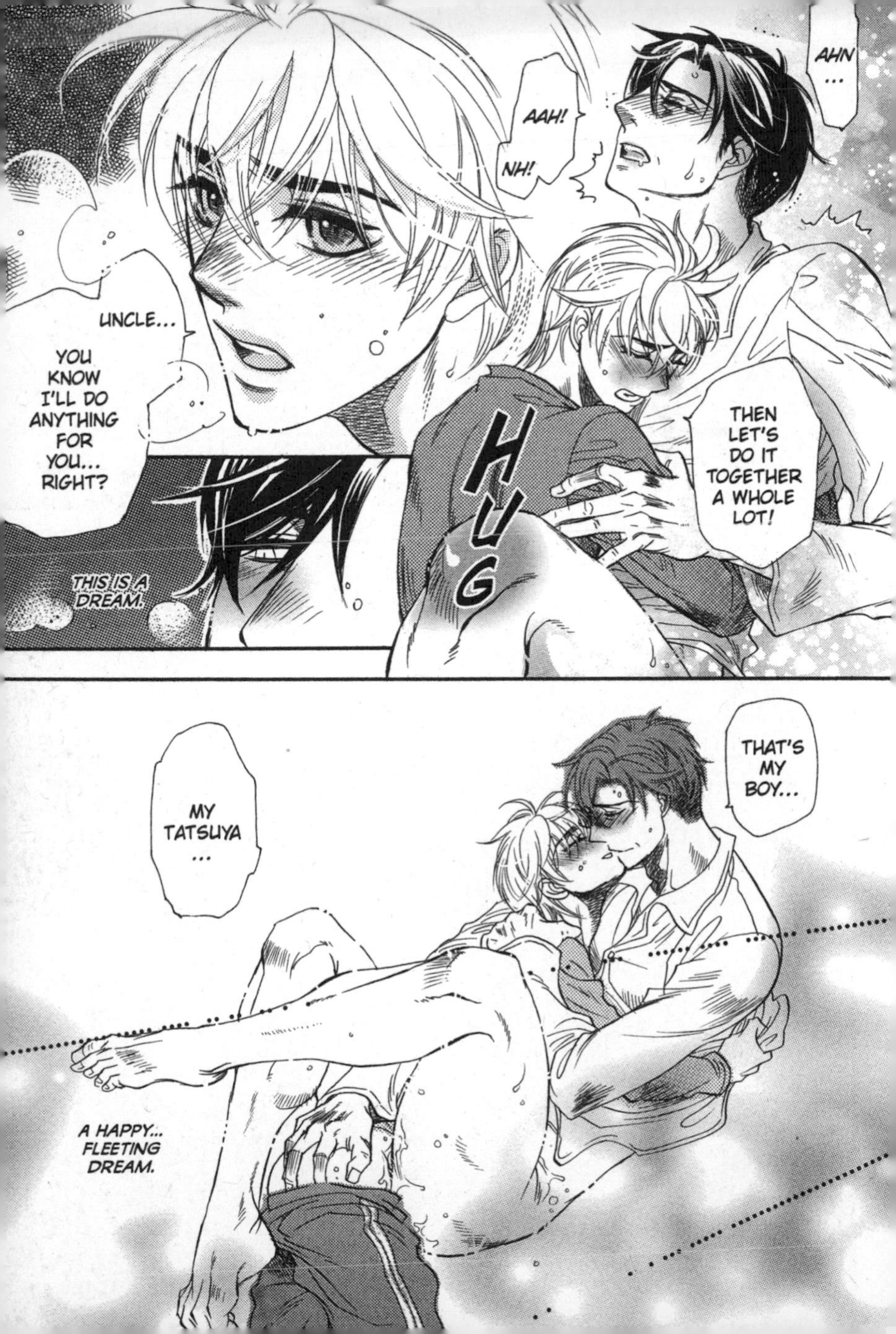
AHN ...
AAH!
NH!
UNCLE...
YOU KNOW I'LL DO ANYTHING FOR YOU... RIGHT?
THEN LET'S DO IT TOGETHER A WHOLE LOT!
HUG
THIS IS A DREAM.
THAT'S MY BOY...
MY TATSUYA ...
A HAPPY... FLEETING DREAM.

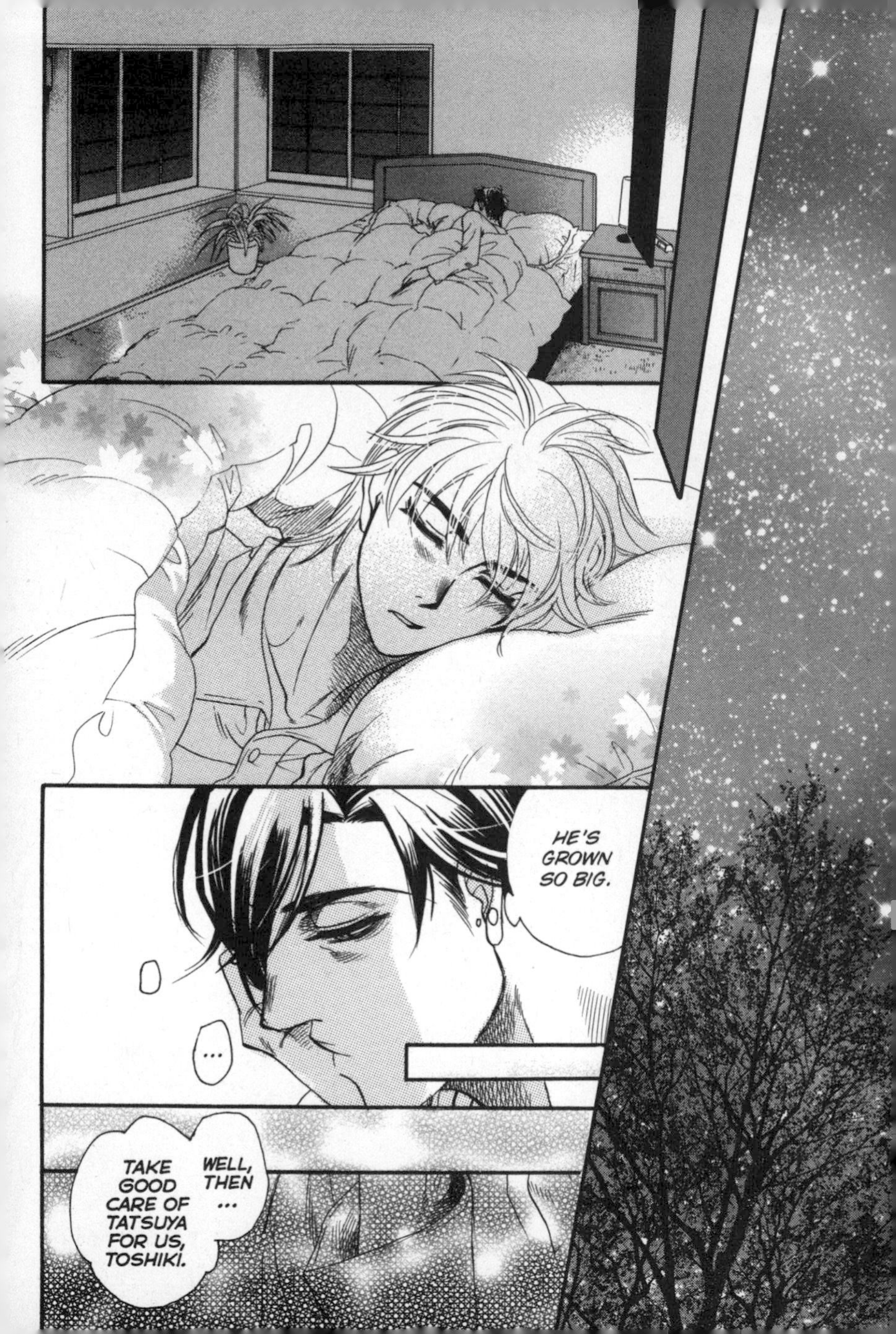
HE'S GROWN SO BIG.
...
WELL, THEN ...
TAKE GOOD CARE OF TATSUYA FOR US, TOSHIKI.

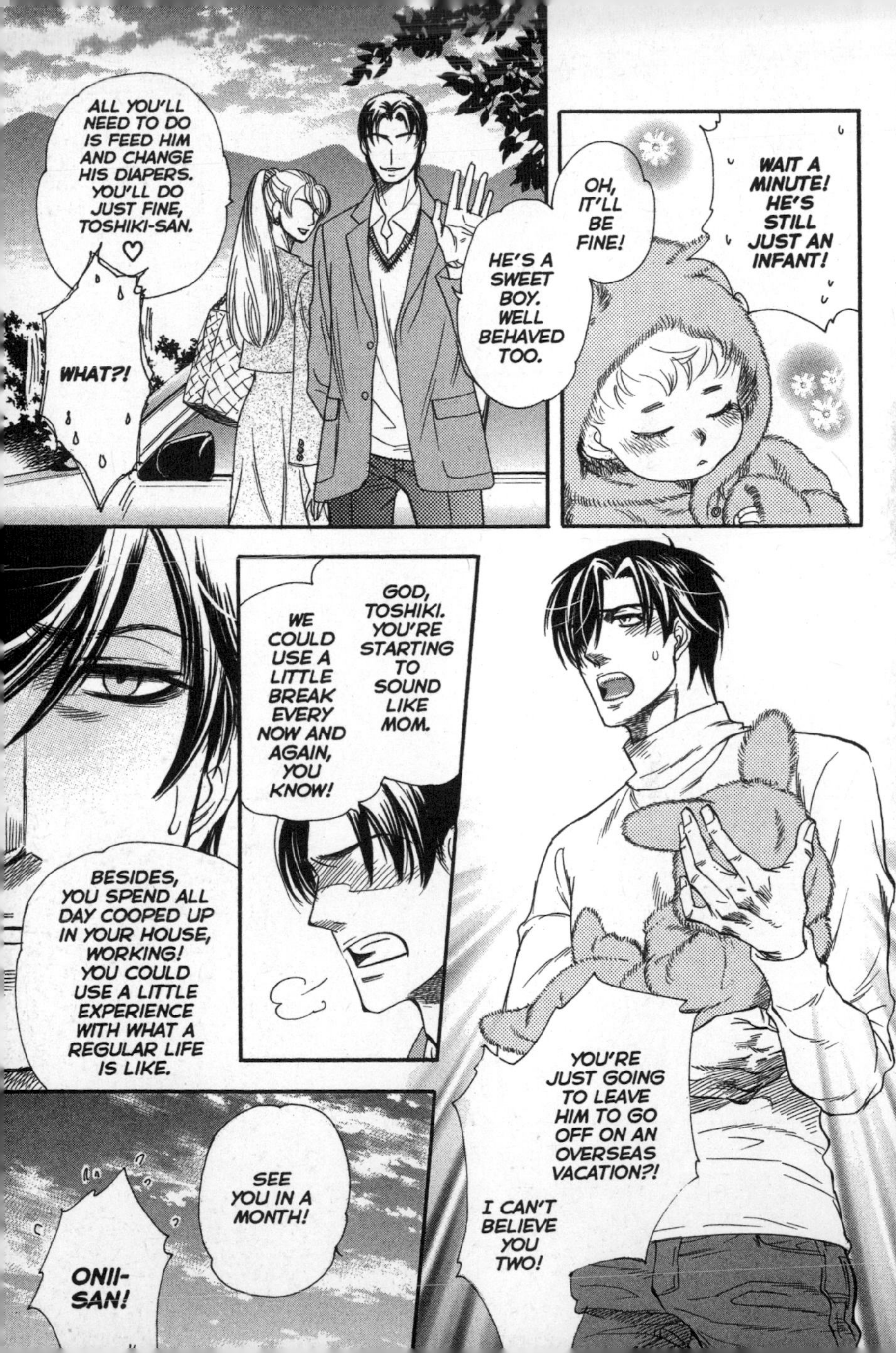
WAIT A MINUTE! HE'S STILL JUST AN INFANT!
OH, IT'LL BE FINE!
HE'S A SWEET BOY. WELL BEHAVED TOO.
ALL YOU'LL NEED TO DO IS FEED HIM AND CHANGE HIS DIAPERS. YOU'LL DO JUST FINE, TOSHIKI-SAN. ♡
WHAT?!
YOU'RE JUST GOING TO LEAVE HIM TO GO OFF ON AN OVERSEAS VACATION?!
I CAN'T BELIEVE YOU TWO!
GOD, TOSHIKI. YOU'RE STARTING TO SOUND LIKE MOM.
WE COULD USE A LITTLE BREAK EVERY NOW AND AGAIN, YOU KNOW!
BESIDES, YOU SPEND ALL DAY COOPED UP IN YOUR HOUSE, WORKING! YOU COULD USE A LITTLE EXPERIENCE WITH WHAT A REGULAR LIFE IS LIKE.
SEE YOU IN A MONTH!
ONII-SAN!

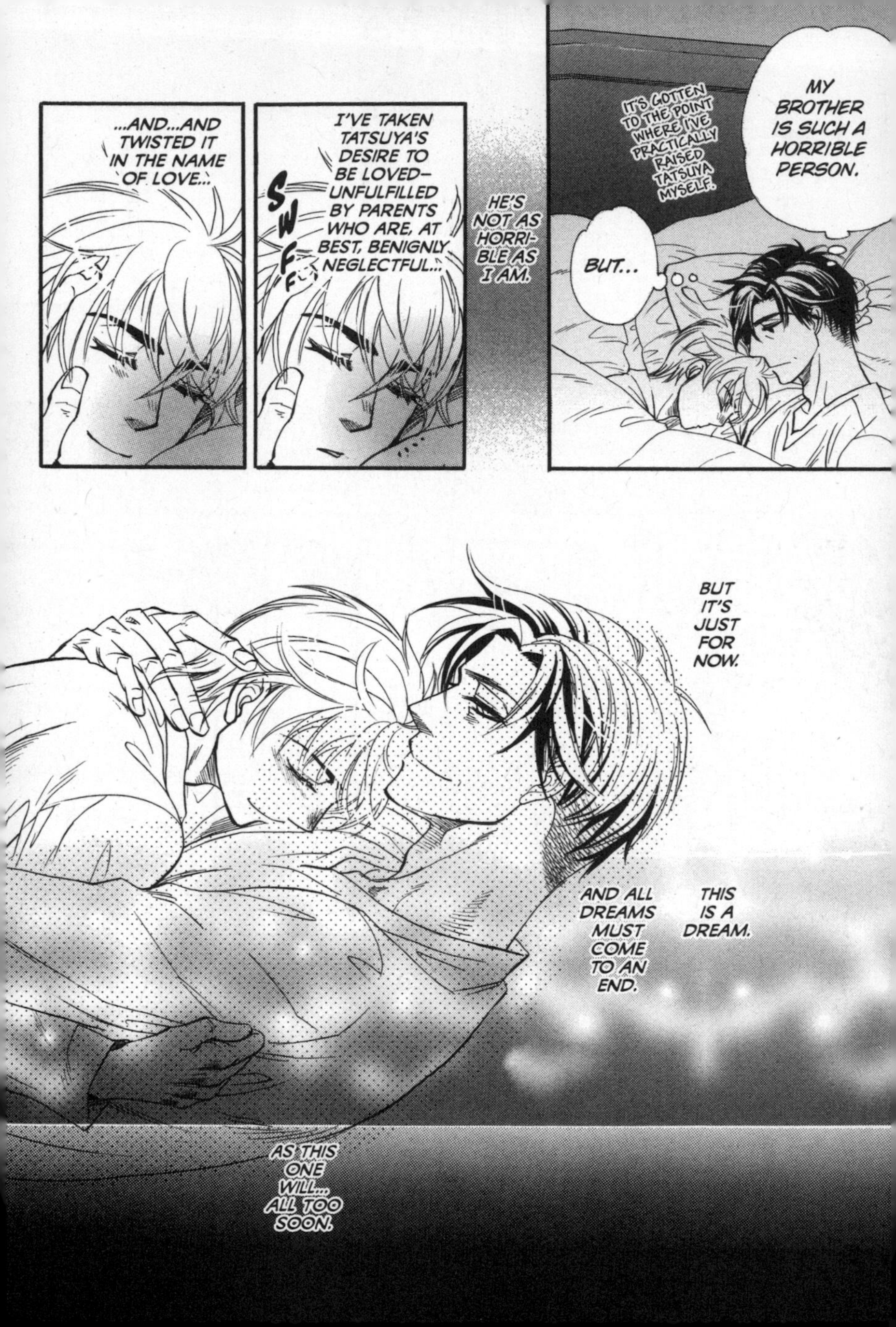
MY BROTHER IS SUCH A HORRIBLE PERSON.
IT'S GOTTEN TO THE POINT WHERE I'VE PRACTICALLY RAISED TATSUYA MYSELF.
BUT...
HE'S NOT AS HORRIBLE AS I AM.
I'VE TAKEN TATSUYA'S DESIRE TO BE LOVED—UNFULFILLED BY PARENTS WHO ARE, AT BEST, BENIGNLY NEGLECTFUL...
SWFF
...AND...AND TWISTED IT IN THE NAME OF LOVE...
BUT IT'S JUST FOR NOW.
THIS IS A DREAM.
AND ALL DREAMS MUST COME TO AN END.
AS THIS ONE WILL... ALL TOO SOON.

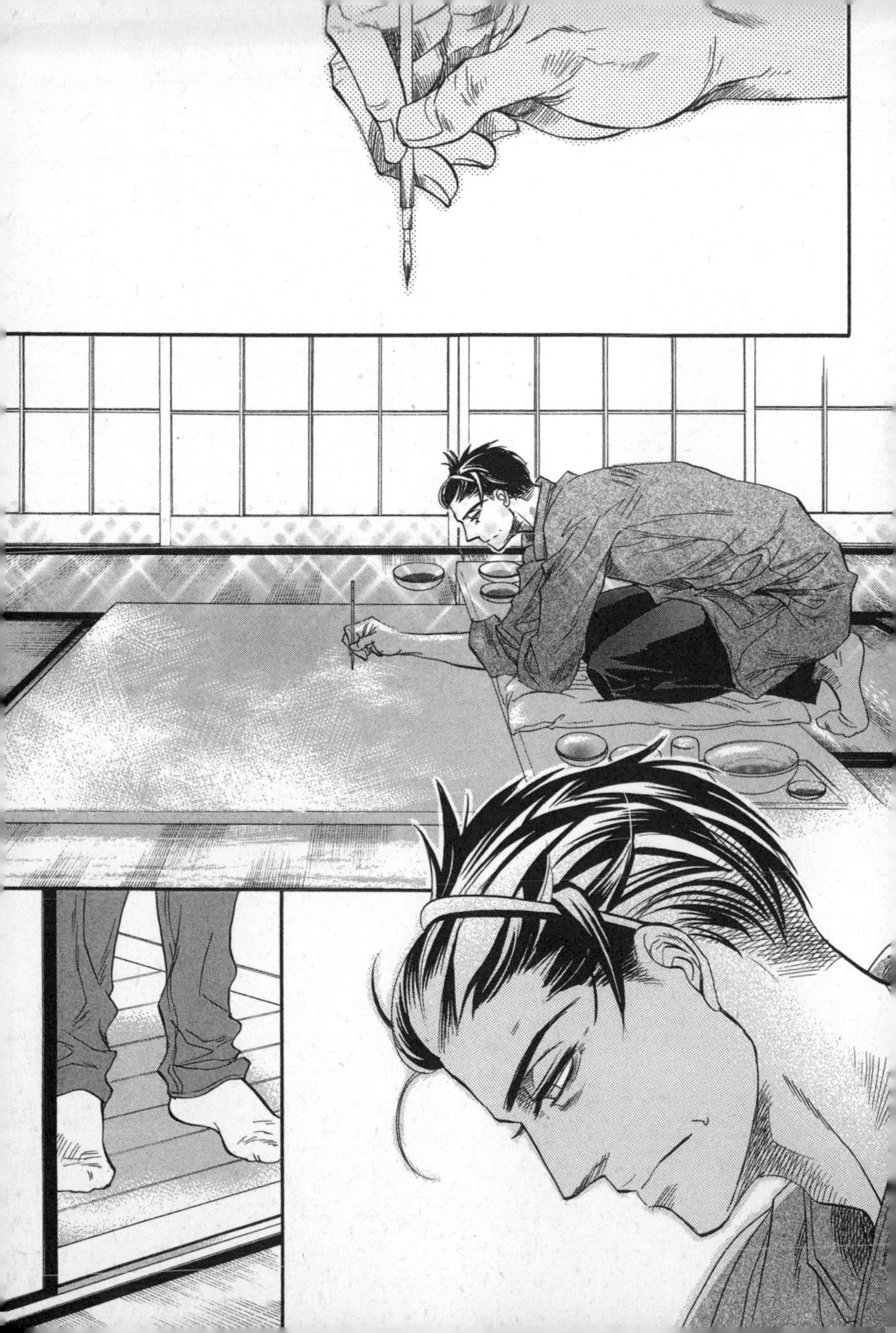

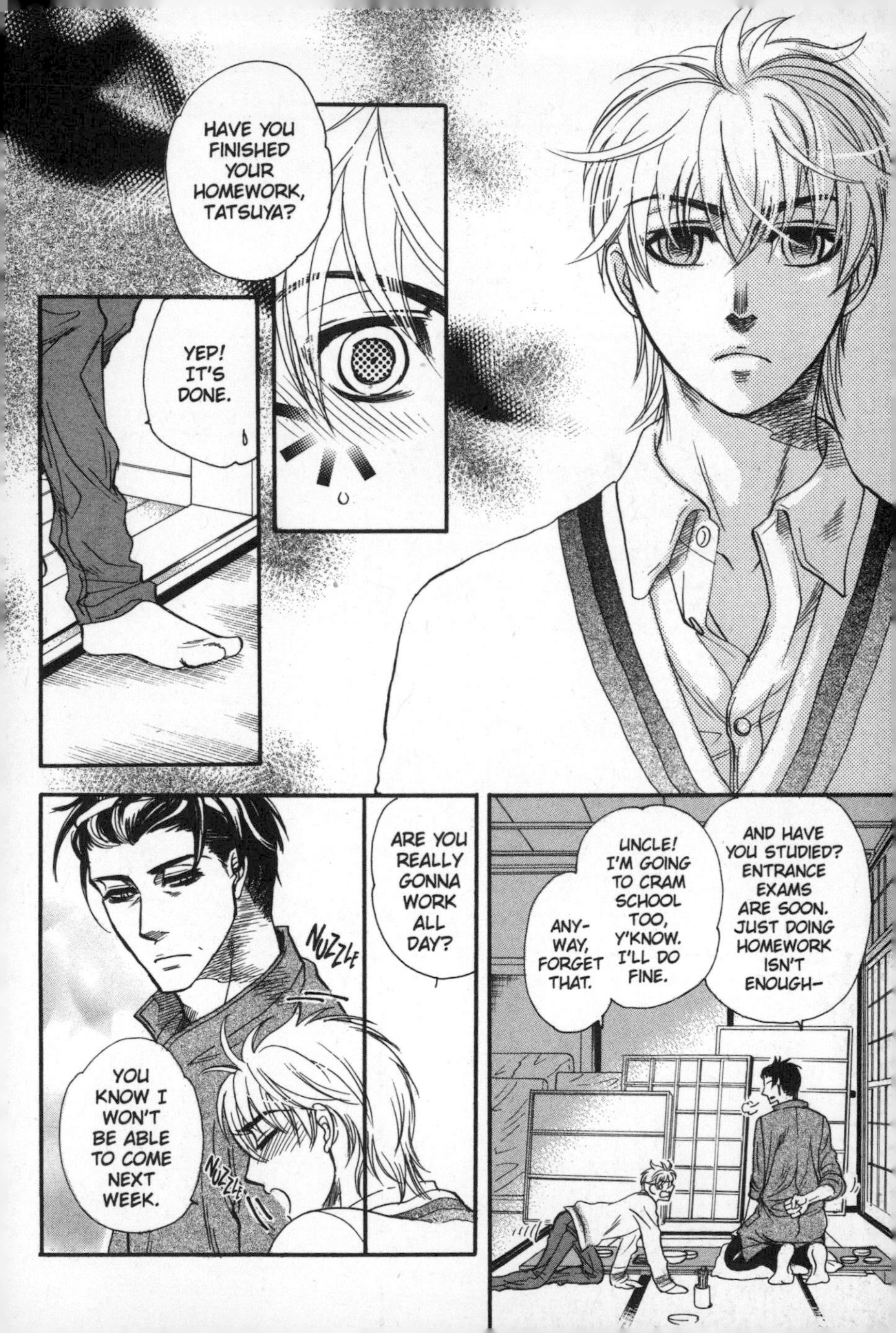
HAVE YOU FINISHED YOUR HOMEWORK, TATSUYA?
YEP! IT'S DONE.
AND HAVE YOU STUDIED? ENTRANCE EXAMS ARE SOON. JUST DOING HOMEWORK ISN'T ENOUGH–
UNCLE! I'M GOING TO CRAM SCHOOL TOO, Y'KNOW. I'LL DO FINE.
ANY-WAY, FORGET THAT.
ARE YOU REALLY GONNA WORK ALL DAY?
NUZZLE
YOU KNOW I WON'T BE ABLE TO COME NEXT WEEK.
NUZZLE

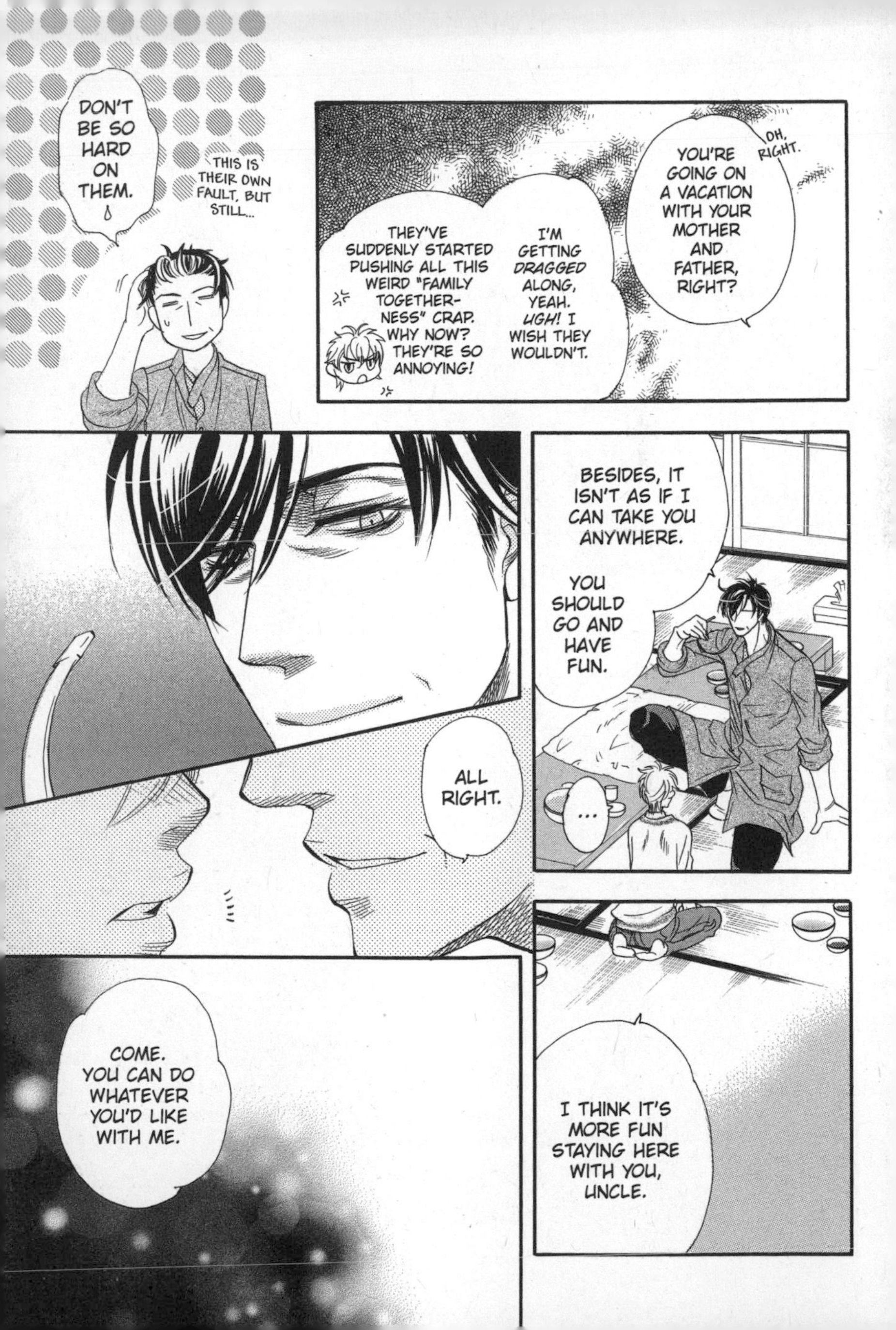
OH, RIGHT.
YOU'RE GOING ON A VACATION WITH YOUR MOTHER AND FATHER, RIGHT?
I'M GETTING DRAGGED ALONG, YEAH. UGH! I WISH THEY WOULDN'T.
THEY'VE SUDDENLY STARTED PUSHING ALL THIS WEIRD "FAMILY TOGETHER-NESS" CRAP. WHY NOW? THEY'RE SO ANNOYING!
THIS IS THEIR OWN FAULT, BUT STILL...
DON'T BE SO HARD ON THEM.
BESIDES, IT ISN'T AS IF I CAN TAKE YOU ANYWHERE.
YOU SHOULD GO AND HAVE FUN.
...
I THINK IT'S MORE FUN STAYING HERE WITH YOU, UNCLE.
ALL RIGHT.
COME. YOU CAN DO WHATEVER YOU'D LIKE WITH ME.

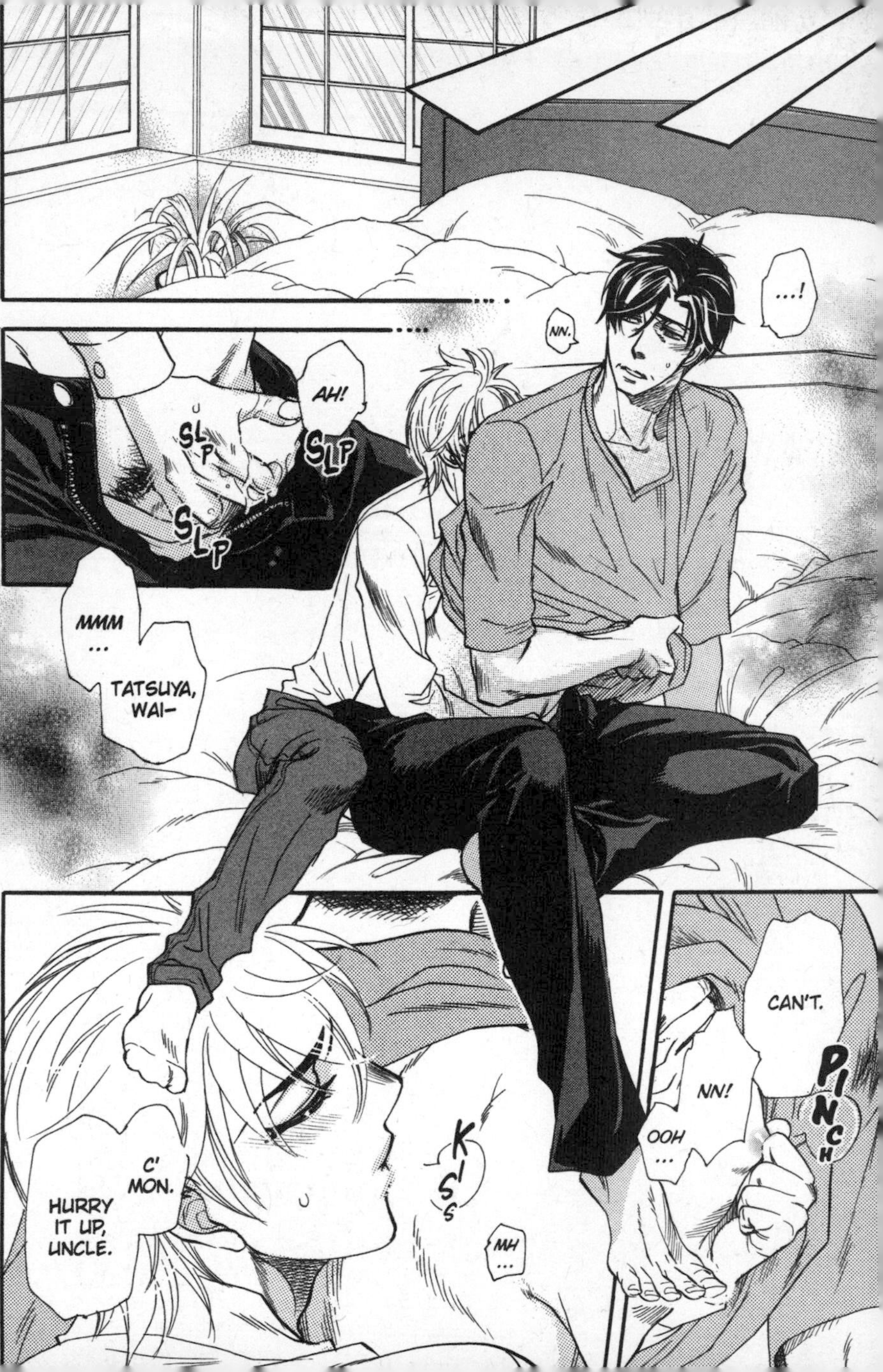
...!
NN.
AH!
SLP
SLP
SLP
MMM... TATSUYA, WAI-
CAN'T.
PINCH
NN!
OOH...
KISS
MH...
C'MON.
HURRY IT UP, UNCLE.

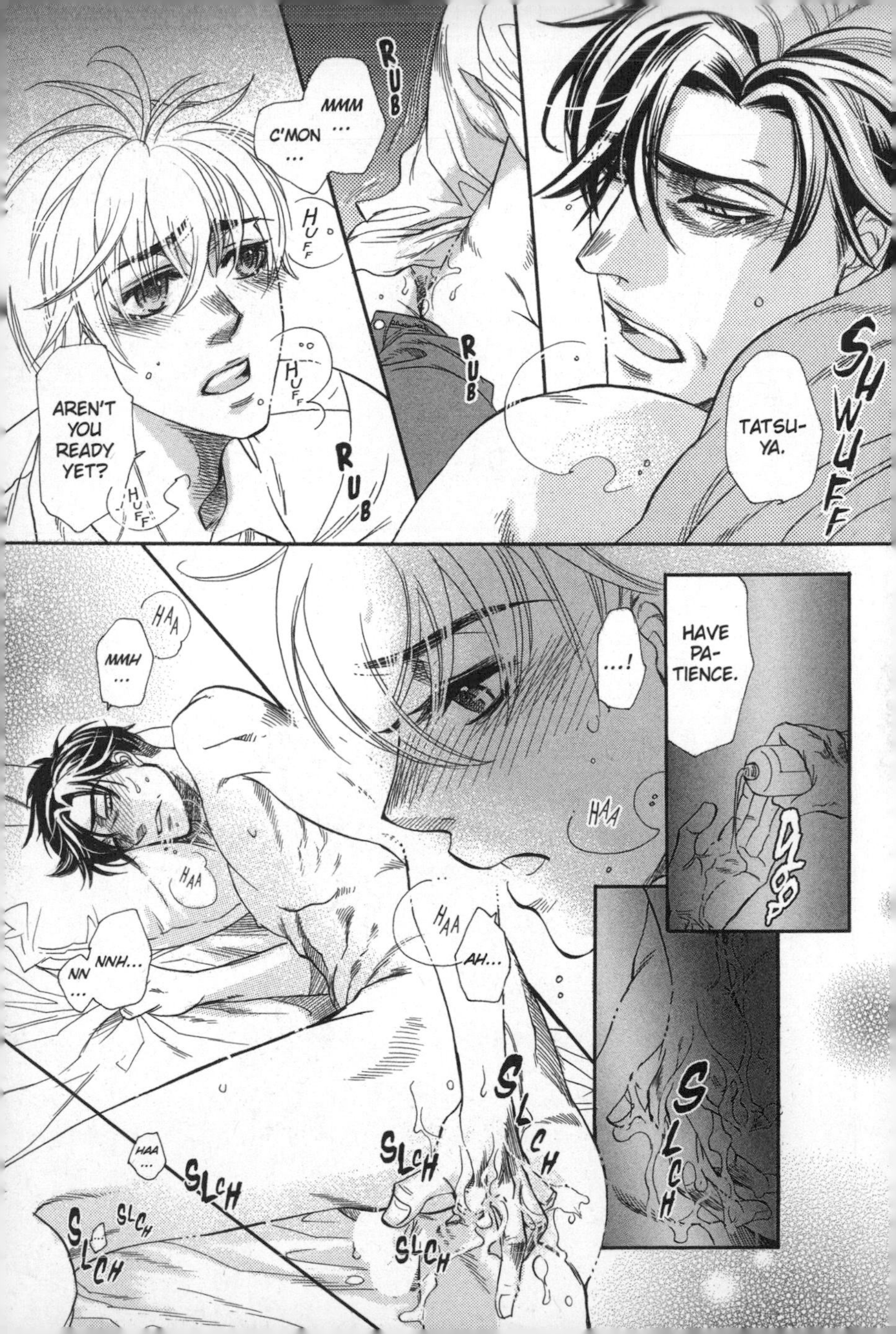
TATSU-YA.
SHWUFF
RUB
RUB
MMM ...
C'MON ...
HUFF
HUFF
AREN'T YOU READY YET?
HUFF
RUB
HAVE PA-TIENCE.
SLCH
...!
HAA
HAA
AH...
HAA
MMH ...
HAA
NNH...
NN ...
SLCH
SLCH
HAA ...
SLCH
SLCH
SLCH
...
SLCH

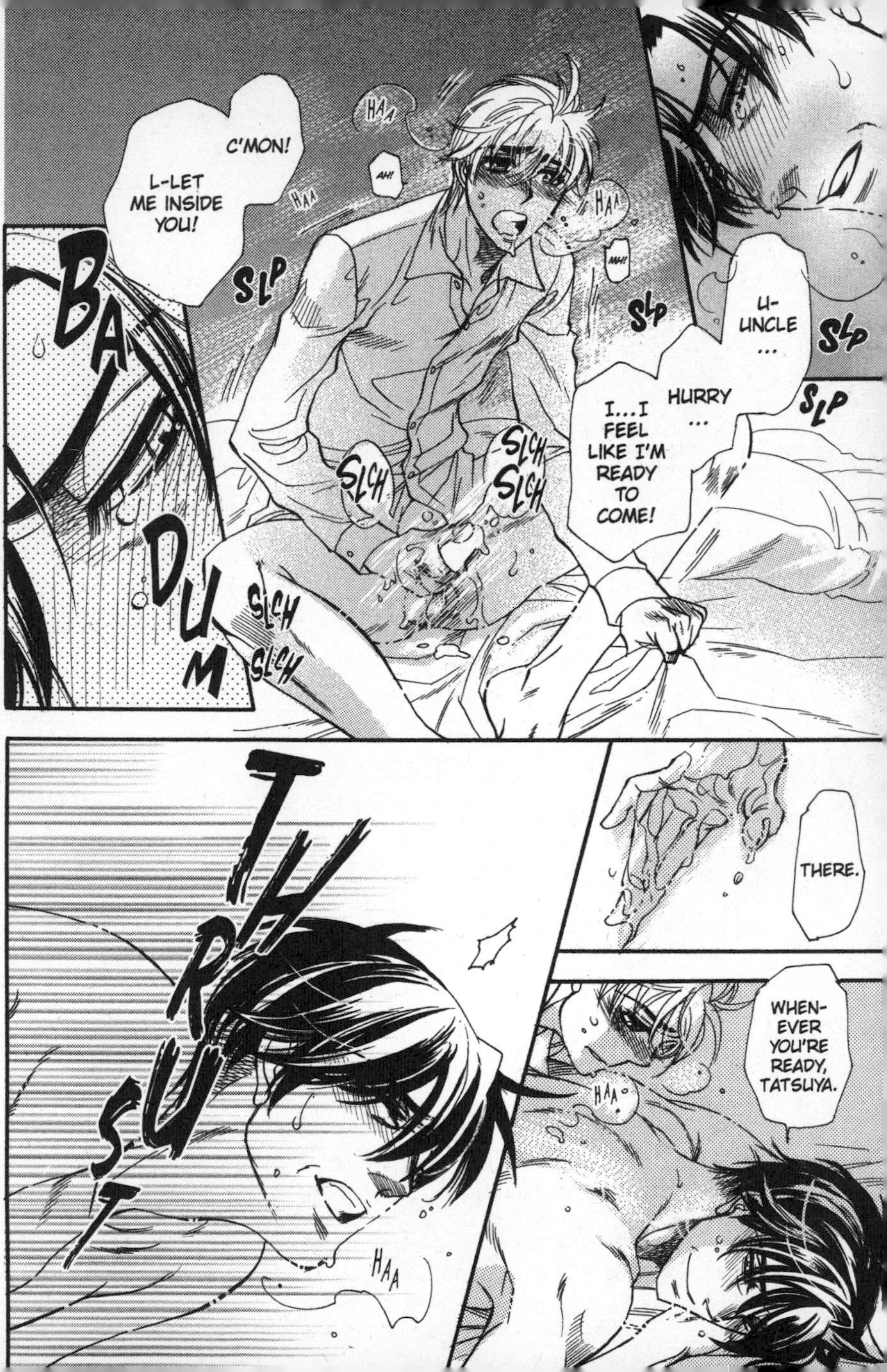
U-
UNCLE
...
SLP
SLP
HAA
AH!
HAA
HAA
MH!
C'MON!
L-LET ME INSIDE YOU!
SLP
SLP
HURRY
...
I...I FEEL LIKE I'M READY TO COME!
SLCH
SLCH
SLCH
SLCH
SLCH
BA DUM
THERE.
WHEN-EVER YOU'RE READY, TATSUYA.
HAA
THRUST
HAA

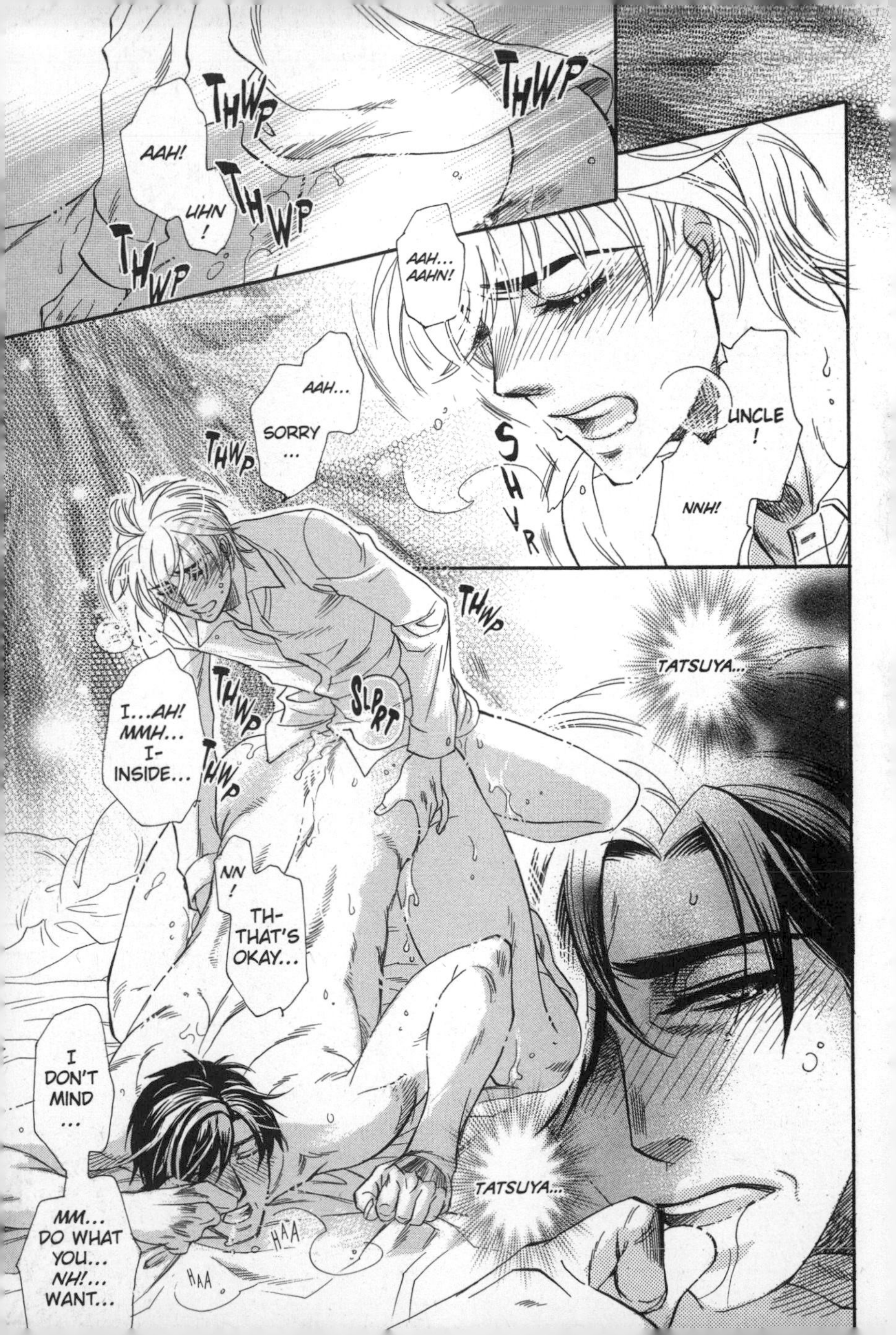
THWP
THWP
AAH!
THWP
UHN!
THWP
AAH... AAHN!
UNCLE!
SHVR
NNH!
THWP
AAH... SORRY...
THWP
TATSUYA...
SLPRT
THWP
THWP
I...AH! MMH... I-INSIDE...
NN! TH-THAT'S OKAY...
TATSUYA...
I DON'T MIND...
HAA
MM... DO WHAT YOU... NH!... WANT...
HAA

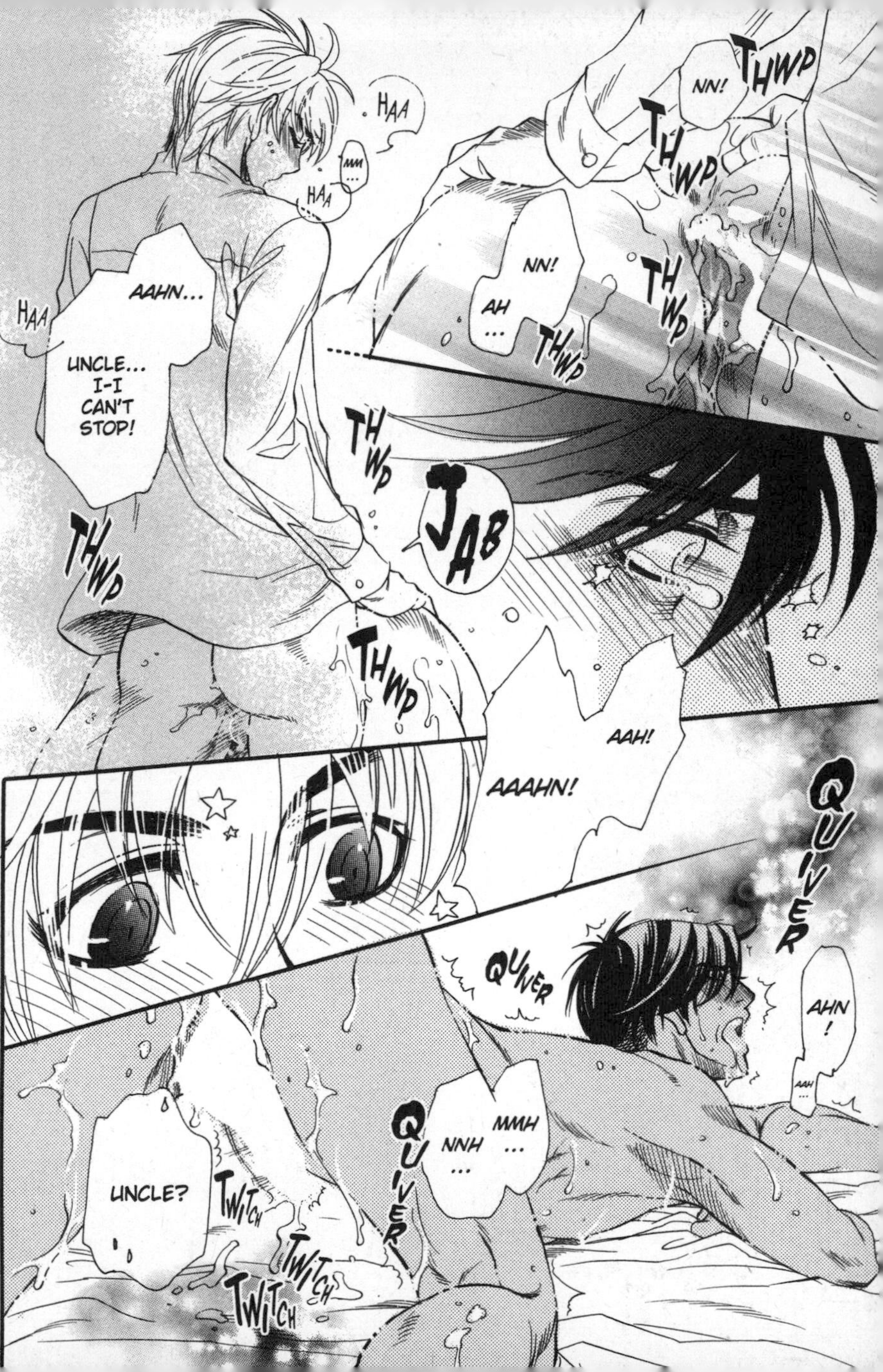
NN!
THWP
THWP
NN! AH...
THWP
THWP
HAA
MM...
HAA
HAA
AAHN...
UNCLE... I-I CAN'T STOP!
THWP
THWP
JAB
THWP
AAH!
AAAHN!
QUIVER
QUIVER
AHN!
AAH...
MMH... NNH...
QUIVER
UNCLE?
TWITCH
TWITCH
TWITCH

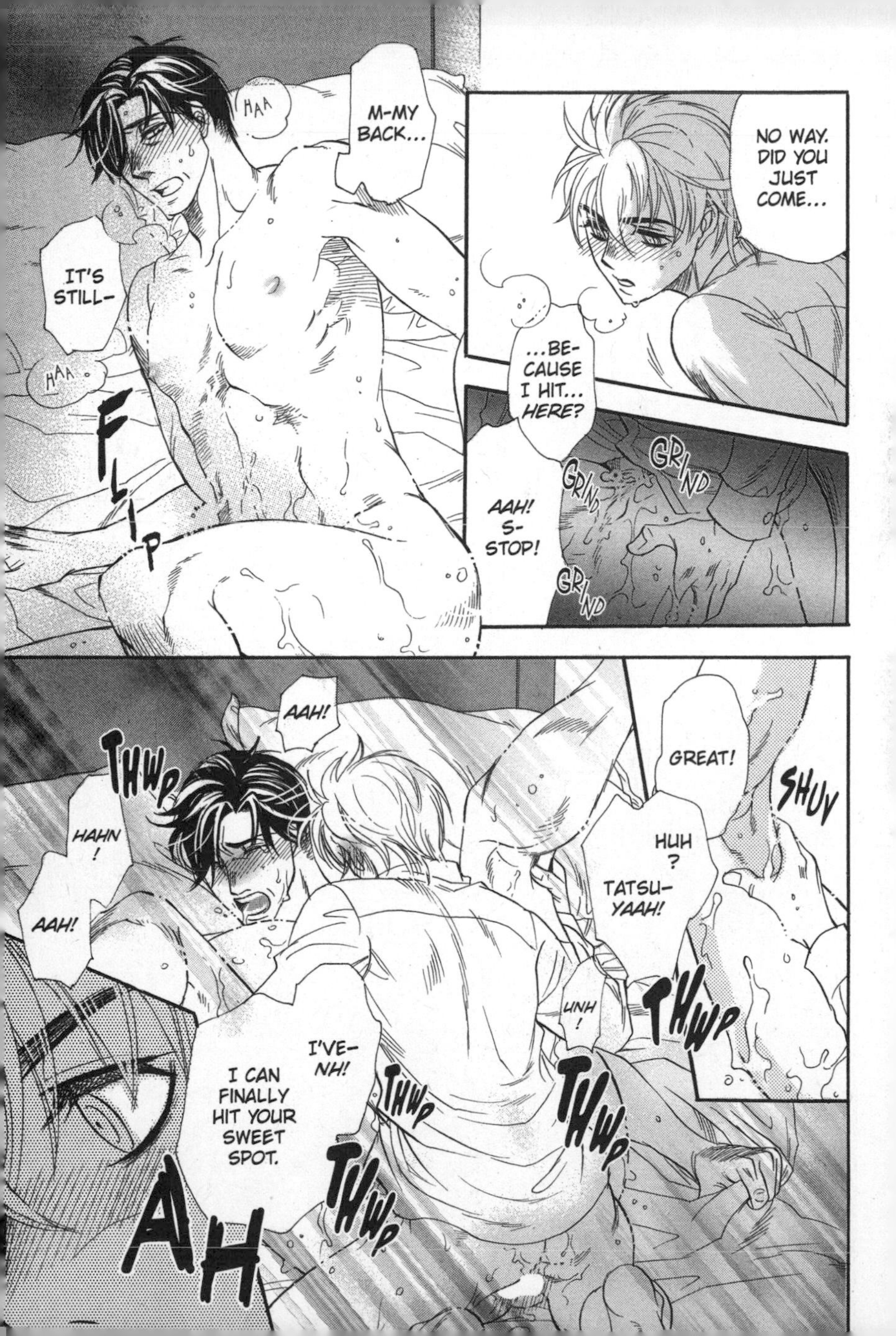
NO WAY. DID YOU JUST COME...
...BE-CAUSE I HIT... HERE?
GRIND
GRIND
AAH! S-STOP!
GRIND
M-MY BACK...
HAA
IT'S STILL-
HAA
FLIP
GREAT!
SHUV
HUH?
TATSU-YAAH!
AAH!
THWP
HAHN!
AAH!
UNH!
THWP
I'VE-NH!
I CAN FINALLY HIT YOUR SWEET SPOT.
THWP
THWP
THWP
AH

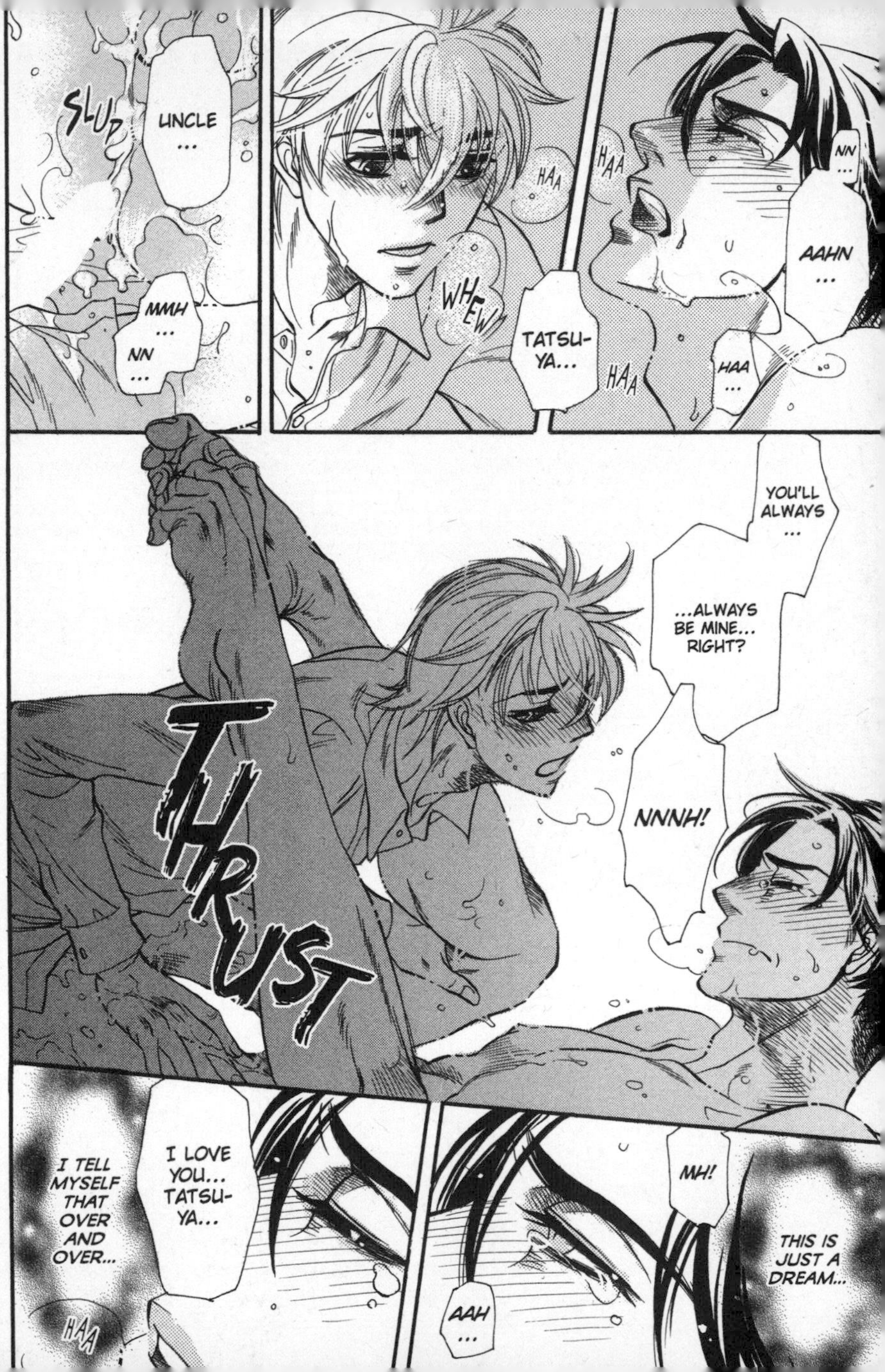
NN ...
HAA
AAHN ...
HAA ...
HAA
HAA
WHEW
TATSU-YA...
UNCLE ...
SLUP
MMH ...
NN ...
YOU'LL ALWAYS ...
...ALWAYS BE MINE... RIGHT?
NNNH!
THRUST
MH!
THIS IS JUST A DREAM...
AAH ...
I LOVE YOU... TATSU-YA...
I TELL MYSELF THAT OVER AND OVER...
HAA

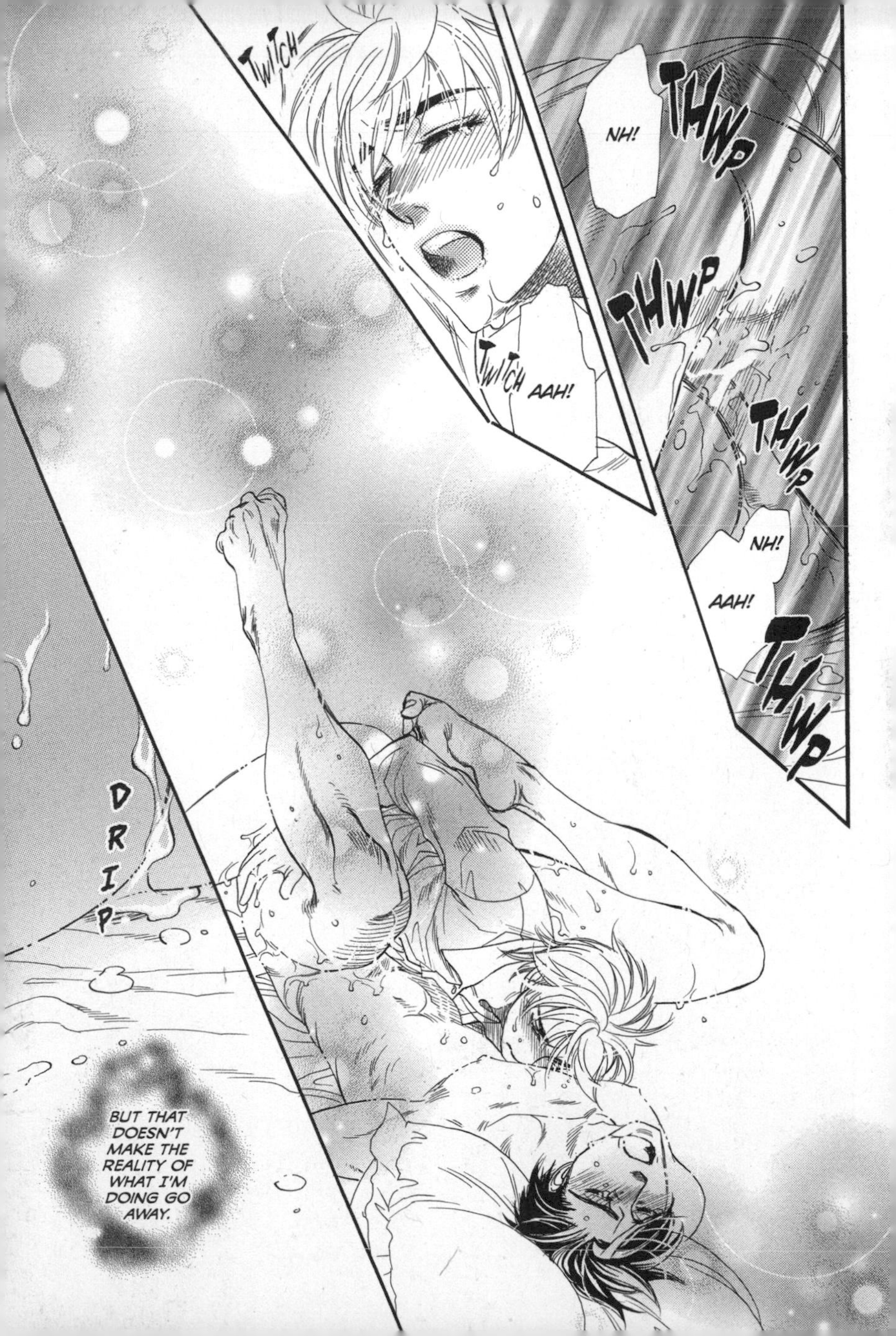
NH!
THWP
THWP
THWP
NH!
AAH!
THWP
TWITCH
TWITCH
AAH!
DRIP
BUT THAT DOESN'T MAKE THE REALITY OF WHAT I'M DOING GO AWAY.

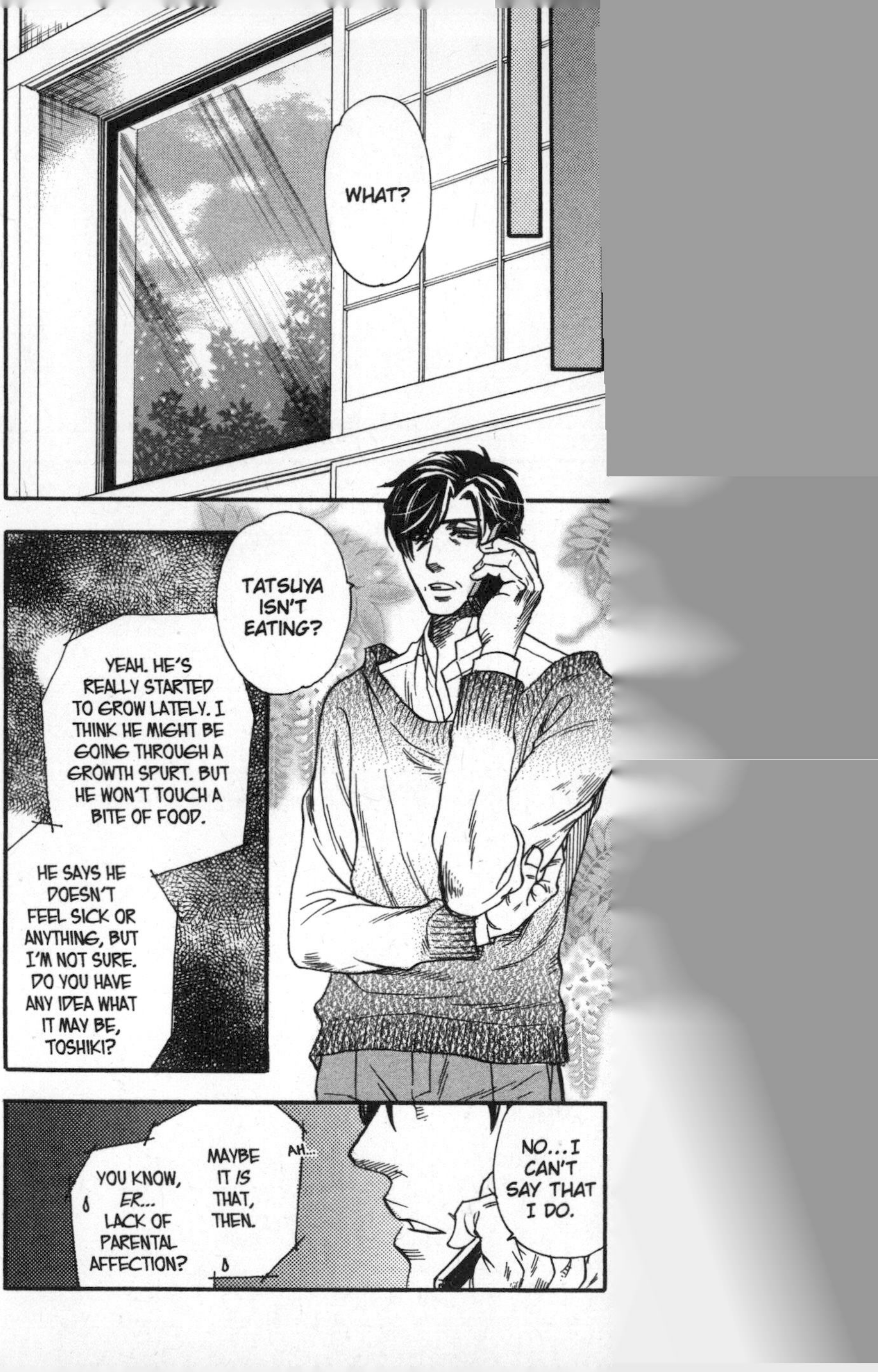
WHAT?
TATSUYA ISN'T EATING?
YEAH. HE'S REALLY STARTED TO GROW LATELY. I THINK HE MIGHT BE GOING THROUGH A GROWTH SPURT. BUT HE WON'T TOUCH A BITE OF FOOD.
HE SAYS HE DOESN'T FEEL SICK OR ANYTHING, BUT I'M NOT SURE. DO YOU HAVE ANY IDEA WHAT IT MAY BE, TOSHIKI?
NO... I CAN'T SAY THAT I DO.
AH...
MAYBE IT *IS* THAT, THEN.
YOU KNOW, *ER*... LACK OF PARENTAL AFFECTION?

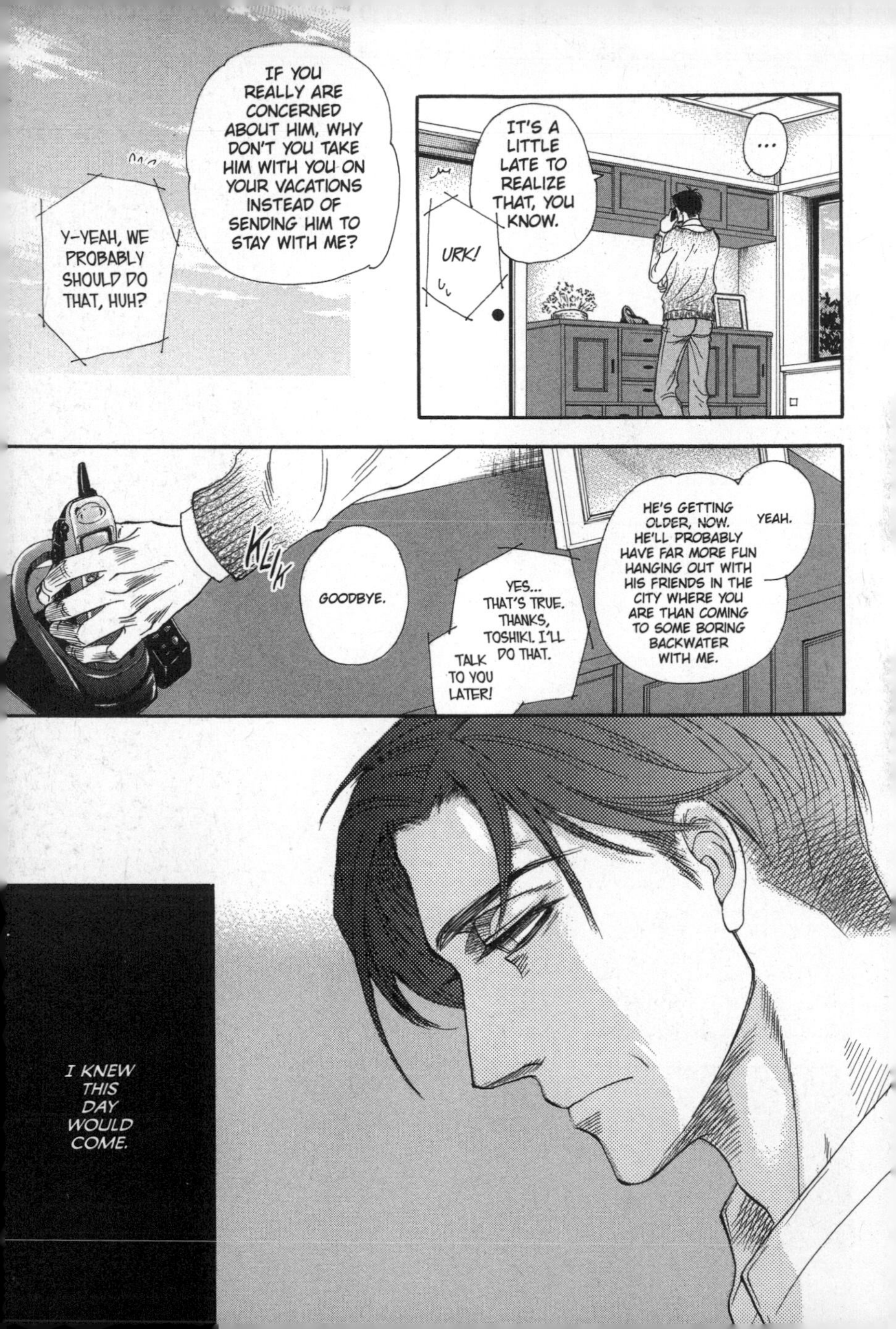
...
IT'S A LITTLE LATE TO REALIZE THAT, YOU KNOW.
URK!
IF YOU REALLY ARE CONCERNED ABOUT HIM, WHY DON'T YOU TAKE HIM WITH YOU ON YOUR VACATIONS INSTEAD OF SENDING HIM TO STAY WITH ME?
Y-YEAH, WE PROBABLY SHOULD DO THAT, HUH?
YEAH.
HE'S GETTING OLDER, NOW. HE'LL PROBABLY HAVE FAR MORE FUN HANGING OUT WITH HIS FRIENDS IN THE CITY WHERE YOU ARE THAN COMING TO SOME BORING BACKWATER WITH ME.
YES... THAT'S TRUE. THANKS, TOSHIKI. I'LL DO THAT.
TALK TO YOU LATER!
GOODBYE.
KLIK
I KNEW THIS DAY WOULD COME.

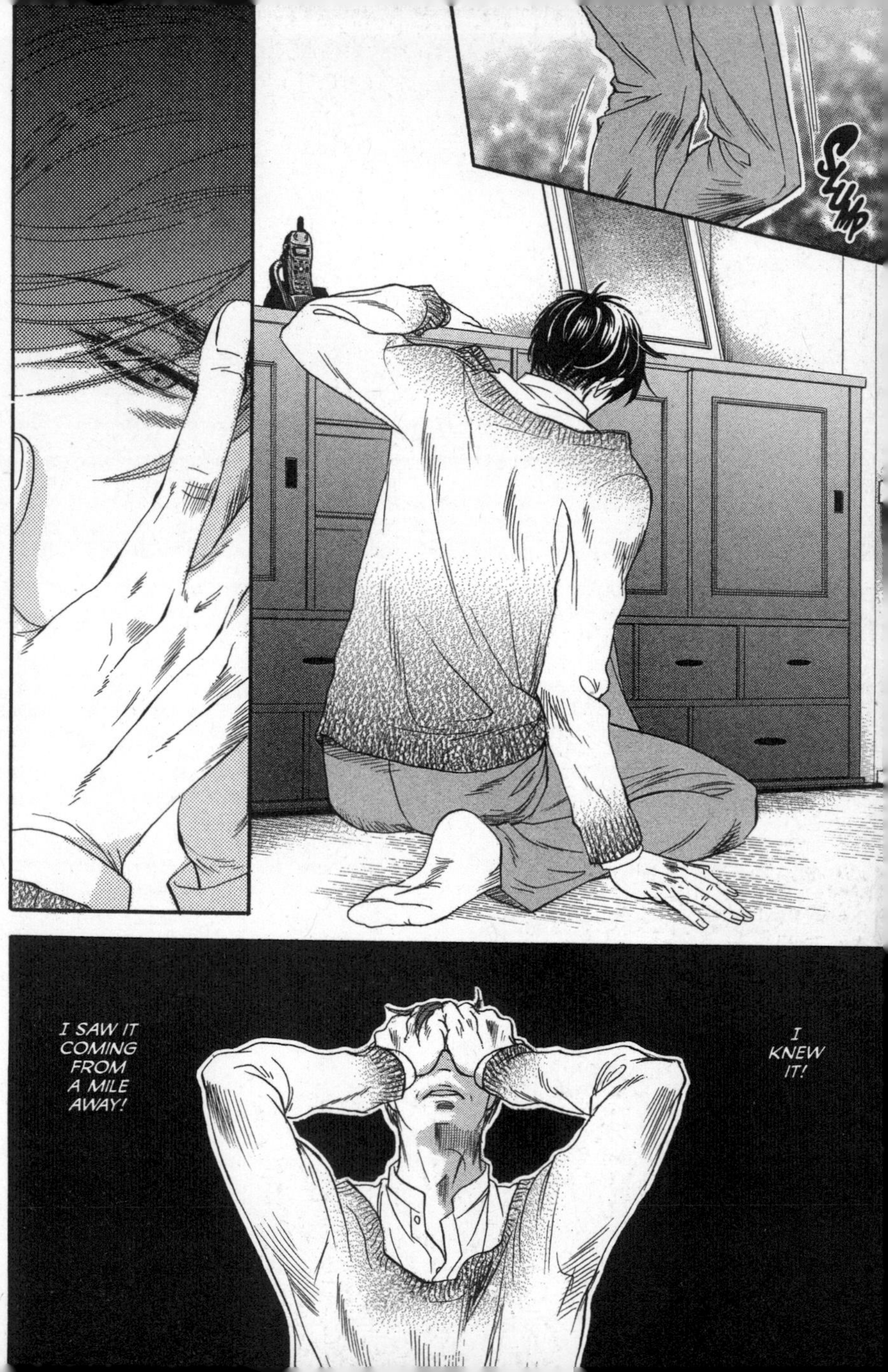
SLUMP
I KNEW IT!
I SAW IT COMING FROM A MILE AWAY!

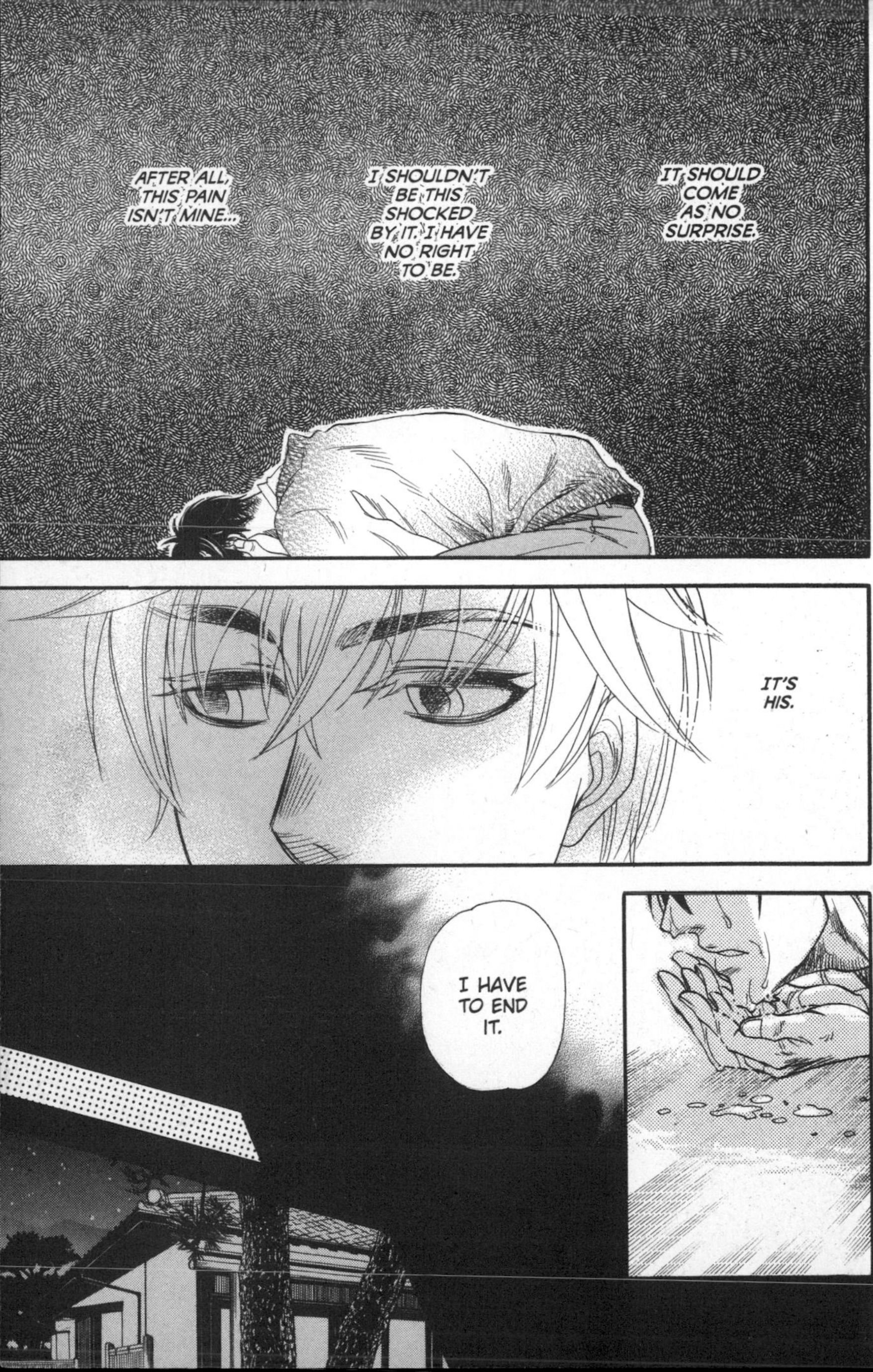
IT SHOULD COME AS NO SURPRISE.
I SHOULDN'T BE THIS SHOCKED BY IT. I HAVE NO RIGHT TO BE.
AFTER ALL, THIS PAIN ISN'T MINE...
IT'S HIS.
I HAVE TO END IT.

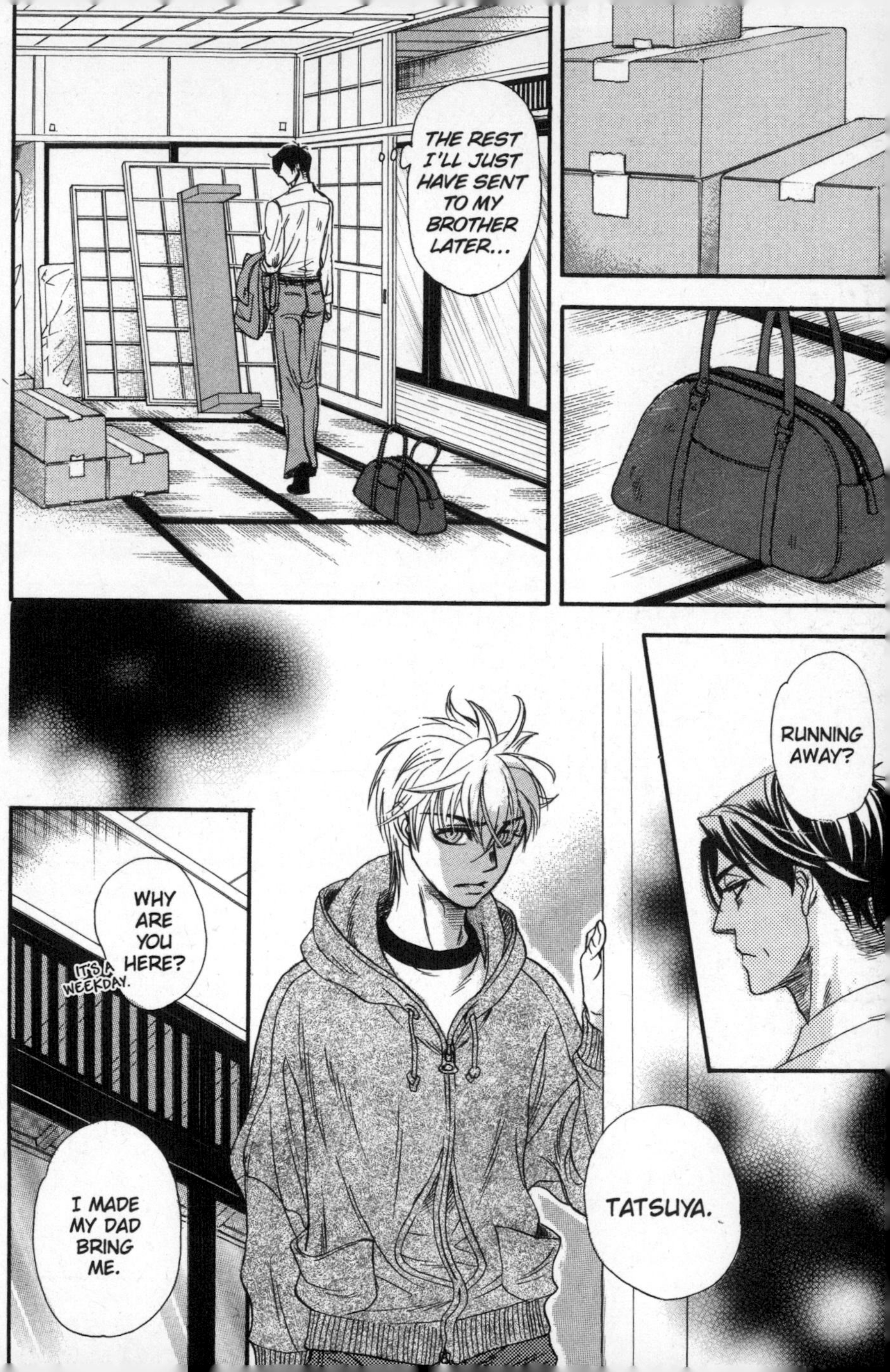
THE REST I'LL JUST HAVE SENT TO MY BROTHER LATER...
RUNNING AWAY?
TATSUYA.
WHY ARE YOU HERE?
IT'S A WEEKDAY.
I MADE MY DAD BRING ME.

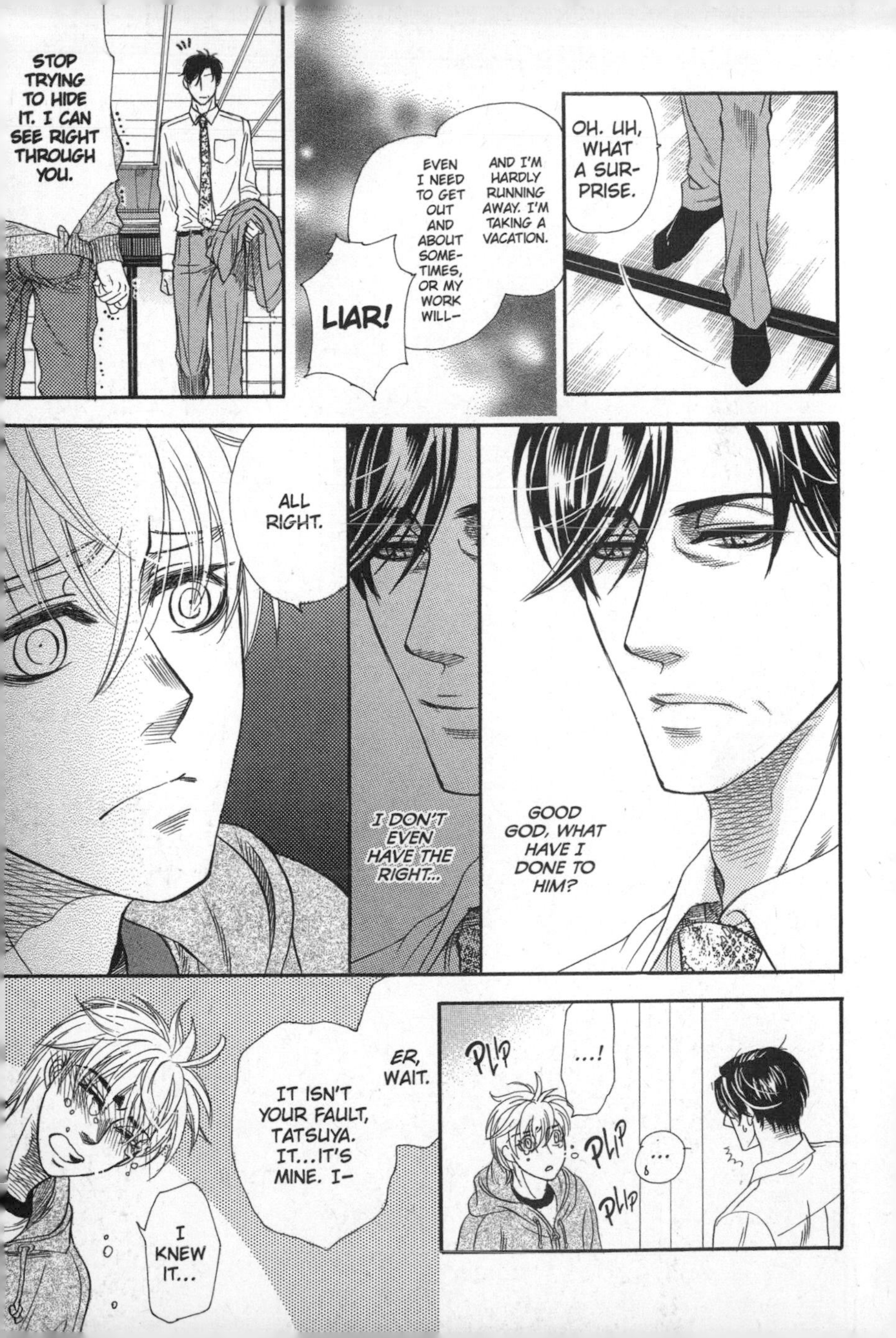
OH. UH, WHAT A SURPRISE.
AND I'M HARDLY RUNNING AWAY. I'M TAKING A VACATION.
EVEN I NEED TO GET OUT AND ABOUT SOMETIMES, OR MY WORK WILL-
LIAR!
STOP TRYING TO HIDE IT. I CAN SEE RIGHT THROUGH YOU.
GOOD GOD, WHAT HAVE I DONE TO HIM?
I DON'T EVEN HAVE THE RIGHT...
ALL RIGHT.
...!
PLIP
...
PLIP
PLIP
ER, WAIT.
IT ISN'T YOUR FAULT, TATSUYA. IT...IT'S MINE. I-
I KNEW IT...

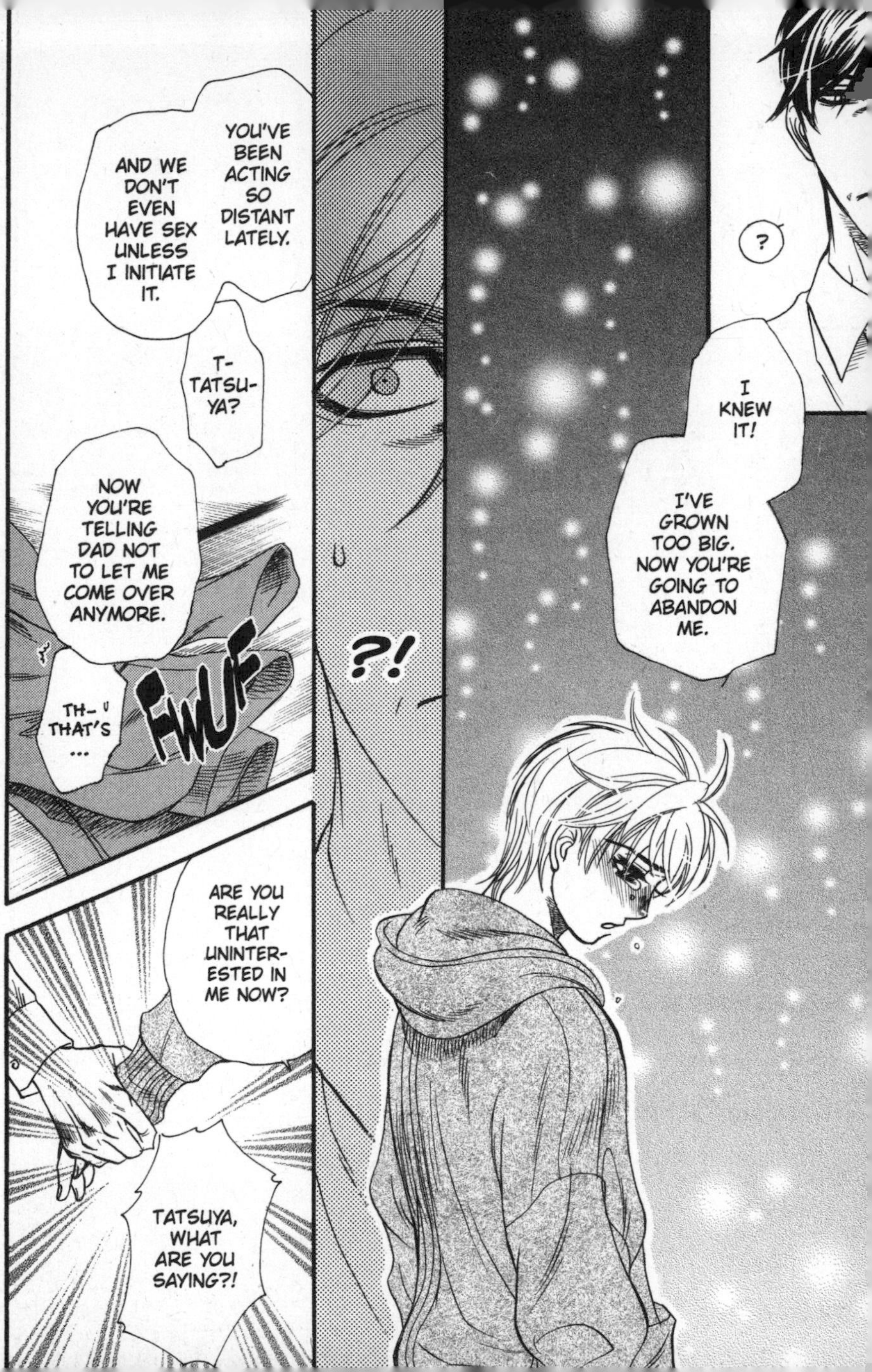
?
I KNEW IT!
I'VE GROWN TOO BIG. NOW YOU'RE GOING TO ABANDON ME.
?!
YOU'VE BEEN ACTING SO DISTANT LATELY.
AND WE DON'T EVEN HAVE SEX UNLESS I INITIATE IT.
T-TATSU-YA?
NOW YOU'RE TELLING DAD NOT TO LET ME COME OVER ANYMORE.
FWUF
TH- THAT'S ...
ARE YOU REALLY THAT UNINTER-ESTED IN ME NOW?
TATSUYA, WHAT ARE YOU SAYING?!

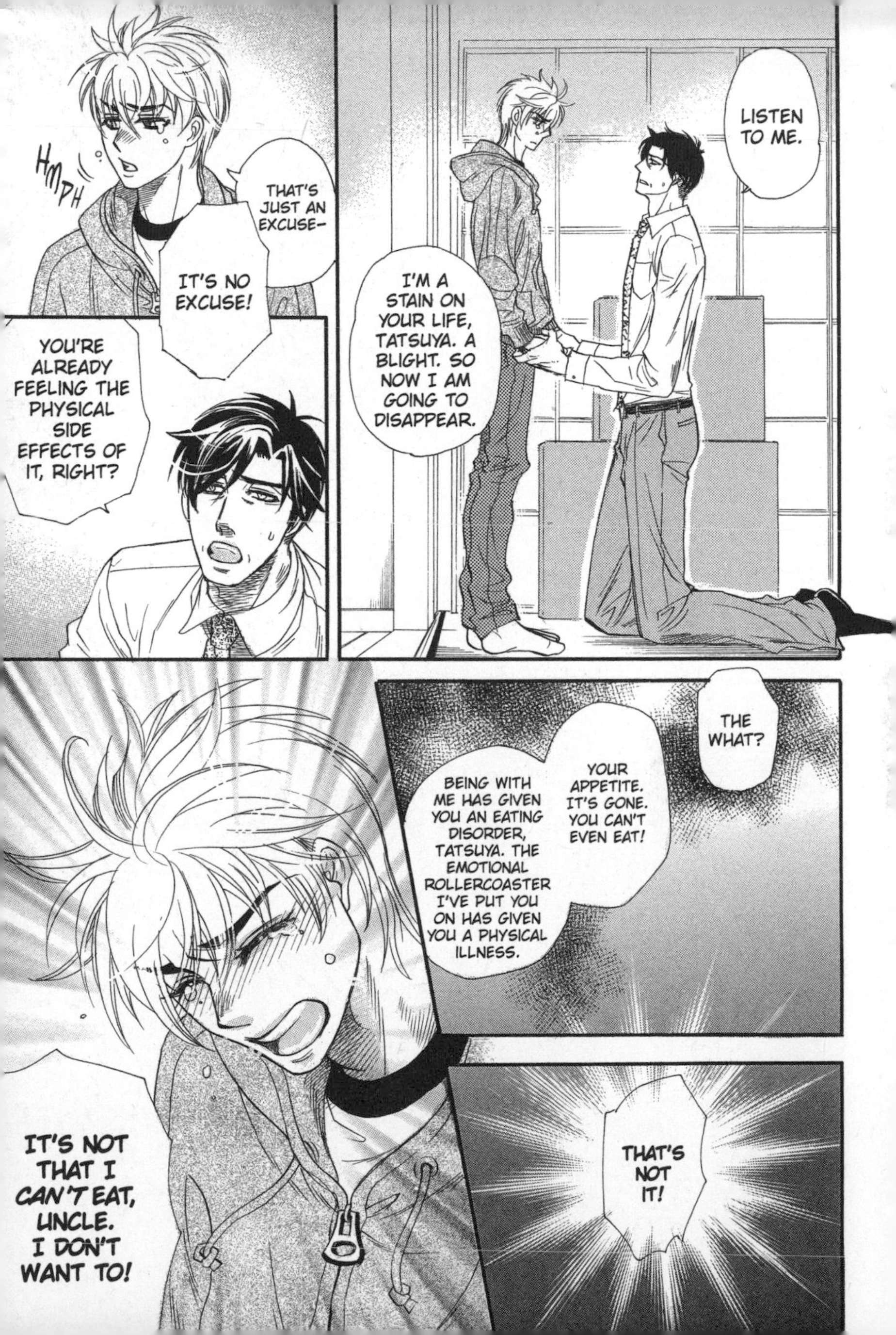
LISTEN TO ME.
I'M A STAIN ON YOUR LIFE, TATSUYA. A BLIGHT. SO NOW I AM GOING TO DISAPPEAR.
HMPH
THAT'S JUST AN EXCUSE–
IT'S NO EXCUSE!
YOU'RE ALREADY FEELING THE PHYSICAL SIDE EFFECTS OF IT, RIGHT?
THE WHAT?
YOUR APPETITE. IT'S GONE. YOU CAN'T EVEN EAT!
BEING WITH ME HAS GIVEN YOU AN EATING DISORDER, TATSUYA. THE EMOTIONAL ROLLERCOASTER I'VE PUT YOU ON HAS GIVEN YOU A PHYSICAL ILLNESS.
THAT'S NOT IT!
IT'S NOT THAT I CAN'T EAT, UNCLE. I DON'T WANT TO!

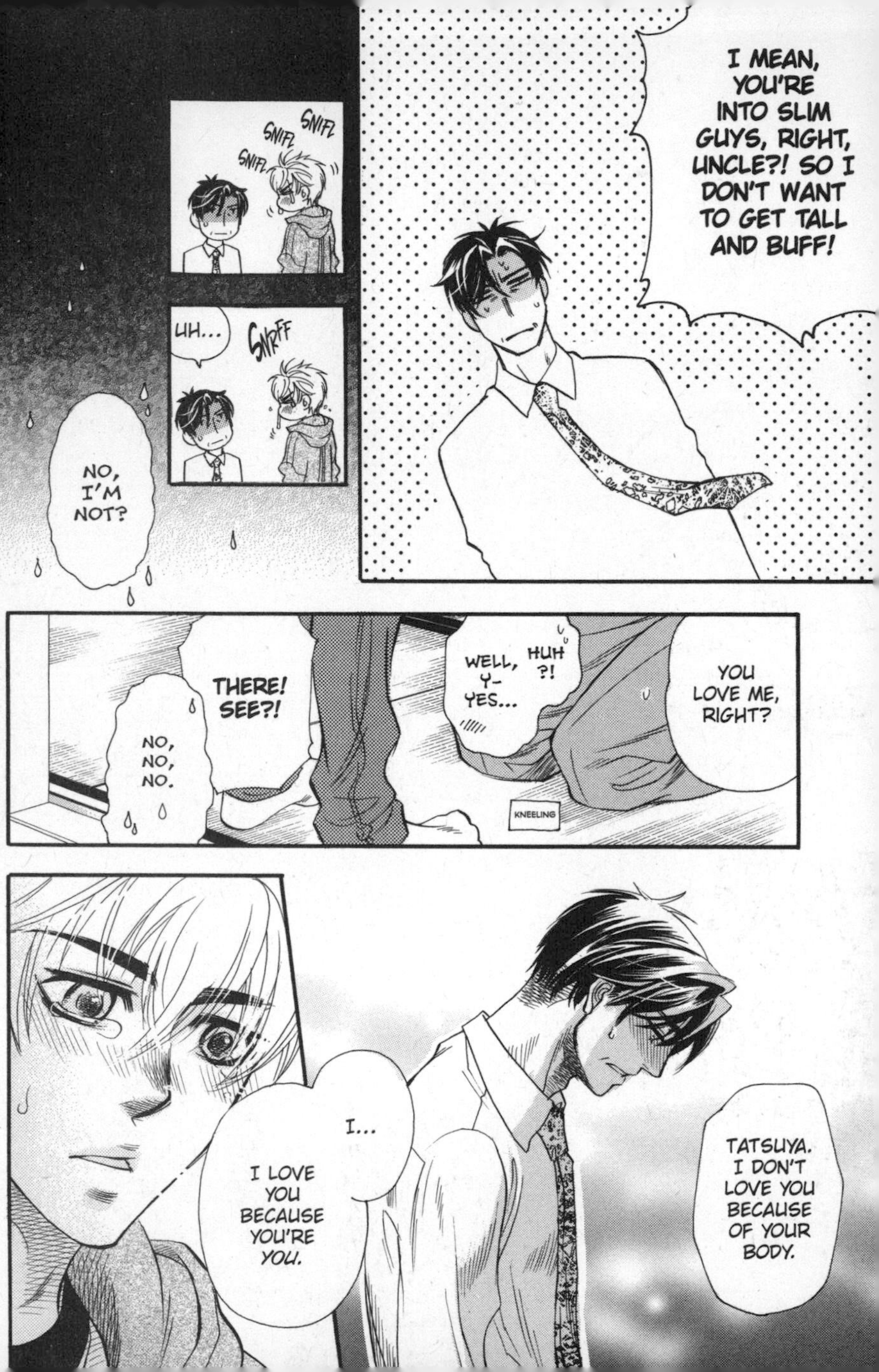
I MEAN, YOU'RE INTO SLIM GUYS, RIGHT, UNCLE?! SO I DON'T WANT TO GET TALL AND BUFF!
SNIFL
SNIFL
SNIFL
UH...
SNRFF
NO, I'M NOT?
YOU LOVE ME, RIGHT?
HUH?!
WELL, Y-YES...
THERE! SEE?!
NO, NO, NO.
KNEELING
TATSUYA. I DON'T LOVE YOU BECAUSE OF YOUR BODY.
I...
I LOVE YOU BECAUSE YOU'RE YOU.

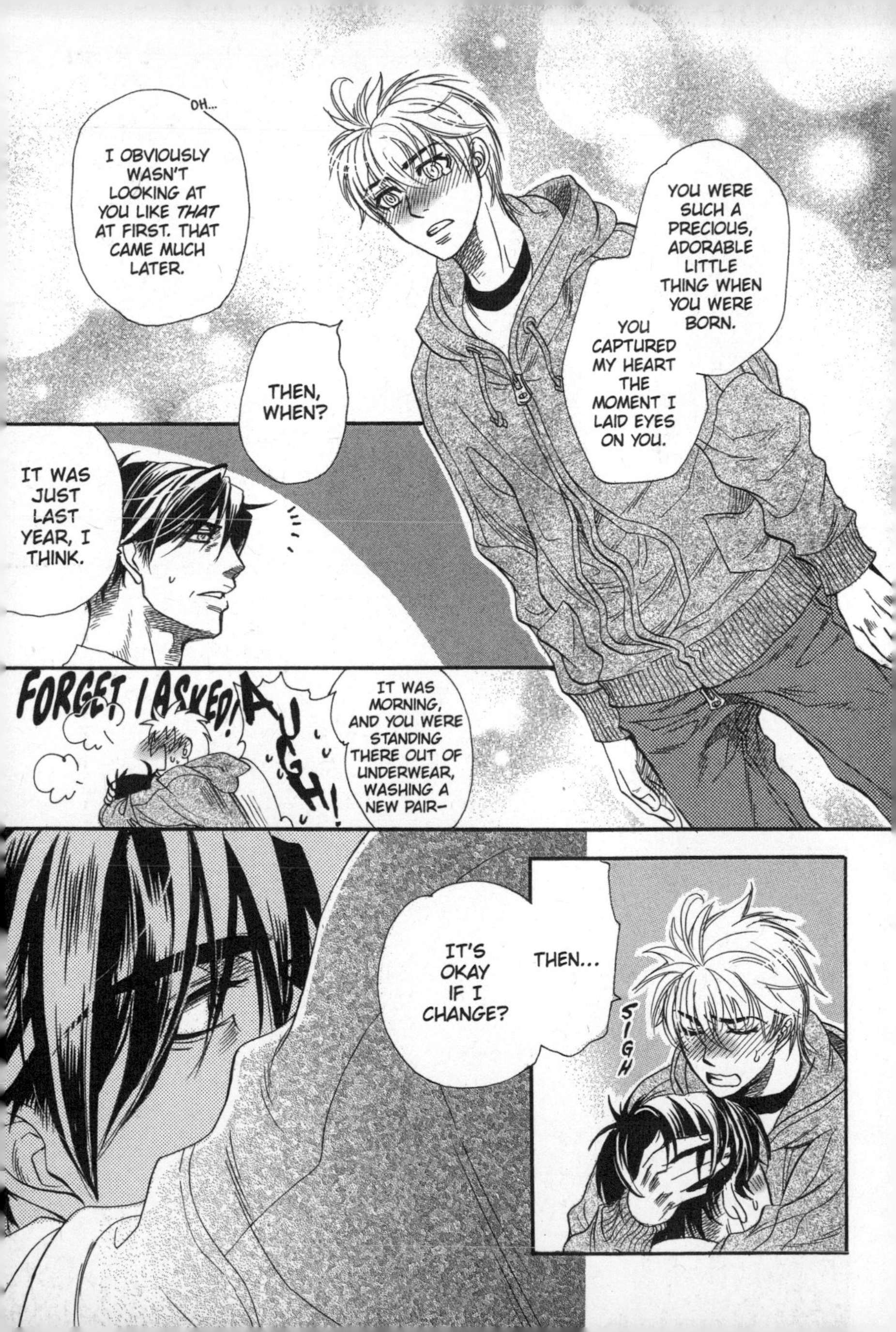
YOU WERE SUCH A PRECIOUS, ADORABLE LITTLE THING WHEN YOU WERE BORN.
YOU CAPTURED MY HEART THE MOMENT I LAID EYES ON YOU.
OH...
I OBVIOUSLY WASN'T LOOKING AT YOU LIKE *THAT* AT FIRST. THAT CAME MUCH LATER.
THEN, WHEN?
IT WAS JUST LAST YEAR, I THINK.
IT WAS MORNING, AND YOU WERE STANDING THERE OUT OF UNDERWEAR, WASHING A NEW PAIR–
AUGH!
FORGET I ASKED!
SIGH
THEN...
IT'S OKAY IF I CHANGE?

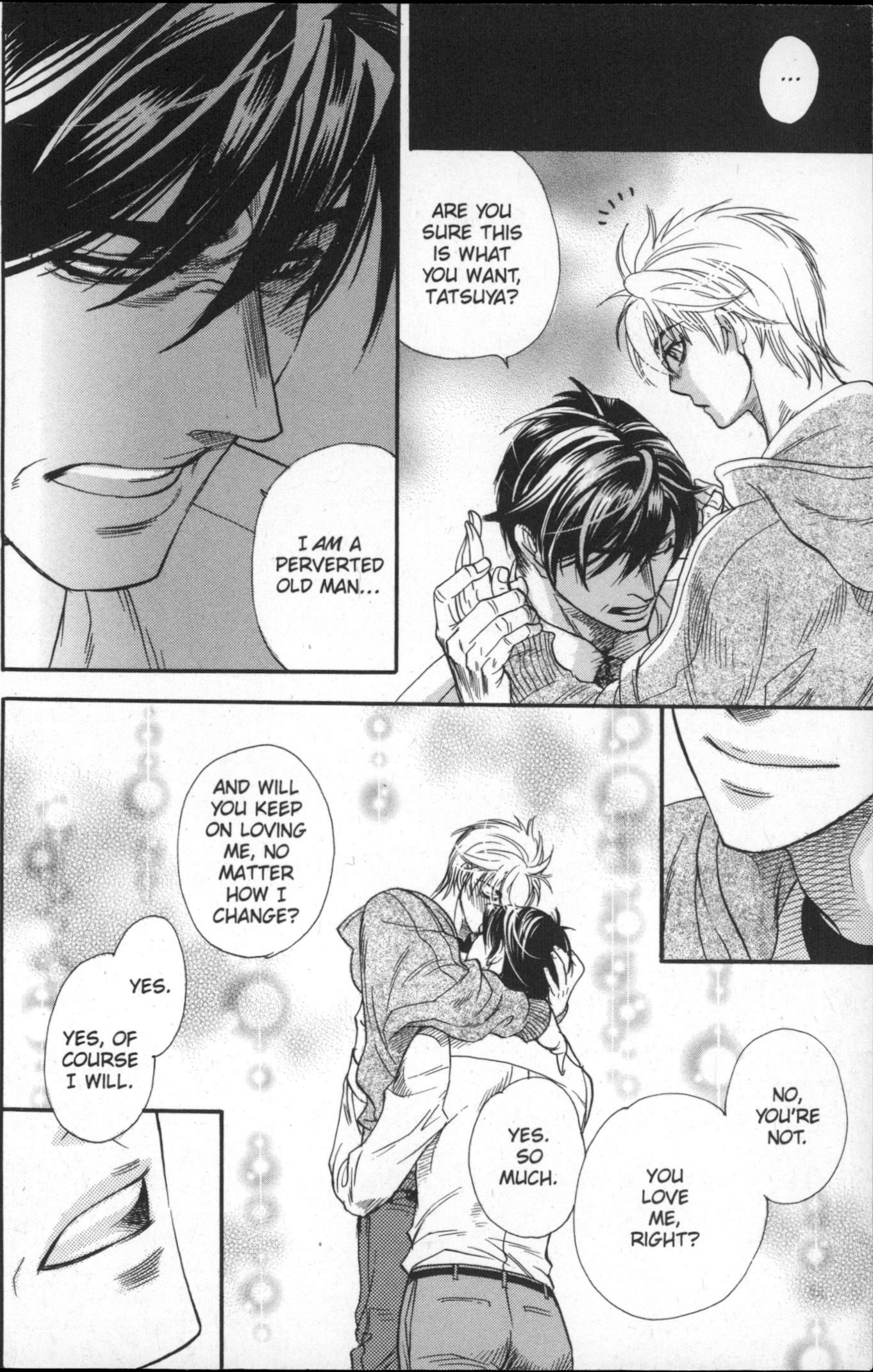
...
ARE YOU SURE THIS IS WHAT YOU WANT, TATSUYA?
I AM A PERVERTED OLD MAN...
NO, YOU'RE NOT.
YOU LOVE ME, RIGHT?
YES. SO MUCH.
AND WILL YOU KEEP ON LOVING ME, NO MATTER HOW I CHANGE?
YES.
YES, OF COURSE I WILL.

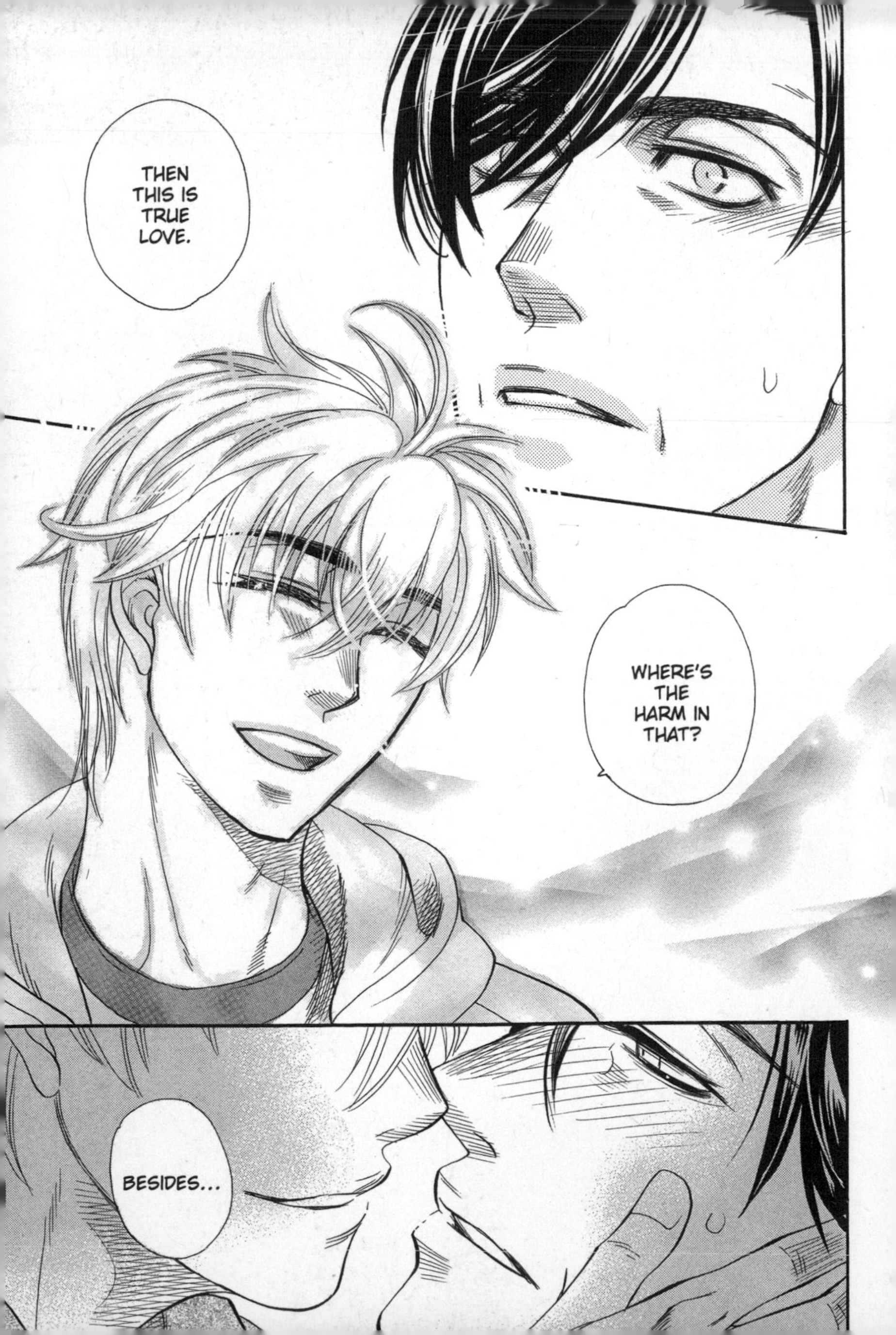
THEN THIS IS TRUE LOVE.
WHERE'S THE HARM IN THAT?
BESIDES...

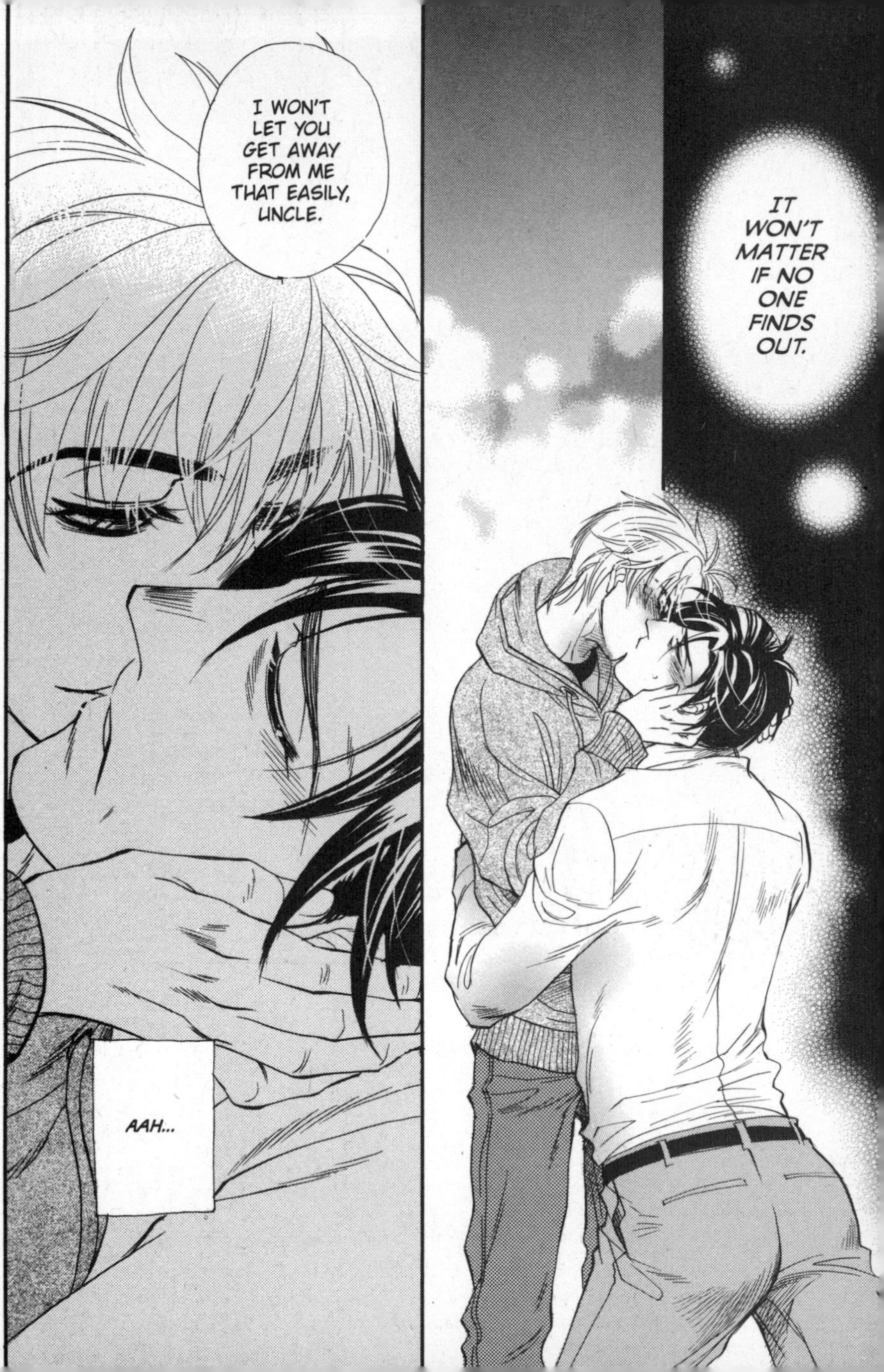
IT WON'T MATTER IF NO ONE FINDS OUT.
I WON'T LET YOU GET AWAY FROM ME THAT EASILY, UNCLE.
AAH...

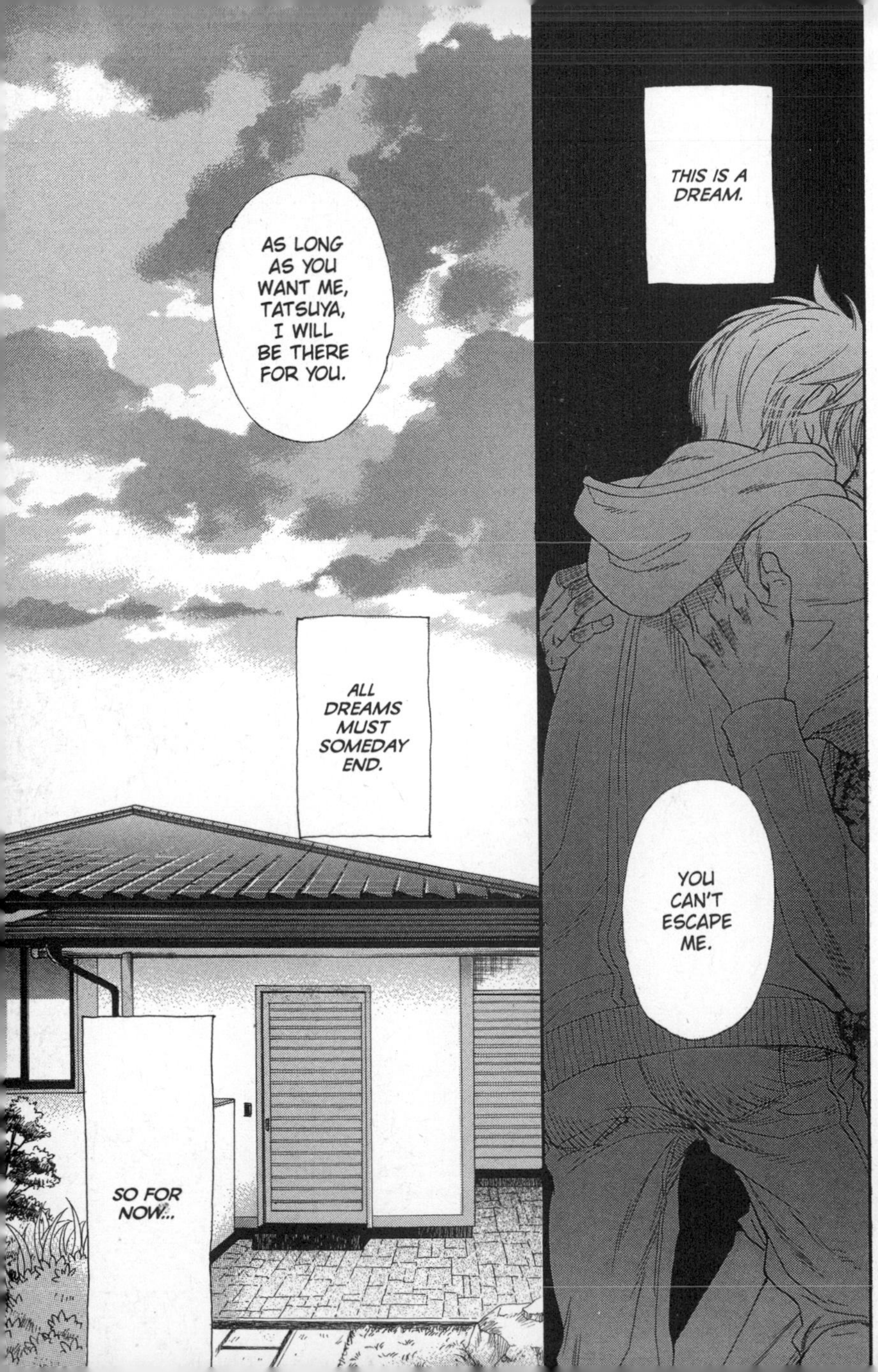
THIS IS A DREAM.
YOU CAN'T ESCAPE ME.
AS LONG AS YOU WANT ME, TATSUYA, I WILL BE THERE FOR YOU.
ALL DREAMS MUST SOMEDAY END.
SO FOR NOW...

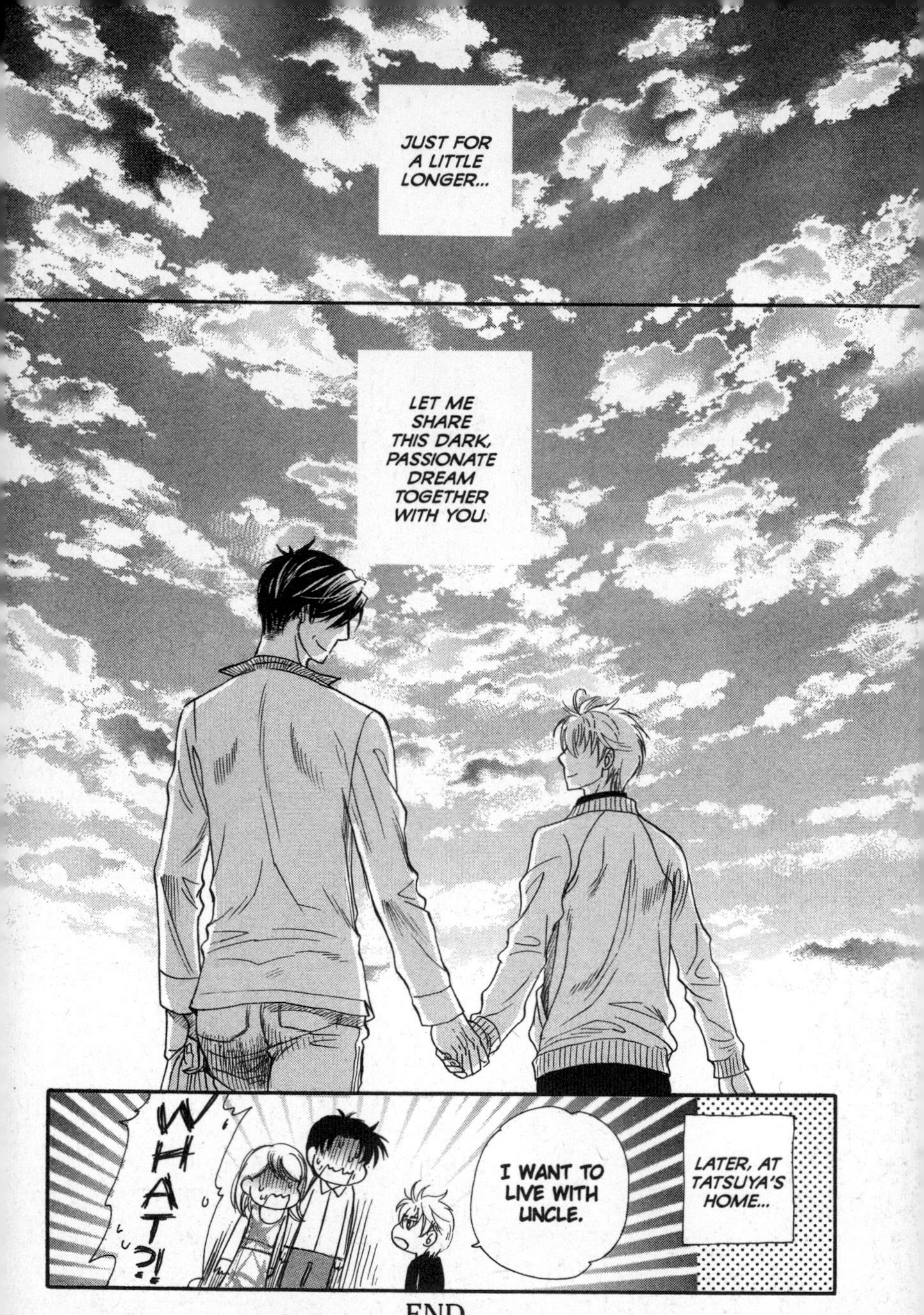
JUST FOR A LITTLE LONGER...
LET ME SHARE THIS DARK, PASSIONATE DREAM TOGETHER WITH YOU.
LATER, AT TATSUYA'S HOME...
I WANT TO LIVE WITH UNCLE.
WHAT?!

END

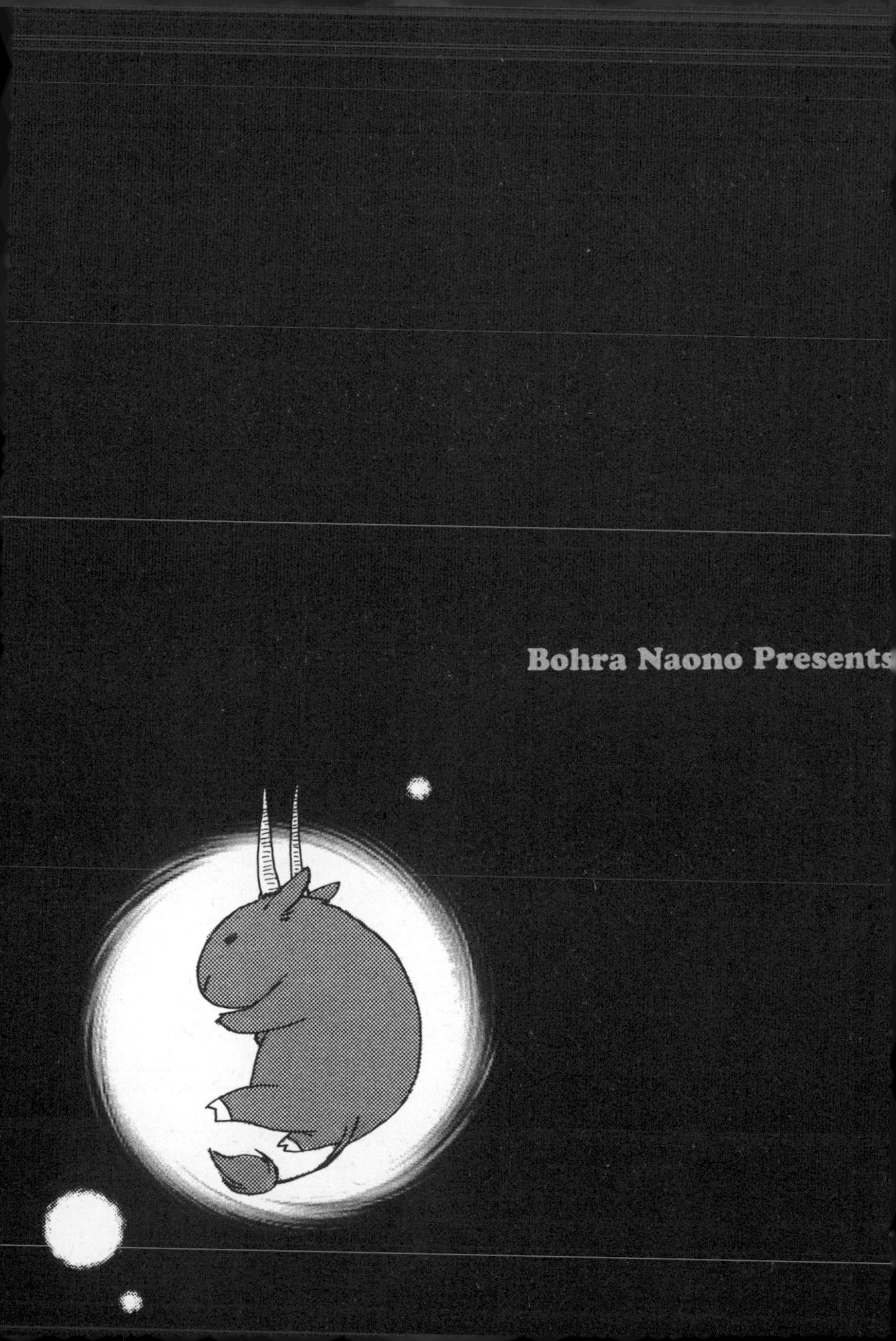
Bohra Naono Presents

The Story Behind the Beard

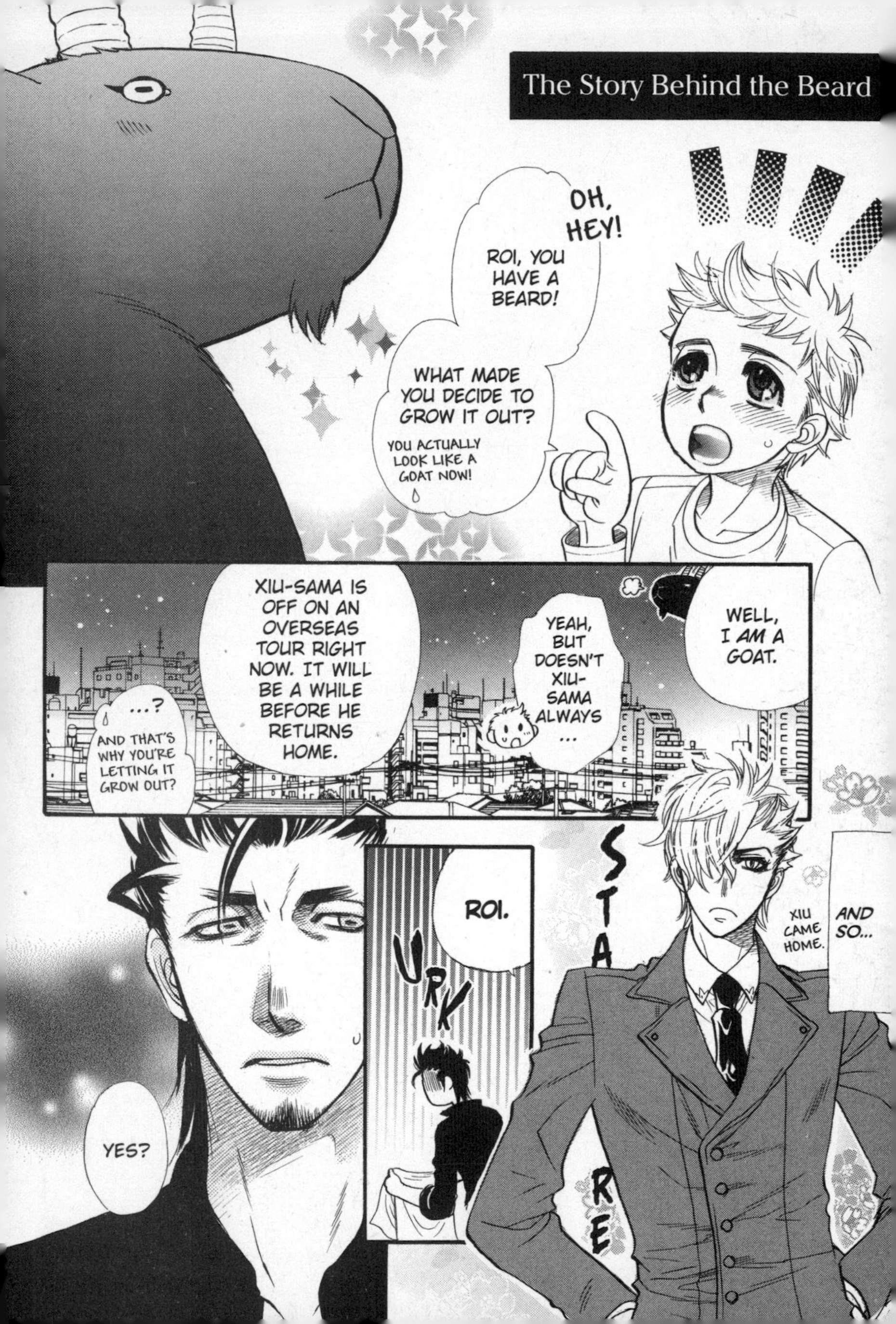

OH, HEY!
ROI, YOU HAVE A BEARD!
WHAT MADE YOU DECIDE TO GROW IT OUT?
YOU ACTUALLY LOOK LIKE A GOAT NOW!
WELL, I AM A GOAT.
YEAH, BUT DOESN'T XIU-SAMA ALWAYS ...
XIU-SAMA IS OFF ON AN OVERSEAS TOUR RIGHT NOW. IT WILL BE A WHILE BEFORE HE RETURNS HOME.
...?
AND THAT'S WHY YOU'RE LETTING IT GROW OUT?
AND SO...
XIU CAME HOME.
STARE
ROI.
URK
YES?

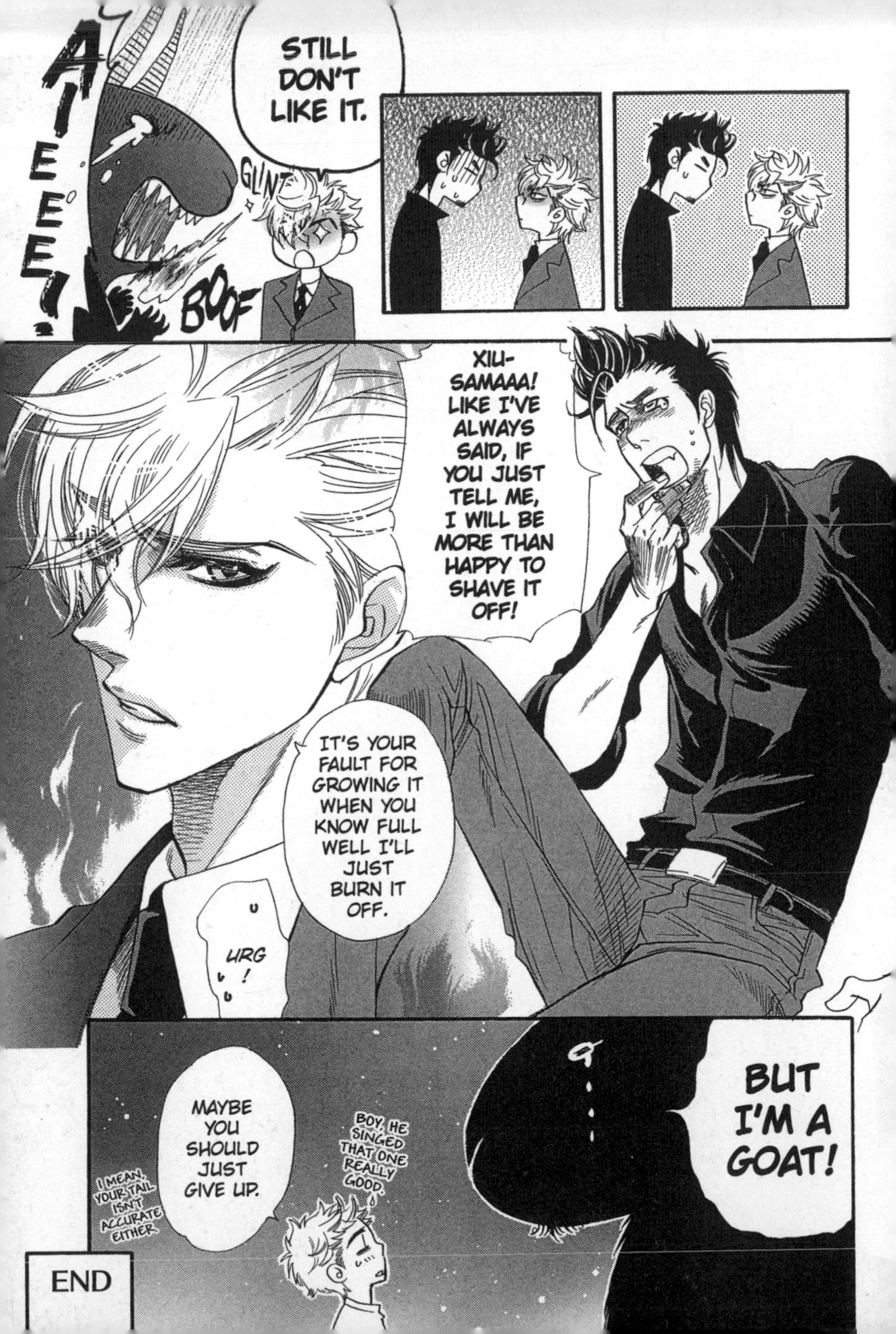
STILL DON'T LIKE IT.
GLINT
AIEEEE!
BOOF
XIU-SAMAAA! LIKE I'VE ALWAYS SAID, IF YOU JUST TELL ME, I WILL BE MORE THAN HAPPY TO SHAVE IT OFF!
IT'S YOUR FAULT FOR GROWING IT WHEN YOU KNOW FULL WELL I'LL JUST BURN IT OFF.
URG!
BUT I'M A GOAT!
MAYBE YOU SHOULD JUST GIVE UP.
BOY, HE SINGED THAT ONE REALLY GOOD.
I MEAN, YOUR TAIL ISN'T ACCURATE EITHER.
END

彼方者の
困惑
あっちものの こんわく

Midnight Stranger

Bohra Naono Presents

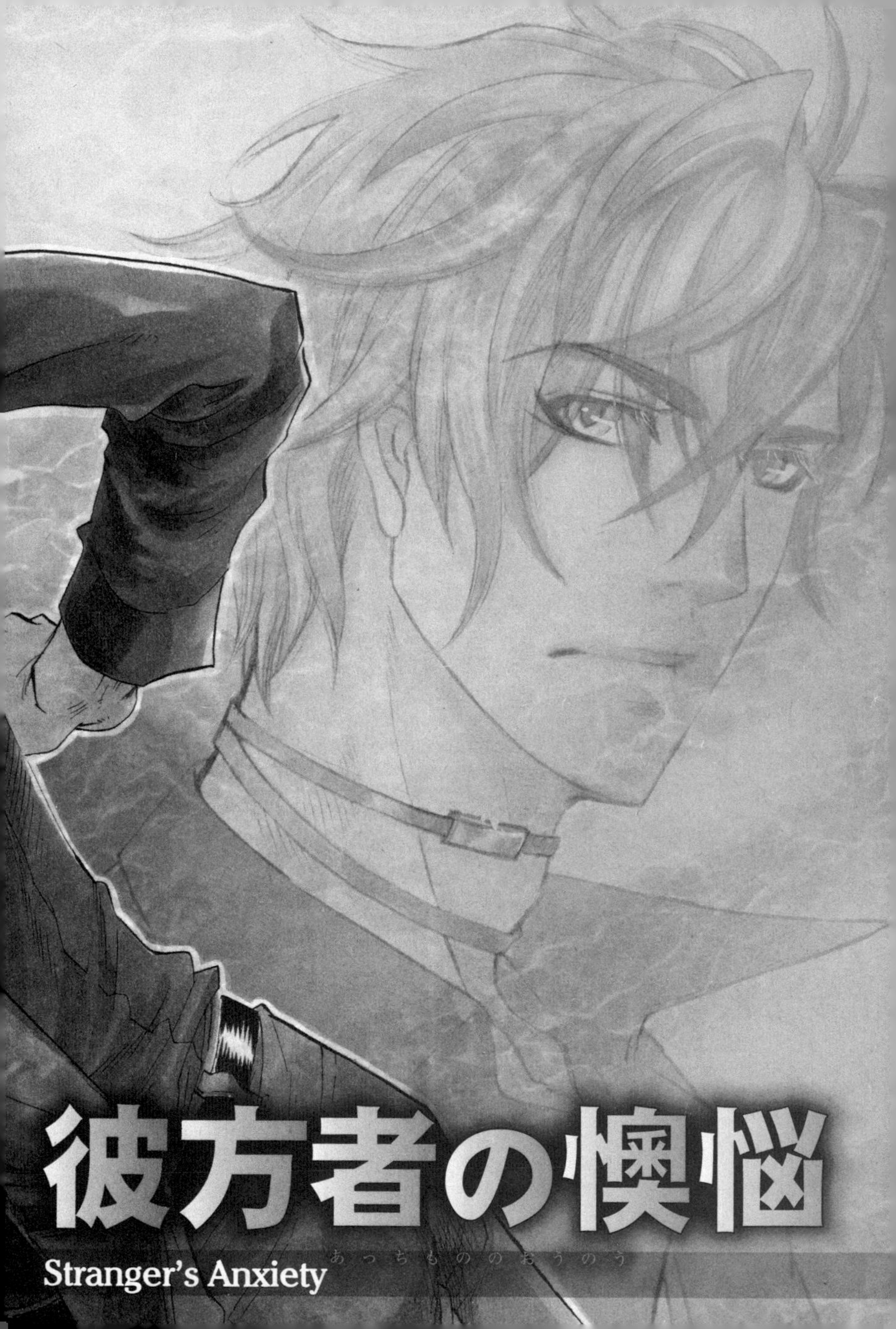
彼方者の懊悩
あっちもののおうのう
Stranger's Anxiety

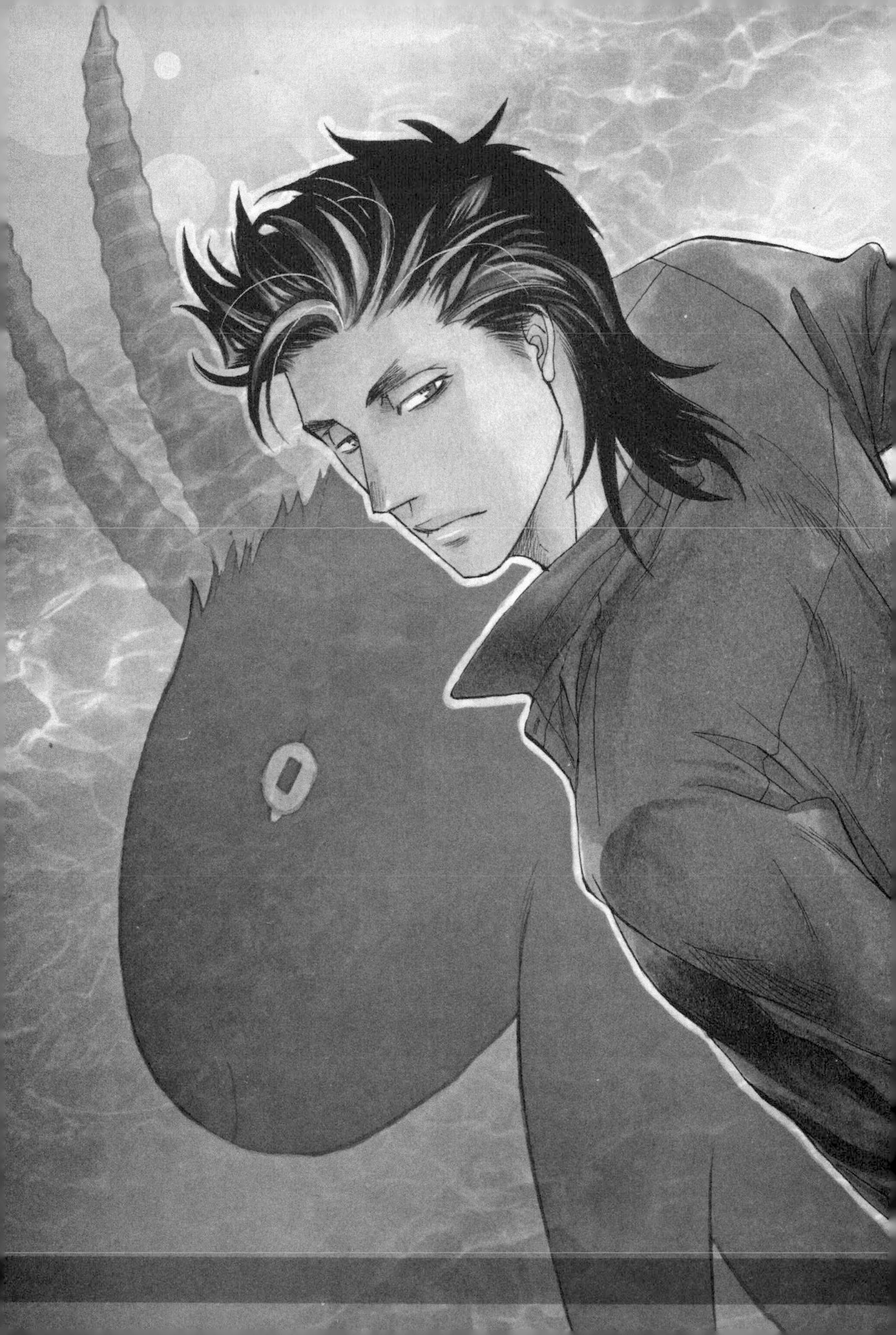

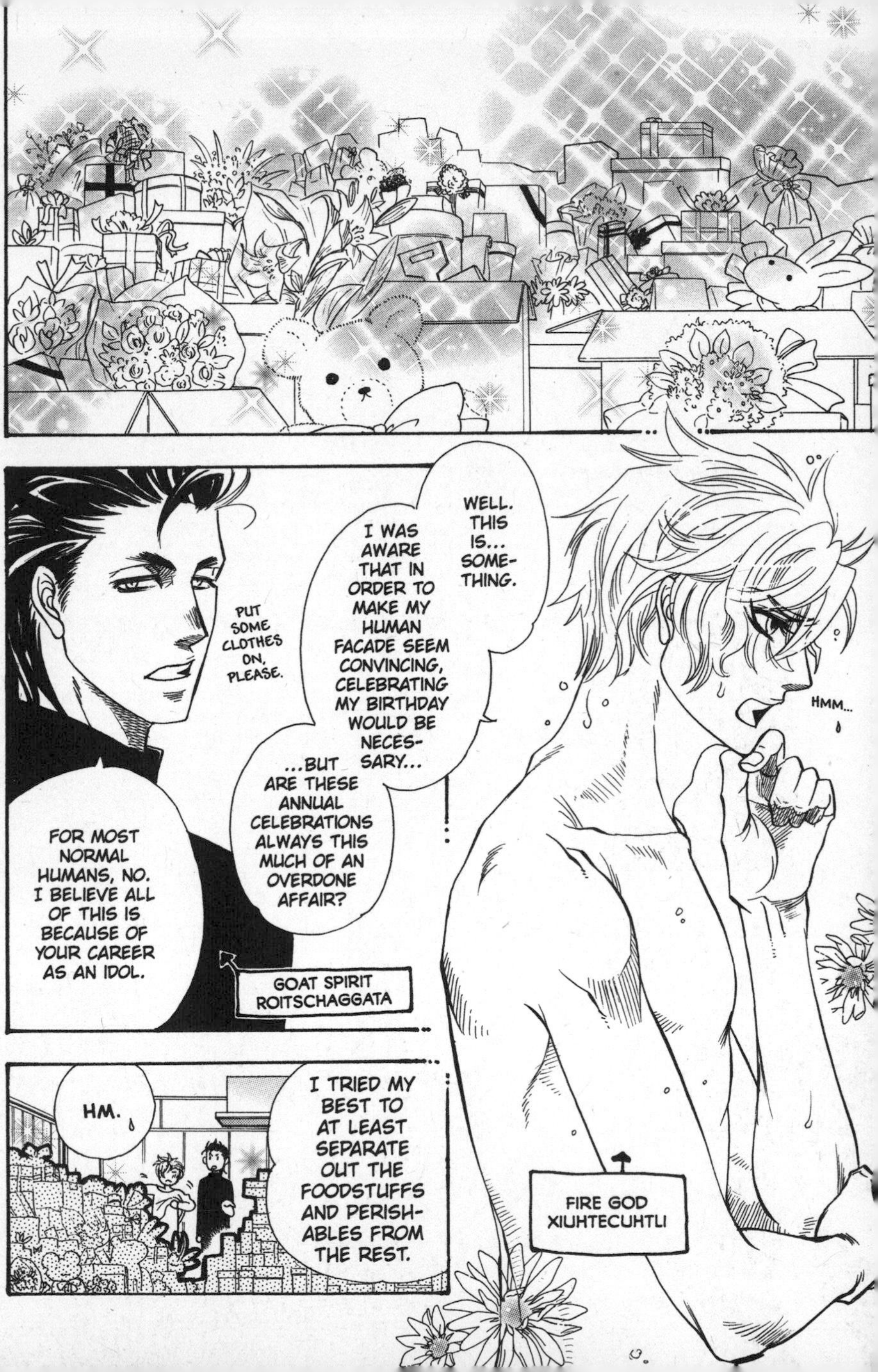

HMM...
FIRE GOD XIUHTECUHTLI
WELL. THIS IS... SOME-THING.
I WAS AWARE THAT IN ORDER TO MAKE MY HUMAN FACADE SEEM CONVINCING, CELEBRATING MY BIRTHDAY WOULD BE NECES-SARY...
...BUT ARE THESE ANNUAL CELEBRATIONS ALWAYS THIS MUCH OF AN OVERDONE AFFAIR?
PUT SOME CLOTHES ON, PLEASE.
FOR MOST NORMAL HUMANS, NO. I BELIEVE ALL OF THIS IS BECAUSE OF YOUR CAREER AS AN IDOL.
GOAT SPIRIT ROITSCHAGGATA
I TRIED MY BEST TO AT LEAST SEPARATE OUT THE FOODSTUFFS AND PERISH-ABLES FROM THE REST.
HM.

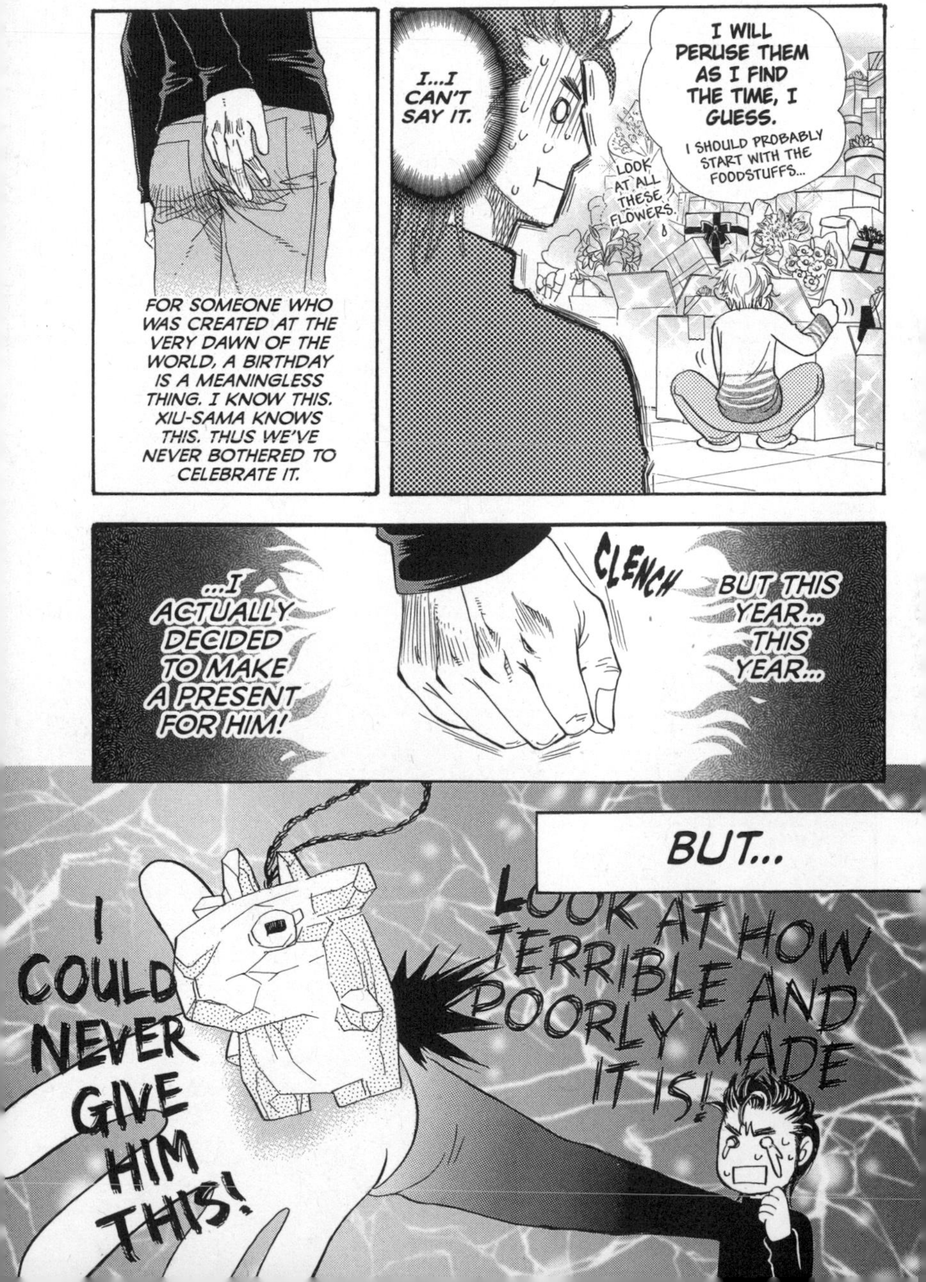
I WILL PERUSE THEM AS I FIND THE TIME, I GUESS.
I SHOULD PROBABLY START WITH THE FOODSTUFFS...
LOOK AT ALL THESE FLOWERS.
I...I CAN'T SAY IT.
FOR SOMEONE WHO WAS CREATED AT THE VERY DAWN OF THE WORLD, A BIRTHDAY IS A MEANINGLESS THING. I KNOW THIS. XIU-SAMA KNOWS THIS. THUS WE'VE NEVER BOTHERED TO CELEBRATE IT.
BUT THIS YEAR... THIS YEAR...
CLENCH
...I ACTUALLY DECIDED TO MAKE A PRESENT FOR HIM!
BUT...
LOOK AT HOW TERRIBLE AND POORLY MADE IT IS!
I COULD NEVER GIVE HIM THIS!

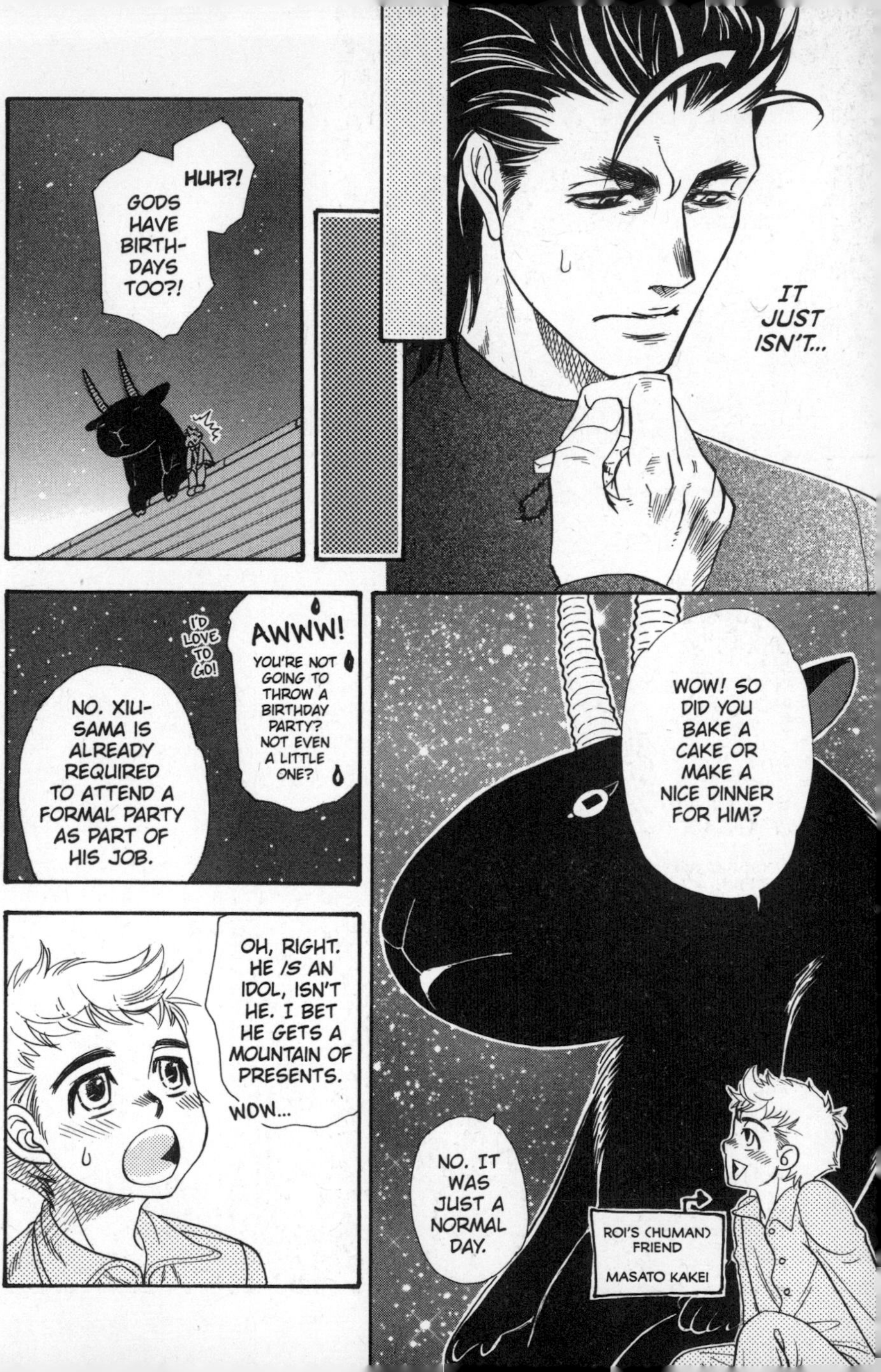
IT JUST ISN'T...
HUH?! GODS HAVE BIRTHDAYS TOO?!
WOW! SO DID YOU BAKE A CAKE OR MAKE A NICE DINNER FOR HIM?
NO. IT WAS JUST A NORMAL DAY.
ROI'S (HUMAN) FRIEND
MASATO KAKEI
AWWW! YOU'RE NOT GOING TO THROW A BIRTHDAY PARTY? NOT EVEN A LITTLE ONE?
I'D LOVE TO GO!
NO. XIU-SAMA IS ALREADY REQUIRED TO ATTEND A FORMAL PARTY AS PART OF HIS JOB.
OH, RIGHT. HE *IS* AN IDOL, ISN'T HE. I BET HE GETS A MOUNTAIN OF PRESENTS.
WOW...

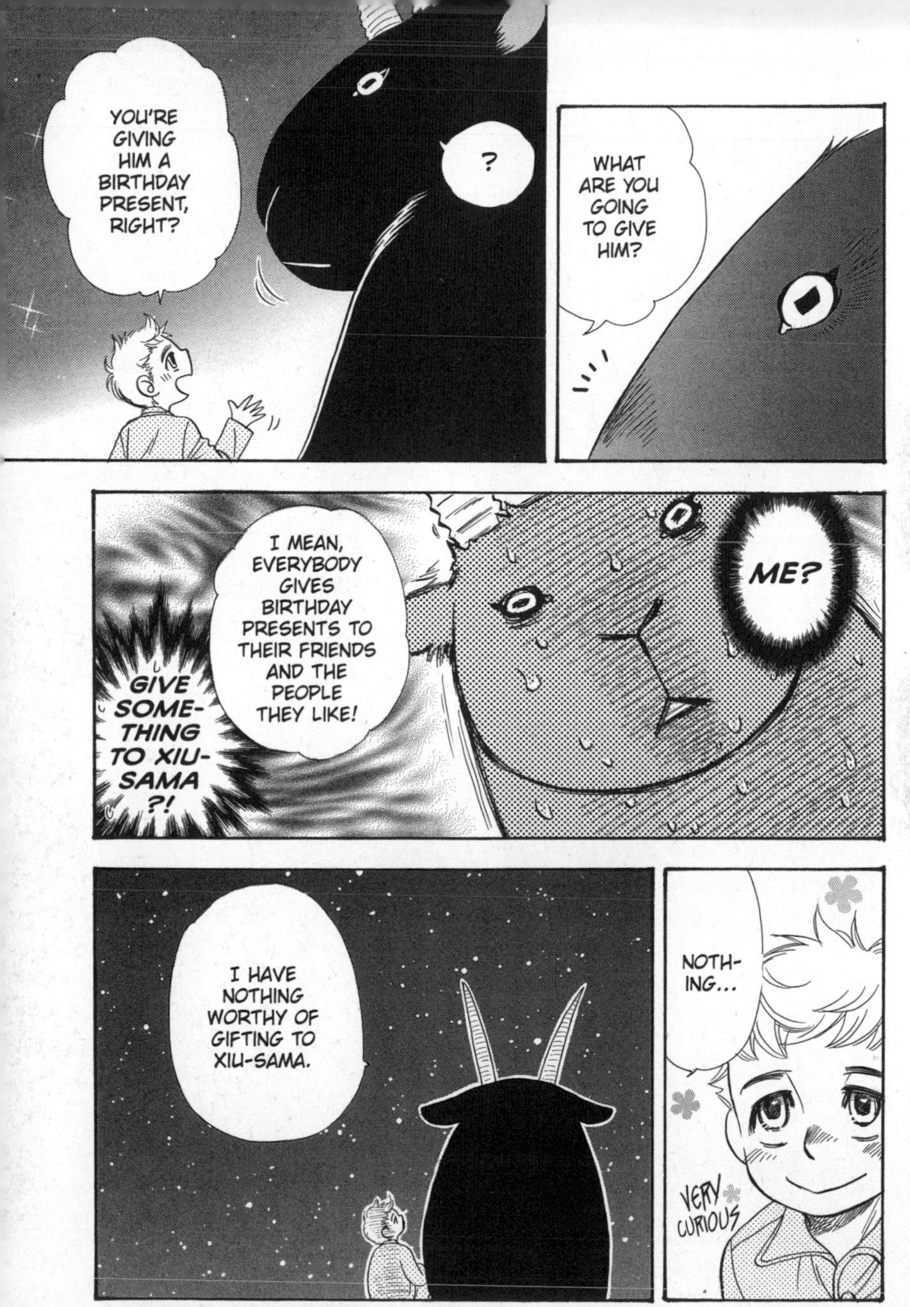
WHAT ARE YOU GOING TO GIVE HIM?
?
YOU'RE GIVING HIM A BIRTHDAY PRESENT, RIGHT?
ME?
I MEAN, EVERYBODY GIVES BIRTHDAY PRESENTS TO THEIR FRIENDS AND THE PEOPLE THEY LIKE!
GIVE SOMETHING TO XIU-SAMA?!
NOTHING...
VERY CURIOUS
I HAVE NOTHING WORTHY OF GIFTING TO XIU-SAMA.

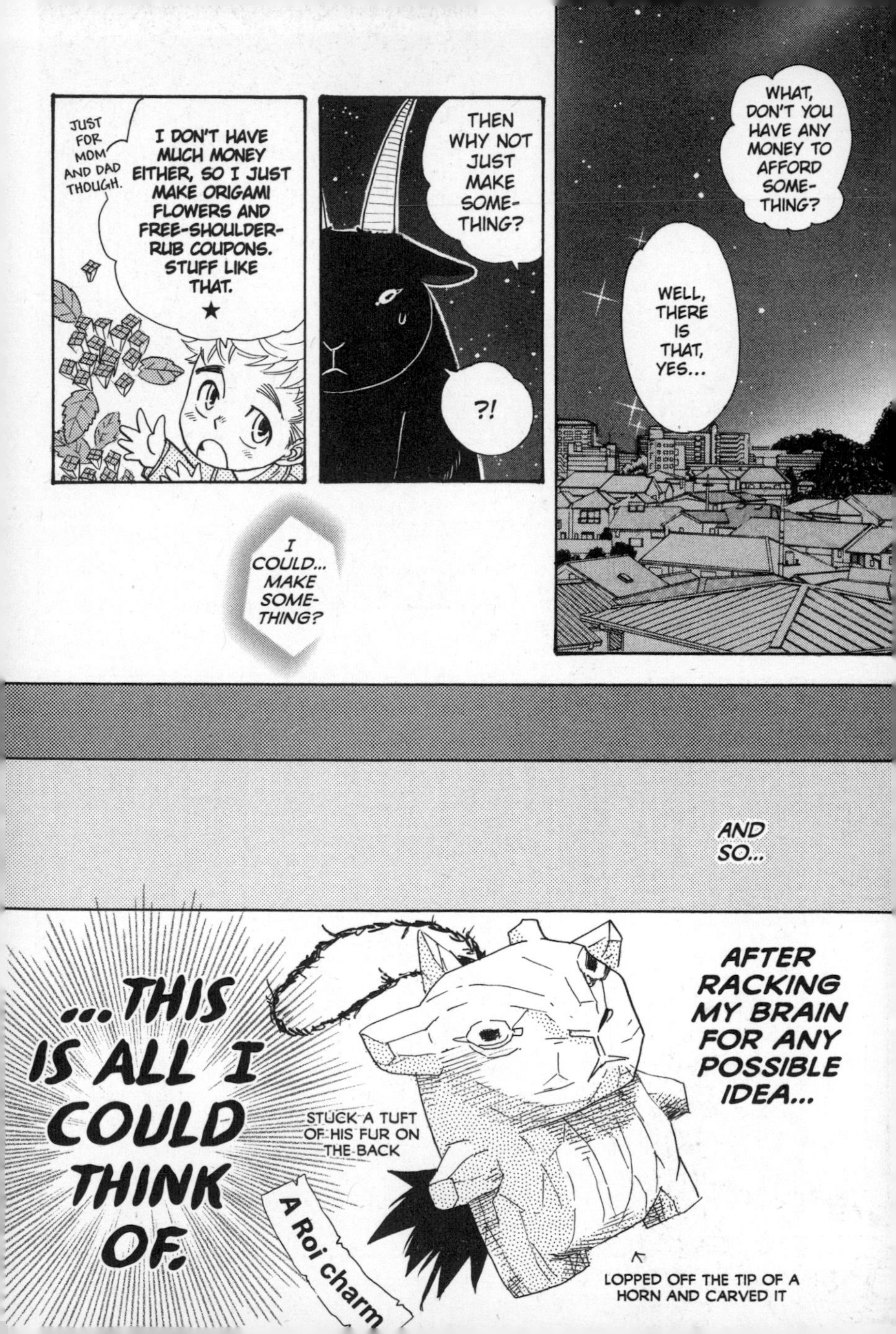
WHAT, DON'T YOU HAVE ANY MONEY TO AFFORD SOME-THING?
WELL, THERE IS THAT, YES...
THEN WHY NOT JUST MAKE SOME-THING?
?!
I DON'T HAVE MUCH MONEY EITHER, SO I JUST MAKE ORIGAMI FLOWERS AND FREE-SHOULDER-RUB COUPONS. STUFF LIKE THAT. ★
JUST FOR MOM AND DAD THOUGH.
I COULD... MAKE SOME-THING?
AND SO...
AFTER RACKING MY BRAIN FOR ANY POSSIBLE IDEA...
...THIS IS ALL I COULD THINK OF.
STUCK A TUFT OF HIS FUR ON THE BACK
A Roi charm
LOPPED OFF THE TIP OF A HORN AND CARVED IT

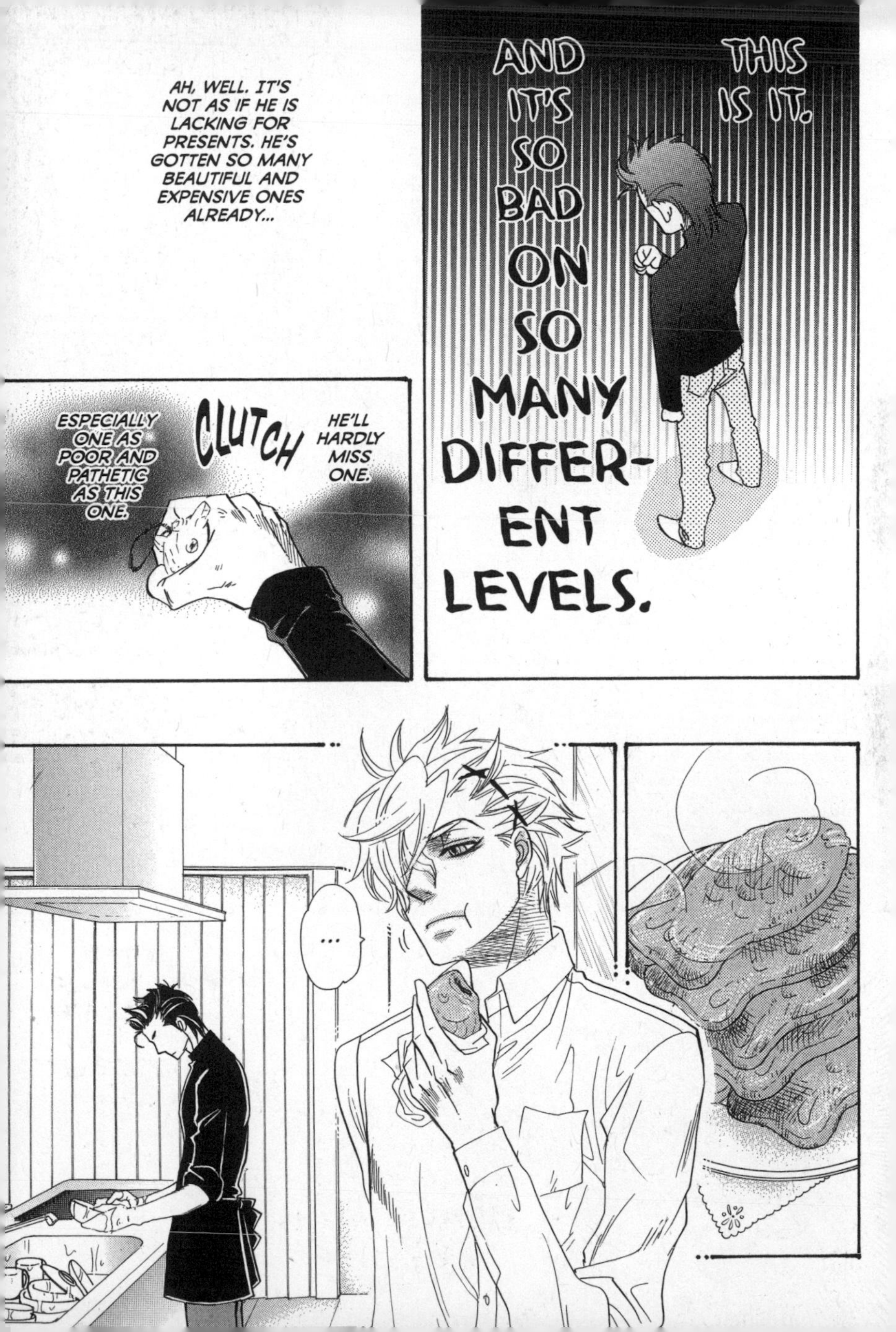
THIS IS IT.
AND IT'S SO BAD ON SO MANY DIFFER-ENT LEVELS.
AH, WELL. IT'S NOT AS IF HE IS LACKING FOR PRESENTS. HE'S GOTTEN SO MANY BEAUTIFUL AND EXPENSIVE ONES ALREADY...
HE'LL HARDLY MISS ONE.
CLUTCH
ESPECIALLY ONE AS POOR AND PATHETIC AS THIS ONE.
...

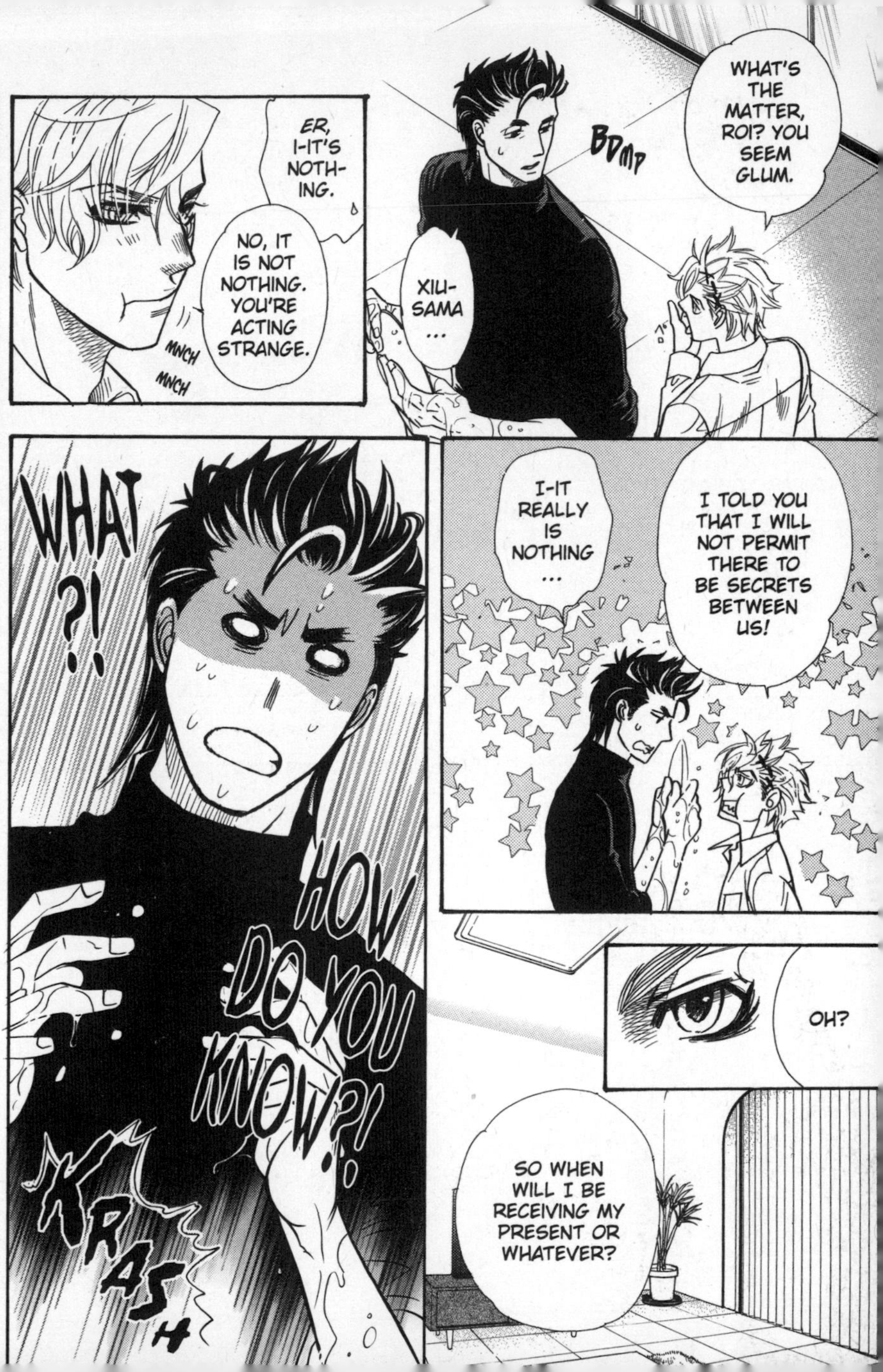
WHAT'S THE MATTER, ROI? YOU SEEM GLUM.
BDMP
XIU-SAMA...
ER, I-IT'S NOTH-ING.
NO, IT IS NOT NOTHING. YOU'RE ACTING STRANGE.
MNCH
MNCH
I TOLD YOU THAT I WILL NOT PERMIT THERE TO BE SECRETS BETWEEN US!
I-IT REALLY IS NOTHING...
OH?
SO WHEN WILL I BE RECEIVING MY PRESENT OR WHATEVER?
WHAT?!
HOW DO YOU KNOW?!
KRASH

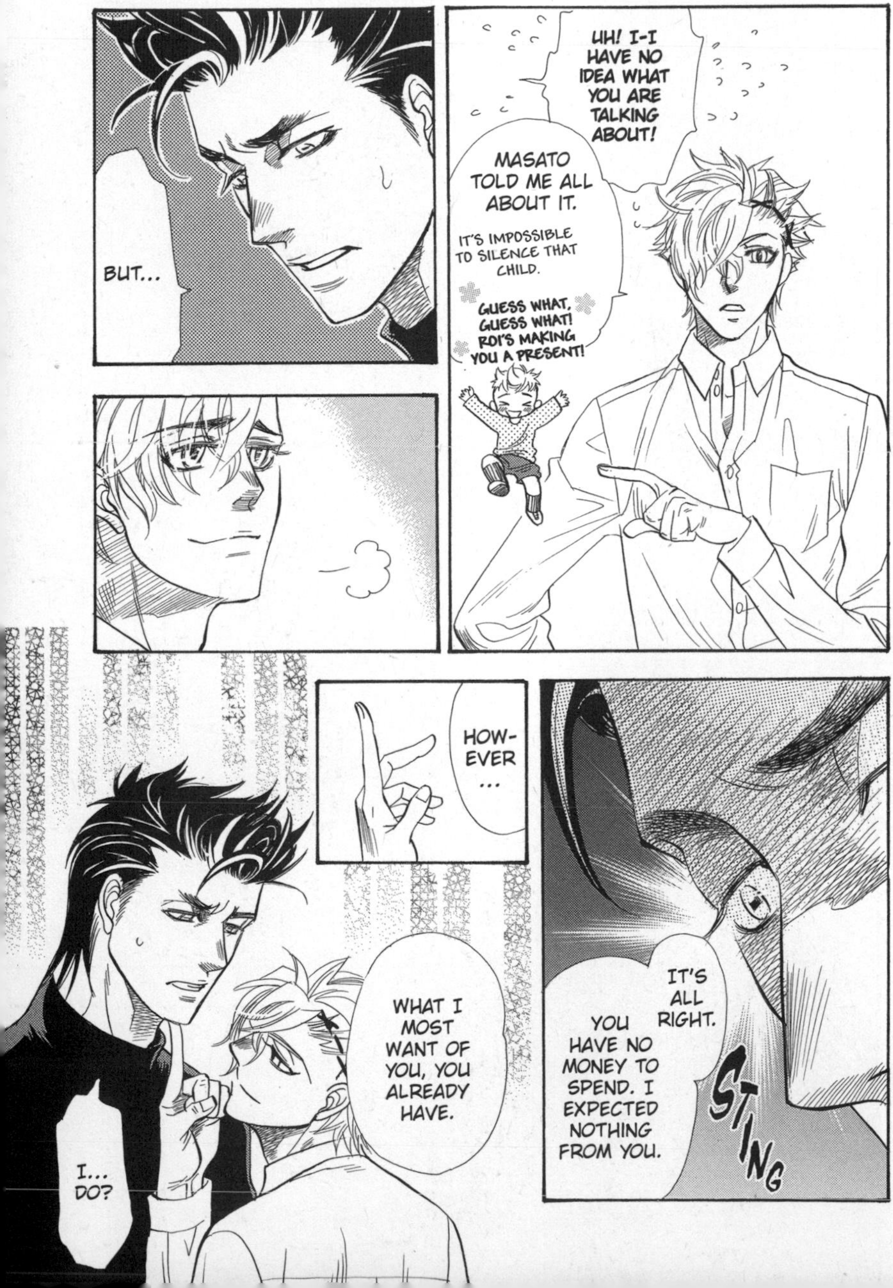
UH! I-I HAVE NO IDEA WHAT YOU ARE TALKING ABOUT!
MASATO TOLD ME ALL ABOUT IT.
IT'S IMPOSSIBLE TO SILENCE THAT CHILD.
GUESS WHAT, GUESS WHAT! RDI'S MAKING YOU A PRESENT!
BUT...
IT'S ALL RIGHT.
YOU HAVE NO MONEY TO SPEND. I EXPECTED NOTHING FROM YOU.
STING
HOW-EVER ...
WHAT I MOST WANT OF YOU, YOU ALREADY HAVE.
I... DO?

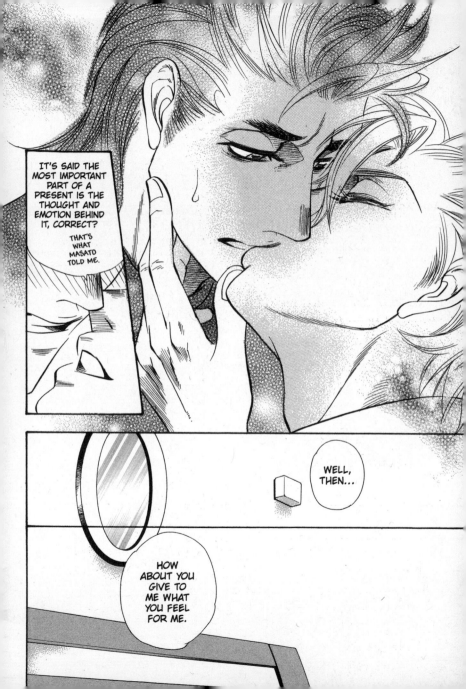

IT'S SAID THE MOST IMPORTANT PART OF A PRESENT IS THE THOUGHT AND EMOTION BEHIND IT, CORRECT?

THAT'S WHAT MASATO TOLD ME.

WELL, THEN...

HOW ABOUT YOU GIVE TO ME WHAT YOU FEEL FOR ME.

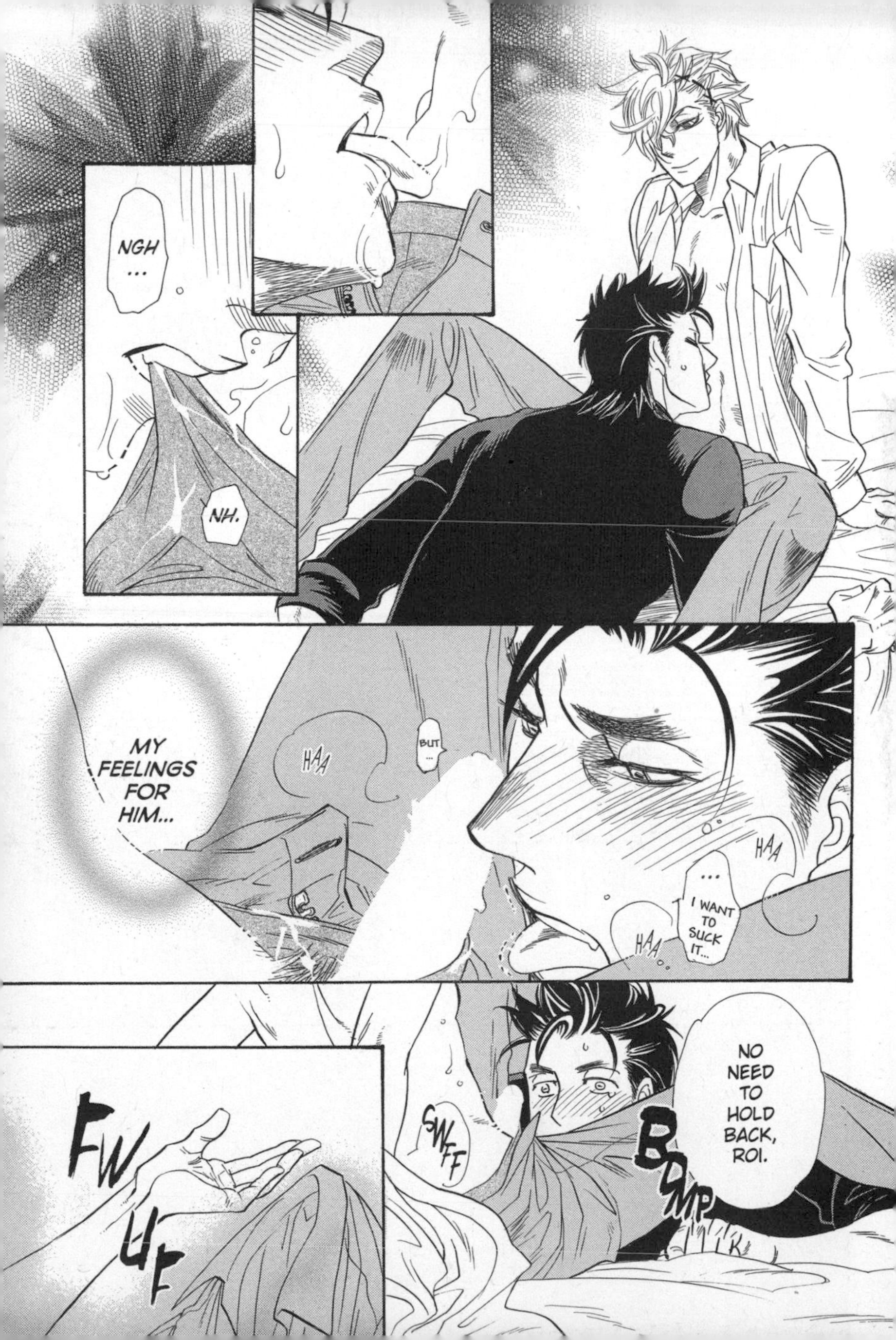
NGH ...
NH.
HAA
... I WANT TO SUCK IT...
HAA
BUT ...
HAA
MY FEELINGS FOR HIM...
NO NEED TO HOLD BACK, ROI.
BOMP
SWFF
FWUF

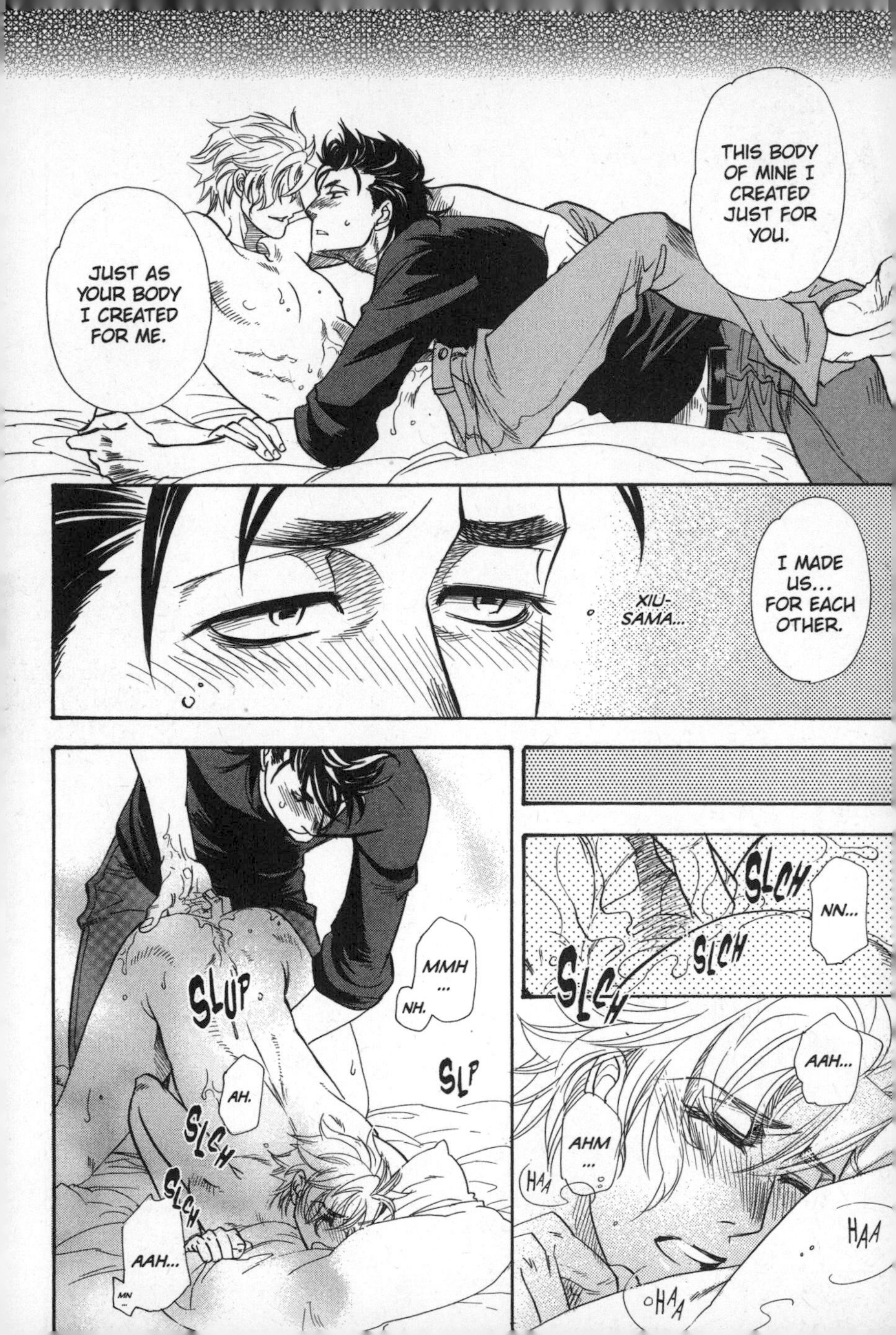
THIS BODY OF MINE I CREATED JUST FOR YOU.
JUST AS YOUR BODY I CREATED FOR ME.
I MADE US... FOR EACH OTHER.
XIU-SAMA...
SLCH
NN...
SLCH
SLCH
AAH...
AHM ...
HAA
HAA
HAA
MMH ... NH.
SLUP
SLP
AH.
SLCH
SLCH
AAH...
MN ...

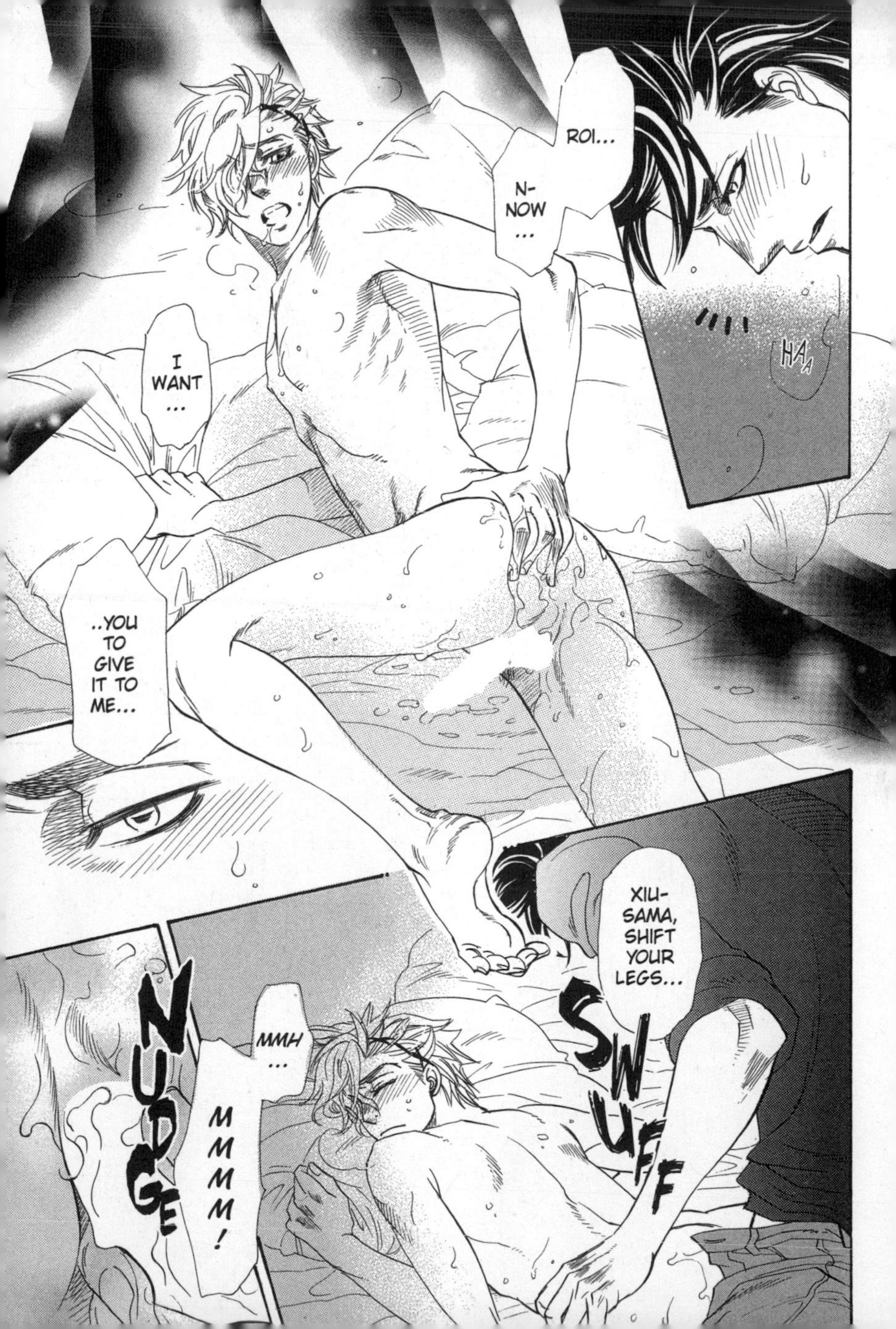
ROI...
N-NOW...
HAA
I WANT...
..YOU TO GIVE IT TO ME...
XIU-SAMA, SHIFT YOUR LEGS...
SWUFF
MMH...
MMMM!
NUDGE

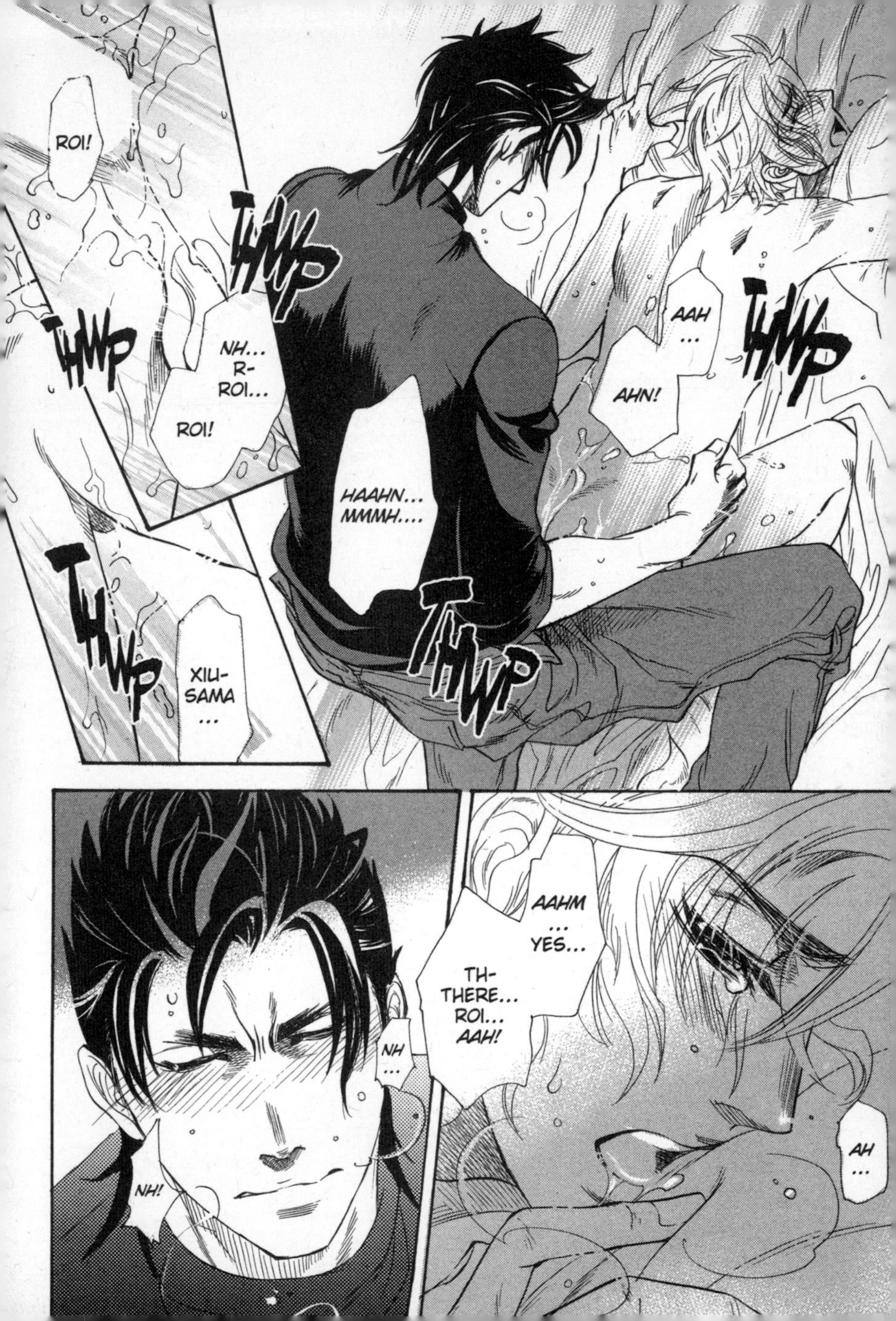
THWP
AAH ... AHN!
THWP
HAAHN... MMMH....
THWP
ROI!
THWP
NH... R-ROI... ROI!
THWP
XIU-SAMA ...
AH ...
AAHM ... YES...
TH-THERE... ROI... AAH!
NH ...
NH!

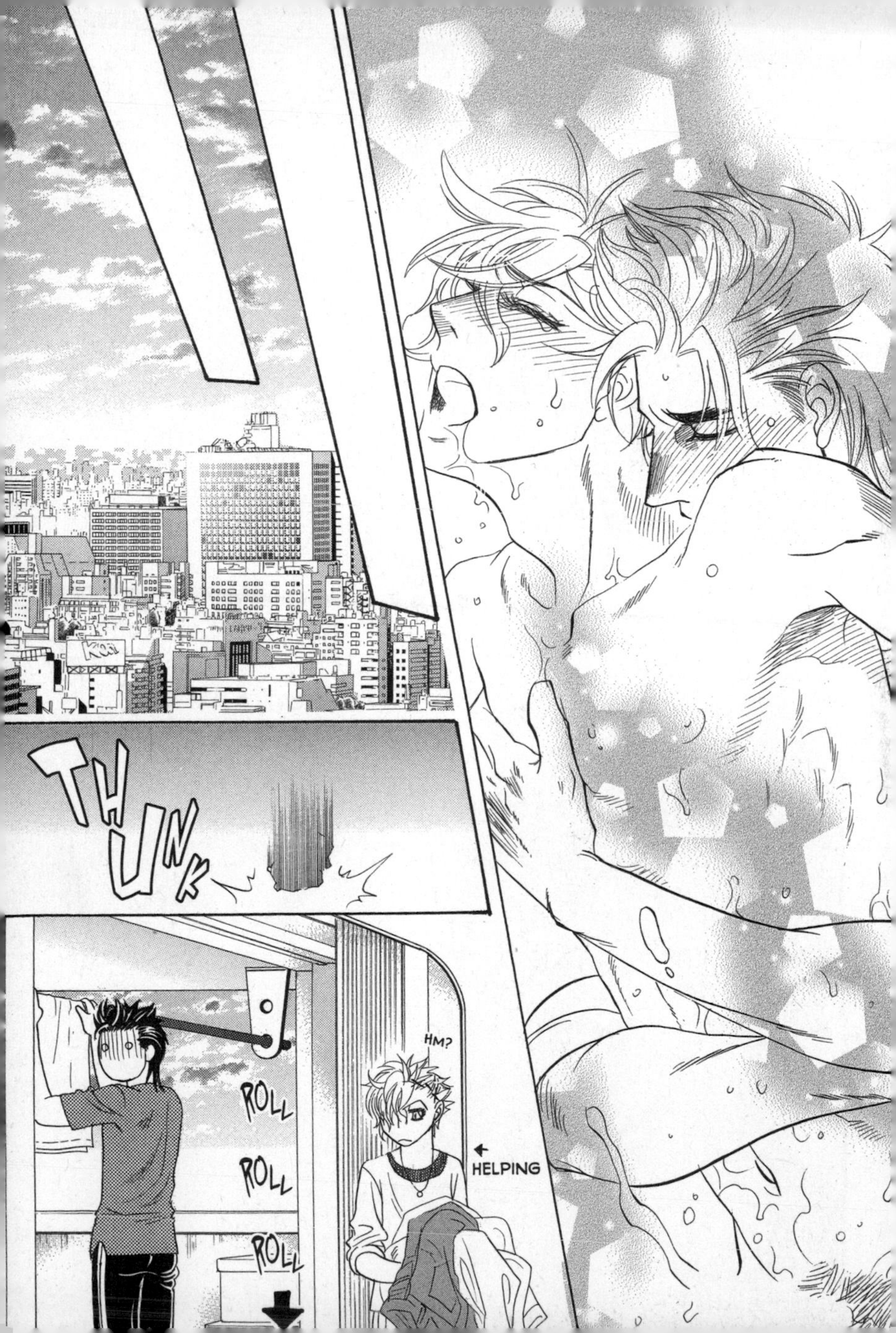
THUNK
HM?
← HELPING
ROLL
ROLL
ROLL

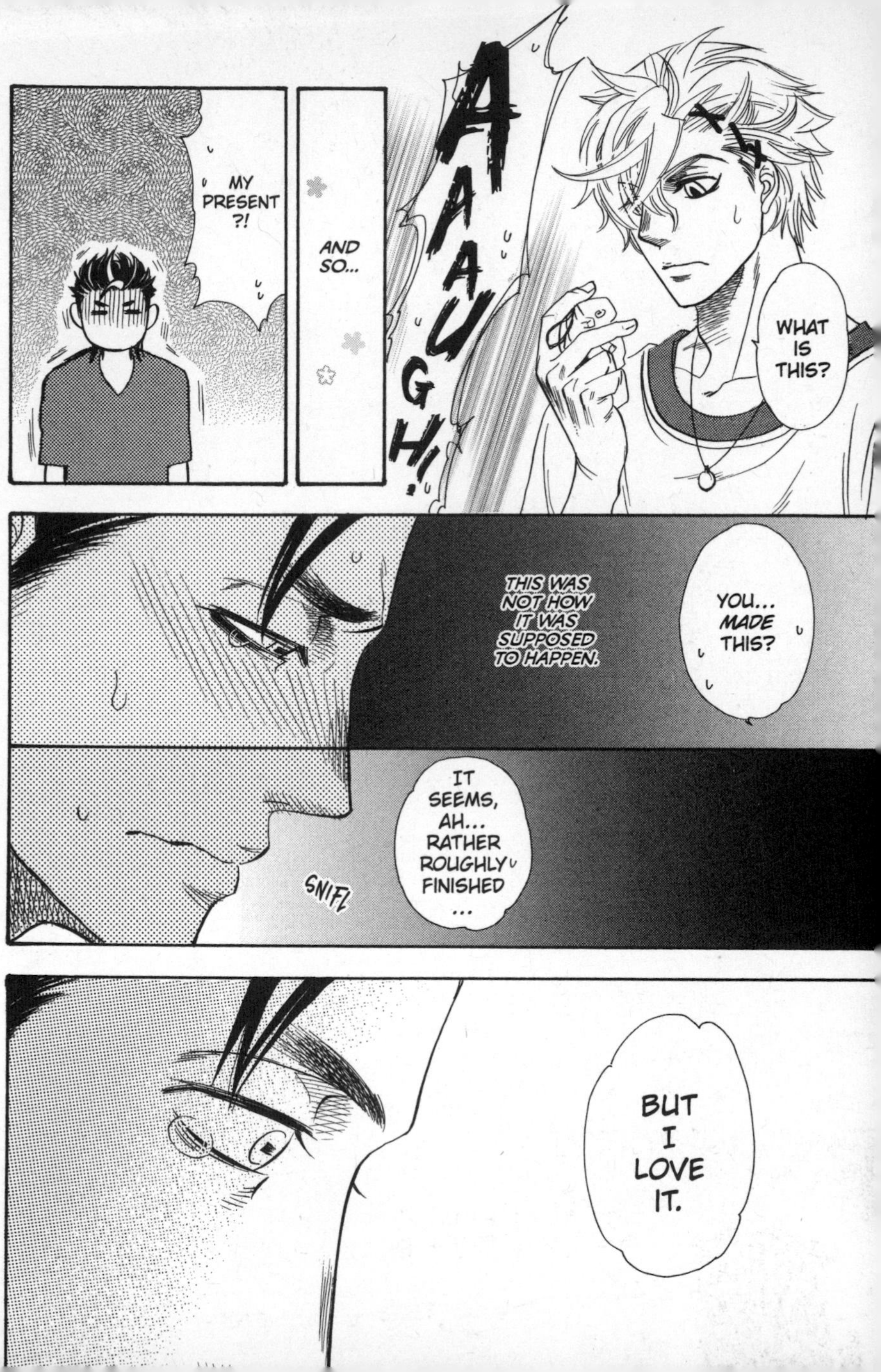
WHAT IS THIS?
AAAUGH!
AND SO...
MY PRESENT?!
YOU... MADE THIS?
THIS WAS NOT HOW IT WAS SUPPOSED TO HAPPEN.
IT SEEMS, AH... RATHER ROUGHLY FINISHED...
SNIFL
BUT I LOVE IT.

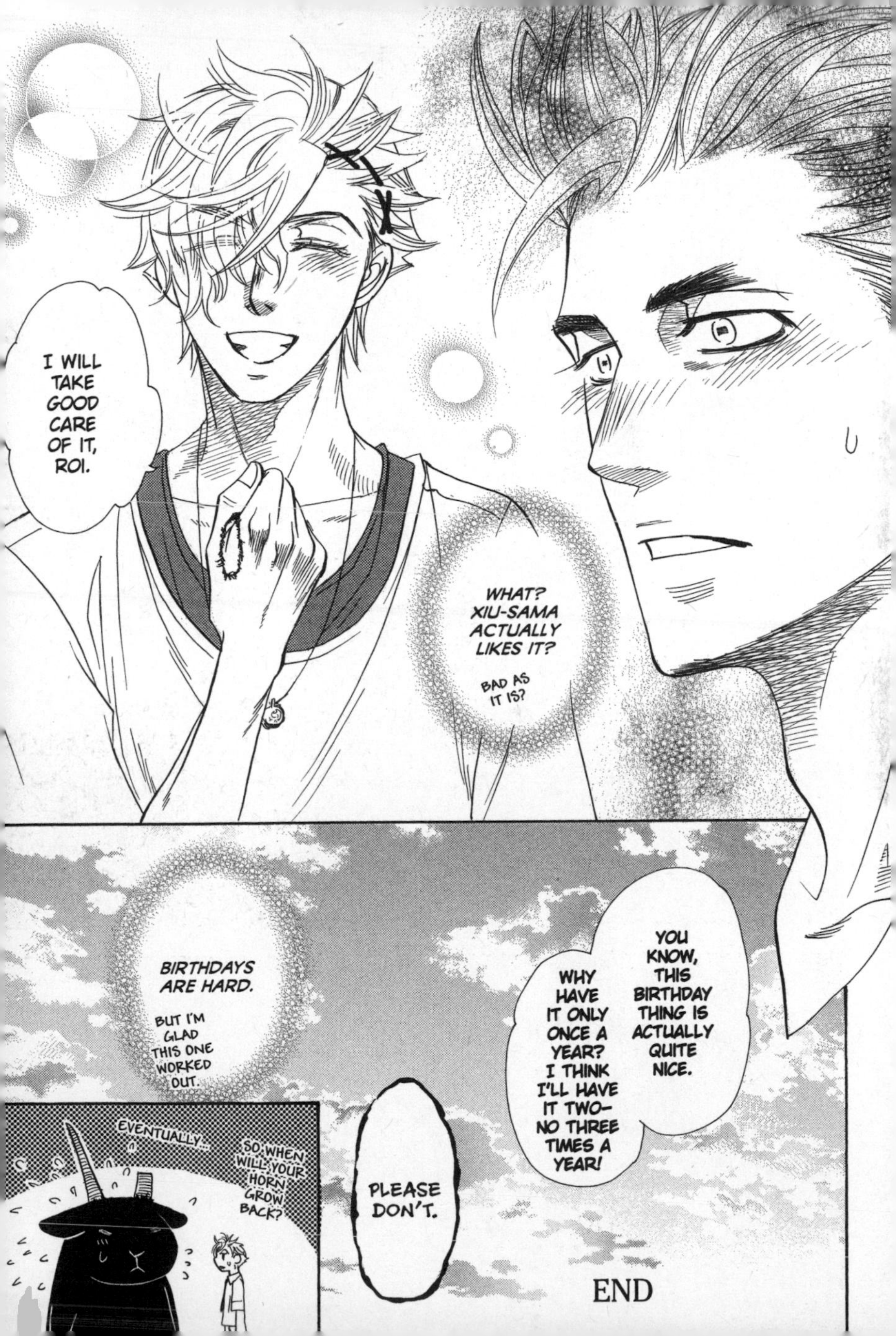
I WILL TAKE GOOD CARE OF IT, ROI.
WHAT? XIU-SAMA ACTUALLY LIKES IT?
BAD AS IT IS?
YOU KNOW, THIS BIRTHDAY THING IS ACTUALLY QUITE NICE.
WHY HAVE IT ONLY ONCE A YEAR? I THINK I'LL HAVE IT TWO—NO THREE TIMES A YEAR!
BIRTHDAYS ARE HARD.
BUT I'M GLAD THIS ONE WORKED OUT.
PLEASE DON'T.
END
SO, WHEN WILL YOUR HORN GROW BACK?
EVENTUALLY...

彼方者の
困惑
あっちものの こんわく

Midnight Stranger

Here 1

XIU-SAMA WENT BACK TO THE DIVINE REALM...
...SO I HAD TO HELP HIM ERASE EVERYONE'S MEMORIES OF HIM, AND...
SEE...
...
Y'KNOW, ONE DAY WE'RE GONNA HAVE TO SAY GOODBYE TOO. I MEAN, I'M STILL A MORTAL HUMAN.
I WONDER HOW MUCH TIME WE HAVE LEFT...
HM?
WHAT? AGING? OH, DON'T WORRY. EVERYTHING WILL BE FINE. SEE, EVERY TIME WE HAVE SEX, I TRICKLE A LITTLE OF MY ESSENCE INTO YOU. YOU SHOULD BE COMPLETELY IMMORTAL BY NOW.♡
I'D LOST MY HUMANITY AND I HADN'T EVEN NOTICED IT...
TODO, WHAT'S WRONG?
TODO?

LOOKS LIKE TODO WAS TAKING IN MORE THAN HE REALIZED.

There 1

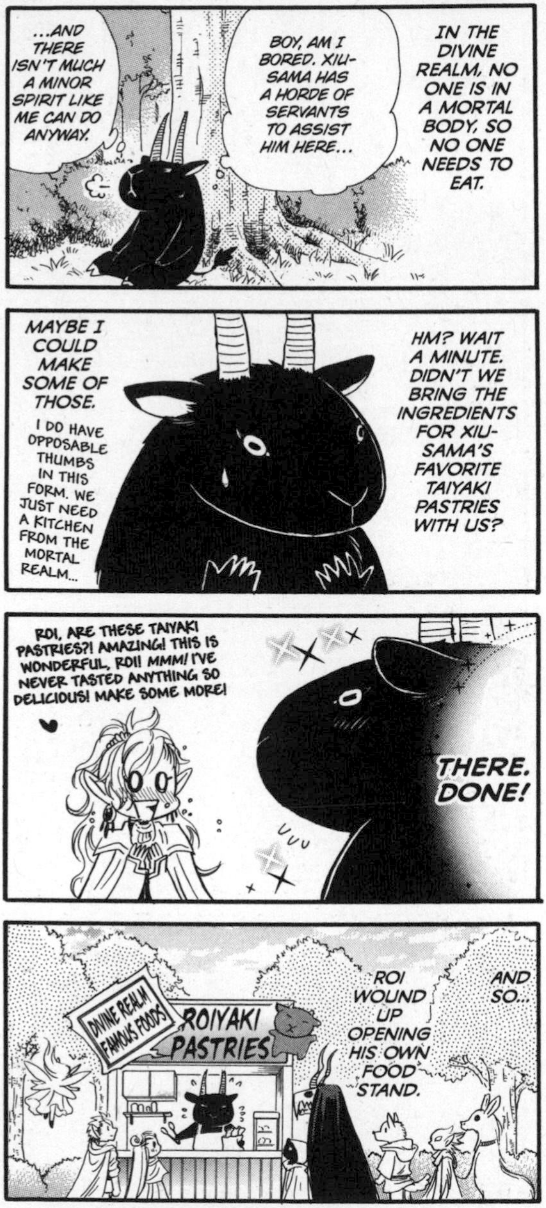
IN THE DIVINE REALM, NO ONE IS IN A MORTAL BODY, SO NO ONE NEEDS TO EAT.
BOY, AM I BORED. XIU-SAMA HAS A HORDE OF SERVANTS TO ASSIST HIM HERE...
...AND THERE ISN'T MUCH A MINOR SPIRIT LIKE ME CAN DO ANYWAY.
HM? WAIT A MINUTE. DIDN'T WE BRING THE INGREDIENTS FOR XIU-SAMA'S FAVORITE TAIYAKI PASTRIES WITH US?
MAYBE I COULD MAKE SOME OF THOSE.
I DO HAVE OPPOSABLE THUMBS IN THIS FORM. WE JUST NEED A KITCHEN FROM THE MORTAL REALM...
THERE. DONE!
ROI, ARE THESE TAIYAKI PASTRIES?! AMAZING! THIS IS WONDERFUL, ROI! MMM! I'VE NEVER TASTED ANYTHING SO DELICIOUS! MAKE SOME MORE!
AND SO...
ROI WOUND UP OPENING HIS OWN FOOD STAND.
ROIYAKI PASTRIES
DIVINE REALM FAMOUS FOODS

THE MOST POPULAR FILLINGS ARE RED BEAN PASTE, CUSTARD, AND CHEESE.

There 2

TO BE BLUNT, WITHOUT OUR HUMAN BODIES (WELL, CERTAIN PARTS OF A HUMAN BODY) WE CAN'T HAVE SEX!
IN HIS GOAT FORM, ROI DOESN'T HAVE A [BEEP]!
FRUSTRATED →
UGH! WHY DID I NOT GIVE HIM ONE WHEN I FIRST CREATED HIS GOAT BODY?!
XIU-SAMA, STOP!
GROSS.
LEWD.
WHY NOT GIVE HIM ONE NOW?
SCALES ↓
??
Please don't look for me.
ROI
I'M SORRY! FORGIVE ME!
KREE
KREE
DWPA
DWPA
DWPA
DWPA
DWPA

THAT...ISN'T THE ONLY PROBLEM. IS IT?

Here 2

IT HAS BEEN MANY DECADES SINCE WE LAST VISITED THE MORTAL REALM. NOT MUCH HAS CHANGED.
HM.
PER-HAPS IT'S THE LACK OF WARS?
XIU-SAMA? XIU-SAMA, IS THAT YOU?!
?!
TCH!
DAMN! THERE'S STILL A HUMAN ALIVE WHO REMEMBERS THIS FORM?
IT'S ME! MASATO!
AAH, TIME. SHE IS A CRUEL MISTRESS.
NUZZLE
AND WHAT GANG DO YOU BOUNCE FOR?
HUGGLE
NUZZLE
HUGGLE
IT'S BEEN FOREVER! IS ROI HERE? WHERE IS HE?

MASATO KAKEI, 98 YEARS OLD AND STILL GOING STRONG.

彼方者の
困惑
あっちものの こんわく

Midnight Stranger

And so the story of Roi and Xiu comes to a close. It feels like the end was less about BL and more about how best to draw Roi as a goat, but oh well. I'm glad they get a happy ending!

About the Author

Bohra Naono has created over 20 manga, some of which have been adapted into drama CDs. She has also published *doujinshi* (independent comics) under the circle name of "NAIFU." Bohra Naono's previous English-language releases include *Yokai's Hunger* and *Three Wolves Mountain.* A native of Oita, she is a Gemini with an A blood type who loves Chinese tea and is obsessed with the neighborhood *yakiniku* restaurant. To find out more about Bohra Naono, visit her website at www.bnlyz.com.

Midnight Stranger
The Trouble with Strangers
Volume 2
SuBLime Manga Edition

Story and Art by **Bohra Naono**

Additional Translation—**Adrienne Beck**
Touch-up Art and Lettering— **NRP Studios**
Cover and Graphic Design—**Izumi Evers**
Editor—**Jennifer LeBlanc**

Acchimono no Konwaku © 2015 Bohra Naono
Originally published in Japan in 2015 by Libre Publishing Co., Ltd. Tokyo.
English translation rights arranged with Libre Publishing Co., Ltd. Tokyo.

Printed in the U.S.A.

Published by SuBLime Manga
P.O. Box 77010
San Francisco, CA 94107

10 9 8 7 6 5 4 3 2 1
First printing, July 2016

PARENTAL ADVISORY
MIDNIGHT STRANGER is rated M for Mature and is recommended for
mature readers. This volume contains graphic imagery and mature
MATURE   themes.

www.SuBLimeManga.com

For more information

on all our products, along with the most up-to-date news on releases, series announcements, and contests, please visit us at:

 SuBLimeManga.com

 twitter.com/**SuBLimeManga**

 facebook.com/**SuBLimeManga**

 SuBLimeManga.tumblr.com

Honey Darling
Story and Art by Norikazu Akira
EXPLICIT CONTENT
Honey Darling

SUBLIME

Your Toys Love Boys' Love

Own your SuBLime book as a convenient PDF document that is downloadable to the following devices:

- ♥ Computer
- ♥ Kindle™
- ♥ NOOK™
- ♥ iPad™, iPhone™, and iPod Touch™
- ♥ Any device capable of reading a PDF document

SUBLIME
www.SuBLimeManga.com

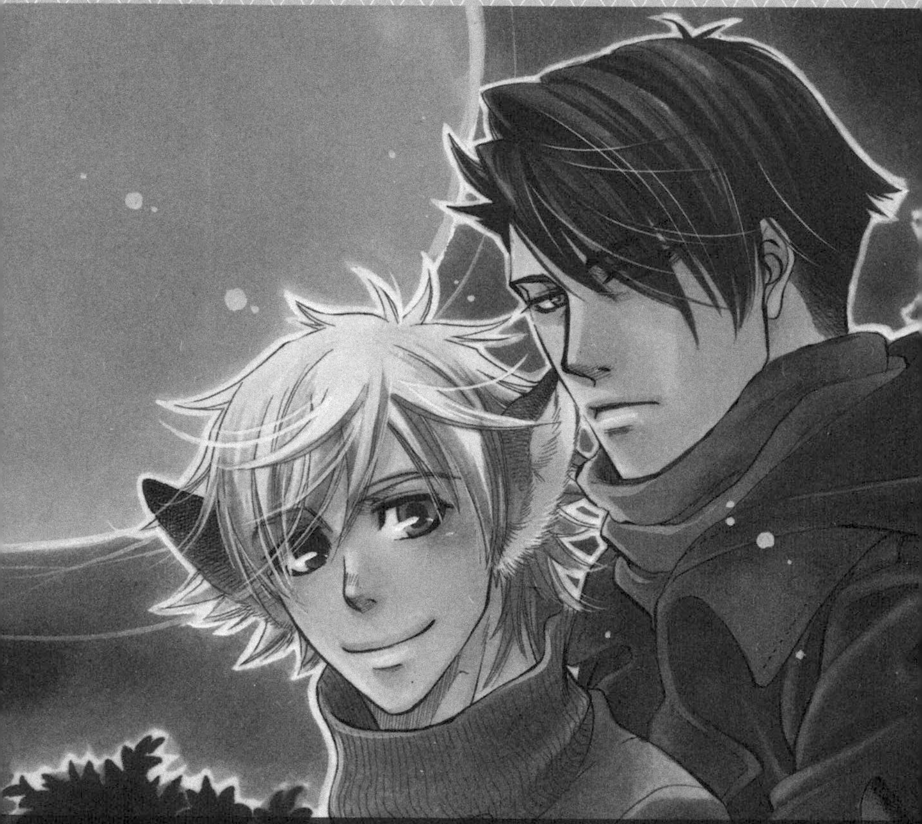

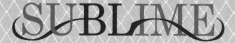